Contents

AENEID

Virgil

AENEID

Translated by
Stanley Lombardo

Introduction by
W. R. Johnson

Hackett Publishing Company, Inc.
Indianapolis/Cambridge

For further information, please address:

Hackett Publishing Company, Inc.
P.O. Box 44937
Indianapolis, IN 46244-0937

www.hackettpublishing.com

Cover design by Brian Rak and Abigail Coyle

Composition by William Hartman

Cover photo: Names on the Vietnam Veterans' Memorial.
Reproduced courtesy of CORBIS.

Library of Congress Cataloging-in-Publication Data

Virgil.
    [Aeneis. English]
    Aeneid / Virgil ; translated by Stanley Lombardo, introduction
by W. R. Johnson.
        p. cm.
    Includes bibliographical references.
    ISBN 0-87220-732-3 (cloth)—ISBN 0-87220-731-5 (pbk.)
    1. Epic poetry, Latin—Translations into English.
2. Aeneas (Legendary character)—Poetry. 3. Legends—
Rome—Poetry. I. Lombardo, Stanley, 1943– II. Title.
    PA6807.A5L58 2005
    873'.01—dc22

                                                    2004022685

    ISBN-13: 978-0-87220-732-5 (cloth)
    ISBN-13: 978-0-87220-731-8 (pbk.)

Ben Graham

insignem pietate virum

The Wanderings of Aeneas

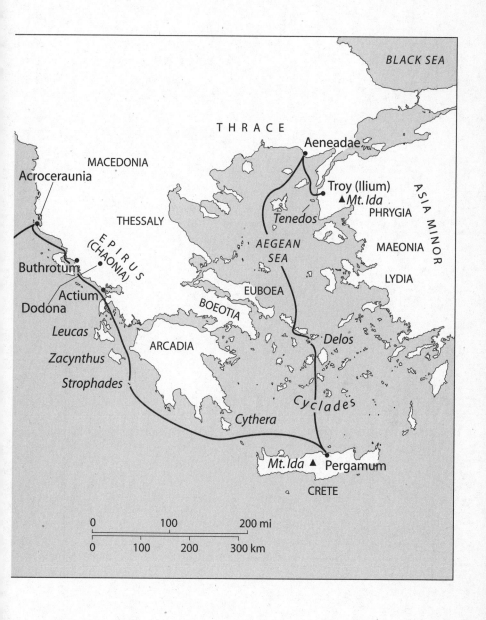

BLACK SEA

THRACE

Aeneadae

MACEDONIA

Acroceraunia

Troy (Ilium)
▲ Mt. Ida

PHRYGIA

ASIA MINOR

Tenedos

THESSALY

E P I R U S
(CHAONIA)

AEGEAN
SEA

Buthrotum

MAEONIA

Actium

EUBOEA

LYDIA

Dodona

BOEOTIA

Leucas

Zacynthus

Delos

ARCADIA

Strophades

Cythera

Cyclades

Mt. Ida ▲ Pergamum

CRETE

| 0 | 100 | 200 mi |
| 0 | 100 | 200 | 300 km |

Translator's Preface

I come to the *Aeneid,* as Virgil did, through Homer. The *Aeneid* is modeled so closely upon Homeric epic that the poet Joseph Brodsky was moved to remark that Homer is the only true audience Virgil can have. And yet, although he adopts the structure, theology, episodes, and even many of the stylistic features of Homeric poetry, Virgil does not merely mimic the old Greek master but transforms everything he takes from Homer—and other poets—into a distinctly Latin and Roman composition. Encouraged by the emperor Augustus to write the national epic of Rome, Virgil settled on a mythological rather than historical approach, choosing Aeneas, a Trojan hero in Homer's *Iliad,* as his central character and picking up the story at the fall of Troy. The first half of the poem traces Aeneas' Odyssean wanderings in his quest to found a new city; the second half brings him to his destiny in Italy, where he must fight a great war as an Iliadic hero before he can found the settlement that was the precursor to Rome. In this way Virgil established Rome as successor to Troy, giving both his city and his poem a Homeric lineage. He had substantially completed his *Aeneid* when he died in 19 B.C.E., leaving behind an epic that was almost instantly monumentalized as a literary and cultural icon, a status it has retained for two thousand years, becoming a standard school text and exerting enormous influence on such major European poets as Dante and Milton.

The primary issues for the translator of the *Aeneid* revolve about the poem's classicism, or "Augustanism." T. S. Eliot expressed a received tradition when in his presidential address to the Virgil Society in 1944 he pronounced the *Aeneid* the exemplar of classic style, by which he meant mature, conservative, morally elevated, sure of its civilized values in language as well as politics— in a word, Augustan. One might think that few would wish to quarrel with this characterization of the *Aeneid,* but there has been in fact a strong minority protest.

Donatus, one of Virgil's ancient biographers, tells us that as the poet lay dying he gave instructions that the manuscript of the *Aeneid* be burned. It is an understandable impulse for an author who was used to polishing his work to the last degree of perfection. But the German novelist Hermann Broch, in *The Death of Vergil,* takes a more interesting, darker view of Virgil's deathbed wish,

representing him as profoundly dismayed over the poem's glorifica-
tion of Augustus' imperial regime. Broch, who began his work in
the shadow of the Nazi regime and published it during World War
II (about the same time as Eliot's address to the Virgil Society),
anticipated a school of Virgilian criticism that took shape during
the Vietnam War and heard the poet's dismay in the very lines of
the great Roman national epic. These critics have pointed to oppo-
sitional and even subversive elements in the *Aeneid,* a species of
pathos that amounts to protest against the Augustan regime, or at
least against the expressions of inhumanity that necessarily found
their way into the epic. Is the poem Augustan, anti-Augustan, or
reluctantly Augustan? Is there one poetic voice in the *Aeneid,* or is
it radically polyphonic? Listening for the discordant voices in the
Aeneid, and making poetic and ideological sense of them, has been
central to Virgilian criticism since the 1960s.

My response to these issues as translator is based on my sense
that Virgil's posture in the *Aeneid* is contemplative. For all of the
action and drama in the *Aeneid,* there is at its core a profound still-
ness, and a subdued light. If, as the ancient critic Longinus says, the
light in Homer's *Iliad* is the intense light of noon, and in the *Odys-
sey* the magical glow of the setting sun, it is in the *Aeneid* a chiar-
oscuro, a play of light amid the shadows of evening, a darkness
visible. This is so not only as Aeneas moves through the Under-
world or the ashes of Troy or seeks shelter from a storm in a cave
with Dido. A twilight mood gathers around almost every scene in
the poem. Like Homer, Virgil reflects a complex world steadily and
as a whole, but, much more so than Homer, he is consciously
reflective as well, both in his melancholy voice as narrator and in
the conflicted voices of his characters. The Roman poet has, in the
words of John Keats, a strong "negative capability," a mind capa-
ble of staying at rest in uncertainties, mysteries, and doubts—like
moonlight reflected in water trembling in a bronze bowl, as Virgil
says of the mind of his poem's hero.

My translation of Virgil necessarily recalls Homer—and, quite
naturally, my translations of Homer. Readers of both translations
will notice that I treat Virgil's similes as I do Homer's, setting them
off in italics to mark their status as semi-independent poetic events
that illumine the main action. The rapidity and immediacy natural
to Homer's Greek is not as pronounced in Virgil's Latin, which is
more considered and distilled. The challenge in translating the

Aeneid is to capture the language's depth and at the same time keep the poem in motion as Virgil does. This is largely a matter of managing the cadences of the lines—modulating the rhythms and sound effects—and being sensitive to nuances of diction. Virgil uses the same meter—dactylic hexameter—as Homer, adapting the metrics to the exigencies of the Latin language. The rhythmic line that I have developed in response to the classical hexameter—a line that I have used for Homer and use for Virgil—is based, like much of modern English and American poetry, on natural speech cadences. This is in keeping with the performative qualities of the *Aeneid,* which although it is literary rather than oral epic was nonetheless intended to be recited, practically sung. Virgil's word music is more than mortal. The biographer Suetonius records a memorable private reading Virgil gave to Augustus and his wife, Octavia. I have continued the practices, which I began with the *Iliad,* of composing for performance as much as for the printed page and of using actual performances to shape the translation process.

In this respect I would like to thank those who convened audiences and lent willing ears: Larry Allums, Director of the Dallas Institute of Humanities and Culture; Elpida Anthan at the University of Missouri Kansas City; Peter Aicher of the University of Southern Maine; and Classics students and colleagues, particularly Tara Welch, at the University of Kansas. Joan McCool was an early and encouraging reader, as was Tony Corbeill, who also provided detailed comments on Book 12. William Levitan cast a critical eye on an early version of Book 1. Linda Frank's brief comments were timely and welcome, as was a suggestion by Anne Shaw that the four traditional introductory lines be somehow included. I am grateful to Daniel Born, editor of *The Common Review,* for publishing an excerpt and an essay. Brad Engelbert compiled the Glossary of Names.

The editorial staff at Hackett Publishing have been, as ever, a band of ministering spirits in times of need. My thanks especially to Brian Rak and Meera Dash. Readers for the press were Gail Polk, David Fredrick, and Tony Corbeill. They not only corrected my errors, supplied my omissions, and pruned my excesses, but also helped tune my ears to Virgil's music and align my words to his soul. I am deeply grateful to them for their work.

To my wife, Judy Roitman, who sustains my own soul, my heartfelt thanks for her constant support.

W. R. Johnson's book, *Darkness Visible,* remains for me the most telling study of the *Aeneid*. I am grateful to him for his Introduction to this translation.

This book is dedicated to my good and noble friend Ben Graham, a man whom Virgil would have appreciated.

Note on the Latin Text

This translation is based on the Oxford text of R. A. B. Mynors. I have consulted the commentaries of T. E. Page and R. D. Williams, and occasionally I have adopted their readings. It was once the custom to begin the *Aeneid* with four introductory lines (first quoted by Suetonius, now rejected by most editors), placing the *Aeneid* in the context of Virgil's earlier works, the *Eclogues* and *Georgics,* so that the poem opened as follows:

I am the poet who once tuned his song
On a slender reed and then leaving the woods
Compelled the fields to obey the hungry farmer,
A pleasing work. But now War's grim and savage
Arms I sing. . . .

Introduction

The *Aeneid* is an epic poem about the destruction of civilizations
and their resurrections. Its insistence on the human capacity to
hope, even when—especially when—that hope is tested on the
brink of ruin, lends the poem what many have felt to be its uni-
versality and has enabled it to exercise its hold on the imagina-
tion of the West for just over twenty centuries. Yet Virgil's epic is
no simple tale of hope and triumph. Most epics concern them-
selves with celebrating the defeat of the enemies who had threat-
ened doom to the community for which the epic poet composes
his victory poem, and the *Aeneid,* in this regard, resembles other
specimens of its genre. But in constructing his celebration of
Rome's empire, Virgil never loses sight of the huge costs of the
victory he is praising and never forgets that most winners were
once losers. Impressed by this steady emphasis on suffering and
loss, some readers of the poem feel that its representations of
imperial glory tend to be overshadowed by an opposing tragic
vision. What fuels the poem, however, is neither triumphalism
nor defeatism but its pervasive tension between exaltation and
lament. This severe dialectic—a counterpoint of defeat and tri-
umph, abjection and salvation, death and rebirth—is the *Aeneid*'s
mainspring. The steady equipoise of this double vision arms the
Aeneid with its unique power to comfort as well as disturb read-
ers even today.

   The enduring appeal of this epic over the past two millennia is
easy to appreciate. Spend an hour or so leafing through the pages
of *The Times Atlas of World History* and you will quickly be
reminded of how, from the earliest days to the present, the bound-
aries of the tribes and nations of Europe (and elsewhere) are con-
tinually and sometimes radically erased, renegotiated, redrawn—
by invasion, by civil war, by "barbaric" incursions. The peoples of
Europe have always understood what it means to be displaced and
exiled, to be conquered, to be an immigrant or an émigré, to lose
one's homeland and to search, desperately, for a new one. To such
readers down the centuries, the closing verses of Book 2—where
Aeneas, the epic's hero, prepares to lead the survivors of burning
Troy to safety—have always spoken with an incomparable and
poignant clarity:

I was surprised by the great number
Of new arrivals I found, women and men,
Youth gathered for exile, a wretched band
Of refugees who had poured in from all over,
Prepared to journey across the sea
To whatever lands I might lead them. . . .
There was no hope of help. I yielded
And, lifting up my father, sought the mountains.
(2.942–47, 951–52)

Yet it is not for the dispossessed alone that this passage has extraordinary resonance; any student of human history knows that Aeneas' speech represents an event all too familiar in human experience and captures an unhappy truth of the human condition: however secure the present may seem, our deepest intuitions—from ancestral memories to the collective consciousness—recognize our communities to be fragile, vulnerable, contingent.

Aeneas is, to be sure, a quintessentially Roman hero in a Roman epic that glorifies the rebirth of a new and better Rome. But if his being a Roman hero were more important than his being a human being, he and his poem would never have managed to transcend the collapse of the Roman Empire and then find a steady welcome in civilizations that replaced it. For diverse readers in very different times, Aeneas has functioned as a sort of epic Everyman, one who escapes by the skin of his teeth from being dispatched on what Hegel would call "the slaughter bench of history" and thereby comes to incarnate the capacity of human beings to endure existence on the brink of ruin—and then to begin again and to flourish. If the tribes and nations of Europe had not kept discovering their need for his story and its message, Aeneas and his poem would long since have joined the many other texts from ancient Rome (and Greece) that have vanished into oblivion or, even if extant, have gone from being revered to ignored—and then all but forgotten.

But for all its appeal to diverse individuals, tribes, and nations over the past two thousand years, it is no accident that the *Aeneid* had its origins in a very particular set of circumstances at a very special moment. As he set about composing his epic, Virgil seized upon a specific cluster of thoughts and feelings about triumph, salvation, and thanksgiving shared by his first readers. This shared outlook had its roots, in turn, in a series of momentous events that took place throughout the century preceding the decade Virgil devoted to writing the *Aeneid* (29–19 B.C.E.). The stability of Rome and of its empire had been shaken by a steady series of civil wars and by the increasingly violent erosion of its political and social institutions. For many observers, eloquently spoken for by the historians Sallust and Livy, a prime cause of this incremental deterioration was the very success that crowned Rome's imperial expansions in the two centuries before the birth of Christ. From this perspective, Rome's blessings were its curse, and its prosperity seemed to generate irreparable damage to its values and its ideals by promoting, particularly among its leaders, a culture of greed and harmful competition—one that left its political, military, economic, and social traditions in shreds. These vicious tendencies spiraled to what seemed their final implosion when Julius Caesar fought his civil war with Pompey and his allies (49–45 B.C.E.); yet they degenerated even further when, after a decade of turbulence and confusion, Marc Antony (Caesar's second-in-command) and Octavian (his grandnephew) fought their own civil war (32–30 B.C.E.); they were finally extinguished only when Octavian, soon to become Augustus, vanquished his adversary and thereafter gradually constructed a throne for himself out of the ruins of what had once been a republic. As monarch of Rome and its empire, Octavian-Augustus was able to impose on his vast realm a stability that was as secure as it was welcome. The Romans and the nations they had conquered sighed with relief. The time was ripe for a monumental epic poem that memorialized their deliverance and gratitude.

Beyond any claims to universality—and centuries after the passing of the historical conditions that gave rise to the epic that celebrates him—Aeneas still enjoys his original renown as the ideal Roman hero. As such he symbolizes (scandalously to some, among them that great reader of the *Iliad,* Simone Weil) the might and right of the Roman Empire just as it was nearing its zenith around the time of Christ's birth. Not surprisingly then, in periods when rulers feel called on to assert their kinship with the Roman Empire and its divinely chosen emperors, this purely Roman Aeneas, rather than his Everyman twin, seems to offer them a powerfully iconic validation. But the figure of Aeneas finds its essential poetic truth not in its value as political propaganda but in the man's capacity to survive, to endure, to cherish good hope. His particular greatness is rooted in his ferocious resolve to win salvation for his people, in the selfless determination that no obstacle thrown in its way can undo. Nevertheless, for all his heroism, he isn't too good to be true. What finally wins him our trust is his troubled humanity. Aeneas is no bloodless, self-righteous automaton. We see him in moments of brooding self-doubt and even near despair. Like Moses, another hero who leads his people to a promised land whose blessings he will not live to enjoy, Aeneas has enough in the way of human error to lend him a surprising verisimilitude. More so than with most epic heroes, his story of escape and struggle, of a fearsome journey's good end rings true; despite his larger-than-life virtues and all the divine guidance he receives, he is sufficiently vulnerable, sufficiently (to paraphrase Housman), "a stranger and alone in a world he never made" that we can see something of him in us and of us in him.

The Legend of Aeneas

According to the legends that grew up about the Trojan War (which took place roughly twelve centuries before the birth of Christ), a great army of Greeks laid siege to the city of Troy, determined to avenge the abduction (or seduction) of Helen, Queen of Sparta, and to restore her to her husband. Homer's *Iliad,* his monumental epic treatment of these legends, takes place toward the end of the war's tenth and final year, but it ends before the Greeks take and burn the city to the ground, slaying all but a few of its males and making slaves of most of its women. Aeneas is one warrior who survives this catastrophe, preserved by fate for a high, mysterious calling.

But despite his being thus singled out, and although in the catalog of Trojan forces in Book 2 of the *Iliad* he is listed second only after Hector, the city's greatest champion, Aeneas plays a relatively small and somewhat ambiguous role in the epic. Aeneas makes a memorable appearance in Book 5, where, having encountered Diomedes in battle and having been wounded by him, he is rescued first by his mother, the goddess Aphrodite (Virgil's Venus), and then, when she fails in her efforts to rescue him, by the god Apollo, who pronounces him "a man . . . honored as much as Hector" (Lombardo's *Iliad* 5.505), an estimate of his value we find echoed when he next appears, in Book 13. There, when Deïphobus, seeking to take vengeance on the killer of a comrade, goes looking for Aeneas to help him, he finds him "in the rear, the last man there, / Angry as always at Priam, / Who utterly failed to honor his worth" (Lombardo's *Iliad* 13.477–79). When Aeneas moves against him, Idomeneus asks his comrades for help, describing Aeneas as "a hell of a fighter / And in his prime" (Lombardo's *Iliad* 13.505–6). Soon after this, though Aeneas fights for a while with genuinely Homeric gusto, he fades into the blur of the carnage. Finally, in Book 20, Aeneas briefly shares the full spotlight with the Greeks' fiercest warrior, Achilles himself, whom he challenges to single combat. Undeterred by Achilles' stinging insult ("Even if you kill me / Priam's not going to hand his kingship to you. / He has sons of his own, and he's not senile yet," Lombardo's *Iliad* 20.188–90), Aeneas answers him with a long piece of bravado, but his spear fails to pierce Achilles' shield, and he is about to suffer a fatal retaliation by Achilles when he is spirited away from death by Poseidon (Virgil's Neptune), who justifies his intervention to other gods by describing Aeneas as "a guiltless man" who "has always / Pleased the gods in heaven with his offerings," and who, further, is destined to get out of Troy alive in order to build a new Troy elsewhere, over which he and his progeny will rule (Lombardo's *Iliad* 20.302–14). These verses explain why Aeneas, almost alone of the Trojan heroes, escapes Troy's doom, and they define the qualities that will henceforth define his character: he is innocent (that is, not guilty of crimes in the eyes of the gods) and he is pious (that is, unlike most men, who sometimes forget or botch their devotion to the gods, Aeneas offers his sacrifices to them with scrupulous reverence). That such a paragon is marked for a special destiny is hardly surprising.

However, it took the figure of Aeneas centuries to find the shape of that destiny. He had some part in the short epics that came to serve as prequels or sequels to Homer's two epics (these are no longer extant). Various historians made mention of him (again, those texts are fragmentary): he wandered about the Mediterranean in search of a new homeland for his tribe, he became especially associated with Sicily (the scene of Book 5), and then, not surprisingly, with Italy. The early writers of Roman epics made use of him (these too are now in the most meager fragments). But it was Virgil, as he cast about for a way of framing what he wanted to say about Rome's empire and its recent tribulations and redemptions, who gave Aeneas his definitive identity and his story its final version, one in which both his piety and his innocence would be tested in ways Homeric epic could never have tested them. The power and precision of Virgil's representation quickly displaced rival versions, ones in which Aeneas escaped from Troy's destruction because he had betrayed it to the Greeks, or, as Virgil's contemporary, the great Roman historian, Livy, relates it, because the Greeks honored him for having constantly recommended that Helen be restored to her husband. Neither of these reasons provides the stuff of heroic drama, so Virgil chooses for his hero a more violent and a more dramatic leave-taking from his burning city. In Virgil's version of Aeneas' flight from Troy, as elsewhere throughout the poem, the hero's piety, his relationship to the gods, is sorely tested by divine interventions into human affairs. More than the Homeric gods, Virgil's gods are crucial to who Aeneas is, to what he thinks and chooses and does.

The Gods, Fate, and Fortune

Like the gods in the *Aeneid*, the gods in Homer's two epics help the humans they are partial to, and they hinder or harm those humans whom for some reason they hate. But Homer's divine machinery functions in more complex ways than Virgil's: it is part plot device, part sheer entertainment, and, not least in importance, it serves as a metaphysical background against which the actions of human beings, their desires, their struggles, and their sufferings gain clarity and meaning. For the most part, Homer's gods, his "deathless ones," are as capricious, selfish, and irresponsible as they are magnificent, powerful, and amusing. The fact that they cannot die, and that their choices (or whims) cannot do them much harm or cause them to grieve for very long, throws into sharpest relief what is at stake for human beings: what Homer's humans value and what they choose because of what they value have immense, sometimes tragic consequences for them and for those whom they love (or hate). It is within the circumference of their mortality, of their lives' brief splendors and ever-threatened losses, that what they want and do takes on its meanings. Paradoxes incarnate, the great Homeric heroes, Achilles no less than Odysseus, are fate-driven but also, in a way, superbly free: within their fated limits, they are free to risk themselves for what they believe in (glory, honor); to wrest meaning, for themselves, from the vicissitudes and constraints they were born into; to become, before they must die, who they are.

This strange tension between freedom and necessity is the hall-mark of a tough and brilliant individualism that characterizes much of what is best and most permanent in our heritage from ancient Greece. Because, on one level at least, the gods often seem like gorgeous, brutal, and spoiled children who are instantly mastered and then released by their inconsequential moods and changing motives, the Homeric heroes, however flawed they may be, take on by contrast a hard-won and admirable authenticity. Whether aided or thwarted by divine agencies, whether admired or reviled by the society whose conventions they dwarf, they reach out for and almost grasp something like an unchanging, highest good. This truth or excellence is not part of the divine machinery; it is beyond it, elsewhere, out of time.

Zeus, the supreme Greek deity whose Roman counterpart is the Jupiter of Virgil's poem, is linked with that truth, with a form of justice that is perfect and eternal, with things as they are. He may banter with the other deathless immortals who are his siblings or his children, he may argue with them, put a stop to their squabbles, threaten them or cajole them, but he also exists in a place apart from them, one where he communes with, or is, something mysterious, unrepresentable, almost unthinkable. At the superb first climax of the *Iliad* in Book 22, Achilles is about to complete his pursuit of Hector around the walls of Troy:

> But when they reached the springs the fourth time,
> Father Zeus stretched out his golden scales
> And placed on them two agonizing deaths,
> One for Achilles and one for Hector.
> When he held the beam, Hector's doom sank down
> Toward Hades.
>   (Lombardo's *Iliad* 22.235–40)

This moment, of course, shows itself as a narrative marker, as a plot device: in the story, it's the time for Hector to die. In terms of the story's framework, however, these scales represent the idea of balance, of Dike, of justice. Hector must now die because all the strands, all the multiple causes that combine to create this war, this struggle, these humans' hopes and fears are now being gathered, ever more swiftly, into the inevitablity that knots them up. But even as the image of the scales represents balance, justice, the way things are and must be, it merely points to—it does not explain—the mystery of the inevitability. Of that mystery, Zeus is the steward, the minister, the guardian.

The *Aeneid*'s parallel scene resembles its Homeric model only superficially. Near the poem's ending, as Aeneas and his rival, Turnus, prepare to battle one another to the death,

> Jupiter himself
> Held up his balanced scales and placed on them
> The destinies of each man to determine whom
> The battle doomed, whose weight sank down to death.
>   (12.872–75)

In the Homeric scene, just before he lifted his scales, Zeus had expressed his grief at what was about to happen to Hector, and had toyed briefly with the notion of deferring the doom of a great hero whom he admires and feels sorry for, but the goddess Athena easily dissuaded him, and he quickly turned to setting Hector's doom in motion. As a symbol, or, rather, as something like the embodiment of Fate, Zeus can, whatever his feelings, only be impartial (it is for the other gods to help or harm humans whenever they can): he is, in the words of Walter Burkert (*Greek Religion,* pp. 130–31), "above all disputes, all faction." Virgil's Jupiter, in contrast, expresses no feeling for Turnus, and there is something ironic in his meticulous care in setting his scales, since he not only knows but heartily approves of the decision the scales are about to make. Jupiter is not "the god of all alike"; he is a tribal god who has been transformed, by a slow and complicated process, first into the chief god of the city of Rome, and then into the universal, supreme god of Rome's universal empire whose capital is Rome.

Very early in the *Aeneid,* just after Aeneas and some of his ships have escaped the storm that his archenemy, the goddess Juno, has unleashed upon him, Aeneas' mother, the goddess Venus, comes complaining to her father, Jupiter, about the dangers that her son has repeatedly endured since he fled from Troy. She addresses him as the "Eternal Ruler of Gods and Men" (1.271), but it is unclear (here as elsewhere in the poem) whether he issues those rules or is, like others, subject to them. In any case, he offers her a soothing reaffirmation of the certainty and splendor of Aeneas' destiny and of the destiny of his progeny:

I have not changed my mind. Your son—
I will speak a length, since you are so worried,
Unrolling Fate's scroll and revealing its secrets—
Your son will wage a great war in Italy,
Crush barbarous nations, and set up laws
And city walls for his own people. . . .
                    (1.311–16)

He then proceeds to sketch for her the long, triumphant history of Aeneas' Trojan descendants after they have merged with the native Italians and become known as Romans, for whom, he proclaims, "I set no limits / In time or space, and have given to them / Eternal empire, world without end"(1.332–34). This supreme deity clearly has no capacity for impartiality; he is the voice, or the mouthpiece, of Rome's version of World Historical Destiny as it was interpreted (and being constructed) at the time Virgil was writing his poem. Continuing his prophetic summary of Roman history, Jupiter makes Venus this promise about her son's descendants:

From this resplendent line shall be born
Trojan Caesar, who will extend his Empire
To the Ocean and his glory to the stars,
A Julian in the lineage of the great Ilus.
And you, Venus, free at last from care,
Will someday welcome him into heaven,
Laden with Oriental spoils of war,
And his name too will be invoked in vows.
                    (1.343–50)

What Jupiter's scales decree at the epic's close is not only the doom of Turnus but also the eventual domination, as beneficent as it is rightful, of the known world by Rome (and by Augustus, who is the greatest of Aeneas' heirs). This view of the ultimate cause of the rise and fall of nations is utterly at odds with Homer's vision of an impartial Zeus, whose evenhandedness finds a memorable echo in Herodotus' introduction to his *Histories:* "Many states that were once great have now become small and those that were great in my time were small formerly. Knowing therefore that human prosperity never continues in one stay, I will make mention of both kinds" (1.5).

In contrast to the Homeric/Herodotean perspective, Virgil's fusion of the guardian of Rome's destiny with the world's fated purpose is at the core of the epic's divine machinery. It would be reasonable enough to suppose that this concept of Rome's divinely ordained mission reflects the poet's own views of divinity and empire. But that reading of the epic ignores the fact that Jupiter is a character in the poem and that what he says and what he does do not necessarily provide us with reliable evidence either of Virgil's attitudes or of his poetic intentions. More to the point here is the moment, again toward the end of the epic, when the poet intrudes into his narrative, just at the point where, thwarted in his efforts to find and close with Turnus, Aeneas slips from frustration into blind rage. In his speech to Venus in Book 1 Jupiter had foretold that someday the Trojans and their Italian opponents would merge into one (Roman) people. This promise he will later repeat in his final confrontation with his wife, Juno, when he forces (or persuades) her to desist from her attempts to destroy Aeneas' settlement in Italy. But at this moment in his poem, as Aeneas and Turnus are about to meet in the fatal encounter that will bring the war and the poem to their bloody finish, Virgil remembers and invites his readers to remember that only very recently, after a dreadful civil war (91–87 B.C.E.), has that union between Rome and its Italian allies been finally effected. Angered and saddened by that war no less than by the war between Aeneas and Turnus, Virgil cries out to Jupiter in a bitter questioning of his divine means and his divine ends:

> What god could now unfold for me
> So many bitter deaths, which poet could tell
> Of all the captains who met their many dooms
> Driven over the plain now by Turnus,
> Now by the Trojan hero? Did it please you,
> Jupiter, that nations destined to live
> In everlasting peace should clash so harshly?
>
>   (12.612–18)

What poetic god, what resource of Homeric epic convention, can help him describe this peculiarly Roman horror, this unrepresentable nightmare? And why did Jupiter not put a stop to it? How could Rome's presiding deity allow it to happen? Virgil's questions here are not rhetorical. They echo the repugnance at violence and pity for its victims that pervade the poem, and they remain unanswered when the poem ends.

This question about divine justice, moreover, echoes another question that the poet voices at his poem's very beginning. There as here, it is with an emphatic Euripidean irony that he links his plea for poetic inspiration to a request for some explanation of divine intervention in human affairs. As he begins his poem, what he wants to know is why Juno was so angry with Aeneas:

> Muse, tell me why the Queen of Heaven
> Was so aggrieved, her godhead so offended,
> That she forced a man of faultless devotion
> To endure so much hardship. Can there be
> Anger so great in the hearts of gods on high?
>
> (1.12–16)

The school of philosophy that left its deepest imprint on Virgil's mind and heart was that of Epicurus, particularly as it had been recently interpreted by the great poet Lucretius in his *On the Nature of Things*. Epicurus believed that the remote and mysterious gods (if they truly exist) spend their serene existences in the contemplation of the realities of nature; they enjoy their being in perfect tranquillity, and they have no interest whatever in human beings and what they want and do. There obtains, then, an irremediable tension between Virgil's Epicurean sensibility and the conventions, specifically the divine machinery, of the epic genre he had undertaken to write in. Though what ultimately matters is the product of this fertile mismatch, one may speculate (however vainly) on the motivations that led Virgil to invest himself so deeply in a form whose conventions were so alien to his own worldview—and on how he came to view that choice in retrospect: blessed with and conflicted by a hybrid identity—Italian and Roman—Virgil wants to believe that Roman Italy's bloody past has ended in a better present. He sets out to write a poem that can help him believe, and perhaps help others to believe, that the nightmare of Roman/Italian history has ended—and he begins, naturally enough, by adopting the only form ready at hand for his purpose. But as he writes in this form and continues writing in it, he has at times the sinking feeling that he is producing what Plato had called "a noble lie." (It was said, after all, that when he died he ordered that his manuscript be destroyed). Seen from this perspective, questioning his poem's divine machinery as to why peace and brotherhood usually emerge only from the killing fields seems all but inevitable.

What usually disrupts the workings of the poem's divine providence (and so furnishes it with much of its tragic power) is, as its opening invocation to the Muse makes clear, the anger of Juno. In the *Iliad* her Greek counterpart Hera hates the Trojans as much as she loves the Greeks, so it is only to be expected that she will continue persecuting Aeneas in his own epic. She is also the patroness of Carthage, Rome's arch-rival in the race for empire after the death of Alexander the Great. And, of course, she tends to dislike heroes in general (see, for example, her vindictive torment of Heracles in Euripides' play of that name, lines 815–85). Her hatred, then, of Aeneas and his Trojans is multiply determined (see her wonderful opening tirade with its laundry list of grievances), and it is not merely a catalyst of epic action (like Apollo's in the *Iliad;* Lombardo's *Iliad* 1.10–15), nor is it temporary (like Poseidon's in the *Odyssey;* Lombardo's *Odyssey* 5.282–92, 380ff.; 9.522–30; 13.129–70): Juno's insatiable wrath is so pervasive that it comes to seem the poem's spine, its very plot.

Juno opens the poem, and she all but closes it. After her angry speech in Book 1, she immediately arranges for the storm at sea in which Aeneas and his Trojans almost drown; in Book 2, she is prominent among the gods who participate, in person and gleefully, in the destruction of Troy; Book 4 finds her colluding with her enemy, Aeneas' mother, Venus, to keep Aeneas with Dido in Carthage, thus preventing him from sailing off to Italy and founding there a new Troy (Venus wants only to assure him temporary safety in Carthage). In Book 5, as he nears his goal, Juno tries in vain to engineer the burning of his ships. But it is in Book 7, when Aeneas has completed his wanderings and has begun to establish himself, that, acknowledging that all her efforts have proved futile, her celestial rage turns hellish:

> But if my powers
> Are not great enough, why should I hesitate
> To seek help from any source whatever?
> If I cannot sway Heaven, I will awaken Hell!
> I concede Aeneas the rule of Latium,

And Lavinia is his bride by iron fate,
But to draw it out and delay the issue,
That I may do, and destroy both nations.
                    (7.378–85)

She understands well enough that she cannot truly alter fate, but she knows she can still cause countless deaths among the Trojans and Latins who are destined to be united, which means that she is in effect fomenting a civil war (a pattern that will endure through the centuries until, under Augustus, Rome and the Italians are, in Virgil's lifetime, united once and for all). Her vindictiveness has now grown so great that, thwarted from achieving any genuine goal, she is committed to doing evil for the sake of evil. For this purpose she summons Allecto, one of the Furies, from hell and commands her to start a war between the Latins and the Trojans: this Allecto proceeds to do with a joyful, demonic efficiency. It is this perverted divinity and her handmaid from hell who are ultimately responsible for what happens throughout the rest of the poem, and it is she who, having dismissed Allecto and sent her back to hell, becomes Discord incarnate as she flings open the gates of war. Having set her gratuitously evil project in motion, Juno is relatively quiet in Books 8 through 11, but she makes a spectacular reappearance in Book 12, where she once again manages to disrupt a new treaty between the opposing sides and to reactivate the (internecine) slaughter.

At last Jupiter persuades Juno to cease and desist her lethal meddlings. He appeals to her vanity, he promises her that the Romans will come to accord her extraordinary worship. In short, he buys her off. She quickly concedes, letting her resentments go (12.996–1008). Or so it seems. Roman readers would have no trouble remembering that, despite her nominal capitulation, in the centuries to come she would side with Carthage against Rome in three wars. Her seeming conversion arises less from Jupiter's powers of persuasion than from narrative expediency: it is time for the story to end, for Aeneas to win, and for Turnus to die. But Juno's submission and Jupiter's success in achieving it in no way answer the questions that Virgil had asked Jupiter a few hundred verses back or at the very beginning of his poem. At this scene's end and at the poem's end, its presentation of theodicy remains clouded in a sinister uncertainty.

One thing Juno clearly represents in the *Aeneid* is fortune (a word often connected with her). As a poetic concept she stands for—and in the poem's narrative she produces—accidents, contingencies, bad luck. She utterly opposes the ordinances of providential fate and contrives whenever possible to derail them—the more violently the better. In contrast, Jupiter represents, in an ambiguous, not wholly satisfying fashion, the power of providential fate, the justice and benevolence that supply the foundations for whatever is decent in the human condition. (Tribal god that Jupiter is, he also represents, of course, an incontestable validation of the Roman Empire.) The power of Juno's fortune cannot triumph over the power of Jupiter's fate, but (as Virgil's anguished question in Book 12 insinuates) Jupiter's fate cannot truly restrain the powers of darkness that Juno and her tamperings with fortune can unleash. One can argue, as the poem's denouement yearns to do, that all the accidents and contingencies, all the rotten, wretched luck that she invents, are, to recall the formulation of Alexander Pope, no more than "partial evils" that contribute to and are eventually gathered into a "universal good." But it is equally plausible that the bad contingencies are as real as they are prevalent and powerful, and that the providential wisdom that claims to transform them into itself is as likely as not to be yet another "noble lie," an illusion, a fiction useful when the tribe comes to (re)write its history, its victor's version of "how it happened." Seen in this latter way, Juno and Jupiter are evenly matched, and what Virgil's divine machine reveals is a tragic dialectic at the heart of history, one that has room both for glory and for the voices of the vanquished and the oppressed.

Aeneas the Wanderer

In the first six books of the *Aeneid*, its hero replicates, in highly condensed form, the travels of the *Odyssey*'s cunning, adventuresome, seriocomic hero. During the welcoming feast given him by Queen Dido of Carthage, Aeneas reluctantly yields to her request to hear about the fall of Troy and his search for the new homeland that numerous omens and prophecies have promised him. In Book 2 he recounts how the treacherous Greeks captured Troy, then indulged themselves in a savage spree of murder, looting, and burning. Troubled by these painful memories, he yet manages to tell of how he was barely able to rescue his son, his aged father, and his household gods and to lead them, together with the rest of the survivors, away from Troy into what turned out to be seven years of dangerous, baffling, and futile voyages. What most characterizes these self-narratives is their extraordinary self-effacement, a style of speech that is exactly counter to the fertile, energetic self-promotion that marks the stories effortlessly spun by Odysseus (that peerless confidence-man) whenever he finds it necessary or possible to recount or embellish or fabricate his adventures. The reader who remembers and expects here the swaggering brio of Aeneas' model in this section of the poem may be surprised and even disappointed by Aeneas as storyteller and hero of his own tale (in his *ABC of Reading,* Ezra Pound sketches a disgruntled reader who cries out in his exasperation: "Aach, a hero, him a hero? Bigod, I t'ought he waz a priest."). But however unheroic they may first strike us as being, Aeneas' laconic utterance and genuine humility are qualities of style and character that Aeneas manifests throughout his epic: here, precisely, the style is the man.

Our first impression of Aeneas in Book 1, when he is terrified that his ships are about to be sunk in the storm Juno has arranged for his destruction, is hardly auspicious. But he quickly recovers his self-possession and his courage once the storm has ended, and what sticks with us from the ensuing scenes are qualities that he will manifest hereafter throughout the poem: his humility (glory is not at all his highest priority), his remarkable instinct for self-sacrifice, and, most unexpected and most attractive of his virtues, his deep concern for the well-being of others. Some readers feel that he grows in discipline and in maturity as the poem progresses, but the degree of his composure and self-assurance seems more nearly a function of the situations he finds himself in. In Book 2, with his city in flames and falling to ruin all around him, he is at times all but hysterical with fear and rage—and too honest to try to conceal it. In Book 3, as he himself recounts it, the frustrations, the sinister people and places he meets with on his journeyings, and, finally, the sudden death of his father, Anchises, all combine to render him, for the most part, morose and querulous. In Book 4, Aeneas surprisingly and briefly imitates, in a somewhat pallid fashion, the robust and protracted philandering of Odysseus. Finally, in Book 6, he repeats his model's descent into the Underworld, but he manifests nothing of Odysseus' curiosity about the afterlife when he questions the newly dead or, after he recovers from his initial terror, his remarkable composure in dealing with the business of making his way through his gruesome ordeal and back out of it to the upper world. Aeneas, unlike Odysseus, behaves in the Underworld like a quiet spectator, or almost like a dutiful tourist, as he passes through the sights and sounds, familiar from Greek poetry, of the worst that hell has to offer. When he comes to the brighter spots in the afterlife and is briefly reunited with his father, Anchises, who has revealed to him, in a sort of splendid pageant, the outlines of his progeny's glory and of Rome's triumphant history, his responses to this amazing spectacle seem rather subdued: though we essentially see the glorious procession of Roman heroes through his eyes, our sense of what he thinks and feels about it is dim.

In Book 5, however, when, after successfully fleeing Dido and Carthage, he has reached Sicily, in imitation of Achilles in *Iliad* 23, he holds belated funeral games for his father, as the greatest of the Greek heroes had held them for his comrade Patroclus. This book shows Virgil's most faithful re-creation of Homer's matter and manner (it was Montaigne's favorite book of the *Aeneid*), and the sudden substitution here of Achilles as heroic model works flawlessly: with his father gone and his mission resumed in earnest he is in a position to behave in a more (conventionally) heroic manner than, for the most part, we have previously seen him behave. Here we find an Aeneas who is, for the first time, relaxed and gentle but clearly in command. In this setting, on this occasion, he has become, finally and fully, the leader of his troops and the father of his people, not so much because he has achieved moral growth as because the condition in which he finds himself has altered.

It is his utter submission of himself to those duties that explains why the adjective *pius* most frequently qualifies his name, and why he automatically chooses it when introducing himself to his mother, Venus (who has wittily disguised herself as her arch-rival, the goddess Diana, a chaste huntress); "I am Aeneas, devoted to my city's gods" (1.461). The English word "pious" fails to address the range of the Latin word's connotations, which center on the purity of an individual's devotion to the performance of the obligations he has to members of his family, to his fellow citizens, and to the gods of his tribe. The word is peculiar because it combines, from a modern point of view, a state of mind that is almost legalistic in its concern with the ties that bind a person to his kin and his comrades and the supernatural powers that can help or harm the place he inhabits with kin and comrades; it also suggests, more subtly, the affection or sympathy (we get "pity" as well as "pious" from *pius*) that a person is likely to have for those, whether mortal or immortal, with whom his life is linked. This complex of feelings, at once familial, patriotic, and religious, may at first seem strange to us (though the closer we regard it the more familiar it may come to seem), yet it lies at the core of the Roman identity. The pious son or father or husband or brother, the pious citizen, the pious wor-shiper, in sacrificing his individual self to this widening collectivity of needs and duties and emotions becomes more than himself: he becomes the incarnation of his family, his tribe, and his nation; he becomes one with what was for a Roman the real absolute, the real eternity, the real good, namely, the Roman State in all its power and glory and hoped-for permanence.

In the tribulations he suffers in the first half of his epic, in his waverings and his vulnerability, Aeneas shows how hard is the pro-cess of accepting the irreversible commitment that Roman piety enjoins on Rome's citizens. Readers in the Middle Ages tended to read the first six books of the poem (it looks as though they were not much interested in the last six) as an allegory in which Aeneas as prototype of a Christian Everyman trudged wearily through temptation and spiritual peril until, at the moment when he plucked the golden bough before venturing down into hell, he was granted moral enlightenment and complete wisdom. But Aeneas does not pluck the golden bough and descend into hell in order to become wise. When the Sibyl of Cumae offers new prophecies of the ordeals that await him in Italy, he cuts her short (6.133–48). He has heard elsewhere about his destiny in Italy, and he is intent on obeying the order that Anchises had given him in a dream (5.820–39): he was to come down into the Underworld and learn what his father's shade had to tell him about his mission and its meaning. And when he meets with his father, his father greets him with these words: "You have come at last! I knew your devotion [*pietas*] / Would see you through the long, hard road" (6.813–14). Here begins the solemn scene in which the father of the family transfers his duties to the son who now becomes the new father of the family. The ghost of the father, in the scenes that follow, relinquishes his powers (and obligations) to his living son who, on his return to life on earth in the upper world, will be the present incarnation of the family's past and of its future. And Aeneas, ancestor of Julius and Augustus Caesar, this particular and fated man, now becomes the incarnation of Rome's future, the sire of its destiny and triumph, the paradigm of its pious sons for as long as Rome itself will endure. This is the place and moment where the wanderer ends his wanderings. In just a few pages, when he ascends to the upper world, he will be ready to assume his role as Rome's warrior, the supreme model of those who, in the coming centuries, will win its empire and whose spirits had paraded past him and Anchises in the final, haunting scene of Book 6.

Aeneas the Warrior

The second half of the *Aeneid* is often described as Iliadic, thus distinguishing it from the first half, where Odysseus was Aeneas' chief model. Books 7 through 12 are primarily concerned with the war between Aeneas, together with the new allies he finds in Italy, and the native Italians, led by Turnus, who regard Aeneas as an invader. One might therefore reasonably expect that Aeneas' heroic model will now become Achilles, but, paradoxically, this does not quite happen. As the invader of Italy, Aeneas seems to take on certain of Achilles' traits in specific situations, but as *pius* defender of hearth and family, he nevertheless often resembles Achilles' enemy, Hector. In contrast, it is Turnus, like Hector the champion of his invaded homeland, who frequently resembles Achilles. But whatever his similarities to Hector or to Achilles, Aeneas differs from conventional Homeric (or Roman) heroes in his seemingly fundamental aversion to warfare.

This quality of Aeneas must not be misunderstood: in no way is he to be thought of as some variety of pacifist (a concept bizarre in the extreme to the Roman mind) or as in any way lacking in bravery or martial excellence. Rather, efficient warrior that he is, he is essentially a man of peace. The day after his arrival in Latium, before he has begun to build a temporary settlement, he sends an embassy to the country's ruler, King Latinus, asking for peace. When this embassy has been warmly welcomed by Latinus, its spokesman asks only for "a safe strip of shore, / A little land for the gods of our country, / And water and air that are common to all" (7.276–78). Latinus happily grants this request, and the embassy returns to Aeneas bringing an offer of the peaceful outcome he had hoped for. We are not, and need not be, told how Aeneas receives this news. Instead, we immediately see and hear Juno's expected reaction to these events: she summons Allecto to incite hostilities, and once Allecto has completed her task, Juno opens the gates of war and hurls Aeneas into a war he did not want.

Desperate for help, Aeneas goes to King Evander, an émigré from Greece who has founded a new city-state on the site where Rome itself will later stand. No sooner has Evander agreed to send his soldiers off under Aeneas' command than Venus signals him with thunder and lightning that she will soon be bringing the divine armor that she has prevailed on her husband, Vulcan, to create for him. Venus' signal shakes Aeneas from the gloomy ruminations that had taken hold of him as soon as Evander promised him the soldiers he had come for: he does not look forward to the carnage that is now close at hand and says to Evander:

> Ask not what the portents forebode,
> My dear host; in truth, do not ask. It is I
> Who am summoned by heaven. . . .
> Ah, the slaughter in store for the poor Laurentines!
> What a price you will pay me, Turnus! How many
> Shields and helmets and bodies of the brave
> Will you, Father Tiber, roll beneath your waves?
> Let them call for battle and break their treaty!
> (8.605–7, 611–15)

These lines recall Aeneas' very first speech in the poem, his cry of anguish when he thinks that he and his ships are about to be destroyed in the storm and remembers the countless deaths that his comrades had suffered years before when Troy fell to the Greeks. In this passage, he seems to be making no distinction between the imminent Trojan deaths and those of his enemies. It is not only the brutality of the coming battles that sickens and grieves him here; he is also saddened by and angered at the futility, the needlessness, of a war that he had tried to avoid by the careful diplomacy of his first overtures to Latinus. He does not yet, and never will, know that Turnus is innocent of the outbreak of a war that Juno and her henchwoman are guilty of having ignited; instead, even when he blames Turnus, he manifests a touch of compassion for the man he thinks guilty of causing the carnage he despises: "What a price you will pay me, Turnus!" (8.612). This is an utterance shaped by an angry pity; it almost a cry of despair.

Aeneas figures only briefly in Book 9. When in Book 10 he returns to Latium with his allies, before he and Turnus manage to encounter one another, the action shifts to Evander's son, Pallas. This young prince is enjoying enormous success in his debut as a warrior when he meets up with Lausus, son of the ferocious Etruscan king, Mezentius. But before they can square off against each other, Turnus rushes forward to save Lausus, challenges Pallas, and quickly dispatches him. Having slain the young warrior, Turnus strips the sword-belt from his corpse. Upon learning of Pallas' death, Aeneas rushes off to avenge him:

> He mowed down everything before him
> With his sword, burning a broad path
> Through the enemy, seeking you, Turnus,
> Flush with slaughter. Pallas, Evander,
> Everything swam in Aeneas' eyes—the table
> He came to as a stranger, the right hands pledged.
>   (10.619–24)

This brief flash of picture-memory in Aeneas' mind's eye marks a crucial moment in the poem. Immediately after it, echoing Achilles in one of his most savage moments, Aeneas grabs eight young enemies whom he will later offer as human sacrifices at the funeral of Pallas. He then charges off after Turnus, slaughtering any Italian he meets in a killing frenzy worthy of Achilles at his most ferocious. But Juno has snatched Turnus out of battle before Aeneas can get to him; cheated of the champion he wants to slay, Aeneas attempts to appease his vengeful wrath by killing any enemy he finds in his path.

It is Mezentius, Turnus' most formidable ally, whom he finally chances on. When Aeneas wounds Mezentius, Lausus rushes bravely to his father's defense, and Aeneas, just before he is forced to kill the young man, cries out to him:

> You're headed for death, Lausus! Why rush it
> By daring what's beyond your strength?
> Your filial devotion is blinding you.
>   (10.968–70)

As a son who loves his father and a father who loves his son,
Aeneas, even as he threatens him, instantly recognizes his own best
virtue in the young man who is about to die at his hands. And
when, while driving his sword through Lausus' body,

> Anchises' son looked on his dying face,
> So strangely pale, he groaned in pity
> And stretched out his hand. There shone in that face
> The image of his own devotion to Anchises. . . .
>   "What now, poor boy,
> Can Aeneas give you for such glorious deeds?
> What is worthy of so great a heart?"
>
>   (10.982–88)

Moved by a curious sense of kinship with this enemy, shaken by
compassion and admiration, Aeneas refuses to strip the corpse and
lifts it tenderly from the ground. This peculiar mix of emotions,
wherein *pietas* all but finds itself divided against itself, goes against
both the epic and the Roman grain. It bespeaks both the poem's
underground Epicurean current and a new kind of hero that it
helps produce. It is this sensitivity, this paradoxical, emergent bias
against violence, that makes Aeneas the strange kind of warrior he
is and that, as we shall presently see, defines the poem's harrowing
final scene where, his emotions again in powerful conflict, he
chooses, or is compelled, to disobey his better instincts.

This peaceable warrior makes one last and powerful appearance
in the poem's final book where once again a treaty has been
arranged between Aeneas and Latinus. This treaty stipulates that
Aeneas and Turnus meet in single combat to decide which of them
will have the king's daughter as his bride and, on the King's death,
his crown. Juno, naturally, has no intention of allowing this solution
to come to its fruition. She summons a new helper, Turnus' own sis-
ter, the fountain-nymph Juturna, to incite Turnus' army to disrupt
the ritual that will ratify the treaty. Then, when Juturna has obeyed
Juno's command and the treaty is in ruins and the bloodletting
begun in earnest, Aeneas rushes forward and shouts to his soldiers:

>   Where are you going?
> What is this sudden surge of strife? Hold in your rage!
> The truce has already been struck, its terms set:

I alone have the right to fight. Let me do it,
Forget your fears; this hand will make the treaty true.
These rites have already given Turnus to me!
                                        (12.381–86)

His *pietas* shines forth here in perfect clarity. He is upset by the dis-
ruption of the ritual that would have sanctified his treaty with Lat-
inus (hostilities have broken out before Turnus could reach the
altar and complete the ritual). But he is also concerned for the lives
of his men, and, as was the case in his similar speech in Book 8, he
is probably also concerned for the lives of the enemy soldiers. This
brave attempt to end violence and restore the rule of law is sud-
denly cut short by a mysterious arrow:

> As Aeneas was saying these things an arrow
> Whistled through the air toward him
> In a long falling arc, shot by whose hand
> No one knows, nor whether it was pure chance
> Or some god who brought the Rutulians
> This glory. Credit for the deed is hidden,
> And no one boasted of wounding Aeneas.
>   (12.387–93)

In their last exchange, a few hundred verses later, Jupiter will
tease Juno about this mysterious wound that brought so much
death to Trojans and Italians alike, asking her if it was right for
an immortal to be wounded by a mortal. Juno indignantly insists
that in persuading Juturna to help her brother she never intended
that such help would include the wounding of Aeneas by a mor-
tal. She hints that Juturna herself may have shot the impious
arrow, then suddenly announces her capitulation to Jupiter and to
Fate. This amazing about-face is perhaps intended to conceal her
own guilt: the angry goddess who opened the Gate of War would
hardly shrink, when she senses herself about to be defeated at
last, from loosing an arrow at the man whose mission she has
moved heaven and hell to destroy. But, whoever shot it ("pure
chance" or "some god"—the poet here is brilliantly equivocal),
the arrow does its work, and Aeneas' passionate hope for bring-
ing the slaughter to an end, for securing a just peace, is once again
destroyed.

Very soon, Aeneas will kill Turnus and the peace he worked for will thereby have been achieved. But, as we will presently see, it is a wrathful not a peaceable warrior who secures that peace, and the poem closes neither with a triumphalist vision of historical necessity nor with a quieter celebration of the coming of a peaceable kingdom. We last see Aeneas in a state of conflicted emotion, and we see him from the perspective of the man he kills. This abrupt and chilling finale does little to brighten our last glimpse of the poem's hero. Which is why, fourteen centuries later, in 1428, Maffeo Vegio decided to add a thirteenth book to the poem, one written in an impeccably correct imitation of the master's style, and one that provided the poem with both a properly triumphalist uplift and (to shore up that triumphalism) a subtle vilification of Aeneas' enemy, the dastardly Turnus.

Turnus

Aeneas' victory over Turnus and the native Italians he led is incontrovertibly fated: Aeneas must establish his people in their new homeland and that settlement, that fusion of Trojans and Italians, must be the origin of the city that will in time come to rule the (known) world. Which means that, as Hector must die in his epic, so Turnus must die in his. But the poetic and the historical necessities that insist on Rome's destiny and Turnus' doom do not require that Turnus die as he does or mean that he merits the death he receives. For some readers, to be sure, Turnus, the villain of the piece, gets no more and no less than he deserves on the poem's final page; however, that response, that judgment, has its roots not so much in Turnus' actions or character as these are presented in the narrative as it does in feelings of the readers in question that for the poem to be successful (for these readers to be content with it) Turnus must be punished by the death that Aeneas inflicts on him. This view of Turnus' death, however, foists on the poem two burdens it doesn't need: by denigrating Turnus it provides Aeneas with an adversary who is unworthy of him, thus cheapening his victory, and it converts a genuine tragedy, one that grapples uniquely with the ambiguities that confront the historical imagination, into a melodrama as cheap as it is predictable.

In the eyes of Turnus, Aeneas is a dangerous immigrant, the leader of a swarm of nasty foreigners wearing funny clothes and speaking gibberish; for Turnus, he is a lying interloper who seeks to hide his real intention, the conquest of Latinus' kingdom, behind preposterous claims that numerous portents and oracles have promised him the possession of a new homeland in Latium. Turnus is entirely ignorant of the truth of Aeneas' claim, and he has some reason to doubt Latinus when, basing his opinion on omens and oracles of his own, he offers confirmation of the truth of Aeneas' claims. Before the arrival of the Trojans, Turnus had given Latinus valuable military assistance, and he feels that he had every reason to believe that Latinus had preferred him to his daughter's other suitors and had in fact betrothed Lavinia to him. He believed, in short, that he would be the king's successor. But Latinus, just before he becomes aware of the Trojans' arrival, consults his father, the rustic deity Faunus, who warns him:

> Seek not, my son, to marry your daughter
> Into a Latin family. Trust not a wedding
> Already prepared. A stranger will come
> To be your son-in-law. His blood will exalt
> Our name to the stars, and his children's children
> Will see the world turn under their feet,
> And their rule will stretch over all that the Sun
> Looks down upon, from sea to shining sea.
> (7.115–22)

His father's promise, another of the prophecies of Rome's unbounded empire that echo throughout the poem, naturally changes Latinus' mind about his choice of son-in-law and heir. But, apparently, he does not bother to tell Turnus about this sudden and crucial alteration in their relationship. Perhaps he assumed that rumors of the newcomers and of the broken betrothal would soon enough reach Turnus' ears. Or perhaps he was too ashamed of himself to approach Turnus directly. In any case, when Aeneas' embassy has explained who the Trojans are and what Aeneas wants, Latinus' response, echoing and inspired by his father's prophecies of empire, is quick and certain:

> "This," he thought, "must be the foreigner
> Whom the Fates have destined to be

My son in marriage and to share my power
Equally. His descendants will excel
In virtue, and rule the world with might."
                    (7.307–11)

Latinus is characteristically timid and indecisive. His haste here
and his failure to consult with Turnus and with his queen, Amata,
to make them understand what compels him to act as he does sets
just the stage that Juno needs for her fatal reentry into the poem.
Bidden by Juno to stir things up, the first thing the Fury Allecto
does is to infect Amata with madness, and the second thing she
does is to cause Turnus' derangement. It can be and has been
argued that both these characters are quite disposed to the behav-
ior she induces in them before she maddens them, but the fact
remains that without the violent transformations that Allecto
effects in them they might have accepted, however reluctantly, Lat-
inus' changed intentions.

Amata is not yet entirely under the influence of the Fury's poison
when she attempts to remind her husband of what she (Turnus'
aunt) regards as his firm commitments to her and to her nephew:

        What of your solemn promise?
    What of your old love for your own, what of
    Your hand so often pledged to Turnus,
    Your kinsman?
                    (7.446–49)

When Latinus refuses to give way, she rushes out from the palace,
and, the effect of Allecto's poison now fully mastering her, she sets
about stirring up war-frenzy in the female population of her city.

Once Allecto has "undone Latinus and all his house" (7.498),
she flies off to Turnus' city, Ardea. There, disguised as an ancient
priestess of Juno (Turnus' patron goddess), she mocks him
viciously as he sleeps: "The king / Denies you the bride you won
with your blood, / And a stranger is sought as heir to your throne"
(7.516–18). She assures him that Juno has sent her to rouse him to
arms (which is in fact true):

        Up then, smile,
    Arm your lads, march them through the gates

> Into the fields, and burn the painted Phrygian ships
> Lying at anchor in our beautiful river!
> Heaven commands it. And unless King Latinus
> Honors his word and gives you your bride,
> Let him feel the full force of Turnus as foe.
>
> (7.523–29)

The dreamer answers her scornfully: he has heard the rumors about the Trojans' coming, but he isn't worried about losing Lavinia since Juno is on his side. This response irritates the Fury, who then flings a torch into his stomach. He wakes in terror, crazed and ready for war, and, "peace be damned" (7.562), he rushes off to collect his troops and march against Aeneas and, if need be, against Latinus. (Note that the peace he damns is one secured by a treaty to which he was not a party and which, in fact, was not fully in force since hostilities between Trojans and Latins broke out before Aeneas and Latinus could formally meet to ratify it.)

While Turnus is gathering his army, Allecto returns to Latium and contrives to set the Trojans and Latins at one another's throats. Just as Turnus arrives on the scene with his army, Latinus looks out from his palace on his people: "Defying the omens and the sacred oracles, / Their minds twisted, they all clamored / For an unholy war" (7.700–2). Responding to the destruction of his plans, he feels himself "powerless / To change their blind resolve" and sees that "all was going / As cruel Juno wished" (7.709–11). Turnus and the Latins have no good reason to think of this war as being "unholy," and Latinus himself has no knowledge whatever of Juno's role in fomenting the chaos that now overwhelms him. But overwhelmed he is, and he calls "the gods and the empty air to witness" (7.712) as he curses Turnus and his people for their wicked disobedience, then shuts himself away inside his palace and all but abdicates his throne.

As we've seen, Aeneas also blames Turnus for the broken treaty in his speech (8.607) when he is "summoned by heaven" and the war is about to begin in earnest. But Latinus and Aeneas are wrong in their condemnation. As we're about to see, Turnus cannot be described as being innocent, but he is not guilty of this particular charge. And only pure prejudice will be unwilling to try looking from his perspective at the situation that confronts him when

Aeneas threatens to take from him Lavinia and the dowry that comes with her—or will persist in regarding the machinations of Juno and Allecto as being nearly ornamental explanations of Turnus' (and Amata's) motives and actions. Whatever his failings, Turnus is not treacherous, and he is hardly in the wrong when refusing to give way to what he regards as Aeneas' invasion of Italy or to countenance Latinus' injustice toward him.

Turnus is a ferocious warrior, and his affinities with Achilles are striking, particularly in the closing scenes of Book 9 where his martial prowess and assured individualism take on a superhuman brilliance. Also like Achilles, Turnus is born of a minor deity: Amata's sister is the nymph Venilia, daughter of a venerable Italian deity. (This aspect of the poem reflects the slow, almost imperceptible displacement of Italy's archaic, rural deities by the Hellenized deities of Rome as it expands its empire.) He also resembles Achilles in being specially marked by his rage, and like Achilles' his killings can be accompanied by what seems gratuitous malice: just before he kills Pallas he expresses the wish that the young man's father, Evander, might be present to witness his son's death. But both the bitterness of this ugly wish and the intensity of rage that he manifests elsewhere in the poem find some explanation in what he says to Pallas' fellow soldiers as he bestrides the young man's corpse:

> Remember, Arcadians, to bring my words
> To Evander. I send him the Pallas he deserves.
> The honor of a tomb, the solace of burial
> I freely grant, but he will pay dearly
> For welcoming Aeneas.
>
> (10.592–96)

His anger here (and elsewhere) is not "a character flaw." Heroes, and epic heroes in particular, are supposed to be angry. The quality and degree of Turnus' anger has its origins in what he sees as Aeneas' invasion of Italy; in his eyes, furthermore, the outrage of that invasion has been compounded by salt in the wound—Latinus' cowardice and duplicity. As for the vindictive message to Evander, Turnus regards him and his son as traitors, for, though they may be Greek émigrés, they are, so to speak, naturalized Italians and ought to help defend their adopted homeland.

These arguments are not offered to make Turnus seem like a nice person or to condone what seem to some his excesses; they are intended only to place his behavior inside the expectations that the genre of epic provide us with and that we should use in arriving at any judgment we may make of him. Thus, however nastily he returns the body to the father, he does return it. And if he first despoils it of its sword-belt and glories in doing so, his action is quite conventional. When the poet intrudes into this scene with a comment on Turnus' despoilment,

> the mind of man
> Knows neither fate nor future doom
> Nor moderation when elated by fortune.
> The hour will come when Turnus will wish
> He had paid handsomely for an unharmed Pallas
> And will curse the day he won those spoils,
>   (10.603–8)

he does so not to rebuke him for acting as epic heroes ordinarily act on the field of battle but to comment (it would be futile to warn him) on the tragic consequences of this particular despoilment; it is a grieving adumbration of the poem's tragic closing scene.

The extraordinary power of the poem's last scene derives from the poet's skillful gathering of his major themes throughout Book 12 into the discordant harmony of its final verses, from his careful husbanding of suspense, and from the superb momentum he sustains until he lets the inevitable happen. Back in Book 11, addressing Latinus and his court, Turnus had ended his magnificent refutation of the slanders heaped upon him by the quisling Drances with an offer to put an end to the war by engaging in single combat with Aeneas:

> To all of you and to Latinus,
> Father of my bride, I, Turnus, second
> In valor to none of my ancestors,
> Dedicate my life. Aeneas calls me out?
> I pray that he does, and that it is not Drances
> But I who appease the gods with death,
> If they are angry, or win glory for valor.
>   (11.523–29)

True hero that he is, with a solemn vow (the ritual is called *devotio*), he devotes himself to the infernal gods, offering his life in exchange for a Trojan defeat. So, at the beginning of Book 12, when Latinus, feckless as usual, suggests that Turnus can avoid single combat (and with it the need for *devotio*) by withdrawing his claim to Lavinia, marrying some other Latin lady of noble birth, and going home to his father, Latinus only succeeds in angering Turnus more. That rising anger is heightened by Amata's tearful plea for him not to risk himself and by the sight of Lavinia's blush (which he rightly takes as a sign of her love for him). Propelled by this complex of emotions, he rushes off to prepare himself for the holy ritual that will sanctify a new treaty, one that will commit him to single combat with Aeneas.

The ratification of this (second) treaty is, as we've seen, disrupted by Juno and her new helper, Juturna. And Book 12 is in fact remarkable (it was a source of huge irritation for the poem's most famous English translator, John Dryden) for the steady intrusions by female representatives of the divine machinery into the resolution of this heroic conflict. In addition to Juno and Juturna, Venus and one of the Furies (Dirae) also get into the action. Divine interventions are commonplace in the *Iliad,* but, aside from Juno's, they are relatively infrequent in this poem. Condensed as they are in Book 12, they take on peculiar prominence, and, in its closing scene, the intervention is peculiarly sinister.

After Juturna provokes hostilities and someone shoots the arrow that wounds Aeneas, Venus comes down to see to his quick healing and recuperation. Thereafter, she returns to help him when he needs it, while Juturna, having carried out the orders of Juno, concerns herself with efforts to help her brother and finally to save him from death. But when Juturna has done all that she can for Turnus and he knows that the tide of battle has turned against his army, realizing that his doom is near, he prepares himself for his fatal encounter and goes off to find Aeneas, like a gladiator entering the arena:

> Now every last man turned and stared—
> Every Rutulian, Trojan, and Italian soldier,
> Both those high on the walls and those below
> Who were battering the walls—and they all
> Took off their armor. Latinus himself
> Was lost in wonder that these two great men,

Born in different parts of the world, had met
And now would settle the issue with steel.
                    (12.848–55)

Their initial engagement produces no victor. Then comes the conversation between Jupiter and Juno that signals her abandon-ment of Turnus (previously, Jupiter had held up his ironic scales just as Turnus and Aeneas first encountered one another). Next, having dealt with Juno, Jupiter decides to frighten Juturna away from her brother and soften him up for Aeneas by sending down a Fury (this time unnamed, and Virgil's deliberate imprecision here renders her all the more sinister). Juno's Fury had to be summoned from the depths of hell where she and her sisters are customarily to be found in Greek and Latin poetry. Now, with another touch of Euripidean irony, Virgil shapes a terrifying anomaly: we learn that two of the Furies—apparently they can be at two places at the same time—also sit by the throne of heaven's "grim monarch" (12.1018), ready to be unleashed as divine justice requires. One of these Furies Jupiter sends down to pay a visit on Juturna and her brother. The description of the Fury's descent, of Juturna's retreat, and of the bird-fiend's assault on Turnus are among the most hor-rific passages in ancient (or any) poetry. The intrusion of Athena in *Iliad* 22 and her cruel deception of Hector bring shivers up and down the spine, but Virgil's celestial demon evokes pure horror. Turnus claims to have recovered from the terror the fiend had instilled in him when Aeneas challenges him (presumably Aeneas is unaware of the ugly help he's getting). With superhuman strength, Turnus hoists an immense stone and flings it at Aeneas, but when he fails to hit him, his nerve suddenly fails him, and he turns to flight. Then follows a simile, borrowed from Homer and here bril-liantly expanded, in which the dread and impotence we feel when being pursued in nightmares evokes Turnus' terror and despair:

> In dreams,
> When night's weariness weighs on our eyes,
> We are desperate to run farther and farther
> But collapse weakly in the middle of our efforts.
> Our tongue doesn't work, our usual strength
> Fails our body, and words will not come.
>   (12.1100–5)

From its very first lines, as we read Book 12, we become gradually ever more aware that we are seeing much of its action through the eyes of Turnus (much as was the case with Dido in Book 4). In this closing scene everything is filtered through his perspective and his feelings. And that is why, when he admits being in the wrong and begs Aeneas to show some mercy ("Give me, or if you prefer, / Give my dead body back to my people," 12.1134–35), some readers feel only horror when the last thing they see is the last thing Turnus sees: his killer's face.

What contributes to that horror, of course, is another, final glimpse, before the wrathful deathblow, of the humane Aeneas, the Epicurean human being who is not much at home in his poem:

> Aeneas stood there, lethal in his bronze.
> His eyes searched the distance, and his hand
> Paused on the hilt of his sword. Turnus' words
> Were winning him over, but then his gaze shifted
> To the fateful baldric on his enemy's shoulder,
> And the belt glittered with its familiar metalwork. . . .
> (12.1139–44)

Aeneas doesn't kill Turnus because Turnus took Pallas' sword-belt or even because Turnus killed Pallas. Aeneas kills Turnus because he, Aeneas, had failed to keep his bargain with Evander, had not protected and guided his son, the novice warrior, and had allowed him to perish on his first battlefield. Aeneas is not angry with Turnus (whose looted sword-belt tells the story, by the way, of how young bridegrooms are sometimes murdered); Aeneas is angry with himself and with war itself and, though he doesn't know it, with Juno and even, or especially, with the Jupiter whom the poem's poet himself had bitterly cried out against. This poem is crowded with victims, and among them are both Turnus and his despairing, reluctant killer.

Dido

In her way as much a threat to Aeneas' mission as Turnus, and far more famous than he, is the woman Aeneas encounters in the first half of his poem. Few women destroyed by their passion can vie with Dido in the duration of their fame or the intensity of the sympathy or condemnation they inspire. In part her eminence here depends solely on her having found a role in a major, enduring epic poem, but her success as an iconic fictional character also arises from the generous imagination and flawless artistry that her creator lavished on her. Two of her ancient readers, Ovid and Augustine, despite the chasm that divides both their literary tastes and their ethical values, agree in making her the center of their experience of the poem. She tends to dominate the first half of the poem, and subtle echoes of her drift through its second half. She is a commanding, unforgettable, tragic figure not only in her own right but also because her tragedy does much to illumine the tragedy of the man whose love destroys her.

But she is hardly tragic when we first see her through the eyes of Aeneas. Like him, she has had to flee her homeland, and like him again she was destined to find a new homeland for herself and for those Phoenicians who escaped with her from her wicked brother. So, a widow and alone in a strange, forbidding place, she is busily engaged in building her new city when Aeneas, just escaped from the sea-storm, comes to her, asking for her help. When Dido first graciously welcomes Aeneas, she proves to be as compassionate as she is wise and effective a ruler. She is a great, good queen. But when he abandons her in obedience to Jupiter's commands and resumes his search for his new Troy in Italy, she becomes a helpless, crazed, vindictive woman who, having forsaken her responsibilities to her city, and having risked everything for her departed lover, now curses him and his progeny and kills herself.

The models for this character, for the forms and feelings that suit it, come not from Homer (Dido is not Calypso or Circe) but from Apollonius of Rhodes' Medea and from Euripidean tragedy (primarily Phaedra in the *Hippolytus*). In Apollonius' charming, truncated epic about callow Jason and his quest for the Golden Fleece, the origins and evolution of young Medea's passion for the handsome Greek stranger emerge from an intricate, exquisite depiction of the young woman's psyche, from the transformations that take place in her heart and her head when she collides with the new, intense erotic experience that Jason, with some divine assistance, inflicts on her. These narrative representations of erotic dynamics depend heavily on the monologues and dialogues that Euripides perfected when he was attempting to solve the problem of how a dramatist can represent inwardness onstage, how he can show what happens in the psyche by representing the hopeless conflicts that Phaedra, for example, ponders and struggles with before she makes her fatal erotic mistake and announces the passion she feels for her stepson. Taking up these Greek models, transporting them into his heroic epic (Apollonius' epic, whatever it is, is not heroic), Virgil fashions the figure of Dido into a powerful obstacle to Aeneas' mission. She is a woman whose qualities of mind and heart, whose splendid passion, could and almost did deflect him from his destiny. Because we have witnessed the growth and workings of her passion (as surely as we witness those of Anna Karenina or Emma Bovary), because we understand the complex causes of her desperation, we care about her, and her death matters to us. As it did to Aeneas.

Or so it seems to me. The precise nature of his feelings for Dido have been the subject of considerable debate over the centuries, female readers often writing him off as worse than a cad, male readers quite frequently defending him by heaping on her the entire wealth of the misogynist's dictionary. This argument will doubtless never find resolution because Virgil's penchant both for delicate shading and for outright ambiguity finds here its fullest freedom. In any case, even more than Book 12 belongs to Turnus, Book 4 belongs to Dido. When we are not listening to her speak, we see most of what happens through her eyes or from her perspective. Which means that, particularly at crucial moments, we know relatively little about what Aeneas is thinking and feeling.

Take, for example, the moment when Dido and Aeneas, driven from their regal hunt, happen to seek shelter from the rain in the same cave. They do not get there by accident.

> Earth herself and bridal Juno
> Give the signal. Fires flash in the Sky,
> Witness to their nuptials, and the Nymphs
> Wail high on the mountaintop. That day
> Was the first cause of calamity and of death
> To come. For no longer is Dido swayed
> By appearances or her good name. No more
> Does she contemplate a secret love. She calls it
> Marriage, and with that word she cloaks her sin.
>   (4.189–97)

Juno, goddess of marriage, is there in the cave already, waiting
with the Earth Mother, for the not-to-be-so happy bride and
groom. It's possible that Dido might have fallen in love with
Aeneas without divine assistance, but, for very different reasons,
first Venus, and then, colluding with her, Juno, have made sure that
Dido will become *madly* enamored of Aeneas. Is this a wedding or
not? Juno apparently thinks so, and who, if not she, goddess of
weddings, should know? Dido thinks of it as a marriage (though
her subconscious mind condemns her use of the word and reproves
her for betraying her vows to her dead husband), and later she will
insist to Aeneas that they are in fact married. Aeneas will deny this
(4.386–87) when she confronts him on discovering his plans to
leave Carthage and abandon her; yet he has, up to this point, been
behaving rather in the manner of her prince consort, which is pre-
cisely why Jupiter sends Mercury to scare him into abandoning her
and then resuming his quest for the promised homeland. When
Aeneas tells his captains to prepare in secret for their departure
from Carthage,

> He explains that—since good Dido knows nothing
> And would never dream that a love so strong
> Could ever be destroyed—he himself will find
> A way to approach her, the right occasion
> To break the news to her gently.
>
> (4.326–30)

Is the "love so strong" in question hers or his or theirs? Apparently
it is theirs. In his conclusion to the laconic, clumsy defense he tries
to offer to her devastating accusations, he states (too) simply: "It is
not my own will—this quest for Italy" (4.415). That brief (sincere)
summation echoes what he had earlier affirmed ("If the Fates
would allow me to lead my own life . . .," 4.388): his fate is his
country's, his country's is his, and there is no choice for him, pious
Aeneas, to make. She, naturally, is not persuaded by these argu-
ments, and in her second speech she curses him and hints at the sui-
cide she will in fact commit:

> And when cold death has cloven body from soul,
> My ghost will be everywhere. You will pay,
> You despicable liar, and I will hear the news;

Word will reach me in the deeps of hell.
(4.445–48)

Saying this, she runs off, "leaving him there / Hesitant with fear, and with so much more to say" (4.451–52). Then,

Aeneas, loyal and true, yearns to comfort her,
Soothe her grief, and say the words that will
Turn aside her sorrow. He sighs heavily,
And although great love has shaken his soul,
He obeys the gods' will and returns to the fleet.
(4.455–59)

Aeneas, loyal and true: *pius Aeneas*. Fearful, with much to say, compassionate, shaken in his soul by great love, and, of course, obedient to the gods. Much feeling and meaning is packed into these few verses, which violently compress what he would have said had Dido (and Virgil) let him say it.

That brief evocation of his true feelings slips from our memories. Whereas Dido's passions persist, vivid and indelible, we recall only the hero's obedience, and we tend to forget the lover's consternation and, above all, his *great love*. And we forget too the split, the division, in his soul's essence, his *pietas*: for if he obeys his duty piously, he feels equal obligation (and pity and compassion) where his beloved Dido is concerned. We forget these few lines (and the passions that are radically condensed in them, that they have been distilled into) because Dido's two tirades have dazzled us, have all but blinded us to his presence in the scene. If Homer had written this scene, Dido and Aeneas would have argued their positions with equal force and at equal length: that is to say, this scene would have been built out of a dramatic confrontation because Homer's poems, particularly the *Iliad,* owe their essential formal structure to passionate, conflicting dialogue. Virgil, by contrast, lets his characters argue with each other briefly and much more rarely; instead, he tends to evoke their emotions (or moods) before or after conflict through monologue and descriptions of his characters' mental landscapes. (Virgil's fondness for imagining inwardness is but one of the ways in which his art contrasts with Homer's: deep affinities between the two poets notwithstanding—Homer never had a better reader—and contrary to misconceptions of the *Aeneid* as a pale imitation of its model, Virgil's psychological sharpness points to a genius that is not merely new, but something unique, something equally incomparable.)

This tendency to replace conflict with psychological description works nowhere to better advantage than here. So sympathetic and so cunning is the artistry that fashions Dido and her erotic rhetoric that we see and judge her nearly taciturn lover as she does; then, condemning him, and letting that condemnation stain, however faintly, what we later see of him, we erase from our memories of him his violently conflicted feelings in this crucial scene, his grief and his great love. (Unless, of course, we take a leaf from *A Streetcar Named Desire* and read Book 4 as Stanley Kowalski would have us read it, thus dismissing Dido as just another crazy lady doing crazy lady things.) Forgetting how this scene really ends *(not* with her dramatic exit) and how Aeneas really feels, we may mark him (unconsciously perhaps) as weak, craven, passionless, a patriotic robot.

That prejudice may cause us to misread him when he encounters Dido in the Underworld, in the Fields of Lamentation, in the company of others whose love has doomed them. When he sees her she seems to him

> *As faint as the new moon a man sees,*
> *Or thinks he sees, through the evening's haze.*
>
> He broke into tears and spoke to her
> With tender love. . . .
>   (6.545–48)

Here, as often in Virgil, feelings are evoked with a delicate, lyrical simile. Aeneas is not sure of what he sees, is not sure he wants to see what he sees. In his confusion and grief, he weeps. Then he tries to absolve himself of her death, desperately swearing "by the stars, by the powers above" (6.551), that he left her (but he fumbles here, saying not her but "her land") only when forced to leave at heaven's orders. "I could not believe that I would cause you / Such grief by leaving"(6.557–58). Hearing this, she starts to go despite his plea to her to stay and hear his excuses. "With such words Aeneas tried to soothe / Her burning soul. Tears came to his eyes, / But Dido kept her own eyes fixed on the ground" (6.561–63), and she hurried off, hostile and cold, to the "darkling grove" and the comforting embrace of her husband. And "Aeneas, struck by the injustice / Of her fate, wept as he watched her / Disappear, and pitied her as she went" (6.569–71). The complex of tensions that shape this scene are easily resolved if we ignore his copious (and genuine) tears and then take his words at face value; if, that is to say, we regard him here as a not much older but much wiser warrior who has "gotten over" a passion that meant much less to him than it did to the doomed lady for whose demise (for which he feels, he says, no responsibility) he now expresses sympathy.

Aeneas, in such a reading of this scene, is a man who, after a final, unfortunate distraction, is now certain of his mission and fully ready to shoulder it. He feels pity for the lost lady, and he sheds a tear or two over her fate, but he then turns back to resume his journey through hell. He is indeed eager to meet his father, and he is in fact more nearly a man with a mission—he knows that he is now on the verge of undertaking it in earnest at last—than he was when he first met Dido in the upper world. But his despairing last words to her ("Fate will never / Let us speak with each other again," 6.559–60) remind us of his final earthly meeting with her, when she also left him before he could say to her what he really wanted to say: not that he had to fulfill his duty but that he loved her. His tears, then, and what he thinks of as his pity for her unjust fate are as much for himself as they are for her. The same fate that took her love from her took his from him.

This had happened to him before, toward the end of Book 2, when in the confusion of his escape from Troy he somehow lost his beloved wife, Creüsa ("Some malignant spirit / Robbed me of my wits. . . . My wife, Creüsa, was taken from me / By some evil fortune" (2.864–68). Virgil is one of the great poets of lost loves, and these moments with Dido and Creüsa echo the superb pathos of the scene near the end of Book 4 of Virgil's short "epic" on farming, the *Georgics,* where the poet Orpheus loses Eurydice, the wife whom he had risked going down into hell to recover. Like Orpheus, like himself toward the end of Book 2, the Aeneas who stumbles into Dido in Book 6 is a man who feels things deeply, as we learned early on in the poem when, in Book 1, we saw him weeping as he looked at representations of the Trojan War ("Here are the tears of the ages, and minds touched / By human suffering" (1.567–68). This hero and lover is a man of feelings that are at once complex and intense: deep sympathies, generous impulses, humane instincts.

For some readers, Aeneas grows ever more stoic, ever more able to control, even to extinguish, his emotions as he moves through the poem. Perhaps it would be closer to the mark to say that, in response to the increasingly harsh demands his mission places upon him, he learns the habit of repressing emotions that hinder him in the performance of his duties. There is a poignant instance of that need to stifle emotion in the interest of duty in the scene in Book 12 when Aeneas arms himself for what may be his last battle and says what may be his final farewell to his son:

> As soon as his breastplate was strapped on
> And his shield was fitted to his side,
> He put his arms around Ascanius, kissed him
> Lightly through his helmet, and said:
> "Learn how to be a man from me, my son;
> Learn good fortune from others."
>
> (12.532–37)

This moment looks like, and almost is, a perfect depiction of the stoic ideal in action. But, for all his stern resolve, here as elsewhere, the hero is conflicted. His need to instill into his son a last, forceful reminder of the warrior's code competes with an equal need to express a father's tenderness. His armor thwarts his embrace; his helmet, his iron mask, deflects his kiss. The hero accomplishes what he needs to, but he does so at the expense of the father.

In recent years, readers of the *Aeneid* have spoken more and more of the cost of Aeneas' victory, the price paid by others for his glory, or rather, for Rome's. But the price Aeneas himself pays should not be ignored. In losing Dido, he loses not a little of himself. That huge loss for the lover foreshadows what his steady pattern of total submission to his nation's demands will finally inflict on him, the diminution of his humanity.

Anthems for Doomed Youth

Among war's worst evils is its appetite for its younger warriors. Homer's *Iliad* doesn't ignore this category of war's victims, but its glimpses at the lost lives of the young are scattered over twenty-four books, whereas the *Aeneid* telescopes most of such carnage into six, and that condensation provides the theme of doomed youth in his poem with its powerful, angry emphasis. In Homer, the pathos of young life blotted out finds its supreme moment in Book 21 when, unarmed, the young prince Lycaon begs for his life and hears Achilles tell him, in "a voice without a trace of softness" (Lombardo's *Iliad* 21.104), that since the death of Patroclus he is no longer in the mood to spare Trojans and sell them into slavery. Then Achilles kills him and, with a sardonic curse, tosses him into the river. What stirs our pity here is all but hidden beneath the pitiless ferocity that consumes Achilles in this scene. At this point in his poem, Achilles wants to murder everything—even, perhaps especially, innocence.

In contrast, the newcomers to Virgil's battlefields are given special prominence and an ample share of the narrative. In Book 10 the actions of Pallas and Lausus serve to shape the plot at one of its most crucial turns, and, at the same time, they illustrate one of the poem's central themes, the quintessentially Roman obsession with the bonds between fathers and their sons. But effective as they are both as engines of plot and as thematic emblems, what most interests Virgil about Pallas and Lausus is their inexperience, their vulnerability, their youth. Just at Book 10's midpoint, when the frenzied violence that will completely overwhelm it is about to be set in motion, the poet affirms their likeness to one another and mourns their shared doom:

> On one side Pallas presses forward, strains,
> Confronted by Lausus, the young heroes
> Nearly equal in age, handsome beyond all,
> Neither destined to return to his homeland.
> But the Lord of Olympus did not permit them
> To meet face to face. Each was fated
> To fall soon to a greater adversary.
>
> (10.525–31)

Pallas had gone off to war with Aeneas in place of his father, Evander, who was too old to lead his contingent into battle. But Pallas was not yet fully ready to perform this function, as Evander well knew when he solemnly entrusted his son to Aeneas' care and tutelage (8.585–88; 11.186–93). Although Pallas, with a sort of beginner's luck, acquits himself superbly in his first (and final) entry into battle, he quickly proves himself in no way a match for Turnus, whom he imprudently attacks and by whose spear he falls dead. It is this death that sets in motion the series of events that will issue in Turnus' end and the poem's.

On learning of Pallas' death, a wrathful Aeneas searches vainly for Turnus, killing as he goes with a savagery that recalls Achilles before and after his slaying of Lycaon. When Juno tricks Turnus into leaving the battlefield, frustrated and beside himself with rage, Aeneas meets up with Mezentius. This banished Etruscan king is, after Turnus, the most formidable adversary that Aeneas has to face. He has just been cutting a bloody swath through the Trojan lines when Aeneas catches sight of him. Undaunted, this scorner of heaven, whose only gods are his right hand and his spear, challenges Aeneas, promising to his son, Lausus, the armor he will strip from "that robber's corpse" (10.925) as spoils. His spear misses its mark, but Aeneas is more skillful or luckier in his throw, and, severely wounded, Mezentius sinks to the ground.

> Aeneas was glad to see the Tuscan's blood
> And, drawing his sword, moved in eagerly
> On an anxious Mezentius. Lausus, watching,
> Groaned deeply for love of his father,
> And tears rolled down his face.
> (10.939–43)

As Lausus moves to rescue his father, the poet cannot help from intruding himself into his poem, not to warn Lausus but to offer him high, heartfelt praise:

> Neither your death,
> Nor your heroic deeds—if antiquity
> Can confer belief in prowess so great—
> Nor you yourself, noble young man,
> So worthy of memory, will I leave in silence.
> (10.943–47)

Aeneas, of course, advances against Lausus and, as we've seen, easily dispatches him. As a warrior, like Pallas, Lausus is brave and initially lucky, but, also like Pallas, he is unseasoned and, in his last fight, much overmatched. Finally, he shares with Pallas a filial devotion that impels him to die in his father's place. Mezentius, no less than Evander, feels both grief and guilt for the sacrifice his son makes for him; with a characteristic twist of convention, Virgil provides Mezentius with superb expression of remorse that, lending his demise an unexpected touch of grace, both ennobles him and adds to the pathos of his son's death. This pair of youthful warriors is crucial to Virgil's plot, and they serve also to vividly embody the father-son thematic that is so close to the *Aeneid*'s core. But it is their youth and the waste and injustice of their slaughter that move him, their poet, to lavish on them so much narrative space and so much artistry. Their destruction points not to the splendors of war but to its miseries, its mindless, meaningless expenditure of life and of promise.

Our second pair of doomed youths are not enemies but comrades-in-arms. The celebration of Turnus' patriotism and prowess takes up much of Book 9, but it is interrupted by the story of Nisus and Euryalus. These young Trojans volunteer to take an urgent message to Aeneas, warning him of the desperate situation that arose when he left to search for allies and that Turnus is vigorously exploiting. Their mission receives the blessings of Ascanius and his counselors, and they sally forth into the night, eager, excited, in high hopes—to their destruction.

In the Homeric model for this story (*Iliad* 10), it is two very formidable soldiers, Odysseus and Diomedes, who undertake a successful counterintelligence mission and manage to combine it with some zestful slaughter of the enemy, which they top off (the tempo is scherzo) with a dash of spectacular horse thievery. In contrast, the mood of Virgil's version is steadily more somber from the moment the pair leave the Trojan camp behind them and become quickly tangled in a fatal web of their own making. They are young and foolish, and their blind stumbling into the poem disrupts—exactly as Virgil intends—both its momentum and its uncertain purchase on epic verisimilitude. But Virgil cares about them, and he wants us to care about them, both because he is (as we've seen) much drawn to pondering the trajectories of unhappy loves and because he seems to have considerable interest in masculine beauty. We have met Nisus and Euryalus briefly before (in Book 5) when they competed in the footraces during the funeral games for Anchises. In Book 9 we see Euryalus with the eyes of his (slightly) older lover, Nisus:

> No one
> More beautiful followed Aeneas
> Or wore Trojan armor. Still a boy,
> His face showed the first hint of a beard.
> One love united them. Side by side
> They would charge into battle. . . .
>   (9.217–22)

It is probably to impress his beloved that Nisus wants to volunteer for the dangerous mission, and he initially refuses Euryalus' wish to join him. But he gives way to his beloved's wish, and they set forth together into the nightmare that will swallow them up. Foolhardy and untested in battle, their imprudence and vainglory quickly trap them, and, killed by the enemies who surprise them, they end their lives not with Homeric grandeur but with a sort of ambiguous poignancy, vanishing as they do into a gently lyrical *Liebestod.* When he was killed,

> Euryalus rolled over, dead. Dark blood
> Ran over his beautiful limbs, and his head
> Sank down onto one shoulder,
>
> *As a purple flower cut by a plow*
> *Droops in death, or as a poppy bows*
> *Its weary head, heavy with spring rain.*
>   (9.517–22)

Rushing to save his beloved and, failing in that, to kill his killer, Nisus also dies, "pierced and slashed, he threw himself / Upon his lifeless friend and there finally / Rested quietly in easeful death" (9.530–32).

Fusing two of the central themes of classical Greek homosexuality (the fashionable pederasty of classical Athens, the loving comrades-in-arms of Thebes), Virgil has here shaped a delicate, dreamlike, and finally terrifying echo of his Homeric model, one that functions almost as a sort of serious parody of it, and one that exposes war's insanities and brutalities even as it deconstructs the conventions of epic by superimposing on epic warfare this pair of attractive and, in this setting, incongruous warriors. Homosexual lovers of hardier mettle than Virgil's could be made to find a place in epic poetry (by Plato's time, Achilles and Patroclus were being misread in this fashion), but Virgil sees to it that his tender young men are mismatched with their poem. Nevertheless, perhaps to underscore this discord, clearly to emphasize this deliberate incongruity, he eulogizes his young lovers, sad in their soldiering but blissful in their shared doom, and he links them, directly and with ironic indecorum, to the grandeur of his poem's imperial theme:

> Happy pair,
> If my poetry has any power
> Never shall you be blotted from memory,
> As long as the house of Aeneas still stands
> On the Capitol's unmoving rock,
> And the Roman Father rules supreme.
> (9.532–37)

No less surprising than his loving and luckless comrades is Virgil's maiden warrior, Camilla. Like them, she appropriates a surprising amount of the poet's time and attention, and like them too she alters, if she does not in fact subvert, the conventions of a genre that is essentially masculine. (Penthesilea, queen of the Amazons, had a major role in one of the minor, now vanished epics that trailed after Homer's masterpieces, but Homer himself had ignored her.) Camilla is used by her creator, again like Nisus and Euryalus, to retard the action of Book 11, whose closure he allows her (almost) to usurp, thereby heightening the suspense that has been steadily building as Turnus heads for his inevitable encounter with Aeneas. But in fashioning this complex figure, what Virgil emphasizes are her naïveté, her fundamental innocence (hence, with her as with Dido and others, the injustice of her death), and her youth.

We first meet Camilla at the end of Book 7, where she is given pride of place, concluding the catalog of all the warriors who have joined with Turnus against Aeneas. The description of her there is lyrical, surreal. She could

> outrun the wind.
> She could sprint over a field of wheat
> And not even bruise the tender ears,

Could cruise above the open sea's waves
And never wet the soles of her feet.
                    (7.963–67)

So remarkable is she that young men and women rush from their
homes to gaze in astonishment "At how the royal purple draped /
Her smooth shoulders, how her hair / Was bound in gold, and how
she carried / A Lycian quiver and an iron-tipped spear"(7.971–74).
The amazement of young men and women arises in part from their
surprise (which we share) at actually seeing a woman warrior (of
whom they had perhaps only heard rumors) and in part from the
pleasure they take (male and female alike) in her loveliness. That
complex beauty depends for its effect on the pure incongruity
between Camilla's male weaponry and her fresh loveliness: the
grace of her movements, her superb skin set off by her military
cloak, her bright hair and its golden clip.

This golden clip foreshadows the love of gold ornamentation
that will prove fatal to her toward the end of Book 11. Just near
the finish of the sequence that represents her in her glory as a war-
rior, she catches sight of a Trojan soldier who is decked out in spec-
tacular panoply, golden all over, from head to foot.

Camilla wanted either to hang these weapons
As spoils in a temple or to wear the gold herself.
In any case she singled out Chloreus
And chased him down like a huntress,
Oblivious to all else and raging recklessly
Through the ranks of men with a woman's passion
For booty and spoils.
                    (11.928–34)

Virgil's deliberately ambiguous explanation of her motives in want-
ing the gaudy plunder reflects the ambiguity of her character as a
whole. Either she wants, as a warrior would, to dedicate the spoils
as a memorial to her prowess or she wants to parade around in
them (that he resolves the ambiguity by opting for sexist slander is
perhaps the poet's ironic deference to the generic demands he keeps
honoring and abusing). More serious is another conflict: Camilla is
a warrior, but she is also a virgin huntress, at home in the forests
and mountains of Italy, in untamed nature. She has been the special

favorite of Diana, goddess of the unspoiled natural world and its creatures, since her exiled father took her with him into the wilderness when she was still a baby. On the one hand, then, she is an Amazonian leader of female warriors (a character drawn from minor Greek epic), but, on the other, she is also an Italian girl, a creature born and reared in rural peace, a devotee of Diana and the good, green world that she governs, a maiden, uncorrupted and utterly alien to civilization, to the concerns of men, their cities, their wars, and their empires. (It is entirely unclear where she and her fellow huntresses gained their anomalous military experience, but, as with Pallas and Lausus and as with Nisus and Euryalus, the discrepancy between Camilla's inexperience in warfare and her assured military prowess, though it tampers a bit with her verisimilitude, in no way diminishes her poetic efficacy.)

Oblivious to any danger, driven by her need to get the golden plunder, Camilla fails to notice an Etruscan who has been stalking her, and she dies, pierced by his javelin. Her death inspires Virgil's lyricism at its purest:

> Camilla's dying hand pulled at the spear,
> But the iron point was stuck deep in her ribs.
> Drained of blood, she sank back; the chill light
> Sank in her eyes; and her face, formerly
> So radiant, turned pale in death.
>
> (11.975–79)

Her last words are those of a warrior (she sends a message to Turnus, offering him some strategy), but her death is that of a maiden cut off in the midst of life:

> As her body grew cold
> She slowly freed herself from all its bonds,
> Relaxing her neck and letting her head fall
> Into the grip of Death. Finally,
> She released her weapons, and with a moan
> Her soul fled resentfully down to the shades.
>
> (11.992–97)

This last verse returns as the poem's final verse, the one that describes the dying moment of Turnus. Like his, Camilla's angry resentment burst from her sense of having been wronged. Turnus, however, is a seasoned, mature warrior whereas Camilla, like the poem's other doomed young people who have been shoved too early onto the fields of battle, has been cheated of her young life.

Turnus' sister, Juturna, after having obeyed Juno and incited hostilities between Latins and Trojans, spends most of the rest of Book 12 trying to help her brother. It might seem paradoxical to speak of her youth since she is immortal, but she was not always so. Her identity as a fountain-nymph who is deathless and eternally young came to her as a recompense from Jupiter, who had ravished her when she was a mortal, a mere girl. Juno snidely reminds her of that rape and its reward when she is enlisting her to ruin the impending treaty between the Latins and the Trojans: "You know how I have given you preference / Over all the Latin girls who have climbed / Into Jove's thankless bed" (12.168–70). In her final, anguished speech to her brother, when she recognizes the monster that is attacking him and realizes that she can no longer help him, she screams at the Fury, bitterly echoing what Juno had said about Rome's patron deity, Father of Gods and Men, Fate's Minister, her spouse, and Juturna's rapist:

> I know the beating of your wings,
> The sound of death, and I do not mistake
> The haughty commands of Jupiter.
> Is this how he compensated me
> For my lost virginity? Why did he give me
> Life everlasting? If I could only die
> I could end this sorrow, go through the shadows
> At my poor brother's side. I, immortal!
> Nothing can be sweet without you, Brother.
> What ground can gape deep enough
> To send a goddess to the deepest shades?
>   (12.1061–71)

Much of the poem's sorrow is condensed into this despairing lamentation. If one has had no sympathy for Turnus up to now, if this cry of pain from his innocent sister cannot win it for him, nothing can. The immortal grief of Juturna recalls that of another minor deity, Thetis, Achilles' mother. But to the incurable, unending suffering of the Homeric figure, Juturna adds the weight of historical destiny. She and her brother are Italians who, along with their country, are being absorbed by, are being swallowed up into, an alien and unforgiving kingdom. Cursed now by her deathlessness, Juturna tries in vain to drown herself and her tears in the depths of the immortal fountain that she is. But she and the bitter accusations she shouts at Jupiter and the grief that drives them are not able to perish. Eternally young and eternally in mourning for her brother and for her vanquished country, hers is a never-ending wrong.

The Shield of Aeneas: Virgil and History

By and large the characters in the *Aeneid* know little or nothing of the historical forces that are shaping the events in which they find themselves making the choices they make, performing the actions they perform. Aeneas himself never gets a real grasp of the extent of Juno's enmity toward him, and the teasing, ambiguous omens, dreams, and prophecies that he encounters before he reaches Italy serve mostly to baffle him. During his visit to the Underworld, however, his father's shade provides him with an elaborate sketch of the glorious history of the nation he will soon found in Italy when his war with its native population has ended:

> Now I will set forth the glory that awaits
> The Trojan race, the illustrious souls
> Of the Italian heirs to our name.
> I will teach you your destiny.
>
> (6.896–99)

That said, a patriotic pageant, made up of souls destined to be reborn as great Romans in future ages, passes in review before Anchises, the Sibyl, and Aeneas. The procession begins with Aeneas' own as yet unborn son, Silvius, whose mother will be Aeneas' future wife, Lavinia; Silvius is followed by the early kings of Alba Longa who are followed in turn by Romulus, Rome's founder and first king: "Under his auspices, / . . . Rome will extend her renowned empire / To earth's horizons, her glory to the stars" (6.924–26). So far the procession is ordered according to a strict chronology, but at this point Anchises suddenly introduces the Julian clan, all of whom are descended from Aeneas' son, Ascanius

(whose second name is Iülus), and from all the clan he singles out
only two figures, Julius Caesar and

> the man promised to you,
> Augustus Caesar, born of the gods,
> Who will establish again a Golden Age
> In the fields of Latium once ruled by Saturn
> And will expand his dominion
> Beyond the Indus and the Garamantes,
> Beyond our familiar stars, beyond the yearly
> Path of the sun, to the land where Atlas
> Turns the star-studded sphere on his shoulders.
>   (6.939–47)

Anchises continues his prophecies of the role Augustus will play in
extending Rome's boundaries throughout the known world, boast-
ing that neither Hercules nor Bacchus in their wide and triumphant
journeyings will surpass the breadth of Augustus' dominions.
Anchises ends this segment of his revelations with a subtle rebuke
to what he apparently takes to be his son's hesitations about the
war in Latium he is about to undertake. Given the worldwide
empire that Aeneas' greatest heir will rule over, should Aeneas have
qualms about gaining a foothold in Italy? "And still we shrink
from extending our virtue, / And fear to take our stand in Auso-
nia?" (6.956–57).
    Augustus is at once the centerpiece of Anchises' pageant and the
zenith of Rome's destiny. Although Rome and its emperors will
know greatness after Augustus is gone (like his adoptive father,
Julius, to his heavenly reward), it is Augustus who will rescue
Rome in its decadence from its enemies and from itself, it is he who
will both restore it to former glories and set it on its new and firmer
foundations. Having made this leap forward in time from Romulus
and Rome's beginnings to Virgil's (and Augustus') present,
Anchises then doubles back to his pageant and to the unborn souls
who will someday become the successors of Romulus, the kings
who will come after him. He then deftly skirts the expulsion of the
last (bad) king of Rome (6.970–73) to focus on the founding of the
Republic, the evolution of its "sweet liberty" (6.977), its slow,
patient conquest of Italy through a series of "defensive" wars, and
its steady string of victories over the Greeks and Carthaginians

who challenged its expansion throughout the Mediterranean. These descriptions of the progress of the Republic's transformation from small (agrarian) city-state into the center of its cosmopolitan world empire are presented through a series of vivid, elliptical images of great moments in Roman history.

It is hard to estimate how much Anchises expects his son to understand and take away from the achronological, swirling succession of events, the blur of unknown names and faces, that Anchises offers to his gaze. But whatever he does or doesn't understand, Aeneas doubtless gets the gist of the fabulous, confusing spectacle his father presents him with because Anchises sums it up with unforgettable clarity:

> Others will, no doubt, hammer out bronze
> That breathes more softly, and draw living faces
> Out of stone. They will plead cases better
> And chart the rising of every star in the sky.
> Your mission, Roman, is to rule the world.
> These will be your arts: to establish peace,
> To spare the humbled, and to conquer the proud.
>   (6.1012–18)

Aeneas, since he is and will remain a Trojan, may be surprised to find his father calling him a Roman. But he has perhaps heard the name enough by now to guess what his father is driving at: Aeneas himself is now Rome incarnate, and it is him and, through him, all true Romans and most especially the man-god, Augustus, greatest of them all, that Anchises is addressing as he explains to his son the nature of Roman identity and of Rome's mission in the world.

If Aeneas' instruction had ended there, we might feel that he had deciphered enough of the pageant's mysteries to grasp something of the meaning of the Roman Empire and his place in it. But it doesn't end there. Coming next to last in the pageant (again out of chronological order) is the great general Marcellus, The Sword of Rome. And following him, the procession's final figure, is the young man who will be the Sword's ancestor, another Marcellus, the son of Augustus' own sister and his prospective heir. Aeneas is much taken by this phantasm ("Beautiful in his gleaming armor / But with downcast eyes and troubled brow," 6.1028–29) and asks his father who he is. Anchises answers him tearfully. In verses that are among the epic's most haunting, Anchises pronounces what is in effect an elegy for the heir apparent, another doomed youth: "Fate will permit him on earth a brief while, / But not for long" (6.1037–38). If Marcellus had not been fated to die just on the brink of his early manhood, he was to have been, could have been, should have been, a great warrior:

> If only you could shatter Fate, poor boy.
> You will be Marcellus! Let me strew
> Armfuls of lilies and scatter purple blossoms,
> Hollow rites to honor my descendant's shade.
> (6.1052–55)

As usual, we are not told what Aeneas feels about the extraordinary conclusion to this splendid vision of Rome's brightest and best. When the pageant vanishes with Marcellus, Anchises fills his son "with longing for the glory that was to come" (6.1060) by describing in detail the war he is about to embark on and by telling him "how to face or flee each waiting peril" (6.1063). Enflamed he may now be with a Homeric "longing for glory" (instead of his usual passion for duty), but by the time Aeneas finds himself embroiled in the war with Turnus and the Latins he seems to have forgotten most of what his father told him. In any case, when Anchises sends him and the Sybil through the Gate of Ivory back to the upper world we don't know what mood he is in or what he has understood about the world that he lives and fights and suffers in. There are numerous opinions about why he returns through the Gate of Ivory. Whatever Virgil's intention (it is well to remember that he has a special fondness for ambiguity), by placing the doomed Marcellus so near the Gate of Dreams (whether they are illusory or improperly interpreted) he shapes a mood that tints the close of Book 6 with an uncanny, ambivalent dissonance, one that clouds our sense of Aeneas' mission and perhaps his own sense as well.

In Aeneas' next and final vision of Roman history, uncertainty seems at first to have no place. Toward the end of Book 8, after Aeneas has concluded his alliance with Evander and is ready to battle the Latins, Venus brings Aeneas the new, divine armor that she has persuaded Vulcan to make for him. He receives these gifts from her hand with much of the gusto that Achilles shows when

Thetis hands him his new armor ("he turned / The polished weap-
ons the god had given him / Over and over in his hands, and felt /
Pangs of joy at all its intricate beauty," Lombardo's *Iliad* 19.26–
29). On taking up his weapons,

> Aeneas gloried
> In the gifts from heaven, in this high honor,
> And he could not satisfy his eyes as they moved
> From one part to another. He was lost in wonder
> As he turned each piece over in his hands
> And cradled it in his arms. . . .
>
> (8.704–9)

But here the similarities between Virgil's scene and its model end.
On the shield of Achilles, the god Hephaestus has engraved the
entire world: earth, ocean, the heavens, and their stars. Then, rep-
resenting the human world, "he made two cities, peopled / And
beautiful" (Lombardo's *Iliad* 18.528–29), one at peace and one at
war. Up to this point, it looks as if Achilles' shield might be sym-
bolizing the *Iliad* itself, which also shows peoples and their cities at
peace and at war (but with a decided emphasis on war). But the
rest of the shield, a little more than half of it, is devoted to the arts
and pleasures of peace: fields being plowed and harvested, vine-
yards, farms and livestock, the business of living; it ends, raptur-
ously, with young men and women in a joyful dance that portends
matrimony and the renewal of the fertile world. There are various
plausible ways of reading Achilles' shield, but a not unreasonable
interpretation might be that the design on the shield of this best,
most fearsome of Greek warriors explains what soldiers (him
included, for all his glamorous individualism and obsession with
glory) are supposed to be fighting to secure, namely, peace and its
blessings for their compatriots and their children's children.

Vulcan's design is rather different. On the shield of Aeneas

> the Fire God had prophetically wrought
> The future of Italy, and Roman triumphs
> In the coming ages, every generation,
> In order, still to be born from the stock
> Of Ascanius, and all the wars they would fight.
>
> (8.716–20)

What the shield will offer Aeneas (and us), then, is a reprise of the parade of phantoms in Book 6. However, instead of being limited to memorializing military glory, it, like the shield of Achilles, will culminate in the blessings of peace. But this peace is not at all the peace that Homer imagined: the absence of war as the ideal condition that all humans yearn for. Instead, what Vulcan portrays at the center of Aeneas' shield is the imperial, universal peace (the *pax Augustana*) that Augustus established when he defeated Antony and Cleopatra and thereby put an end to Rome's hundred years of civic strife.

Vulcan's pictures begin, much as Anchises' pageant had begun, with early Roman history, but he skips quickly from Ascanius to Romulus, devotes much of his space to Romulus' successors and to the great (dim) heroes of the early Republic, ending this segment with the fateful day when the Gauls actually sacked Rome (387 B.C.E.). Abruptly, he then includes a snippet of the Underworld:

> Far below he set the hells of Tartarus,
> The high gates of Dis, and the wages of sin.
> You, Catiline, were hung from the frowning
> Face of a cliff and trembled at the Furies
> While Cato, set apart, gave laws to the good.
>   (8.762–66)

Between them, Catiline, one of Rome's worst traitors, and Cato the Younger, one of its greatest moral champions, summon up so briefly that they function only to extinguish the ugly story of the disintegration of the Republic in its last years, the turmoil and violence that both produced Augustus and was ended by him. It is this sleight of hand that allows Vulcan (and Virgil), in another sudden shift of mood and topic, to begin their depiction of the triumph of Augustus, which will take up more than half of the rest of the shield.

The sea-battle that made Augustus ruler of the world and bringer of the peace it had longed for begins with a deceptive, lyrical loveliness:

> These scenes were lapped by the swelling sea,
> Pure gold, yet the water was blue, and flecked
> With whitecaps. Circling dolphins picked out in silver
> Cut through the waves and their tails flicked the spume.
>   (8.767–70)

At the fateful Battle of Actium, engraved on one side, stands Caesar Augustus, leading a united Italy along with Rome and its people, its senate and its gods, against Antony and his Egyptian wife, who are figured on the opposite side, with all their maddened Oriental hordes. Cleopatra has summoned the monstrous, bestial gods of her kingdom to aid her, but, "chiseled in iron at the eye of the battle" (8.802), ranged against them are Neptune, Minerva, Venus, Mars, the Furies, Discord, and the war goddess Bellona. It is Apollo, however, the god with whom Augustus most identified himself, the god who would come to best symbolize the style of his governance and his incontestable right to power, it is Apollo who bends his bow, it is his arrow that puts an end to the Battle of Actium. (Virgil's contemporary, the poet Propertius, provides us with a delicious parody of this moment in his poem on Actium, *Elegies* 4.6.) Terrified, the wicked Queen deserts Antony along with her motley squadrons and is gathered up (like Dido before her, whom she echoes in other ways) into a pretty, lyrical demise. "Pale as death," completing her flight to Egypt, she sails into the Nile where "The great rivergod had opened all the folds / Of his copious robe and welcomed the vanquished / Into the sheltering waters of his azure lap" (8.815–17).

Unlike the pageant of Book 6, the shield of Aeneas is carefully directed toward and ends vividly in pure narrative. This heavily stylized, condensed, elliptical representation of the Battle of Actium and its aftermath may be all that is left of the germ of an epic about Augustus that Virgil seems to have considered composing before he hit upon the (subtler, more artistic) idea of framing the story of Augustus, like a jewel in its setting, by the story of Aeneas. The picture of Augustus in triumph after his return to Egypt, benevolent and wise, graciously welcoming a grateful humankind as it throngs from all over the known world to do him homage (or rather to worship him) is possessed of a poetic beauty as splendid as it is delicate and concise. It is an astonishing, unforgettable portrait of the Augustan Peace.

But it is far from clear that Aeneas understands the meaning of Actium any better than he understands the rest of his shield (or any better than he had understood the Underworld pageant). He rejoices in the beauty of his armor when he first receives it, but we are told (8.715), even as he delights in it, that its design is "ineffable [*non enarrabile*]," beyond description or explanation. It is, of course, the perfection of the shield's craftsmanship, the beauty of the artifact, that is "ineffable," but what it represents is also beyond the power of art (both Vulcan's and poetry's) to imitate, to order, to clarify. And even it were not, even if the uncertainties and anomalies of history could be distilled through art to clarity, Aeneas still could not understand them:

> Such was the design of the shield Vulcan made,
> Venus' gift to her son. Aeneas was moved
> To wonder and joy by the images of things
> He could not fathom, and he lifted to his shoulder
> The destiny of his children's children.
>
> (8.840–44)

So different from the feelings he had back in Carthage when he gazed at the pictures of the Trojan War, it is an ironic sort of joy he feels in the pictures of wars and triumphs that he does not understand and that he does not and cannot connect with the procession he saw in the Underworld. As he once lifted his father on his shoulders in their flight from Troy to a new homeland, so also he now hoists onto his shoulders these pictures (puzzling to him, clear to Augustus and to us) of a glorious future that he comprehends dimly if at all, one that his actions will ensure but that he will not live to partake of. At this moment, though he is near his goal, he is still what he was when we first glimpsed him, "exiled by Fate" (1.3), "a man battered / On land and sea" (1.4–5). Courageous, dutiful, compassionate, in proud possession of his beautiful and baffling shield, he is as much an existential Everyman as an epic hero when he departs from Evander's city to resume his struggles in a world whose workings and meanings he cannot grasp.

Virgil's first readers, of course, could read the shield expertly, and among them who more expertly than Augustus himself, the center of the shield, its real meaning, the man-god emperor who was to Aeneas little more than one of the more splendid of the ghostly creatures in the Underworld parade—that, and a mere name? As he read the shield, he, the real purpose of Aeneas' mission, Augustus would have seen nothing disconcerting in Aeneas' failure to understand the significance of the actions that he was, as an instrument of Fate, required to perform. Some of his contemporaries, however, probably did notice that fissure, and some of them may have sensed that it pointed to other places in the poem—among them, the poet's cry to Jupiter in Book 12, Anchises' elegy for Marcellus, Juturna's lament, Aeneas' encounter with Dido in the Underworld, his anguished speech over the corpse of Lausus—where the poem's patriotic grandeur conflicts with its more private, human face, moments in it when its sense of suffering outweighs its sense of imperial imperative, where Aeneas the human being and Aeneas the progenitor of all-conquering Rome split apart.

But there were probably more readers among Virgil's first readers (and there have been many more since) for whom, as for Augustus, such ambiguities were of no real importance. For these readers, any doubt about the centrality of Augustus on Aeneas' shield, and what they took to be his centrality in the poem, was unthinkable. Like any reader of Appian's *Civil Wars* (his terrifying history of Rome in the hundred years before the Battle of Actium), these readers knew in their blood and their bones why Augustus deserved to be, needed to be, at the center of a poem that celebrated Rome and its destiny. It was not hard to persuade them that his birth was a miracle, that his sudden intervention in Rome's self-destruction, just at the moment of what seemed its complete destruction, was providential. They understood why some Greeks hailed him as "savior" and were prepared to call him a god and to worship him as a god. For these readers, what might appear to be the poem's fissures or gaps or ambiguities, if they could not be explained (away), could be safely and easily ignored (after all, Virgil had not had a chance to put his finishing touches to his epic). So, for these readers, Augustus was at the center of Aeneas' shield because he became and remained and would remain the still center of Rome and its world, which was at the center of the universe and of history; he was the actuality toward which all the world's potentialities had always been moving.

Exactly what Virgil intended by the shield and by the poem that accords it such prominence we will never know. (One of its very best modern readers, the wonderful W. F. Jackson Knight, was so eager to learn what the poet really meant that he asked a friend to hold seances with a view to finding the answers to his questions "in the beyond.") We can assume that Virgil had some sympathy with those of his readers who would be pleased with the grandeur of his shield, who felt comfort in the world that Augustus had (as he claimed) rescued from ruin and remade, who felt unable to express their gratitude sufficiently and welcomed a poet and a poem that would say what they themselves were incapable of saying in praise of the return of law and order and the blessings of peace. But he may very well have shared some of the thoughts and feelings of those who paused to ponder those places in his poem where its tensions reveal themselves, where there glimmer, under the surfaces of the poem, worries about the fate of empires, about what happens when delight in prosperity turns into the dangerous notion that greed is good, and when joy in victory morphs into mere hubris. We cannot know whether he deliberately crafted those tensions, thus setting the truth of human misery against the truth of human achievement, or whether he was merely reflecting, merely recording (almost unconsciously) the tensions and uncertainties that continued to haunt Rome in the first decade of Augustus' reign, before it began to seem likely that he would *not* join his predecessors in being swept away in the chaos of Rome's recent history, before it began to seem possible, even probable, that the settlement he was planning would be successful and permanent.

Whether by his own design or as a reflection of anxieties in Rome's collective consciousness (whether he shared them or didn't), interwoven in the poem's epic texture, countervailing its celebration of the warrior in triumph, is the persistent memory of the outcast, the exile, who speaks with the voice of the dispossessed, of Trojan, not Roman, Aeneas. In recent years, some readers, this reader among them, have been struck with what they take to be Virgil's Epicurean strain and the deep, unfailing imprint on his mind and art by Lucretius' *On the Nature of Things*. One line from that poem could serve as a useful motto for this aspect of Virgil's vision of the human condition: *"imbecillorum est aequum miserarier omnes"* (5.1023), "it is just for all of us to feel compassion for those who are weak." The *Aeneid* imagines how the world, how any society, any time, anywhere, can be saved by depicting (and celebrating) how Rome, Virgil's own (adopted) city, was once saved. Though ambiguous about the nature of victory, it is hardly contemptuous of prosperity and ordinary happiness. But it is never forgetful of the prevalence of human suffering, it never ignores the pain and the loss of the defeated or the huge cost of victory, to the victor no less than to the vanquished. Aeneas is the right hero for this strange, almost unepical epic, an odd and improbable hero, perhaps, but more credible than many and more admirable than most.

W. R. Johnson
University of Chicago

AENEID ONE

Arms I sing—and a man,
The first to come from the shores
Of Troy, exiled by Fate, to Italy
And the Lavinian coast; a man battered
On land and sea by the powers above   5
In the face of Juno's relentless wrath;
A man who also suffered greatly in war
Until he could found his city and bring his gods
Into Latium, from which arose
The Latin people, our Alban forefathers,   10
And the high walls of everlasting Rome.

Muse, tell me why the Queen of Heaven
Was so aggrieved, her godhead so offended,
That she forced a man of faultless devotion
To endure so much hardship. Can there be   15
Anger so great in the hearts of gods on high?

There was an ancient city, Carthage,
Colonized by Tyrians, facing Italy
And the Tiber's mouth far across the sea;
A city rich in resources, fierce in war,   20
And favored by Juno more than any other
Place on earth, even more than Samos. Here
Were her arms, her chariot; this was the city
The goddess cherished and strove to make
Capital of the world, if the Fates permitted.   25
But she had heard that a scion of Trojan blood

Would someday level Carthage's citadel;
That a Trojan people, an imperial power,
Would destroy Libya: so the Parcae
Were spinning out Fate. The Goddess   30
Brooded on this and on the Trojan War,
Which she herself, Saturnian Juno,
Had waged on behalf of her beloved Greeks,
Ever mindful of the Judgment of Paris—
The cause of the war—and her savage grief   35
Over her beauty scorned by that hateful race.
Nor could she forget the spiteful honor given
To ravaged Ganymede.
                    Incensed with these memories,
The Goddess kept the Trojan remnant
That had escaped the Greeks—and Achilles' rage—   40
Tossed all over the sea's expanse,
Far from Latium, doomed to wander
The circling waters year after year.

So massive was the labor of founding Rome.

Sicily had scarcely dropped out of sight,   45
And they were sailing joyfully on the open sea,
Bronze prows shearing the seaspume,
When Juno, nursing her heart's eternal wound,
Said to herself:

          "Am I to admit defeat,
Unable to keep these Trojans and their king   50
From Italy? Forbidden by the Fates, am I?
Pallas could burn the Argives' fleet
And drown all hands for one man's offense—
Oïlean Ajax's fit of passion.
She herself hurled Jupiter's fire from heaven,   55
Splintered the ships, churned up the sea,
And whirled up Ajax, exhaling flames
From his pierced lungs, and impaled him on a crag.
But I, who walk among the gods as their queen,
Sister of Jupiter and Jupiter's wife—I   60

Have to wage war for years on end
Against this one race. Who will worship Juno
After this, or bow down before her holy altars?"

Her heart inflamed, the Goddess went
To Aeolia, a country of clouds   65
And raging winds. Here in a vast cave
Aeolus rules the squalls and gales,
Keeping them chained in vaulted cells.
The indignant winds roar at their prison doors,
Rumbling deep in the mountain. But Aeolus   70
Sits on high and with his scepter calms
Their frenzied souls. If he did not,
They would swoop over land and sea
And through the deep sky, sweeping
Everything before them. Fearing just this,   75
The Father Almighty hid them away
In dark caves and piled above them
A mountain massif. And he gave them a king,
One who would know by chartered agreement
When to restrain and when to unleash them.   80
It was to Aeolus that Juno came as a suppliant:

"Aeolus, by order of the Father of Gods and Men
You calm the waves or provoke them with wind.
A race I despise sails the Tyrrhenian Sea,
Bringing Ilium's conquered gods to Italy.   85
Hit them hard with a storm and sink their ships,
Or scatter the fleet and litter the sea with corpses.
I have fourteen Nymphs with lovely bodies,
The most radiant of which, Deiopeia,
I will pronounce your wife, to have and to hold,   90
In return for this favor. She will live with you
All her years and bear you beautiful children."

And Aeolus:

        "It is yours to consider what you want,
My Queen, and mine to fulfill your commands.
To you I owe this modest realm and Jove's good will.   95

You grant me a seat at the table of the gods,
And you make me master of cloud and storm."

With that, he drove the butt of his spear
Against the cavernous mountainside, and the winds,
In battle formation, rushed out of all ports   100
And whirled over the earth. Swooping down,
They fell on the sea. Eurus and Notus
Churned up the depths, and with them Africus,
Whose dark squall line rolled huge waves shoreward.
The crews began to shout, the rigging creaked,   105
And then, in an instant, clouds stole the daylight
From the Trojans' eyes. Night lay black on the sea.
The sky's roof thundered and flashed with lightning,
And everywhere men saw the presence of death.

Aeneas' limbs suddenly went numb with cold.   110
He groaned and, lifting both palms to heaven, said:

"Three times, four times luckier were those
Who died before their parents' eyes
Under Troy's high walls! O Diomedes,
Bravest of the Greeks, if only I had been killed   115
By your right hand on Ilium's plain,
Where Hector went down under Achilles' spear,
Where huge Sarpedon lies, where the Simois rolls
So many shields and helmets caught in its current
And the bodies of so many brave heroes!"   120

As he was speaking a howling wind from the North
Struck against the sail. Waves shot to the stars.
The oars shattered. The prow swung around,
Exposing the side to the waves, and then
A mountain of water broke over the fleet.   125
The crews of some ships bobbed high on the crest,
While the wave's deep trough revealed to others
The deep seafloor churning with sand.
The South Wind twirled a trio of ships
Onto the Altars—the Italians' grim name   130
For the hulk of reef lurking under the sea.

The East Wind pushed another three ships
Into the shallows and ground them onto
The Syrtes' shoals, bedding them down
In pockets of sand. Another ship,   *135*
Which carried the Lycians and trusted Orontes,
Sank before Aeneas' own eyes. A wall of water
Crashed onto the deck, and the pilot flew headfirst
Into the sea. The ship spun around twice, three times,
Caught in a whirlpool that sucked it down quickly.   *140*
You could see men swimming here and there
In the vast gulf. Wicker shields, plaques,
And Trojan finery floated on the waves.
And now Ilioneus' strong ship, now Achates',
Now the ships that carried Abas and old Aletes   *145*
Were battered by the storm. Their joints sagged,
And they took on water through their splitting seams.

Meanwhile, the news filtered down to Neptune
Of the turmoil above. He heard the murmur
From the churning surface, and he felt   *150*
The still, bottom water rise in upheaval.
Lifting his serene face above the waves,
He peered out and saw Aeneas' fleet
Scattered, and the Trojans overwhelmed
By rough seas and the sky's downpour.   *155*
His sister's treachery was all too obvious.
Calling Eurus and Zephyrus, he said to them:

"Do you have so much confidence, Winds,
In your family connections? Do you dare
Overturn heaven and earth and raise tons of water   *160*
Up to the sky—without my divine sanction?
Why, I ought to . . . ! But settling the waves comes first.
You won't get off so lightly next time.
Now clear out of here! And tell your king this:
The sea and the trident were allotted to me,   *165*
Not to him. His domain is the outsized rock
That you and yours, Eurus, call home. Aeolus
Can puff himself up there, in his own hall,
And lord it over the prison of the winds."

Thus Neptune, and—no sooner said than done—   170
He calmed the sea, chased off the massed clouds,
And brought back the sun. Cymothöe and Triton,
Working together, pushed the ships off the jagged reef.
Neptune himself levered them up with his trident,
Cut channels through the shoals, and eased the swells,   175
His chariot's wheels skimming the whitecaps.

>   *Riots will often break out in a crowded assembly*
>   *When the rabble are roused. Torches and stones*
>   *Are soon flying—Fury always finds weapons—*
>   *But then all eyes light upon a loyal citizen,*   180
>   *A man of respect. The crowd stands still*
>   *In hushed expectation. And with grave words*
>   *He masters their tempers and calms their hearts.*

So too the crashing sea fell silent, as its sire,
Surveying the watery expanse, drove his chariot   185
Under a clear sky, giving the horses free rein.

Aeneas' men, numb with fatigue,
Made for the nearest land, the coast of Libya.

They found a deep bay, across whose mouth
An island stands and makes a good port: 190
The waves that roll in from the open sea
Break on its sides and ripple on to shore.
The bay is flanked by high cliffs. Twin crags
Rise like threats toward the sky, but the water below
Is sheltered and silent. Above, shimmering woods,   195
And, rising higher, a dark grove with sinister shadows.
Opposite the looming crags is a cave,
With sweet-water springs and stone seats inside,
A haunt of the Nymphs. Sea-weary ships
Need not be tied in this harbor, nor moored   200
By hooked anchors that bite the seafloor.

Aeneas puts in here with the seven ships
That are left of his fleet. Lusting for dry land,
The Trojans disembark on the welcome beach,

Laying their brine-soaked bodies on the sand.   205
Achates strikes a flint and catches a spark
In leaves, then feeds the flames with dry tinder.
The men bring out whatever grain they can salvage
From the spoiled stores and, weary of it all,
Parch the kernels and grind grain on stones.   210

Aeneas now climbed up to an isolated point
With a view of the sea spread out below,
Hoping to see where the storm might have left
The Phrygian galleys of Antheus
Or of Capys, or to glimpse Caicus' armor   215
Mounted high on the stern. There was no ship in sight,
But he did see three stags browsing on the shore
And behind them an entire herd, feeding
In a long line down through the valley. Aeneas
Stood still, as did faithful Achates,   220
Who passed over feathered arrows and bow.
He brought down the leaders, each standing tall
With a thicket of antlers, and then he shot
At the herd itself, scattering them with his arrows
Into the woods. He did not stop shooting   225
Until he had triumphantly brought down
Seven good-sized animals, one for each ship.
Back at the port, Aeneas divided the meat
Among all of his men and distributed wine
That the hero Acestes had stored in jars   230
And given to them at their departure
From Sicily's shores. And then Aeneas
Spoke to his men to ease their hearts:

"Trojans! This is not our first taste of trouble.
You have suffered worse than this, my friends,   235
And God will grant an end to this also.
You faced Scylla's fury in her thundering crags
And braved the Cyclops' rocks. Recall your courage
And put aside your fear and grief. Someday, perhaps,
It will help to remember these troubles as well.   240
Through all sorts of perils, through countless dangers,
We are headed for Latium, where the Fates promise us

A peaceful home, and where Troy will rise again.
Endure, and save yourselves for happier times."

Aeneas said this, and though he was sick   245
With worry, he put on a good face
And pushed his anguish deep into his heart.
They set about preparing a feast from the kill.
Some did the skinning and butchering
And skewered the still quivering flesh on spits.   250
Others set cauldrons on the shore and tended fires.
The meal revived their strength. Spread out
Along the grass, they took their fill of old wine
And fat venison. When the feast was finished,
They talked long about their lost companions,   255
Hoping they were still alive, but fearing
They had met their end and would hear no more
When their names were called.
Loyal Aeneas grieved especially
For bold Orontes, and lamented in silence   260
The bitter loss of Amycus and Lycus,
Of brave Gyas and brave Cloanthus.

The day was at an end, and Jupiter
Was looking down from heaven's zenith
At the sail-winged sea and at the shores   265
Of all the peopled lands spread far and wide,
And as he looked he paused at the sky's pinnacle
And turned his luminous eyes toward Libya,
Pondering the world's woes. And Venus, sad,
Her eyes shining with tears, said to him: 270

"Lord of Lightning, eternal Ruler of Gods and Men,
What has my Aeneas done to offend you?
What have my Trojans done? They have suffered
One disaster after another, and still the whole world
Is barred to them to keep them out of Italy.   275
Surely someday, in the turning of time,
The Romans are to arise from this race.
They will continue Teucer's bloodline

And give birth to rulers who will hold
Earth and sea under their dominion.   280
You promised. What has changed your mind,
Father? That promise was what consoled me
At Troy's heartrending downfall. I balanced one fate
Against another. But the fortunes of these men,
After all their mishaps, have still not changed.   285
What end, O Lord, will you grant to their toils?
Antenor was able to escape the Greeks,
Cross safely over the Illyrian gulfs,
Pass the Liburnians' inmost realms,
And skirt the springs of the Timavus   290
Where it bursts through nine roaring mouths
And floods the fields under a sounding sea.
There he founded the town of Padua,
Settled his Teucrians, named his race,
And fixed the arms of Troy on a temple wall.   295
Now he is at rest and enjoys peaceful ease.
But we, your own flesh and blood,
To whom you have opened the heights of heaven,
Have lost our ships—O the infamy!—
And because of one deity's anger are betrayed   300
And disbarred from the shores of Italy.
Is this the reward for devotion? Is this
How you restore our ancestral power?"

Smiling at her with the look that calms storms
And clears the sky, the Father of Gods and Men   305
Kissed his daughter lightly and said:

"Spare your fears, Cytherean. Your people's destiny
Remains unmoved. You will see Lavinium
And its promised walls, and you will raise
Great-souled Aeneas to the stars on high.   310
I have not changed my mind. Your son—
I will speak at length, since you are so worried,
Unrolling Fate's scroll and revealing its secrets—
Your son will wage a great war in Italy,
Crush barbarous nations, and set up laws   315
And city walls for his own people, reigning

In Latium until three summers have passed
And three winters since the Rutulians' defeat.
But the boy Ascanius, surnamed Iülus—
His name was Ilus while Ilium still stood—   320
Will be in power for thirty great cycles
Of the rolling months, will move his throne
From Lavinium, and build the mighty walls
Of Alba Longa. This kingdom will endure
For three hundred years under Hector's race,   325
Until Ilia, Vesta's royal priestess,
Pregnant by Mars, shall give birth to twins.
Then Romulus, proud in the tawny hide
Of the wolf who nursed him, will continue
The lineage, build the walls of Mars,   330
And call the people, after his own name,
Romans. For these I set no limits
In time or space, and have given to them
Eternal empire, world without end.
Even Juno, who in her spite and fear   335
Now vexes earth, sea, and sky, shall adopt
A better view, and with me cherish the Romans,
Lords of the world, the people of the toga.
That is my pleasure. And there will come a time
As the years glide on, when the descendants   340
Of Trojan Assaracus shall subdue
Glorious Mycenae, Phthia, and Argos.
From this resplendent line shall be born
Trojan Caesar, who will extend his Empire
To the Ocean and his glory to the stars,   345
A Julian in the lineage of great Ilus.
And you, Venus, free at last from care,
Will someday welcome him into heaven,
Laden with Oriental spoils of war,
And his name too will be invoked in vows.   350
Then war shall be no more, and the ages
Will grow mild. Grey-haired Faith, and Vesta,
And Quirinus with his brother Remus
Will make laws. The Gates of War,
Iron upon bolted iron, shall be closed,   355
And inside, impious Fury will squat enthroned

On the savage weapons of war, hands bound tight
Behind his back with a hundred brazed knots,
Howling horrible curses from his blood-filled mouth."

Thus Jupiter, and from heaven he dispatched   360
Mercury, Maia's winged son, so that Carthage,
With its newly built towers, would lie open
To welcome the Trojans, and that Dido,
In her ignorance of Fate, would not ban them
From her land. The god wings his way   365
Through the vast sky, quickly touches down
On Libya's shore, and just as quickly
Accomplishes his mission. At the god's will
The Phoenicians put aside their fighting spirit,
And, above all, the Queen conceived   370
A great benevolence toward the Trojans.

Aeneas, meanwhile, aware of his duty,
Was up thinking the whole night through.
When Dawn kissed his face with light, he resolved
To set forth and explore the strange coastline   375
To see which way the wind had blown him
And to see who lived there, man or beast,
In the untilled land that lay before him.
Then, he would report back to his men.
He hid the fleet under a rocky overhang   380
Steeped in a forest's shimmering shade.
Then he strode forth, with Achates
His only companion, gripping in his hand
A pair of javelins tipped with flared iron.

And there, in the middle of the forest,   385
Was his mother, coming toward him.
She looked and dressed like a young woman
And bore a huntress's weapons. She could have been
A Spartan girl, or Harpalyce of Thrace,
Who outruns horses and the Hebrus' rapids.   390
A supple bow was slung over her shoulders
In the style of a huntress, and she let her hair

Fly loose in the wind. Her flowing robe was cinched up
In a knot, offering a glimpse of her knees.
She spoke first:

              "Have either of you seen   *395*
Any of my sisters? They're sporting quivers
And lynx hides. They may have wandered here,
Or are hot on the trail of a frothing boar."

Thus Venus, and the son of Venus responded:

"I've neither heard nor seen any of your sisters.   *400*
But how should I address you, Maiden? Your face
Is hardly mortal, and your voice does not sound human.
Surely you are a goddess. Apollo's sister?
One of the Nymphs? Whoever you are, Goddess,
Be gracious to us, lighten our burden,   *405*
And tell us, under what sky are we now?
Into what part of the world have we been tossed?
We are strangers in a strange land, lost,
Driven here by the wind and immense seas.
Many victims will fall by my hand at your altars."   *410*

And Venus:

              "I am hardly worthy of such honor.
It is customary among Tyrian girls
To carry quivers and lace on high scarlet boots.
What you see around you is Tyrian country
And a Punic city from Agenor's bloodline,   *415*
But it borders on Libya, a warlike nation.
Dido rules here, having left her city, Tyre,
To escape from her brother. It's a long story,
Full of intrigue, but I will sum it up for you.
Dido's husband, Sychaeus, was the richest man   *420*
In Phoenicia, and loved dearly
By ill-starred Dido. Her father, with good omens,
Had given her to him untouched and virgin.
But her brother, Pygmalion, who ruled the land,
Was a most wicked man. A feud rose up   *425*

Between the two men, and impious Pygmalion,
Blind with gold-lust and contemptuous
Of his sister's love, secretly cut down Sychaeus
Before the altars, alone and off guard.
The villain hid his crime for a long time   430
And with many pretenses cruelly kept alive
Poor Dido's vain hopes. But the actual ghost
Of her unburied husband visited her dreams,
Lifting his pale face in wondrous ways.
He showed her the bloodstained altars,   435
Bared his pierced chest, and revealed the crime
At the dark heart of the noble house.
Then he urged her to flee the country,
And, to aid her journey, he showed her where
An ancient, secret treasure was buried,   440
Untold tons of silver and gold. Roused by all this,
Dido prepared for flight, joined by others
Who either feared or hated the cruel tyrant.
They commandeered ships, loaded them with gold,
And all the wealth of avaricious Pygmalion   445
Was shipped out to sea. A woman did this.
They arrived at the place where now you see
The soaring walls of a new city—Carthage.
They bought as much land as they could surround
With the hide of an ox, and so its name Byrsa.   450
But who are you? From what shores did you sail,
And where are you going?"

           Faced with such questions,
Aeneas sighed and drew his voice from deep within:

"Goddess, if I were to start from the beginning
And tell you the whole tale of our suffering,   455
Dusk would gather over the dying day.
We are from Troy. Perhaps the name
Of that ancient city means something to you.
We have wandered the seas, and a storm
Has driven us to the coast of Libya.   460
I am Aeneas, devoted to my city's gods,
Refugees I rescued from enemy hands,

And my ship's most precious cargo. My fame
Has reached the heavens above. My quest
Is for Italy to be our fatherland, and to found   465
A race descended from Jove most high.
I embarked on the Phrygian sea with twenty ships,
My mother charting my course
As I pursued my destiny. Scarcely seven
Have survived the winds and the waves.   470
Lost, destitute, I wander the Libyan desert,
A man expelled from both Europe and Asia."

Venus would not endure any further self-pity
And interrupted him in mid-complaint:

"Whoever you are, I can hardly believe   475
You draw your breath cursed by the gods.
After all, here you are at our Tyrian town.
Just get yourself to the Queen's doorstep.
I foretell that your ships and comrades are safe,
Driven to shore by winds from the North—   480
Unless I've learned nothing about reading birds.
Observe the serenity of those twelve gliding swans.
An eagle, Jove's bird, swooped down from above
And disturbed their flight in the open sky,
But now they are flying in a long line again.   485
Some have landed, and you can see the others
Looking down for a good place to alight.
Just as those birds, in formation again,
Sport with wings whirring, rimming the sky
And issuing their song, so too your ships,   490
With their hearty crews, are either in port
Or entering the harbor under full sail.
Well, go on. Just let your feet follow the road."

She spoke, and as she turned, her neck
Shone with roselight. An immortal fragrance   495
From her ambrosial locks perfumed the air,
Her robes flowed down to cover her feet,
And every step revealed her divinity.

Aeneas knew his own mother, and his voice
Fell away from her as she disappeared: *500*

"You! Do you have to cheat your son
With empty appearances? Why can't we
At least embrace and talk to each other
In our own true voices?"

                  With this rebuke,
Aeneas turned toward the city.   *505*
Venus, for her part, enclosed both her son
And his companion in a dark cloud,
Cloaking them in mist so that none would see them
As they walked along and so detain them
With questions about their reasons for coming.   *510*
And then she was gone, aloft to Paphus,
Happy to see her temple again, where Arabian
Incense curls up from one hundred altars
And fresh wreaths of flowers sweeten the air.

The two heroes, meanwhile, followed the path   *515*
And ascended a hill high above the city.
Looking down, Aeneas was amazed
At the sheer size of the place—once a few hovels—
The city gates, the bustle on the paved streets.
The Tyrians were hard at work, building walls,   *520*
Fortifying the citadel, rolling boulders by hand,
Marking out sites for houses with trenches.
As Aeneas watched, they made laws, chose officials,
Installed a senate. Some were dredging
The harbor, others laying the foundation   *525*
For a theater, carving huge columns out of a cliff
To grace the stage that was yet to be built—

   Like bees under an early summer sun
   Leading a new swarm out to the wildflowers,
   Or stuffing honey into the comb,   *530*
   Swelling the cells with nectar, or unloading
   The pollen other bees bring to the stall,
   Or warding off the worthless brood of drones:

The busy hive seethes with all their activity
And the fragrant honey is redolent of thyme.   535

"Happy are they whose walls are rising."

Thus Aeneas, as he surveyed the city's heights.
And then, hidden in the miraculous cloud
He mingled with the citizens, invisible to all.

At the city's center there was a shady grove.   540
It was here the Phoenicians when they made land,
Refugees from the surge and storms of the sea,
Had dug up the token foretold by Juno,
The head of a spirited horse, an augury
Of success in war and a prosperous people.   545
Here Sidonian Dido had dedicated
A huge temple to Juno, rich with offerings
And the goddess's presence. A bronze threshold
Surmounted the steps; the joints and beams glowed
With bronze, and bronze doors slowly groaned open   550
On heavy hinges. It was in this grove that Aeneas
Could finally relax; here he first dared
To hope for safe harbor and have confidence,
After all his trials, in a turn for the better.
For while he was waiting for the Queen,   555
Touring the temple, marveling at the city's
Great good fortune and at the work
Of various artisans blended together,
He saw pictured on the walls the whole Trojan War,
Whose fame had already spread through the world.   560
There were the sons of Atreus, there Priam,
And there Achilles, raging at each of them.
Aeneas stopped and said with tears in his eyes:

"Is there any place on earth, Achates,
Not filled with our sorrows? Look,   565
There is Priam! Here, too, honor matters;
Here are the tears of the ages, and minds touched
By human suffering. Breathe easy, my friend.
Troy's renown will yet be your salvation."

                                        Thus Aeneas,
And he fed his soul on empty pictures,   570
Sighing, weeping, his face a flood of tears
As he scanned the murals of the Trojan War.

   On one panel the Greeks are in full retreat,
With the Trojan youth hard on their heels.
In the other direction crested Achilles   575
   Bears down on the Trojans with his chariot.

   A little farther on he sees through his tears
The snowy canvas of Rhesus' tents,
His camp betrayed in their first night at Troy
And savaged by the blood-soaked son of Tydeus,   580
Who then drove the fiery steeds of Rhesus
To the Greek camp, before they ever tasted
   Trojan fodder or drank from the Xanthus.

   On another panel Troilus, just a boy
And no match for Achilles in combat,   585
Has lost his armor and is being dragged
By his stampeding horses. Fallen backward
From his empty chariot, he still holds the reins
While his neck and hair trail in the dust
   And the plain is scored by the tip of his spear.   590

   Meanwhile, Trojan women, their hair streaming,
Are going to the temple of implacable Pallas,
Bearing a robe and beating their breasts
In supplication. The goddess's head is turned away,
   And she keeps her eyes fixed on the ground.   595

   And now Achilles has dragged Hector
Three times around the walls of Troy
And is selling the lifeless body for gold.
Aeneas is choked with grief when he sees the spoils,
The chariot, the corpse of his friend,   600
   And Priam stretching out weaponless hands.

   And now Aeneas recognizes himself
In close combat with the foremost Achaeans

And sees the eastern ranks, dark Memnon's armor,
And Penthesilea among her thousands of Amazons 605
With their crescent shields. Burning with fury,
She binds a golden belt below one naked breast,
    A warrior queen daring to do battle with men.

While Aeneas' gaze was fixed on these marvels,
The Queen was making her way to the temple, 610
The most beautiful Dido, and as she walked
A throng of youths crowded around her.

> On the Eurotas' banks or the ridges of Cynthus
> Diana leads the dances, and a thousand Oreads
> Circle around her this way and that. A quiver 615
> Hangs from her shoulder, and as she treads
> She towers above the other goddesses,
> And Latona's heart beats with secret joy.

So too Dido, moving through their midst,
Urged on the work of building a kingdom. 620
Then, under the temple's vaulted entrance
And flanked by guards, she ascended her throne.
She was making laws for her people,
Distributing duties or assigning them by lot,
When suddenly Aeneas saw, coming toward him 625
In a crowd, Antheus, Sergestus, and brave Cloanthus
Along with other Trojans whom the black storm
Had scattered and driven to distant shores.
Aeneas was stunned, Achates too, with joy and fear.
They burned with desire to clasp hands with them 630
But were confused and uncertain of the situation.
They kept themselves hidden inside the cloud
And watched. What has happened to their comrades?
On what shore did they leave their ships?
Why have they come here? These are chosen men 635
From all the ships, making for the temple
With loud cries and prayers for indulgence.

When they had entered and were allowed to speak,
The eldest, Ilioneus, calmly began:

"Queen, whom Jupiter has permitted   640
To found a new city and to curb with justice
The arrogance of the surrounding tribes,
We are Trojans, blown by winds over the sea.
In our misery we pray you to prohibit
The burning of our ships. Spare a pious race,   645
And look with grace upon our fortunes.
We have not come to pillage your homes
And carry the booty down to the shore.
There is no such violence in our hearts
And no such arrogance in a conquered race.   650
There is a place the Greeks call Hesperia,
An ancient land, strong in war and rich in soil.
Oenotrians once lived there. Now, it is said,
A younger race has named it Italy
After their leader. We were on course   655
For that land, when a sudden squall
Rose up—Orion behind it—and drove us
Onto blind shoals, scattering our ships
Amid trackless rocks and overwhelming waves.
We few drifted along and came to your shores.   660
But what race of men is this? What land
Is so barbarous that it allows this conduct?
We are denied access to the very shore!
These warmongers forbid us to set foot
On the border of their land. You may scorn   665
Our common humanity and mortal arms,
But the gods will remember good and evil.
We had a king, Aeneas, no one more just
Or devoted, no one greater in battle.
If Fate still preserves him, if he still breathes   670
The sky's pure air and does not yet lie with the shades,
We have no fear, nor would you regret
Being first to contend with him in courtesy.
    There are cities in Sicily too, and arms,
And a hero of Trojan blood, Acestes.   675
Allow us to beach our storm-battered fleet,
To mill planks and trim oars from your woods,
So that if we find our comrades and leader,
And we are destined to go to Italy, to Italy

And to Latium we may gladly set forth.   680
But if all is lost, and you, noble father
Of the Trojan people, have gone down
In the Libyan sea, and Iülus
Is our hope no more, then at least we can seek
The straits of Sicily—whence we came here—   685
And our homes there, with Acestes as our king."

Thus Ilioneus, and all the Trojans
Murmured in approval.

Dido, eyes lowered, responded briefly:

"Fear no more, Teucrians, ease your hearts.   690
Stern necessity and my kingdom's newness
Force me to such measures to protect our frontier.
Who does not know of Aeneas and Troy,
Of that city's warriors and its exploits,
Of the conflagrations of that great war?   695
Punic hearts are not so dull and unfeeling,
Nor is Tyre so far from the course of the sun.
Whether you choose great Hesperia, land of Saturn,
Or Sicily, the realm of Acestes,
I will speed you safely on your journey.   700
Or would you like to settle here, share my kingdom?
The city I am founding is yours. Draw up your ships.
Trojan and Tyrian I will treat the same.
I only wish that Aeneas himself were here,
Driven in by the same South Wind. Be sure   705
I will dispatch our best men to scour the coast
And search every corner of Libya.
He may have been cast ashore and
May be wandering now in some wood or town."

Aeneas and Achates, alert to every word,   710
Had long been burning to burst from the cloud,
And now Achates turned to Aeneas and said:

"What do you think, Goddess-born? You see
That all is safe, our ships and men restored.

Only one is missing, and he went down in the gulf   715
Before our own eyes. Everything else agrees
With your mother's words."

                        He had scarcely finished
When the enveloping cloud parted
And dissolved into thin air. There stood Aeneas,
Gleaming in the clear light, his face and shoulders   720
Like a god's. His mother breathed upon him
The radiance of youth, breathed glory on his hair,
And she gave his eyes an exultant luster
Like the sheen of hand-rubbed ivory,
Or Parian marble, or silver set in gold.   725
Unforeseen, unexpected, he addressed the Queen:

"The man you seek is before you. I am
Aeneas, of Troy, saved from Libyan seas.
Dido, you alone have pitied Ilium's
Unutterable woes, and now you offer us—   730
The remnant left by the Greeks, outworn
By every misfortune on land and sea,
A destitute band—you offer us
A share of your city and your home.
We do not have the means to render worthy thanks,   735
Nor do any Trojan survivors anywhere
In the wide world. May the gods—
If any powers above look down on the pious,
If there is any justice anywhere—may the gods
And your good conscience reward you   740
As you deserve. What happy age bore you?
What noble parents gave birth to such a child?
While rivers run to the sea, while shadows
Move over mountainsides, while the sky
Pastures the stars, ever shall your honor,   745
Your name, and your praises endure,
Whatever the lands that summon me."

Aeneas spoke, and he reached out
For dear Ilioneus with his right hand,

Serestus with his left, and then the others,   750
His brave Gyas and brave Cloanthus.

Dido, stunned by his sudden appearance
And his great ill fortune, responded:

"Goddess-born, what misfortune has plagued you,
What force has driven you onto savage coasts?   755
You, then, are Aeneas, whom Venus bore to Anchises
Near the waters of the Simois river in Troy?
I remember well when Teucer came to Sidon,
Exiled by his father and seeking new realms
With the aid of Belus, my own father,   760
Who was waging war in Cyprus then,
Establishing his power in that rich land.
Since that time I have known about Troy,
Known you by name, and the Pelasgian leaders.
The Trojans' enemy sang Troy's praises   765
And wanted it known that he was of Trojan stock.
And so, young men, come under my roof.
My fortune too has long been adverse
But at last has allowed me to rest in this land.
My own acquaintance with suffering   770
Has taught me to aid others in need."

Thus Dido, and as she led Aeneas into her palace
She proclaimed sacrifices in his honor
In all the temples. Meanwhile, she sent
To his comrades on the shore twenty bulls,   775
A hundred boars with great, bristling backs,
And as many fat lambs with their dams,
The day's joyful gifts.
                          The palace gleamed
With luxurious furnishings as the great hall
Was being prepared for a banquet: 780
Coverlets embroidered with royal purple,
Heavy silver on the tables, gold cups engraved
With the heroic deeds of a long lineage
Stretching back to the origin of the race.

But Aeneas' love for his son, Ascanius,   785
Would not allow his mind to rest. He sent
Achates, on the run, to the ships
To report the news and to bring the boy
Back to the city. Ascanius was all Aeneas' care.
He also told Achates to bring presents   790
Snatched from ruined Ilium: a mantle
Stiff with gold-stitched figures, and a veil
Fringed with saffron acanthus, both worn
By Helen, who brought them from Mycenae—
Wondrous gifts from her mother, Leda—   795
When she sailed for Troy and her illicit wedding;
The scepter, too, of Priam's eldest daughter,
Ilione; and a pearl necklace; and a coronet
With a double band of jewels and gold.
And so Achates hurried off to the ships.   800

Venus, meanwhile, was busily concocting
Another scheme. She would send Cupid—
Transformed to look just like Ascanius—
To come in the place of that sweet boy
And with his gifts enflame the Queen's heart   805
And infiltrate her bones with fire.
The Cytherean feared this dubious union,
Tyrians speaking two tongues. She chafed
Under Juno's arrogance, and at nightfall
Her anxiety mounted. She turned, therefore,   810
To the winged God of Love and spoke to him:

"My son, my strength and my power, you alone
Scorn your father's Typhoean lightning blasts,
And so to your godhead I come on bended knee.
You know how your brother, Aeneas,   815
Is beaten about the sea by Juno's wrath,
And you have often grieved at my grief for him.
Phoenician Dido now has him, and detains him
With soft words. I dread the outcome
Of Juno's hospitality. She will not be idle   820
During this great turn of events. And so,
I plan to catch the Queen off guard and by guile

Encircle her with passion, so that no power
Can change her, and she will be bound to me,
By her great love for my Aeneas.   825
Now here is how I think you can do this.
The young prince, my pride and joy and all my care,
Is preparing to go, at his father's summons,
To the Sidonian city, bearing such gifts
As have survived the sea and the flames of Troy.   830
I will wrap him in slumber and tuck him away
In my sacred shrine, either high on Cythera
Or on Idalium, so that he will never know
Of my trickery or get in the way.
For a single night, no more, feign his looks.   835
Boy that you are, wear the boy's familiar face.
And when amid the royal feast and flowing wine
Dido, her joy knowing no bounds, takes you
Onto her lap, embraces you and plants
Sweet kisses on your mouth, breathe into her   840
Your secret fire and poison her unobserved."

Love obeyed his dear mother, donned his wings,
And walked off joyously with Iülus' gait.
Iülus himself Venus bathed in the waters
Of calm repose and, holding him to her breast,   845
Lifted him up to Idalia's high groves,
Where soft marjoram breathed upon him,
Nestled in blossoms sweet in the shade.

And so Cupid, obedient to his mother's word,
And delighting in the company of Achates,   850
Carried the royal gifts to the palace.
When he arrived, the Queen had already
Taken her place amid gorgeous tapestries,
Reclining on a golden couch in the great hall.
Father Aeneas and the Trojan youth gathered   855
And were made to recline on purple coverlets.
Servants poured water on their hands, served bread
From baskets, and brought them soft napkins.
There were fifty maids working in the kitchen
To prepare all the banquet's dishes in order   860

And to keep the hearth-fire for the Penates.
Another hundred, and as many male servants,
All the same age, laid the food on the table
And set out the cups.
            The Tyrians too
Crowded the festive hall and were told to recline   865
On embroidered couches. They marveled
At Aeneas' gifts, and they marveled at Iülus,
At the god's glowing complexion, at the words
He feigned, and at the robe and the veil
Elaborately stitched with saffron acanthus.   870
Dido especially, doomed to a wretched end,
Could not satisfy her soul. The ill-fated Phoenician
Burned with desire when she gazed at the boy
And was equally moved at the sight of the gifts.
The boy, when he had hung on Aeneas' neck   875
And satisfied the deluded father's love,
Went to the Queen. And she clung to him
With all her heart, her eyes were riveted on him,
And she cuddled him on her lap. Poor Dido.
She had no idea how great a god had settled there.   880
Mindful of his Acidalian mother,
Little by little he began to blot out Sychaeus
And tried to captivate with a living passion
Her slumbering soul and her heart long unused.

At the first lull in the feast the tables were cleared.   885
Great bowls were set out and crowned with wine.
The palace grew loud, and the guests' voices
Echoed through the halls. Glowing lamps
Hung down from the fretted gold ceiling,
And flaming torches vanquished the night.   890
Dido called for a heavy gold drinking bowl
Crusted with jewels and filled it with wine—
A bowl used by Belus and Belus' descendants.
Then silence reigned in the great hall again.

"Jupiter, Lord of Hospitality,   895
Grant that this day be a happy one
For Tyrians and Trojan travelers alike,

And may our children remember it!
May Bacchus, giver of joy, be near,
May Juno bless us, and may all Tyrians   900
Favor our gathering with grace and good cheer."

Dido prayed and then poured a drop
Onto the table. After this libation,
Her lips were the first to touch the bowl's rim.
Then she passed it to Bitias with a challenge,   905
And he promptly drained the foaming bowl,
Soaking himself in the brimming gold.
Then the other lords drank.
                              Long-haired Iopas,
A bard taught by mighty Atlas,
Now sounded his golden lyre.
                              He sang   910
Of the wandering moon and the sun's toils,
Of the origin of human and animal kind,
Of how rain falls and why lightning flashes,
Of Arcturus, the Bears, and the misty Hyades,
Of why the winter sun rushes down to Ocean,   915
And why long winter nights are so slow to end.

The Tyrians applauded again and again,
And the Trojans joined in. And Dido,
Unhappy woman, prolonged the night
With varied conversation   920
And drank deeply the long draught of love.
She asked about Priam over and over,
Asked much about Hector, wanted to know
What armor Memnon wore when he arrived,
What the horses of Diomedes were like,   925
And how great was Achilles.

                              "Still better,"
She cries, "Tell us, my dear guest,
The whole story from the beginning—
The treachery of the Greeks, the downfall
Of your people, and your own wanderings.   930
Seven summers have now seen you roving
Through every land and over all the seas."

AENEID TWO

The room fell silent, all eyes on Aeneas,
Who from his high couch now began to speak:

"My Queen, you are asking me to relive
Unspeakable sorrow, to recall how the Greeks
Pulled down Troy, that tragic realm   5
With all its riches. I saw those horrors myself
And played no small part in them. What Myrmidon
Or Dolopian, what brutal soldier of Ulysses
Could tell such a tale and refrain from tears?
And now dewy night is rushing from the sky,   10
And the setting stars make sleep seem sweet.
But if you are so passionate to learn
Of our misfortunes, to hear a brief account
Of Troy's last struggle—although my mind
Shudders to remember and recoils in pain,   15
I will begin.

Broken by war and rebuffed by the Fates
For so many years, the Greek warlords
Built a horse, aided by the divine art
Of Pallas, a horse the size of a mountain,   20
Weaving its ribs out of beams of fir.
They pretended it was a votive offering
For their safe return home. So the story went.
But deep within the Horse's cavernous dark
They concealed an elite band, all their best,   25
Stuffing its huge womb with men at arms.

Within sight of Troy lies a famous island,
Tenedos, prosperous while Priam's kingdom stood,
Now just a bay with poor anchorage for ships.
The Greeks sailed there and hid on the desolate shore;　　30
They were gone, we thought, sailed off to Mycenae.
And so all of Troy shook off its long sorrow.
The gates were opened. It was a joy to visit
The Doric camp, the abandoned beachhead,
The deserted sites. Here the Dolopians　　35
Pitched their tents, here fierce Achilles,
Here lay the ships, here were the battle-lines.
Some of us gaped at the virgin Minerva's
Fatal gift, amazed at the massive Horse.
Thymoetes wanted it dragged inside the walls　　40
And installed in the citadel. Treason perhaps,
Or Troy's doom was already in motion.
But Capys, and other wiser heads, urged us
To either pitch this insidious Greek gift
Into the sea, or burn it on the spot, or else　　45
Pierce and probe the belly's hidden hollows.
The crowd took sides, uncertain what to do.

And now Laocoön comes running down
From the citadel at the head of a great throng
And in his burning haste he cries from afar:　　50

'Are you out of your minds, you poor fools?
Are you so easily convinced that the enemy
Has sailed away? Do you honestly think
That any Greek gift comes without treachery?
What is Ulysses known for? Either this lumber　　55
Is hiding Achaeans inside, or it has been built
As an engine of war to attack our walls,
To spy on our homes and come down on the city
From above. Or some other evil lurks inside.
Do not trust the Horse, Trojans! Whatever it is,　　60
I fear the Greeks, even when they bring gifts.'

With that, he hurled his spear with enormous force
Into the vaulting belly of the beast. The shaft

Stood quivering, and the hollow insides
Reverberated with a cavernous moan.   65
If we had not been on the gods' wrong side,
If we had been thinking right, Laocoön
Would have driven us to hack our way into
The Greek lair, and Troy would still stand,
And you, high rock of Priam, would remain.   70

But at that moment a band of Dardan shepherds
Came up with loud shouts, dragging to the king
A prisoner with his hands bound behind his back.
This man had deliberately gotten himself captured
With one purpose in mind, to open Troy to the Greeks,   75
Ready to either work his deceits or face certain death.
The Trojan youths streamed in from all sides
To see the captive and jeer at him.
                              Hear now
The treachery of the Greeks, and from one offense
Learn all their evil.
                              The man stood in full sight   80
Of the crowd, dismayed, unarmed, and glancing
Around at the ranks of men he cried out:

'Ah, what land, what sea, can receive me now,
What will be my final wretched fate?
I have no place among the Greeks,   85
And the Trojans are clamoring for my blood.'

At this our mood changed, and we prodded him
To tell us what he meant. Who were his people,
And what was he counting on to save him
Now that he was our prisoner? Finally,   90
He stopped trembling and began to speak:

'Come what may, King, I will tell you all
And not deny, first, that I am a Danaan.
Fortune may have damned Sinon to misery,
But she will not make him a liar as well.   95
You may have heard the name Palamedes,
Belus' glorious son, whom the Greeks

Condemned to death, under false charges,
Because he opposed the war. He was innocent.
Now they mourn him, now that he is dead.　　　　　　　*100*
He was my kinsman, and my father,
A poor man, sent me here in his company
When I was just a boy. While Palamedes
Was still in good standing, still thrived in council,
I too had somewhat of a name, some honor.　　　　　　　*105*
But when through the malice of cunning Ulysses — mentioned
(Everyone knows this) he passed from this world,　in Odyssey?
I was a ruined man and dragged on my life
In darkness and grief, eating my heart out
Over the fate of my innocent friend.　　　　　　　　　*110*
Nor was I silent, but I raved
That if I ever had the chance, ever returned
As victor to Argos, I would have my vengeance.
My words aroused resentment, and my life
Was now infected. Ulysses made it his mission　　　　　*115*
To terrorize me with countless new charges,
Sowing rumors in everyone's ears, searching
In his guilt for weapons against me. In the end
He found Fortune's tool, Calchas the soothsayer—
But you don't want to hear all this. And why　　　　　*120*
Should I stall? If you paint all Greeks
With the same stripe, if "he's Achaean"
Is all you need to hear, take your vengeance
At once. This is what the Ithacan would want,
And what Atreus' sons would pay dearly for.'　　　　　*125*

Now indeed we burned to know more,
Strangers as we were to infamy so great
And to Greek guile. Trembling, he went on: — He is playing
　　　　　　　　　　　　　　　　　　　　　manipulative
'Weary with the long war, the Greeks　　　　　　　　deception
Often wanted to quit Troy and sail home.
If only they had! But stormy weather　　　　　　　　*130*
And rough seas would scare them from leaving.
And when they'd hammered together
The maple horse, the sky rumbled even more.
Anxious, we sent Eurypylus to consult　　　　　　　　*135*

The oracle of Phoebus Apollo,
And he brought back these dismal words:
You placated the winds with a virgin's blood
To come, O Danaans, to the shores of Troy.
Your return must be won with an Argive life.   140
When the god's words reached the army's ears
Everyone was dazed, and an icy fear
Seeped into their bones. Which man was doomed,
Whom would Apollo claim? The Ithacan
Dragged Calchas out into the roaring crowd   145
And demanded to know what heaven portended.
Many divined that this despicable ploy
Was aimed at me and saw what was coming.
Five days and five more the seer sat in his hut,
Silent, refusing to sentence anyone to death.   150
Finally, forced by the Ithacan's cries,
Calchas broke his silence and, as agreed,
Doomed me to the altar. Everyone approved,
And the ruin each had feared for himself
They bore well when it devolved upon one.   155

'And now the dark day dawned. The salted grain,
The sacral headbands were being prepared
For my ritual slaughter, when, I confess,
I broke my bonds and snatched myself from death.
I skulked all night in a muddy swamp,   160
Hidden in the sedge, holding my breath
Until they sailed. Now I have no hope
Of seeing my homeland, my sweet children,
The father I long for. And the Greeks
May make them pay for my escape, poor things,   165
And by their death expiate my sin.
And so I pray, by whatever powers above
Still witness Truth, and by any Faith we men
Still have uncorrupted, show mercy
To a suffering soul, guiltless and wronged.'   170

We spared him for his tears and pitied him
Of our own accord. Priam himself ordered
His shackles removed and spoke to him kindly:

[handwritten annotation at top: while very kind, he is also too trusting]

'Whoever you are, take no further thought
Of the Greeks. You are one of us now.　　　　175
But tell me, and speak the whole truth:
Why did they erect this monstrous horse?
Who devised it, and to what purpose?
Is it a religious offering or an engine of war?'

[handwritten annotation in right margin: hes successfully convinced Troy that he was not with the Greeks]

Thus Priam. And Sinon, the consummate liar,　　180
Lifting his unchained hands to the stars:

'Eternal fires of heaven, I summon you
And your inviolable Power to witness,
And you altars and nefarious blades
Which I escaped, and you consecrated fillets　　185
Which as victim I wore: it is just for me
To break the sacred oaths of the Greeks,
Just to abhor those men, and to lay bare to the sky
Every secret they would conceal. I am bound
By no law of my country. But you, Troy,　　190
Stand by your word and keep your faith,
If what I say proves to be your salvation.

'From the war's beginning, Pallas Athena
Was the Greeks' entire hope. But when
Wicked Diomedes and Ulysses,　　　　195
With his criminal mind, entered
Her high temple, murdered the guards,
And stole the fateful Palladium,
Daring to handle her virgin fillets
With bloodstained fingers—then　　　　200
The Danaans' fortunes began to falter,
Their strength was broken, and the goddess
Turned her back on them. Tritonia
Gave us clear portents of her displeasure.
As soon as her statue was set up in camp,　　205
Flames glittered from her upturned eyes,
Sweat poured down her limbs, and three times
She flashed up from the ground, miraculous,
Holding her shield and quivering spear.
Calchas at once began to prophesy:　　　210

"The Greeks must attempt a retreat by sea.
Troy cannot be taken by Argive weapons
Until they seek new omens in Argos
And return the godhead carried away
In curved keels over open water."

'They are sailing over to Mycenae now,   215
And when they have recruited soldiers and gods
They will recross the water all unforeseen.
So Calchas sifted the omens and counseled the Greeks
To erect this Horse, in expiation   220
Of the Palladium's theft and the godhead wronged.
And he ordered them to build its oaken bulk
Up to the sky, so it could not be brought
Through the city's gates or walls and there protect
The Trojan people under the old religion.   225
For if you lay violent hands
Upon this offering to Minerva,
Destruction will fall—may the gods turn this omen
Against the Greeks—upon Priam's realm.
But if your hands bring it into the city,   230
Asia will wage war upon Pelops' walls,
And this fate awaits our children's children.'

And so through Sinon's treacherous art
His story was believed, and we were taken
With cunning, captured with forced tears,   235
We whom neither great Diomedes
Nor Achilles of Larissa could subdue,
Nor ten years of war, nor a thousand ships.

What happened next was more horrible still
And threw us into deepening chaos.   240
Laocoön, serving by lot as Neptune's priest,
Was sacrificing a great bull at the god's altar,
When we saw, coming from Tenedos
Over the calm water, a pair of serpents—
I shudder to recall them—making for shore.   245
Trailing huge coils they sheared through the sea,
And their bloody crests arched over the waves

As they writhed and twisted in the seething surf.
They were almost ashore. Their eyes
Were shot with blood and fire, and their tongues   250
Hissed and flickered in their open mouths.
We scattered, pale with fear, as the sea-snakes
Glided through the sand straight for Laocoön.
First, they entwined the priest's two sons — *great* He spared
In great looping spirals, and then they sank their fangs *no one who*   255
Into the boys' wretched bodies and began to feed.   *prayed to him*
Then they seized Laocoön as he ran to their aid,
Weapon in hand, and lashed their scaly bodies
Twice around his waist and twice around his neck,
Their heads reared high. As the priest struggled   260
To wrench himself free from the knotted coils,
His headbands were soaked with venom and gore,
And his horrible cries reached up to the stars.   *meant for someone else,*
                                                   or unfair

   Wounded by an ill-aimed blow, a bull will bellow
    As it flees the altar and shakes the axe from his neck.   265
                                        the animal
                                        he was
So too Laocoön. But the twin serpents   *sacrificing*
Slithered off to the high temple of Pallas
And took refuge at the grim goddess's feet,
Vanished behind the disk of her shield.

An inhuman terror coiled through our hearts.   270
Shuddering with horror, everyone said Laocoön
Had received the punishment he deserved — *even though he*
For wounding the sacred wood of the Horse *tried to save*
With his accursed spear. All proclaimed   *everyone*
The Horse should be drawn to Minerva's temple   275
And her godhead appeased. We breached the walls,
Everyone girding themselves for the work,
And set wheels beneath the feet of the Horse.
A noose was made taut around its neck
And the fateful contraption inched up the battlements,   280
Pregnant with arms. Boys and unwed girls
Circled around it, singing hymns
And touching the rope with glee. On it moved,

sort of like a good luck charm

Gliding like a threat into the city.
O my country! O Ilium, home of the gods!   285
O walls of Troy famed in war! Four times
At the very threshold of the city gate
The Horse halted, and four times
Weapons clattered in its belly. Yet we pressed on
Mindlessly, blind with passion, and installed   290
The ill-starred monster on our high holy rock.
Even then Cassandra opened her lips
Against the coming doom, lips cursed by a god
Never to be believed by the Teucrians,
And we pitiful Trojans, on our last day,   295
Wreathed the shrines of the gods with flowers.

— glory before a tragedy

The sky turned, and night swept up from Ocean,
Enfolding in its great shadow earth and heaven—
And the Myrmidons' treachery. The Trojans
Spread out along the wall were dead silent now,   300
Slumber entwining their weary limbs,
And the Argive fleet started to sail from Tenedos
Through the silent, complicit moonlight,
Making for the shore they knew all too well.
The flagship raised a beacon, and at this signal   305
Sinon, cloaked by the gods' unjust decrees,
Stealthily unlocked the pine trapdoor,
And the Horse released from its open womb
The enclosed Danaans, glad to push themselves out
Of the hollow oak into the cool night air,   310
Thessandrus and Sthenelus and grim Ulysses—
Sliding down the rope—Acamas and Thoas,
Achilles' son, Neoptolemus, great Machaon,
Menelaus, and Epeos himself,
The fabricator of the insidious horse.   315
They fanned out through a city drowned in sleep,
Slit the guards' throats, opened all the gates,
And joined as planned the invading Greeks.

— the gods were helping the Greeks

familiar name

At that late hour, when sleep begins to drift
Upon fretful humanity as grace from the gods,   320
Hector appeared to me in my dreams,

at least they were sleeping when it happened

Pitiful spirit, weeping, black with blood
And dust from the ruts of Achilles' chariot,
Thongs piercing his swollen ankles. Ah,
How he looked, how different from that Hector
Who returned to Troy wearing Achilles' armor,   325
The Hector who threw fire on the Danaan ships!
His beard was matted, his hair clotted with gore,
And he bore all the wounds he had received
Fighting before his country's walls. In my dream   330
I blurted out to him these tearful words:

'Light of Dardania, Troy's finest hope,
What has delayed you? From what shores have you come
To answer our prayers? We have suffered
Many losses since you left us, Hector.   335
Yet, we have labored on, and now we see you
At the end of our strength. Why has your face
Been defiled, and what are these wounds I see?'

My empty questions meant nothing to him.
With a heavy sigh from deep within, he said: 340

'Run, child of the goddess, save yourself
From these flames! The enemy holds the walls.
Great Troy is falling. Enough has been given
To Priam and his country. If Pergamum's height
Could be defended by a hero's hand,   345
Its defense would have been this hand of mine.
Troy commends to you the gods of the city.
Accept them as companions of your destiny
And seek for them the great walls you will found
After you have wandered across the sea.'   350

He spoke, and brought out from the sanctuary
Great Vesta, her chaplets, and her eternal fire.

By now the lamentation in the city
Had grown to such proportions that it reached
My father Anchises' house, secluded though it was   355
Among the pines. The sickening sound of battle

Startled me from sleep, and I climbed to the roof
And stood at the very top, upright and listening.

> It was as if the South Wind were fanning fire
> Through the fields, or a mountain torrent had leveled   360
> The farmlands and swept away the oxen's tillage,
> Flattening the hedgerows, and I was a shepherd
> Listening in the dark from some towering rock.

Then the truth was revealed. The Danaans' treachery
Lay open before me. Deïphobus' great house   365
Was collapsing in flames, as was Ucalegon's
Next door. The Sigean straits burned
With the inferno's reflected light.
Men's shouts rose with the shrill sound of horns.
Out of my mind, I took up arms—no battle plan,   370
But my soul burned to gather a war party
And storm the citadel. Rage and fury
Sent my mind reeling, and my only thought
Was how glorious it is to die in combat.

At that moment Panthus, priest of Apollo,   375
Ran up to my door, dragging his grandson
Away from Greek swords, the sacred images
Of our vanquished gods clutched in his arms.

'Where is the fighting thickest, Panthus?
What position should we try to hold?'

                              My words   380
Were scarcely out when he answered, groaning:

'Troy's last day and final hour have come.
We are Trojans no more. Ilium is no more.
The great glory of the Teucrians is gone.
Jupiter in his rage has given all to Argos,   *terrifying*   385
And Greeks are lords of our burning city.   *gods*
High stands the Horse, pouring forth armed men,
And Sinon, insolent in victory,
Sets fires everywhere. Thousands of troops,

As many as ever came from Mycenae,   390
Are at the wide-open gates. Others patrol the streets.
A line of unsheathed, glistening steel
Stands ready for slaughter. Our night guard
Is barely resisting and fighting blind.'

Panthus' words and will of the gods   395
Drove me through the inferno of battle
Wherever the grim Fury called, wherever
The roars and shouts rose to the sky.
Falling in with me in the moonlight
Were Rhipeus and Epytus, one of Troy's best,   400
Hypanis and Dymas, a little throng now,
And young Coroebus, son of Mygdon.
He had come to Troy in those last days,
Madly in love with Cassandra, and brought
Aid to Priam, a sturdy son-in-law. Poor boy,   405
If only he had listened to the warnings
Of his raving bride.
When I saw them close ranks, eager for battle,
I began:

        'Brave hearts—brave in vain
If you are committed to follow me to the end—   410
You see how we stand. All the gods
Who sustained this realm are gone, leaving
Altar and shrine. You are fighting to save
A city in flames. All that is left for us
Is to rush onto swords and die. The only chance   415
For the conquered is to hope for none.' ~leavewhite
                                          / ar can

This added fury to the young men's courage.
Like wolves in a black mist, blind with hunger,
Their whelps waiting with dry throats, we passed
Through the enemy's swords to certain death   420
And held our course to the city's center.
Ebony night swirled around us. Who could tell
That night's carnage, or match it with tears?
The ancient city fell, that had for many years
Been queen. Corpses lay piled everywhere,   425

In the streets, the houses, the hallowed thresholds
Of the temples. And it was not only Trojans
Who paid in blood. At times the vanquished
Felt their valor pulse through their hearts,
And the conquering Greeks fell. Raw fear   430
Was everywhere, grief was everywhere,
Everywhere the many masks of death.

Androgeos offered himself to us first.
Heading up a large company of Greeks,
He mistook us for an allied band and called: 435

'On the double, men! What took you so long?
We're burning and looting Pergamum here,
And you're just arriving from the ships?'

He realized at once from our tentative reply
That we were the enemy. He froze, choked   440
On his own words, and then tried to backpedal,

> *Like a man who has stepped on a snake*
> *Hidden in briars and in sudden terror cringes*
> *When it rears and puffs out its purple hood.*

Androgeos was shaking and backing away *—that was weirdly edit?*   445
When we charged and hedged them in.
Unfamiliar with the terrain, they panicked.
And we cut them down, Fortune smiling
On our first effort. Flushed with success,
Coroebus cried:

                    'Let's follow Fortune's lead   450
And exchange our armor for Danaan gear.
Who cares if this is deceit or valor?
The enemy will supply us with weapons.'

With that he put on Androgeos' plumed helmet,
Hefted his emblazoned shield, and hung   455
An Argive sword by his side. So too Rhipeus,
Dymas, and my other boys, their spirits high

As they armed themselves in new-won spoils.
We moved out, mingling with the Greeks
And with gods not ours. In the blind night   460
We engaged in many skirmishes, and sent
Many a Greek into the jaws of Orcus.
Some scattered to the safety of the shore
And the ships. Others, like terrified children,
Climbed back up into the belly of the Horse.   465

Never rely on the gods for anything
Against their will. The next thing we saw
Was Cassandra, Priam's daughter,
Being dragged, hair streaming, from the shrine
Of Minerva's temple, lifting to heaven   470
Her burning eyes—her eyes only,
For her tender hands were bound. Coroebus
Could not endure this. He threw himself
Into the midst of the band, determined to die.
We closed ranks and charged, but were overwhelmed.   475
First, our countrymen targeted our uniforms,
The misleading crests on our Greek helmets,
Picking us off from the roof, a piteous slaughter.
Then the Greeks themselves, grunting with anger
At the attempted rescue of Cassandra,   480
Came at us from all sides, Ajax most viciously,
Then the two sons of Atreus and Ulysses' men.

  It was like a hurricane when winds clash
  From every direction, Winds West and South
  And the East proud with his colts of Dawn.   485
  The forests groan, and Nereus foams with rage
  As he stirs with his trident the lowest depths.

The men we had routed with our stratagem
In the dim of night rematerialized, the first
To recognize our mendacious shields   490
And discordant accents. We were outnumbered.
Coroebus fell first, killed by Peneleos
At the war goddess's altar. Then Rhipeus,
Of all Teucrians the most righteous (but the gods

Saw otherwise) went down. Hypanis   495
And Dymas were run through by friends; *of whom?,*
And you, Panthus, neither your piety
Nor Apollo's fillet protected you
When you fell. O ashes of Ilium!
O last flames of my people! Be witness   500
That in your fall I shunned neither fight nor chance,
And had my fate been to die by Greek hands
I had earned that fate. We were torn from there,
Iphitus, Pelias, and myself, we three,
Iphitus heavy with years, Pelias slowed   505
By a wound from Ulysses. Without pause
We were called by the clamor to Priam's house.

Here was an enormous battle, so intense
It was as if there was no fighting anywhere else,
And men were not dying throughout the city.   510
Here we saw the War God unchained. Greeks
Scrambled to the roof, and the threshold
Was besieged by a bulge of shields. Ladders
Hugged the walls, and men inched their way
Upward on the rungs, left hands holding up shields   515
Against projectiles, right hands clutching
Posts and battlements. Above, the Trojans
Tore down the towers and all the rooftop
To use as missiles—they saw the end was near—
Defending themselves to the death, rolling down   520
Gilded rafters, their fathers' splendors of old.
Other troops, swords drawn, massed around the doors,
Blocking the entrances. Our pulses quickened
With new energy to protect the palace
And come to the aid of our vanquished men.   525

There was a secret entry in the rear,
A passageway through Priam's palace
By which Andromache, poor soul,
Would come unattended to her husband's parents
While Troy still stood and lead her boy,   530
Astyanax, to see his grandfather.
I scaled the roof, where the Teucrians

Were lobbing their useless missiles to little effect.
Rising to the sky from the roof's sheer edge
Stood a tower from which all Troy   535
Could once be seen, and in the distance
A thousand Greek ships and their beachhead camp.
We pried at its upper stories with our swords
Until the joints gave way, wrenched it loose,
And sent it crashing down like rolling thunder   540
Onto the ranks of the Greeks. But more Greeks
Kept coming, and more stones kept falling.

Framed by the portal to the entrance court
Pyrrhus stood in his glory, haloed in bronze,   *Symbol*

> *As a snake raised on poison basks in the light*   545
> *After a cold winter has kept him underground,*
> *Venomous and swollen. Now, having sloughed*
> *His old skin, glistening with youth, he puffs out*
> *His breast and slides his lubricious coils*
> *Toward the sun, flicking his three-forked tongue.*   550

At his side loomed Periphas, and Automedon,
Once Achilles' charioteer, now the armor-bearer
Of Achilles' son. Massed around them
Were all the tough troops from Scyros,
Hurling torches onto the roof as they closed in   555
On Priam's palace. Pyrrhus led the charge,
Cleaving through the solid threshold
With a battle-axe, tearing the brass-bound doors
From their hinges, and hatcheting a hole
The size of a window in a huge oaken panel,   560
Revealing all the house in a grim tableau.
Open to view were the long halls; laid bare
Was the inner sanctum of Priam
And the kings of old, who now saw
Armed men standing on their very threshold.   565

A tumultuous roar tore through the house;
Its vaulted halls echoed with women's wails,
And the din reverberated to the golden stars.

Greeks are breaching Priam's palace

Trembling matrons roamed lost through the rooms,
Clinging to the doors, lips pressed against them.   *570*
Pyrrhus moved on with all his father's might,   — *motivation*
And nothing could stop him. The gate gave way
Before the battering ram, and the doors,
Wrenched from their sockets, fell to the floor.
The Greeks forced their way in, butchered   *575*
The Trojans who stood up against them,
And filled the whole space with their soldiery,

Worse than a river bursting through its banks,
The water churning in overwhelming fury,
Flooding the fields and sweeping herds and folds   *580*
Over the plain.   ← *destroying everything no matter what*

        I saw with my own eyes
Neoptolemus, lusting for slaughter,
And Atreus' two sons, there on the threshold.
I saw Hecuba, with her hundred daughters,
And Priam, polluting with his blood   *585*
The very altars he had consecrated himself.
Those fifty bedchambers, that promise of offspring,
The doorposts proud with barbarian gold—
All lost. The Greeks held what the fire spared.

And what, you may ask, was Priam's fate?   *590*
When he saw that his city had fallen,   *experiencing great tragedy before death*
The doors of his palace shattered,
And the enemy at his very hearth,
The old man slung his long-unused armor
Over his trembling shoulders, strapped on   *595*
His useless sword, and, bound to die,   — *dying virtuous even though his fate is sealed*
Charged the enemy.
        In the middle of the palace,
Under heaven's naked wheel, an enormous altar
Lay beneath the branches of an ancient laurel
Whose shade embraced the household gods.   *600*
In this sacred place Hecuba and her daughters
Huddled like doves driven by a black storm,
Clutching the gods' images. But when she saw

Priam's death on the horizon

Priam himself clad in the armor of his youth,
She cried out:

                    'My poor husband,   605
What insanity has driven you
To take up these weapons? Where
Are you rushing to? The hour is past
For defense like this, even if my Hector
Were still here. Come to this altar, please.   *still holding*   610
It will protect us all, or you will die with us.' *onto the gods*

Hecuba said these things, took the aged man
In her arms, and placed him on the holy seat.

And now Polites, one of Priam's sons,
Pursued by Pyrrhus, came running   615
Through the colonnades, wounded.
When he reached the vast atrium
Pyrrhus was breathing down his neck,
And yet he slipped away to face his parents' eyes.

There he fell, Pyrrhus' spear in his back,   620
And poured out his life in a pool of blood.
Then Priam, in death's grip as he was,
Did not hold back his anger or spare his voice.

'For this heinous crime,' he cried, 'this outrage,
May the gods in heaven—if there is in heaven   625
Any spirit that cares for what is just and good—
May the gods treat you as you deserve   *experiencing*
For making me watch my own son's murder   *tragedy*
And defiling with death a father's face.
Not so was Achilles, whom you falsely claim   630
To be your father, in the face of Priam his foe,
But honored a suppliant's rights and trust,
And allowed the bloodless corpse of Hector
Burial, and sent me back to my own realm.'

And the old man threw his feeble spear. Its tip   635
Clanged against the bronze of Pyrrhus' shield

priam middles *think of trojan*
after anna *to he sees his sons*
death

And dangled uselessly from its boss. And Pyrrhus:

'Then you can take this news to my father,
The son of Peleus. Be sure to tell him
About my sad behavior and how degenerate   640
His son has become. Now die.' *—Seems to be bored with this*

              So saying,
He dragged Priam, trembling and slipping
In his son's blood, up to the altar. Winding
His left hand in the old man's hair, with his right
He lifted his flashing sword and buried it   645
Up to its hilt in his side. So ended Priam,
Such was his fated doom, as Troy burned
Before his eyes and Pergamum fell.
Once the lord of so many peoples,
The sovereign of Asia, he lies now   650
A huge trunk upon the shore, head severed
From his neck, a corpse without a name. *—he wants us to mourn and pity Priam*

Then an awful sense of dread enveloped me.
I stood in a daze, and there rose before me
The image of my dear father, the same age   655
As the wounded king whom I was watching
Gasp out his life. Before me rose Creüsa,
Abandoned, the pillaged house, and the plight
Of little Iülus. I looked around
For my troops. They had all deserted me.   660
Too fatigued to fight, they had either jumped
To a welcome death or dropped limply into the flames.

Now I alone was left, when I saw, *the one who started it all*
Hiding in the shadows of Vesta's shrine,
Helen, daughter of Tyndareus. The bright fires   665
Gave me light as I wandered here and there
Casting my eyes over everything.
Fearing the Trojans' anger for Troy's fall,
The vengeance of the Greeks, and the wrath
Of her deserted husband, Helen, destroyer   670

Priam has a tragic death Aeneas spots Helen

Alike of her own country and ours,
This detestable woman, crouched by the altars.
My soul flared with a burning desire
To avenge Troy and make her pay for her sins.

'So she will look upon Sparta unscathed   675
And enter Mycenae as a triumphant queen?
She will get to see her husband and home,
Her parents and children, attended
By Trojan women and Phrygian slaves?
Was it for this that Priam was slaughtered,   680
Ilium burned, and our shore soaked with blood?
Never! Although there is no heroic name
In killing a woman, no victory,
I will be praised for snuffing out evil
And meting out justice. And it will be sweet   685
To quench my soul with vengeful fire
And satisfy my people's ashes.'

I was carried away by this frenzy, when,
Shining through the dark in a halo of light,
My mother appeared before my eyes, more clearly   690
Than ever before, revealing herself
As a radiant goddess, just as the great ones
In heaven see her, so beautiful, so tall.
She caught me by the hand and, in grace,
Spoke these words from her pale-rose lips: 695

'What anguish is behind this uncontrollable rage?
Why so angry, my son? And where has your love
For our family gone? Will you not first see
Where you left your father, Anchises,
Feeble with age, or whether Creüsa   700
And your child, Ascanius, are still alive?
They are surrounded by Greek soldiers
And but for my loving care would have died
In the flames by now, or the swords of the enemy
Would have tasted their blood. It is not   705
The detestable beauty of Tyndarean Helen
Or sinful Paris that is to blame. No, it is the gods,

[handwritten: — no blame is on him, he's a hero for not killing Helen]

The remorseless gods, who have ruined Troy
And burnt the topless towers of Ilium.
See for yourself. I will dispel the mist   710
That enshrouds you and dulls your mortal vision.
You might not trust your mother otherwise,
And disregard her kind instructions.

[handwritten: also, aren't you a part of these gods?]

                          Here,
Where you see piles of rubble, stones
Wrenched from stones, and plumes of smoke and dust,   715
Is Neptune, shaking the walls he has pried up
With his great trident and uprooting the city
From its foundations. Over here, Juno,
Ferocious in her iron vest, first to hold
The Western Gates, summons with her usual   720
Fury reinforcements from the ships.
And now look up. Tritonian Pallas
Is already seated on the highest towers,
Glowing from a thunderhead, grim
With her Gorgon. The Father himself   725
Gives the Greeks courage and strength
And incites the gods to oppose the Trojans.
Hurry away, my son, and end your struggle.
I will bring you safely to your father's door.'

And she plunged into night's shadows.
                              Dire faces,   730
Numinous presences hostile to Troy, now loomed
In the darkness visible.

To my eyes it seemed that all Ilium *[handwritten: and he is the lone, divine survivor]*
Was sinking in flames, and Neptune's Troy
Was being overturned from its base.   735

    It was just like an ancient mountain ash
    That woodsmen are straining to fell. Iron axes
    Ring thick and fast on its trunk, hacking it through,
    And it threatens to fall, nodding from its crest,
    Its foliage trembling, until, bit by bit,   740
    Overcome with wounds, it gives one last groan
    And torn from the hillside comes crashing down.

[handwritten: Venus shows Aeneas that the gods are causing the fall of Troy]

I descended and, guided by a god,
Somehow got through fire and foe.
Weapons gave way; the flames receded.   745

When I reached the doors of my father's house,
My old home, I sought him first and wanted
More than anything to lift him up
Into the mountains—but he refused   *courage to die*
To draw out his life and suffer exile   *with city*   750
With Troy in ashes.

                    'You are young,'
He cried, 'and still strong; you must take flight.
If the gods wanted to prolong my life
They would have preserved this home of mine.
It is enough and more that I have seen   755
Such destruction once before and have survived
One capture of my city. Say farewell
To my body lying just as it is
And depart. I shall die by my own hand.
The Greeks will pick over my spoils and pity me.   760
Loss of burial is light. Despised by heaven
And useless, I have lived too many years
Since the Lord of Gods and Men breathed winds
Of lightning upon me and touched me with fire.'

He kept repeating words such as these   765
And would not move. We were all in tears,
My wife, Creüsa, Ascanius, all our household,
Pleading with my father not to compound
Our desperate plight and destroy us with him.
He refused, and remained just as he was.   770
I reached for my gear, wanting only to die.
What hope was there for deliverance now?

'Did you think I could leave without you, Father?
How could such a thing come out of your mouth?
If it pleases the gods that nothing be left   775
Of this great city, and if you are determined,
If it is your pleasure, to throw yourself

Aeneas's father refuses to leave Troy

And all of us into Troy's holocaust—
The door to that fate is wide open. Pyrrhus,
Grimed with Priam's gore, will be here soon; 780
Pyrrhus, who mutilates the son — *just as Athena*
Before the father's eyes, butchers the father
Like a beast at the altar. O my merciful mother,
Was it for this you saved me from the enemy,
So I could see the enemy in my own home 785
And Ascanius, and my father, and Creüsa
Slaughtered in each other's blood?
                                   To arms, men!
The last light calls the vanquished. Take me back
To the Greeks. Let me start the battle again.
Never this day shall we all die unavenged!' 790

Once more I strapped on my sword, gripped my shield
In my left hand, and was hurrying out of the door,
When Creüsa embraced my feet at the threshold
And held up little Iülus to his father, saying:

'If you go to die, take us with you, 795
To whatever fate. But if experience has taught you
To rely on your weapons, guard first this house.
To whom do you leave us, little Iülus,
Your father, and me, once called your wife?'

Her voice filled the house with moaning, 800
And then, without warning, a strange portent
Flickered between the faces and hands
Of Iülus' anxious parents: a light tongue of flame
Gleaming above his head. Harmless to the touch,
It licked his soft locks and grazed his temples. 805
Trembling with fear, we shook the fire from his hair
Quickly and doused the holy flames with water.
But my father, Anchises, enraptured,
Raised his eyes to the stars above
And lifted his hands and his voice to heaven: 810

'Almighty Jupiter, if you are moved
By any prayers, only look upon us,

Aneas fails to convince his father
his wife convinces him not to leave
using his son

And if by our piety we have earned it,
Give us your aid and confirm this omen.'

His aged words had just finished, when suddenly   815
Thunder crashed on our left, and a star
Shot down from the sky, sliding through the dark
And trailing a luminous flood of sparks.
We watched it glide over the palace roof
And bury its splendor in Ida's forest,   820
Leaving a shining furrow in its wake.
The air reeked with sulfur all around.
Overwhelmed, my father lifted himself up
In adoration of the star and spoke to heaven:

'No more delay. I follow, and where you lead,   825
There I am. Gods of our fathers, save this house,
Save my grandson. Yours is this omen,
In your power is Troy. And now, my son,
I am ready to go as your companion.'

while they fear the gods,
they still obey them

He spoke, and now the sound of the fire   830
Could be heard more clearly, and the inferno
Rolled its seething heat ever closer.

'Come, dear Father, onto my shoulders now.
You will not weigh me down, and come what may
We will face it together, peril or salvation.   835
Little Iülus will walk beside me, and my wife
Will walk in my footsteps some distance behind.
Now listen to me, all of my household:
Just outside the city there is a mound,
And a temple of Ceres, long deserted.   840
Beside these stands an ancient cypress
Worshiped by my ancestors for many years.
There, by our separate ways, we will meet.
Take into your hands, Father, the sacred gods
Of our country. It would be a sacrilege   845
If I touched them before I washed away
The bloody filth of battle in a living river.'

gives a sense of the proper dynamic in the family

A sign from Jupiter convinces them to leave

This said, I spread upon my shoulders
A golden lionskin and bent to my burden.
Little Iülus held my hand and kept up,   850
Although his stride could not match his father's,
And my wife followed behind.
                        We kept
To the shadows and I undisturbed before
By any number of weapons thrust my way
And whole platoons of Greeks, now was frightened   855
By every breeze and startled by every sound,
Afraid for my companion and my burden.

We were nearing the gates, and it looked like
We had made it through, when suddenly
The sound of marching feet drifted on the wind.   860
Squinting through the gloom, my father cried:

'Run for it, Son! They're getting close.
I can see the bronze glitter of their shields.'

I panicked. Some malignant spirit
Robbed me of my wits, for while I ran   865
Down back alleys, leaving the familiar streets,
My wife, Creüsa, was taken from me
By some evil fortune. Had she stopped,
Or got lost and sat down exhausted?
I never saw her again, didn't even look back   870
Or think of her behind me until we arrived
At the mound by Ceres' ancient temple.
When finally we were all gathered there,
She alone was missing. No one had seen her,
Not her husband, not her son, no one.   875
What man or god did I not accuse
In my delirium? What crueler thing
Had I seen in our overturned city?
I entrusted Ascanius, Anchises,
And the gods of Troy to my companions   880
And hid them in a bend of the valley.
Myself, I strapped on my glittering armor
And went back to the city, hell-bent

[Handwritten annotations:]

portrayed as cowards

plot twist, builds evermore on "he's the lone heroic survivor" unvirtuous similar to that Greek myth with Hades

Creüsa is gone and they escape more Greeks

On running every risk again,
Combing through all of Troy,   885
And putting my life on the line once more.

I started at the walls and the dark gate
Where I had escaped and retraced my steps
Through the night, looking everywhere by torchlight.
Everywhere there was fear. The very silence   890
Was terrifying. Then I turned homeward,
In case, just in case, she had gone there.
The Greeks were there in force, and the house
Consumed with fire. Fanned by the wind,
It spiraled up past the eaves and gnawed at the roof,   895
Blasting the sky with its heat. I moved on
And saw once more the palace of Priam —*going through*
On the citadel. There, in the empty court   *and seeing all*
Of Juno's sanctuary, stood Phoenix
And dire Ulysses, chosen to guard the spoils, *the ruins*   900
Treasures from every part of Troy, ripped
Out of burning temples—tables of the gods,
Solid gold bowls, and plundered robes—
All in a heap. Boys and trembling matrons
Stood around in long rows.   905

I even risked casting my voice into the night
And filled the streets with shouts, calling
'Creüsa' over and over again
In my misery, all in vain.
                        But as I rushed
Through the empty shells of buildings, frantic   910
To find her, there rose before my eyes
The sad ghost of Creüsa herself, an image
Larger than life. I was transfixed,
My hair stood on end, and my voice choked.
Then she spoke to me and calmed my fears: 915

'What good does it do, my sweet husband,
To indulge in such mad grief? These things
Do not happen without the will of the gods.
You may not take your Creüsa with you;

After searching he finds the ghost of his wife

The Lord of Olympus does not allow it.   920
Long exile is yours, plowing a vast stretch
Of sea. Then you will come to Hesperia,
Where the Lydian Tiber runs gently
Through fertile fields. There, happy times,
Kingship, and a royal wife shall be yours.   925
Dry your tears for your beloved Creüsa. — *speaking in third person*
I shall not look upon the proud domains
Of the Myrmidons or Dolopians,
Nor go to be a slave for Greek matrons,
I, a Trojan woman, and wife of the son   930
Of the goddess Venus. No,
The Great Mother keeps me on these shores.
Farewell, and keep well your love for our child.'

Creüsa spoke, and then left me there,
Weeping, with many things yet to say.   935
She vanished into thin air. Three times
I tried to put my arms around her; three times
Her wraith slipped through my hands,
Soft as a breeze, like a vanishing dream.

The long night was spent, and at last   940
I went back to rejoin my people.

I was surprised by the great number
Of new arrivals I found, women and men,
Youth gathered for exile, a wretched band
Of refugees who had poured in from all over,   945
Prepared to journey across the sea
To whatever lands I might lead them. — *beginning of Rome, dawn of hope*
The brilliant morning star was rising
Over Ida's ridges, ushering in the day.
The Greeks held all the city gates.   950
There was no hope of help. I yielded
And, lifting up my father, sought the mountains." — *beginning of new time*

He begins his exile

AENEID THREE

"After the gods saw fit to overthrow
The power of Asia and Priam's guiltless race,
After proud Ilium fell, and Neptune's Troy
Lay smoking on the ground, we were driven
By signs from heaven to seek another home   5
On far, desolate shores. We built a fleet
Close to Antandros and the mountains
Of Phrygian Ida. There, with no idea
Of our destiny, we mustered our men,
And when summer came my father, Anchises,   10
Ordered us to spread our sails to Fate.
With tears in my eyes, I left my native shores
And harbors and the plains where once was Troy.
An exile, I took to sea with my men, my son,
And the great gods of my country and home.   15

There lies at a distance a land dear to Mars.
Its wide fields, once ruled by Lycurgus,
Are tilled by Thracians, old allies of Troy
While Fortune still smiled. There I sailed
And on its curving shore began to build,   20
Under adverse auspices, my first city,
And named it after myself, Aeneadae.

I was bringing offerings to Venus
And the gods who bless new beginnings,
And I was preparing to slaughter a sleek bull   25
To the Lord of Heaven there on the shore.

Nearby was a mound, its summit crowned
With cornel shrubs and bristling myrtle.
I went over to it and bent down to pull
Some greenery from the soil to deck the altars,   30
When I witnessed an awful portent:
The first bush that I uprooted oozed drops
Of black blood that clotted on the ground.
A cold horror numbed my limbs, and icy fear
Coursed through my veins. Still, I pulled up   35
Another sapling, trying to understand
The mystery within. This one bled too.
Greatly troubled, I prayed to the Nymphs
And Father Mars, lord of Thracian fields,
To lighten this omen and turn it to good.   40
But when I pulled, with greater effort,
Upon a third branch, struggling on my knees
In the sand (should I speak or be silent?)
I heard a groan from deep within the mound,
A piteous voice that sighed on the air: 45

'Why are you rending my flesh, Aeneas?
Spare a buried man, do not commit
This sacrilege. I am no stranger to you,
But Trojan born, nor is it wood and bark
That wells with blood. Flee this savage land,   50
This avaricious coast. For I am Polydorus,
Transfixed by spears and overgrown
With an iron crop of sprouted blades.'

Fear now pushed me to the breaking point.
My hair stood on end, my voice choked.   55
This Polydorus had been sent by Priam,
With a fortune in gold, to be reared
By the king of Thrace. This was when Priam
Had lost all hope that his besieged city
Could be saved by arms. But the Thracian,   60
Seeing that Troy's power was broken,
Joined forces with victorious Agamemnon
And broke all faith. He cut down Polydorus
And seized the treasure. O cursed lust for gold,

To what do you not drive the human heart!   65
When the fear had ebbed from my bones
I reported these portents to the elders,
My father especially, and sought their judgment.
They were of one mind: to quit this accursed land
Where hospitality had been desecrated   70
And sail with the wind. We held a funeral
For Polydorus, heaping the mound high with earth
And erecting to his shade somber altars
Dark with cypress and deep purple ribbons.
The Trojan women stood around them,   75
Hair unbound in ceremony, while we offered cups
Foaming with warm milk and bowls brimming
With sacrificial blood. So we interred his spirit
And called his name for the very last time.

As soon as we had good sailing weather   80
And a whispering southerly called us to sea,
The crews launched the ships. Out from shore
We watched cities and lands fade in the distance.

In the middle of the sea lies a hallowed island,
Dear to the Nereids and Aegean Neptune.   85
The Archer God, loyal to the isle of his birth,
Stopped its wandering and moored it in place
Close to Myconos and Gyaros—the island
Delos, secure at last from the winds.
I pulled in there, and the island welcomed   90
Our weary men in its peaceful haven.
Onshore we paid homage to Apollo's city.
Anius, both king and priest of Phoebus,
Ran up to meet us, his brows bound with fillets
And sacred laurel. He recognized Anchises   95
As an old friend and, clasping our hands
In welcome, led us under his roof.

I began to pray in the god's ancient stone temple:

'Grant us, God of Thymbra, a home of our own,
Grant our weary band walls, a nation,   100

A city that will endure. Preserve a second Troy
For the remnant left alive by the Greeks
And merciless Achilles. Whom shall we follow?
Where shall we go? Where settle down?
Give us an omen, Father, slip into our hearts.'   *105*

These words were barely out when it seemed
Everything trembled. The door, the god's laurel,
The whole mountain shook, and the holy tripod
Bellowed loud as the shrine was laid open.
We fell to the ground, and a voice filled our ears: *110*

'Enduring sons of Dardanus,
The land that bore you from paternal stock
Will welcome you back to her fruitful bosom.
Seek your ancient mother. From that land
The house of Aeneas will rule the world,   *115*
His son's sons and their sons thereafter.'·

Thus Apollo, and amid tumultuous joy
Everyone asked, 'To what land, what city,
Does Phoebus mean we should finally return?'
Then my father, searching old memories, said: *120*

'Listen, my lords, and learn what to hope for.
Crete, the island of great Jupiter, lies
In the middle of the sea. Mount Ida is there,
And there too is the cradle of our race.
Men live in a hundred cities there,   *125*
The realm most rich from which Teucer came,
Our earliest ancestor. If I remember rightly,
He sailed from Crete to our Rhoetian shores
And chose a site for his kingdom. Ilium
And high Pergamum had not yet been built.   *130*
Men lived in the lowlands. And from Crete came
The Great Mother Cybele, the Corybants' cymbals,
Our own wooded Mount Ida, the Mysteries' silence,
And the lions yoked to Cybele's chariot.
We must follow where the god leads,   *135*
Appease the winds, and sail for Cnossus.

It is not a far run. If Jupiter is with us,
The third dawn will anchor us off Cretan shores.'

Anchises spoke, and offered due sacrifice:
A bull to Neptune and to you, Apollo;   140
A black sheep to the Storms, a white to the Zephyrs.

A rumor reached us that Idomeneus,
The Cretan hero, had gone into exile,
That the island was deserted, our enemy gone
And the houses abandoned and empty.   145
We left Ortygia and flew over the sea,
Past Naxos ridged with Bacchic revels,
Past green Donysa and Olearos,
Past gleaming Paros and the Cyclades,
Threading the straits between the islands.   150
The seamen outdid each other chanting,
'On to Crete, the land of our fathers!'
And a following wind pushed us along
Until we glided up to the ancient shores
The Curetes once haunted. And so I began   155
To build my city. I called it Pergamum
And urged my people, who loved the old name,
To cherish their homes and raise the citadel
High with buildings.
                        Our ships were just dry,
Drawn up on the beach, our youth beginning   160
Their families and farms, and I was busy
Making laws and parceling land, when suddenly
Heaven's air turned foul and pestilential,
And we were afflicted with a wretched plague,
A season of death that spread even to our crops.   165
Our people lost their sweet lives, or dragged
Their bodies around like corpses. Then Sirius
Scorched our sterile fields. The grass withered,
And the sickly crops denied us sustenance.
My father urged us to recross the sea   170
And ask Delian Apollo what end he might put
To our weary fate, where we might seek aid
In our distress, where to bend our course.

It was night, and all living things slept,
When the sacred images of the gods,   *175*
The Phrygian Penates I took with me
Out of burning Troy, seemed to stand
Before my sleeping eyes, clear in the moonlight
That flooded through the latticed windows,
And with these words they dispelled my cares: *180*

'What Apollo would tell you on Ortygia
He tells you now, sending us unbidden
To your very door. We followed you,
Followed your arms when Ilium was burned;
Under you we traversed the swelling sea;   *185*
And we will exalt your coming descendants
To heaven's stars and give to their city
Empire over all. Prepare great walls
For the great, and do not shirk exile's long toil.
You must change your home. These are not the shores   *190*
Delian Apollo counseled; not on Crete
Did he bid you settle. There is a place
The Greeks call Hesperia, an ancient land,
Strong in arms and rich of soil. Oenotrians
Once lived there. Their descendants now   *195*
Have named it after their leader—Italy.
This is our true home. Here Dardanus was born,
The father of our race, and his brother Iasius.
Arise, then, be glad, and bring these tidings,
True beyond doubt, to your aged father: *200*
Seek Corythus and the land of Ausonia.
Jupiter denies you the Dictaean fields.'

Awed by this vision and the voice of the gods—
It was not just a dream; I saw them clearly,
Their veiled heads and living faces,   *205*
And a cold sweat poured down my body—
I leapt out of bed, lifted both palms to heaven,
And with a prayer to the gods made pure offerings
Upon my hearth. This rite completed,
I rose with joy and told my father   *210*
All that had happened. He acknowledged

Our twofold lineage and his confusion
About our ancestry in two ancient lands.
Then he said:

        'My son, steeled by Ilium's fate,
It was Cassandra, Cassandra alone   215
Who foretold to me our race's destiny,
Often naming Hesperia, naming Italy.
But who would believe that Teucrians would come
To Hesperia's shores? Who would be moved
By Cassandra's prophecies? Let us yield   220
To Apollo, and pursue the better course.'

My father finished, and we all cheered.
We abandoned this home too,
And, leaving a few behind, we spread our sails
And raced our hollow keels over the barren sea.   225

When our ships were sailing out on deep water
With no land in sight, but only sea and sky,
A brooding thunderhead settled in above us,
Bringing dark squalls to the shuddering waves.
Huge seas rolled under the winds, heaving us   230
All over the swirling abyss. Dark clouds
Shrouded the day, and foggy night
Blotted out the sky while jagged lightning
Split the air again and again. We were thrown
Far off course, wandering the blind waves.   235
Even Palinurus could not tell day from night
Or remember our heading. Three sunless days
We drifted the misty sea, three starless nights.
On the fourth day we raised land at last and saw
Mountains in the distance and curling smoke.   240
Down came the sails, and we manned the oars,
Churning the blue seawater into foam.

Delivered from the sea, I first made shore
In the Strophades, the Greek name given
To the islands set in the Ionian Sea,   245
Which dark Celaeno and the other Harpies

Made their home after they fled in fear
From the tables they kept in Phineas' palace.
No monster, no curse, no plague more grim
Ever raised itself from the water of Styx.   250
These birds have maiden faces, they drop
Foulest excrement, their hands are claws,
And their faces are pale with hunger.
When we entered the harbor we saw sleek cattle
Scattered over the plains and flocks of goats   255
Untended in the meadows. Swords drawn,
We rushed upon them, calling the gods
And Jove himself to share the bounty.
Then we built couches on the curved shore
And began to feast. But suddenly the Harpies   260
Swooped down from the mountains, beating
Their clanging wings, and plundered our feast,
Fouling every dish with their filthy touch,
And from the loathsome stench came hideous screams.
We set up the tables again, this time under   265
An overhanging rock deep in a hollow,
And relit the altar fires—and again they came
From their hidden lair, a clamorous flock
Circling above their prey with taloned feet,
And then they polluted the feast with their maws.   270
I ordered my men to take up arms and wage war
Against these dread creatures. We hid our swords
In the long grass and concealed our shields.
When they swooped down screeching along the shore,
Misenus gave the signal from his high lookout,   275
Sounding his brass horn, and my men charged
Into strange combat, determined to despoil
Those filthy birds of the sea. But their feathers
Felt nothing, they could not be wounded,
And they soared to the sky leaving their prey   280
Half-eaten and foul. One only, Celaeno,
A bird of ill omen, perched high on a cliff
And broke into prophetic speech:

'Sons of treacherous Laomedon,
Is this how you pay us for killing our cattle,   285

By waging war on the innocent Harpies
And driving us from our ancestral land?
Mark my words well. What the Father Almighty
Told to Apollo, and Phoebus Apollo to me,
I, first of the Furies, reveal now to you.   290
You are sailing the seas to reach Italy,
And so you shall, and enter her harbors.
But you shall not surround your city with walls
Until terrible hunger—and the way you wronged us—
Drives you to chew and swallow your tables.'   295

Celaeno spoke and then winged her way
Back to the forest. My men felt their blood
Turn icy with fear. Their spirits fell,
And they pleaded with me to sue for peace,
Resort to vows and prayers rather than arms,   300
Whether these were goddesses or hellish birds.
Father Anchises, with hands outstretched,
Called from the beach upon the great gods,
With proclamations of due sacrifice:

'Gods, stop their threats. Gods, avert harm.   305
Save the pious, O Gracious Ones.'

                              And he ordered
The stern cables torn from the shore
And the rigging uncoiled. A strong southerly
Stretched the sails and we escaped on sea-surge,
Where wind and pilot called our course.   310
Wooded Zacynthus appeared in mid-sea,
Then Dulichium, Samê, and craggy Neritus.
We passed Ithaca's cliffs, the realm of Laertes,
And cursed the island that nursed Ulysses.
Leucate's storm-whipped peaks soon came into view,   315
And Apollo's temple, dreaded by sailors.
Weary, we sailed up to the little town
And cast anchor. Our sterns fringed the shore.

Safe on land we never hoped to gain,
We purified ourselves with rites of Jove   320

And made the altars blaze with sacrifices.
Then we thronged the shore for Trojan Games.
My men, stripped and oiled, competed
In their age-old wrestling matches,
Glad to have slipped past so many Greek towns   *325*
And still be on their journey.
                          Time went by.
The sun rolled through the year's great circle,
And winter roughened the sea with icy winds.
I affixed a bronze shield, once borne by Abas,
To the doorposts and inscribed this verse: *330*

          THESE ARMS AENEAS DEDICATES
             FROM VICTORIOUS GREEKS

Then I gave the order to man the benches
And pull out from the harbor. The crews
Outdid each other, sweeping the sea with oars.   *335*
In no time we dropped the peaks of Phaeacia,
Grazed the shores of Epirus, and entered
The Chaonian port of towering Buthrotum.

There we heard the incredible report
That Priam's son Helenus ruled   *340*
Over Greek cities, having won the bride
And kingdom of Pyrrhus, son of Achilles,
And that Andromache again had passed
To a Trojan husband. I was amazed
And burned with desire to question him   *345*
About this strange turn of events.
I was making my way up from the harbor
Just when, as it happened, Andromache
Was offering a ritual feast for the dead
In a grove outside the city, beside the waters   *350*
Of a pretend Simois, pouring libations
To the ashes of Hector and calling his ghost
To the empty mound of green turf
Hallowed with twin altars and with her tears.
She saw me coming, saw the Trojan arms,   *355*

And could not believe her eyes. She stiffened,
The warmth left her body, and she fainted.
After a long time she gasped out these words:

'Is the face I see real? Are you a true messenger,
Goddess-born? Are you alive? Or if the light   360
Has left you, where is Hector?'

                                    She spoke
And poured forth her tears, filling the place
With her cries, so frantic I was scarcely able
To reach her with my few stammered words:

'Yes, I am alive, through all my trials.   365
You can believe what you see is true.
O, what has happened to you since you lost
Your noble husband? What fortune could be
Worthy of you—Hector's Andromache?
Are you still married to Pyrrhus?'

                            Eyes downcast,   370
Andromache lowered her voice and said:

'Priam's virgin daughter, Polyxena,
Was most fortunate of all, condemned to die
At an enemy's tomb beneath Troy's walls,
And never a slave in a conqueror's bed.   375
We, our city burnt, were taken overseas
And bore the disdainful pride of Achilles' son,
Giving birth in slavery. Later, he courted
Leda's Hermione and a Spartan marriage
And transferred me to Helenus,   380
A slave to a slave. Orestes, inflamed
With jealousy over his stolen bride
And hounded by the Furies, caught Pyrrhus
Off guard and killed him at his father's altar.
Helenus inherited part of Pyrrhus' realm   385
And called it Chaonia after Chaon of Troy
And built upon its hill a Pergamum,
This Iliadic citadel.

                   But you, what winds
Drove you on your fated course? What god
Has pushed you to our shores all unaware?   390
And what about your boy, Ascanius?
Is he alive and breathing heaven's air?
Even in Troy he . . .
Still, does he miss his lost mother?
Do his father, Aeneas, and his uncle Hector   395
Inspire him to ancestral valor?'

These words poured out of her as she wept,
And she was raising a futile lament
When the hero Helenus, Priam's son,
Came from the city with a great company.   400
He recognized us as kin and led us
Joyfully to the city's gates, yet weeping
Profusely at every word. As I advanced
I recognized a little Troy, a Pergamum
Modeled on the great one, a dry creek   405
Named after the Xanthus, and I embraced
Another Scaean gate. My fellow Teucrians
Enjoyed the friendly city as much as I did.
The king welcomed them in a broad colonnade,
And they poured libations in the center   410
Of a great hall, holding their wine-bowls
As the feast was served on platters of gold.

Day followed day, the breeze called the sails,
And a strong southerly bellied the canvas.
I approached the seer and made this request: 415

'Helenus, son of Troy, you speak for the gods.
You know the will of Clarian Apollo,
His tripod and laurel, and you know the stars,
The sounds of birds and birds on the wing.
All the omens concerning my journey   420
Have been favorable. All the oracles
Have counseled me to make for Italy
And distant lands. Only the Harpy,
Celaeno, has prophesied a portent

Horrible to speak of and threatened   425
Wrath and famine. Tell me now yourself,
What are the main perils I must shun,
And how may I overcome my trials?'

At this, Helenus first offered sacrifice,
Prayed for grace, and unbound his sacred brow.   430
Then he led me by the hand to the gates
Of your temple, Apollo, my mind soaring
With your presence, and prophesied:

'Goddess-born, it is clear that your journey
Over the deep is sanctioned on high, for so   435
The Lord of the Gods has ordained,
And so the wheel of destiny turns. I will,
Therefore, unfold for you a few things
Out of many, so you may more safely
Traverse the welcoming oceans and find   440
Haven in Ausonia. The Fates forbid
Helenus to know more, and Saturnian Juno
Censors my speech.
                    First, the Italy
That you, unknowing, think is near,
And whose ports you are preparing to enter   445
As if they were close, can only be reached
Along long coastlines and a long, pathless path.
You must first bend your oar in Sicily's waves
And sail your ships in the Ausonian sea
Past the netherworld lakes and Circe's isle   450
Before founding your city in a land secure.
I will now list signs for you to remember:
In great distress you will find a huge sow
Lying under oaks near a hidden stream
With a litter of thirty, a white sow   455
Lying on the ground nursing white young.
That shall be the site of your city,
And a sure rest from all of your labors.
Have no fear of gnawing your tables;
The Fates will find a way, Apollo will come.   460
Avoid the near coast of Italy

Washed by our sea. All of the towns are held
By evil Greeks. The Narycian Locri
Have built a city there. Cretan Idomeneus
Has occupied the Sallentine plains.   465
The famous town of Philoctetes is there,
Little Petelia, defended by her walls.
But when your ships have crossed the high seas
And stand moored, and you have built altars
And fulfill vows on the shore, veil your hair   470
With a purple robe, so that no hostile face
May appear in the fires and spoil the omens.
Both you yourself and your men should hold
To this manner of sacrifice. Let your children,
And theirs after, remain pure in religion.   475
        When you leave, and the wind has borne you
To the coast of Sicily, and the straits of Pelorus
Begin to widen, make for land on the left
And seas on the left in a long circuit round.
Shun the shore and water on the right.   480
These lands, they say, broke apart from each other
Long ago, in a catastrophic
Upheaval (the ages can bring titanic changes),
When the two countries were a continuous whole.
The sea surged between, cutting off Sicily   485
From Hesperia, and in a seething channel
Washed fields and cities on separate coasts.
Scylla lurks on the right shore, and on the left
Insatiable Charybdis. At the bottom
Of her swirling abyss she sucks down   490
Tons of saltwater in three gulps, then spews
All of it up again, spraying the stars.
Scylla, though, lies in her cave's dark gloom,
Extruding neck and jaws, and dragging ships
Onto her rocks. She looks human above,   495
A beautiful woman down to her loins.
Below, she is a scaly monster, joining
A belly of wolves to dolphins' flukes.
Better to round Pachynus slowly,
Make the turn at this promontory,   500
And double back to complete the long lap,

Than even to glimpse Scylla's hideous form
In her vast cavern, or to come within sight
Of the rocks that echo with her cyan hounds.
    And this above all: If Helenus possesses   505
Any foresight, if I have as a seer
Any claim to belief, if Phoebus Apollo
Fills my soul with his truth—this one thing,
Goddess-born, this one thing before all,
I will foretell and repeat again and again: 510
Worship Juno. Pray to her first. Joyfully
Chant vows to Juno. Shower her majesty
With suppliant gifts and win her grace.
    At last you will leave Sicily behind
And be sent to the shores of Italy.   515
When you come to Cumae, its mystic lakes,
And the woods of Avernus, you will meet
A prophetess who in her frenzy
Chants the future and commits it to leaves
With marks and signs. Whatever verses   520
The virgin priestess scratches on leaves
She arranges in order and stores in her cave.
There they remain in their numbered ranks.
But if the door is opened and a light breeze
Disturbs the soft leaves and scatters them,   525
She does not bother to gather them up
As they fly through the cave, does not care
To arrange them again and order the verse,
And so those who inquired receive no advice
And learn to hate the Sibyl and her shrine.   530
Here you must spare no expense of time.
Though your men complain and your journey calls
And you have the chance to fill your sails with wind,
You must visit the prophetess. And plead with her
To open her lips and prophesy in person.   535
She will unfold for you Italy's nations,
The wars to come, how to flee some toils
And how to face others. Venerated,
She will also grant you a favorable voyage.
This counsel you are allowed to hear from my lips.   540
Go, and by your deeds lift Troy to the stars.'

Helenus finished his kindly advice,
And then ordered that gifts of heavy gold
And sawn ivory be brought to our ships,
And he himself stowed in our hulls   545
Massive silver and cauldrons from Dodona,
A coat of golden mail, and a superb helmet
Crested with plumes, arms of Pyrrhus himself.
There were gifts, too, for my father, and horses,
And pilots to guide us. . . .   550
Extra oarsmen, and gear for my crews.

Meanwhile, Anchises ordered the ships
Rigged with sails, so we could catch the wind,
And Helenus addressed him with deep respect:

'Anchises, worthy of wedlock with Venus,   555
Cherished by the gods, twice rescued from Troy,
Before you lies Ausonia. Sail to seize it!
Yet you must drift past this shore. Far is that part
Of Italy promised by Phoebus Apollo.
Go forth, blessed by the love of a pious son.   560
My long speech delays the rising wind.'

Andromache, too, sad at this last parting,
Brought robes embroidered with woven gold
And for Ascanius a Phrygian cloak,
And paid him more honor, loading him   565
With gifts from her loom, saying:

'Take these also, the work of my hands, child,
And let them remind you of the enduring love
Of Andromache, the wife of Hector.
Take these last gifts of your people, you,   570
The sole surviving image of my Astyanax!
He was just like you in his eyes, his hands,
The expression on his face. He would be
The same age as you are now, a growing boy.'

Tears welled up as I said my good-byes: 575

'Live happily. Your destiny is complete,
We are still called from one fate to another.
Your rest is won. You have no seas to plow,
No quest for ever-receding Ausonian fields.
Before your eyes is an image of the Xanthus   580
And a Troy that your own hands have built,
Under better auspices, I hope and pray,
And less vulnerable to the Greeks.
If I ever enter the Tiber and its valley
And look upon walls granted to my race,   585
We will have sister cities and be allies,
Hesperia allied to Epirus
With the same Dardanus as ancestor
And the same tragic past. We will make them
One Troy in spirit, and may it pass   590
Into the care of our children's children.'

We sailed past the near Ceraunian cliffs
Along the shortest sea-lanes to Italy.
Evening fell, and the hills grew dark.
We allotted the next day's rowers   595
And spread out on the dry sand
For refreshment and rest.
                              Sleep flowed
Through our bodies like a river. Night,
Driven by the Hours, was just half through,
When Palinurus woke. He rose   600
And tested the winds, listening.
His eyes scanned all the stars
Gliding in the sky, Arcturus,
The rainy Hyades, the two Bears,
And Orion armored in gold.   605
He saw their steady light in the clear air
And gave a piercing signal from his ship.
We broke camp quickly and headed out,
Spreading our sails. Soon the stars faded
In the roselight of Dawn, and we saw   610
Dim on the horizon the hills of Italy.
'Italy!' Achates was the first to call,

And all the crews cheered 'Italy, Italy!'
Father Anchises wreathed a great bowl,
Filled it with wine, and called on the gods   615
From his ship's high stern:

'Lords of Sea and Earth and Storm, O Gods,
Make easy our way with wind at our backs!'

The winds he prayed for freshened, a haven
Opened before us, and a temple of Minerva   620
Appeared on the heights. The crews furled sail
And turned the prows shoreward. The harbor
Curved like a bow away from the eastern surge,
Hidden behind rocky breakwaters
That foamed with salt spray. Towering cliffs   625
Let down two craggy arms, and the temple
Retreated between them back from the shore.
I saw there our first omen, four snow-white horses
Grazing on the plain. And Father Anchises:

'War, you bring us war, O Promised Land.   630
Horses are armed for war. And yet,
Horses sometimes are reined in concord.
There is still hope for peace.'

                              Then we prayed
To the holy power of the warrior goddess,
Pallas, who first welcomed our cheers,   635
Veiling our heads with Phrygian robes
Before her altar. And, remembering
Helenus' tense commands, we offered
The prescribed sacrifice to Argive Juno.

Our devotions done, we pointed our ships   640
To the open sea, hauled up the sails,
And left behind the mistrusted Greek lands.
We scanned the gulf of Tarentum,
Founded by Hercules (if the tale is true).
Across the bay, in Lacinia, rose   645
A temple of Juno, the towers of Caulon,

And Scylaceum, with its wreckage of ships.
Then, cresting a wave, we sighted far off
Trinacrian Aetna and heard the sound
Of the moaning sea crashing on rocks   650
And breaking over the speaking shore.
The shoals surged high and seethed with sand.
Then Father Anchises:

     'This surely must be
Charybdis; these are the crags and dread rocks
Foretold by Helenus. Lean on the oars   655
And pull us away, men!'

     They did just that.
First Palinurus swung the groaning prow
Hard to leeward, and the whole crew
Held us to the left with sail and oar.
The ship rode the arcing waves to the sky   660
And sank with them to the depths of hell.
Three times the hollowed cliffs roared,
Three times we saw spray strike the very stars.
With evening the wind died, and, bone-tired
And lost, we drifted to the Cyclopes' coast.   665

A huge harbor lies there, the water sheltered
And still, but Aetna thunders nearby
With horrific crashes and darkens the sky
With swirls of black smoke and glowing ash.
Globes of flame rise to lick the sky's dome,   670
And then the mountain retches up rocks,
Its own wrenched-out entrails, and whirls
Molten stone up with a skyward groan,
Boiling and churning in its innermost depths.
The story is told that Enceladus' body,   675
Charred by the thunderbolt, is weighed down
Under all that mass. Above, great Aetna
Breathes out flame from its ruptured furnace,
And when Enceladus turns over,
All Trinacria trembles and groans   680
And shrouds the sky with smoke.

That night,
We lay in the woods enduring endless horrors
And never saw where the sound came from.
There were no stars, no light at all in the sky,
And misty clouds had buried the moon.   685

Dawn melted away the night's damp shade
And rose in a clear sky. At break of day
A strange figure came from the woods,
Gaunt with hunger, squalid, and pitiful.
He stretched his hands toward the beach.   690
We stared at him in horror. Filthy,
Beard matted, clothing fastened with thorns,
But in all else a Greek, who once
Had been sent to Troy in his country's arms.

When he saw by our clothes and weapons   695
That we were Trojans, he stopped in fear
For a moment, then rushed to the shore
With tears in his eyes and prayed:

                         'By the stars,
By the gods above, and by the light we breathe,
Take me away, Trojans, anywhere at all.   700
That will be enough. I know I am a Greek
Who shipped out to Troy, I admit that I fought
Against the gods of Ilium. If my guilt for that
Is so great, cut me to pieces, and throw me
Into the sea. At least I will die by human hands.'   705

He spoke, and then clasped our knees, groveling
At our feet. We urged him to tell us
Who he was, where he was born,
And what fate dogged his steps. My father,
Anchises himself, with just a moment's pause,   710
Gave the man his hand, encouraging him
With this pledge of friendship. At last,
The man put aside his fear and said to us:

'I am from Ithaca and served under Ulysses,
That unlucky man. My name is Achaemenides,   715

And because my father Adamastus was poor
(If only I were still a poor man in Greece!)
I set out for Troy. Here, my shipmates left me
In Cyclops' cave, forgetting me when they ran
From the gruesome entrance, half mad with fear.   720
That cave is a house of gore, dark and huge,
And he is gigantic, towering to the stars.
O Gods, rid earth of this monster! No one
Could bear to look at or speak to him. He feeds
On men's flesh and drinks their black blood.   725
I myself saw him seize two of my friends
In his huge hand, as he sprawled in his cave,
And smash them to bits, spattering the rock
With their gore. I watched while he chewed
Their dripping limbs, I saw the warm muscle   730
Quiver in his jaws. But he has not gone unpunished!
Ulysses did not stand for this, the Ithacan
Did not forget who he was when the time came.
Gorged with his feast and soused with wine,
The monster lay stretched on the floor of his cave   735
With his head bent sideways belching out gore,
Wine, and bits of flesh. We prayed to the great ones,
Drew lots, took our positions, and gouged
The huge eye set beneath his frowning brow
Like an Argive shield or the disk of the sun.   740
We were glad to avenge our dead comrades.
Now run, you poor fools, cut your cables
From the shore. . . .
For there are a hundred other Cyclopes here
Along these curved shores and in the high hills,   745
The same size and shape as Polyphemus
When he pens his sheep in the cave and milks them.
The moon has filled her horns with light
Three times since I began to drag out my life
In the woods, among the lonely lairs of beasts.   750
I watch the Cyclopes from a high rock
And tremble at their voices and tramping feet.
Berries and wild plums are my sorry fare,
Roots grubbed from the ground. From my lookout
I saw your fleet coming to shore, and now   755

I have surrendered myself, come what may.
It is enough to have escaped those savages.
Take my life by any death whatever.'

These words were no sooner out than we saw
Polyphemus himself, moving his vast bulk   760
Down the mountain, a shepherd among his flock,
Heading down to the shore he knew too well,
A hideous monster, hulking in his eyeless dark.
He used a lopped pine tree as a walking staff,
And his fleecy sheep, his only joy and solace,   765
Kept him company. When he reached the water
He washed his oozing eye socket out with brine,
Gritting his teeth and groaning, and then waded
Through the open sea, the waves barely wetting
His towering flanks. We took our worthy suppliant   770
On board and moved fast to get out of there.
We cut the cable silently and began to row hard.
The Cyclops heard and turned toward the sound,
But when he couldn't lay hands on us
Or match the pace of the Ionian waves,   775
He let out a great roar that shivered the sea.
The heartland of Italy shuddered, and Aetna
Bellowed from within its winding caverns.
The Cyclopes' tribe was roused and came down
From the wooded mountains to fill the shore.   780
We saw them standing helpless, lone eyes glaring,
These brothers of Aetna, heads reaching the sky,
An unnerving conclave,

                    like aerial oaks
      On a mountaintop, or coniferous cypresses
      In a high grove of Jupiter or woods of Diana.   785

We pitched headlong under full sail
In whatever direction the wind took us.
But Helenus' words rang in my ears:
Not to steer between Scylla and Charybdis,
Where the slightest mistake would mean our death.   790
We had decided to sail back, when a northerly

Came blowing down the straits of Pelorus.
Our course took me past Pantagia's mouth
With its living rock, past the bay of Megara
And low-lying Thapsus. Achaemenides　　　　　　　　*795*
Pointed out these coasts, which he had seen before
When he sailed as luckless Ulysses' companion.

An island lies stretched before a Sicilian bay
Opposite wave-washed Plemyrium. Ortygia
Is its ancient name. The story is told　　　　　　　*800*
That the river Alpheus channeled his water
Under the sea to this very island, mingling
His waters with yours, Arethusa.
We worshiped, as told, this land's great gods.
Then we passed the loam of Helorus' wetlands,　　　*805*
Skirted the jutting rocks of Pachynus, and saw,
Far in the distance, Camerina—which the Fates
Will not allow to be moved—the Geloan plains,
And Gela, named after its rushing river.
Then steep Acragas, breeder of noble horses,　　　*810*
Showed off its great walls, and with a tailwind
I left you behind, palmettoed Selinus,
And grazed Lilybaeum with its hidden shoals.
Then the sad harbor of Drepanum
Took me in. Here I, who had weathered　　　　　　*815*
So many storms at sea, lost my father,
Anchises, solace of all my cares.
Best of fathers, rescued from such great perils
In vain, you abandoned me in my weary hour.
The seer Helenus foretold many horrors　　　　　　*820*
But not this grief; nor did Celaeno.
This was my final trial, the goal and end
Of all my long journeys. We left Drepanum
And some god drove me here to your shores."

Thus Aeneas, the father of our race,　　　　　　　*825*
Before an audience who hung on every word,
Told the tale of heaven's dooms, and the story
Of his wanderings. He stopped now, and rested.

AENEID FOUR

But the Queen, long sick with love,
Nurses her heart's deep wound
With her pounding blood, and dark flames
Lick at her soul. Thoughts of Aeneas—
The man's heroic lineage, his noble character—   5
Flood her mind, his face and words transfix
Her heart, and her desire gives her no rest.

When Dawn had spread the sunlight over earth
And dispelled night's damp shadow from the sky,
Dido, deeply troubled, spoke to her sister: 10

"Anna, my nightmares would not let me sleep!
This guest who has come to our house—
His looks, the way he carries himself, his brave heart!
He has to be descended from the gods. Fear
Always gives away men of inferior birth.   15
What the Fates have put him through at sea,
The wars he painted, fought to the bitter end!
If I were not unshakable in my vow
Never to pledge myself in marriage again
After death stole my first love away—   20
If the mere thought of marriage did not leave me cold,
I might perhaps have succumbed this once.
Anna, I must confess, since my husband,
Poor Sychaeus, fell at my brother's hands
And stained our household gods with blood,   25
Only this man has turned my eye,
Only he has caused my heart to falter.

I recognize the old, familiar flames.
But may the earth gape open and swallow me,
May the Father Almighty blast me   30
Down to the shades of Erebus below
And Night profound, before I violate you,
O Modesty, and break your vows.
The man who first joined himself to me
Has taken my love with him to the grave."   35

Thus Dido, and her tears wet her bosom.

And Anna:

         "O sister dearer than light itself,
Will you waste your youth in spinsterhood
Alone and grieving, never to taste love's joys,
The sweetness of children? Do you think   40
Any of this matters to ghosts in the grave?
True, in your mourning no potential husbands
Have caught your eye, neither back in Tyre
Nor here in Libya. You've looked down your nose
At Iarbas and Africa's other heralded chieftains.   45
But does it make sense to resist someone you like?
Has it crossed your mind just where you've settled?
The Gaetulians, invincible in war,
And Numidian horsemen are on one frontier.
Just off the coast are the Syrtes' quicksand shoals,   50
Desert to the south, and wild Barcaean nomads
Ranging all over. Need I mention the war clouds
Gathering over Tyre, and your brother's threats?
I think the providential gods, with Juno behind them,
Have blown these Trojan ships our way.   55
With a husband like this, what a city, Sister,
What a kingdom you would see rise! With Trojan allies
What heights of glory our Punic realm would climb!
Just beg the gods' indulgence, and when you have
Good omens from the sacrifices, pamper   60
Your guests, and invent reasons for them to linger:
'Stormy Orion vexes the dim sea, your ships
Are battered, the weather just won't cooperate.'"

With these words Anna fanned the flames of love
That flickered in Dido's heart and gave resolve   65
To her wavering mind, dissolving her sense of shame.

First they make the rounds at shrines, soliciting
Divine approval. To Ceres the lawgiver, Apollo,
And father Bacchus the sisters slaughter
Choice sheep in perfect rituals. But they honor   70
Above all Juno, goddess of marriage. Dido herself,
With her great beauty, holds the wine-bowl
And pours it out between a glossy heifer's horns.
She glides past statues of gods to rich altars,
Ushers in each day with offerings, consults in awe   75
The steaming entrails of disemboweled bulls.
But what do prophets know? How much can vows,
Or shrines, help a raging heart? Meanwhile, the flame
Eats her soft marrow, and the wound lives,
Silent beneath her breast.

                              Dido is burning.   80
She wanders all through the city in her misery,
Raving mad,

                    like a doe pierced by an arrow
          Deep in the woods of Crete. She is unwary,
          And the arrow, shot by a shepherd who has no idea
          Where it has landed, finds the animal,   85
          And as she runs all through the Dictaean forest
          The lethal shaft clings to her flank.

                                   So too Dido.

Now she leads Aeneas on a tour of the walls,
Shows him what the wealth of Sidon can build.
She begins to speak, but her voice cracks.   90
As dusk comes on her royal desire is a banquet.
Mad to hear once more the labors of Ilium,
She demands the story again, and again she hangs
On every word. When her guests have left,
And the waning moon has set, and the westering stars   95

Make slumber sweet, she pines away
In the empty hall, lying alone on Aeneas' couch,
Seeing and hearing him although he is gone.
Or she holds little Ascanius in her lap
To fill in the features of Aeneas' face   100
And in this way cheats her unspeakable love.

The half-built towers rise no higher, the men no longer
Drill at arms or maintain the city's defensive works.
All work stops, construction halts on the huge,
Menacing walls. The idle derricks loom against the sky.   105

When Jove's dear wife saw Dido so lovesick
That her good name no longer mattered to her
As much as her passion, she approached Venus and said:

"An outstanding victory! What a memorable display
Of divine power by you and your little boy,   110
Two devious deities laying low a single woman!
Your fear of Carthage and your suspicion
Of its noble houses hardly escapes me, my dear.
But to what purpose? Why are we at odds?
Why not instead work out a lasting peace—   115
Sealed with a royal marriage? You have what you want:
Dido burning with love, her very bones enflamed.
I propose, therefore, that we rule this people jointly,
With equal authority. Dido can submit
To a Trojan husband, with Carthage as her dowry."   120

The Goddess of Love detected a ploy
To divert power away from Italy
And to Libyan shores. She responded this way:

"Only a fool would refuse such an offer
And prefer to oppose you—provided, of course,   125
That your plan meets with success. But I remain
A little unclear about the intentions of Fate.
Does Jupiter want the Tyrians and Trojans
To form one city? Does he approve

This mingling of races? You are his wife,   130
And so you should persuade him. Lead on,
And I'll follow."

               And the Queen of Heaven:

"Leave that to me. Now listen, and I'll outline
Exactly how we will deal with the business at hand.
Aeneas and the most unfortunate Dido   135
Are preparing a woodland hunt for tomorrow,
As soon as Titan lifts his luminous head
And dissolves with his rays the curtains of the world.
Just as the beaters start flushing out game
I'll pour down a black rain laced with hailstones   140
And make all the heavens rumble with thunder.
The hunters will scatter in the enveloping gloom,
And Dido and Aeneas will find themselves
In the same cave. I will be there too,
And with your consent I will unite them   145
In holy matrimony. This will be their wedding."

The Cytherean approved and nodded her assent,
Smiling all the while at Juno's treachery.

Dawn rose from the river Ocean,
And at first light the hunting party   150
Spills out from the gates with nets and spears.
Massylian horsemen and keen hounds surge ahead,
But the Carthaginian nobles await their Queen.
She pauses at the threshold of her chamber
While her stallion, resplendent in purple and gold,   155
Champs the foaming bit. Finally, she steps forward
With her retinue, wearing a Phoenician cloak
Finished with embroidery. Her quiver is gold,
Her hair is bound in gold, and the purple cloak
Is pinned with a clasp of gold.
                              Then out ride   160
The Trojans with Iülus, excited to be among them.
Aeneas himself, handsome as a god,

Takes the lead and joins his troops to Dido's.

In winter Apollo leaves Lycia and the streams
Of Xanthus and goes to his birth-isle, Delos.   165
There he renews the circling dances,
And Cretans, Dryopes, and painted Scythians
Whirl around his sacred altars while the god
Paces the ridges of Mount Cynthus, braiding
His flowing hair with soft leaves and gold,   170
And the arrows rattle in the quiver on his back.

                  No less majestic
Was Aeneas, and his face shone with equal glory.

When they came into the high, trackless hills,
Mountain goats, dislodged from the rocks above,
Ran down the ridges. Elsewhere, herds of deer   175
Streamed across open country, kicking up
Billows of dust in their flight from the hills.
Young Ascanius rode his spirited mount
Up and down the valleys, in high spirits himself,
Chasing deer and goats but hoping all the while   180
That something less tame, a wild boar or tawny lion,
Would come down from the mountains.

Meanwhile, the sky begins to rumble,
And a rainstorm, turning to hail, sweeps in.
The Tyrians and Trojans, with Iülus among them,   185
Venus' own dear grandchild, scatter through the fields
In search of shelter. Streams gush down the mountain,
And Dido and the Trojan leader make their way
To the same cave. Earth herself and bridal Juno
Give the signal. Fires flash in the Sky,   190
Witness to their nuptials, and the Nymphs
Wail high on the mountaintop. That day
Was the first cause of calamity and of death
To come. For no longer is Dido swayed
By appearances or her good name. No more   195
Does she contemplate a secret love. She calls it
Marriage, and with that word she cloaks her sin.

Rumor at once sweeps through Libya's great cities,
Rumor, the swiftest of evils. She thrives on speed
And gains power as she goes. Small and timid at first,   200
She grows quickly, and though her feet touch the ground
Her head is hidden in the clouds. The story goes
That Mother Earth, vexed with the gods, bore this
One last child, a sister to Coeus and Enceladus.
Fast on her feet, her beating wings a blur,   205
She is a dread, looming monster. Under every feather
On her body she has—strange to say—a watchful eye,
A tongue, a shouting mouth, and pricked-up ears.
By night she wheels through the dark skies, screeching,
And never closes her shining eyes in sleep.   210
By day she perches on rooftops or towers,
Watching, and she throws whole cities into panic,
As much a hardened liar as a herald of truth.
Exultant now, she fills the people's ears
With all kinds of talk, intoning fact and fiction: 215
Aeneas has come, born of Trojan blood;
Dido, impressed, has given him her hand,
And now they indulge themselves the winter long,
Neglecting their realms, slaves to shameful lust.
The loathsome goddess spreads this gossip   220
Far and wide. Then she winds her way to King Iarbas,
And with her words his rage flares to the sky.

Iarbas, a son of Jupiter Ammon
By a Garmantian nymph the god had ravished,
Had built in his vast realm a hundred temples   225
For his Father, and on a hundred altars
Had consecrated sacred fire, an eternal flame
In honor of the gods. Blood from sacrificial victims
Clotted the soil, the portals bloomed with garlands,
As Iarbas, they say, insane with jealousy at Rumor's   230
Bitter news, knelt at these altars surrounded by gods,
Upturned his palms and prayed, prayed to his Father:

"Almighty Jupiter, to whom the Moors now offer
Libations of wine as they feast on brocaded couches—
Do you see these things? Why should we shudder   235

At you, Father, when you hurl your thunderbolts,
Or when lightning flashes blindly in the clouds
And stammering thunder rolls through the sky?
This woman, a vagrant in my land, who established
Her little town on a strip of coast we sold to her,   240
With acreage on lease—this woman has spurned
My offers of marriage and embraced Aeneas as her lord.
And now this Paris, with his crew of eunuchs,
The bonnet on his pomaded hair tied with ribbons
Beneath his chin, makes off with the prize   245
While we, who bring offerings to temples—
Your temples—are worshiping an empty name."

So Iarbas prayed, clutching the altar.
And the Almighty heard him, and turned his eyes
To the royal city and the lovers oblivious   250
Of their better name.

                Then Jupiter said to Mercury:

"Go now, my son, summon the Zephyrs,
Glide down on your wings and speak to the Trojan
Idling in Carthage. He seems to have quite forgotten,
In his infatuation, the cities given him by Fate.   255
Carry my words down through the rushing winds.
This is not the man his lovely mother promised us.
Not for this did she rescue him twice from the Greeks,
But that he should be the one to rule Italy, a land
Pregnant with empire and clamorous for war,   260
And produce a race from Teucer's high blood,
And bring all the world beneath the rule of law.
If his own glory means nothing to him, if he will not
Take on this labor for his own fame's sake,
Does he begrudge Ascanius the towers of Rome?   265
What is he hoping for? Why does he linger
Among a hostile people and have no regard
For Ausonia's race and Lavinian fields?
In sum, he must sail. That is my message."

Jupiter had spoken, and his son prepared   270
To fulfill his commands. He bound on his feet

The golden sandals whose wings carry him over
Landscape and seascape in a blur of wind.
Then he took the wand he uses to summon
Pale ghosts from Orcus or send them down   275
To Tartarus' gloom—the same wand he uses
To charm mortals to sleep and make sleepers awake
And unseal the dead's eyelids. Holding this wand
He now rides the wind, sailing through thunderheads.
As he flies along, he makes out the summit   280
And steep slopes of Atlas, who shoulders the sky.
His pine-clad head is forever dark with clouds
And beaten by storms. Snow mantles his shoulders,
And icy streams drip from his frozen grey beard.
Mercury glided to a halt here, poised in the air,   285
And then gathered himself for a dive to the sea,
Where he skimmed the waves

                    like a cormorant
        That patrols a broken shoreline hunting for fish.

And so the god flew from the mountain giant, Atlas,
(Whose daughter, Maia, was Mercury's mother)   290
And came at last to the beaches of Libya.

The wing-footed messenger stepped ashore,
And when he reached the huts he saw Aeneas
At work, towers and houses rising around him.
His sword was enstarred with yellow jasper,   295
And from his shoulders hung a mantle blazing
With Tyrian purple, a splendid gift from Dido,
Who had stitched the fabric with threads of gold.

Mercury weighed in at once:

                        "Are you, of all people,
Laying the foundations of lofty Carthage   300
And building a beautiful city—for a woman?
What about your own realm, your own affairs?
The ruler of the gods—and of all the universe—
Has sent me down to you from bright Olympus,

Bearing his message through the rushing winds.   *305*
What are you thinking of, wasting your time in Libya?
If your own glory means nothing to you,
Think of the inheritance you owe to Ascanius—
A kingdom in Italy and the soil of Rome."

With these words on his lips, Mercury vanished   *310*
Into thin air, visible no more to human eyes.

Aeneas stood there amazed, choking with fear.
He bristled all over, speechless, astounded,
And he burned with desire to leave that sweet land,
In awe of the commandment from the gods above.   *315*
But what should he do? What can he say
To the Queen in her passion? How will he choose
His opening words? His mind ranges all over,
Darting this way and that, and as he weighs
His options, this seems the best choice: *320*
He calls his captains, Mnestheus, Sergestus,
And brave Serestus, and he orders them
To prepare the fleet for silent running, get the men
To the shore and the gear in order, but conceal
The reason for this change of plans. Meanwhile,   *325*
He explains that—since good Dido knows nothing
And would never dream that a love so strong
Could ever be destroyed—he himself will find
A way to approach her, the proper occasion
To break the news to her gently.
                     The captains   *330*
Were more than happy to fulfill his commands.

But the Queen (are lovers ever really fooled?)
Had a presentiment of treachery. Fearing all
Even when all seemed safe, she was the first
To detect a shift in the wind. It was evil Rumor   *335*
Who whispered that the fleet was preparing
To set out to sea.
                She went out of her mind,
Raging through the city

as wild and furious
As a maenad when the holy mysteries have begun,
Her blood shaking when she hears the cry "Bacchus!" 340
In the nocturnal frenzy on Mount Cithaeron,
And the mountain echoes the sacred call.

Finally she corners Aeneas and says:

"Traitor! Did you actually hope to conceal
This crime and sneak away without telling me? 345
Does our love mean nothing to you? Does it matter
That we pledged ourselves to each other?
Do you care that Dido will die a cruel death?
Preparing to set sail in the dead of winter,
Launching your ships into the teeth of this wind! 350
How can you be so cruel? If Troy still stood,
And you weren't searching for lands unknown,
You wouldn't even sail for Troy in this weather!
Is it me? Is it me you are fleeing?
By these tears, I beg you, by your right hand, 355
Which is all I have left, by our wedding vows,
Still so fresh—if I have ever done anything
To deserve your thanks, if there is anything in me
That you found sweet, pity a house destined to fall,
And if there is still room for prayers, I beg you, 360
Please change your mind. It is because of you
The Libyan warlords hate me and my own Tyrians
Abhor me. Because of you that my honor
Has been snuffed out, the good name I once had,
My only hope to ascend to the stars. 365
To what death do you leave me, dear guest
(The only name I can call the man
I once called husband)? For what should I wait?
For my brother Pygmalion to destroy my city,
For Gaetulian Iarbas to lead me off to captivity? 370
If you had at least left me with child
Before deserting me, if only a baby Aeneas
Were playing in my hall to help me remember you,
I wouldn't feel so completely used and abandoned."

Dido finished. Aeneas, Jupiter's message   375
Still ringing in his ears, held his eyes steady
And struggled to suppress the love in his heart.
He finally made this brief reply:

                    "My Queen,
I will never deny that you have earned my gratitude,
In more ways than can be said; nor will I ever regret   380
Having known Elissa, as long as memory endures
And the spirit still rules these limbs of mine.
I do have a few things to say on my own behalf.
I never hoped to steal away from your land
In secret, and you should never imagine I did.   385
Nor have I ever proposed marriage to you
Or entered into any nuptial agreement.
If the Fates would allow me to lead my own life
And to order my priorities as I see fit,
The welfare of Troy would be my first concern,   390
And the remnants of my own beloved people.
Priam's palace would still be standing
And Pergamum rising from the ashes of defeat.
But now the oracles of Gryneian Apollo,
Of Lycian Apollo, have commanded with one voice   395
That the great land of Italy is my journey's end.
There is my love, my country. If the walls
Of Carthage, vistas of a Libyan city,
Have a hold on you, a Phoenician woman,
Why do you begrudge the Trojans   400
A settlement in Ausonia? We too have the right
To seek a kingdom abroad.
                    The troubled ghost
Of my father, Anchises, admonishes me
Every night in my dreams, when darkness
Covers the earth, and the fiery stars rise.   405
And my dear son, Ascanius—am I to wrong him
By cheating him of his inheritance,
A kingdom in Hesperia, his destined land?
And now the gods' herald, sent by Jove himself,
(I swear by your head and mine) has come down   410
Through the rushing winds, ordering me to leave.

I saw the god myself, in broad daylight,
Entering the walls, and heard his very words.
So stop wounding both of us with your pleas.
It is not my own will—this quest for Italy."   *415*

While he is speaking she looks him up and down
With icy, sidelong glances, stares at him blankly,
And then erupts into volcanic fury:

"Your mother was no goddess, you faithless bastard,
And you aren't descended from Dardanus, either.   *420*
No, you were born out of flint in the Caucasus,
And suckled by tigers in the wilds of Scythia.
Ah, why should I hold back? Did he sigh as I wept?
Did he even look at me? Did he give in to tears
Or show any pity for the woman who loved him?   *425*
What shall I say first? What next? It has come to this—
Neither great Juno nor the Saturnian Father
Looks on these things with impartial eyes.
Good faith is found nowhere. I took him in,
Shipwrecked and destitute on my shore,   *430*
And insanely shared my throne with him.
I recovered his fleet and rescued his men.
Oh, I am whirled by the Furies on burning winds!
And now prophetic Apollo, now the Lycian oracles,
Now the gods' herald, sent by Jupiter himself,   *435*
Has come down through the rushing winds
With dread commands! As if the gods lose sleep
Over business like this! Go on, leave! I'm not
Arguing with you any more. Sail to Italy,
Find your kingdom overseas. But I hope,   *440*
If there is any power in heaven, you will suck down
Your punishment on rocks in mid-ocean,
Calling Dido's name over and over. Gone
I may be, but I'll pursue you with black fire,
And when cold death has cloven body from soul,   *445*
My ghost will be everywhere. You will pay,
You despicable liar, and I will hear the news;
Word will reach me in the deeps of hell."

With these words she breaks off their talk
And in her anguish flees from the daylight   450
And out of his sight, leaving him there
Hesitant with fear, and with so much more to say.
Her maids support her as she collapses, take her
To her marble room, and lay her on her bed.

Aeneas, loyal and true, yearns to comfort her,   455
Soothe her grief, and say the words that will
Turn aside her sorrow. He sighs heavily,
And although great love has shaken his soul,
He obeys the gods' will and returns to the fleet.

Then the Trojans redouble their efforts   460
And haul their ships down all along the shore.
Keels are caulked and floated, leafy tree limbs
Are brought in for oars, and beams left rough
In the men's impatience to leave. You could see them
Streaming down from every part of the city.   465

Ants, preparing for winter, will busily plunder
A huge pile of seeds and store it in their nest.
The black line threads through the fields as the insects
Transport their spoils on a narrow road through the grass.
Some push the huge grains along with their shoulders,   470
Others patrol the line and keep it moving,
And the whole trail is seething with their work.

What was it like, Dido, to see all this? What sighs
Escaped your lips, when from your high tower
You saw the shoreline crawling with Trojans,   475
And the sea roiled with the shouts of sailors?

Cruel Love, what do you not force human hearts to bear?
Again Dido collapses into tears, again feels compelled
To beg Aeneas and to bow down to Love,
Lest she leave something untried and so die in vain: 480

"Look at them, Anna, scuttling across the shore,
Streaming down from every direction. The canvas

Can hardly wait for the breeze, and the sailors
Are laughing as they hang the sterns with garlands.
I had the strength to foresee this sorrow,   485
And I will have the strength to endure it, Sister.
There is one more thing I will ask of you.
You are the only one that traitor befriended,
Confiding in you even his deepest feelings.
Only you will know the best way to approach him.   490
Go, my dear, bend your knee before our archenemy.
Tell him I never joined the Greek alliance at Aulis
To burn down Troy, never sent my warships
To Pergamum, nor defiled his father's ashes
Or disturbed his ghost. Why, then, does he refuse   495
To admit my words into his obstinate ears?
What is his hurry? Is he too rushed to grant
The final request of his wretched lover:
To wait for favorable winds for his flight?
I am no longer asking for our marriage back—   500
The marriage he betrayed—nor that he do without
His precious Latium or relinquish his realm.
All I want is time, some breathing room for my passion,
Until Fate has taught me how the vanquished should grieve.
Beg from him this last favor, Sister. If he grants it,   505
I will pay it back with interest—by my death."

Thus Dido's prayer, and her sister sadly
Bore it to Aeneas, then bore it again. Unmoved
By her tears, he made no response to her words.
Fate stood in the way, and a god sealed the man's ears.   510

> *Alpine winds swoop down from the North, struggling*
> *To uproot an ancient oak. They blow upon it*
> *From every side, until its leaves strew the ground*
> *And the strong trunk-wood creaks. But the tree*
> *Clings to the crag, and as high as its crest reaches to*
> *   heaven,*   515
> *So deep do its roots stretch down into Tartarus.*

So too the hero, battered with appeals
On this side and that. His great heart feels

Unendurable pain, but his mind does not move,
And the tears that fall to the ground change nothing.   520

And now Dido, in awe of her doom,
Prays for death. She is weary of looking upon
The dome of heaven, and, furthering her resolve
To leave the light, she saw as she placed offerings
On the incense-fumed altar a fearful omen: 525
The holy water turned black, and the wine,
When she poured it, congealed into gore.
She told no one of this, not even her sister.
There was more. Dido had in the palace
A marble shrine to her deceased husband,   530
A shrine she honored by keeping it wreathed
With snow-white wool and festal fronds.
Now she heard, or seemed to hear, her husband's voice,
When dusk had melted the edges of the world,
Calling her. And the owl, alone on the rooftop,   535
Would draw out its song into an eerie wail.
And the sayings of seers from days gone by
Would fill her with terror. And then in her sleep
A fierce Aeneas would pursue her as she raved.
And then she would be alone, abandoned forever,   540
Forever traveling a long, lonesome road
Through a desert landscape, searching for her Tyrians—

> *Like mad Pentheus when he sees the maenads,*
> *And sees a double sun and a duplicate Thebes;*
> *Or like Orestes stalked by Furies on an empty stage,*   545
> *Pursued by his mother with torches and snakes*
> *While the avenging Fiends lurk in the doorway.*

And so Dido, worn down by grief, went mad.
Determined to die, she worked out by herself
The time and the means, and only then   550
Did she address her sister, hiding her plan
Behind a face radiant with serenity and hope:

"O Sister, I have found a way—be glad for me—
Either to get him back or free myself from love.

On the shore of Ocean, near the setting sun,   555
Lies farthest Ethiopia, where gigantic Atlas
Turns on his shoulders the star-studded heavens.
A priestess from there, of the Massylian tribe,
Has been presented to me. She guarded the sanctuary
Of the Hesperides, protected the golden apples   560
On their tree, and feasted the dragon
On honey and the poppy's drowsy opium.
She claims her incantations can set hearts free
Or plunge them into the depths of despair,
All as she chooses. She can stop rivers cold,   565
Make the stars turn backward, and conjure up
The spirits of night. You will hear the ground bellow
Under your feet, see elms stroll down mountains.
I swear by the gods, Anna, and by your dear head,
I am reluctant to resort to black magic. Still,   570
Build a pyre secretly in the central courtyard
Under the open sky and pile upon it
The weapons our impious hero left
On our bedroom walls, and all his forgotten clothes,
And the marriage bed that was my undoing.   575
It will do me good to destroy every reminder
Of that evil man—as the priestess told me."

She fell silent, and the color drained from her face.

In spite of everything, her sister Anna
Did not believe that Dido was inventing   580
These strange rites to disguise her own funeral.
She could not conceive of passion so great
And feared no worse for Dido now
Than at the death of Sychaeus.
                              And so,
Anna prepared the pyre.   585

But the Queen, out in the open courtyard—
Where the pyre now reared heavenward,
Vast with billets of pine and sawn oak—
Hangs the place with garlands and funeral fronds.

Upon the bed she arranges his clothes, the sword   590
That he left, and his picture, knowing well
What was to come.
                            There were altars
Around the courtyard, and the priestess
Shook her hair out free and chanted thunderous prayers
To three hundred gods, to Erebus and Chaos,   595
To three-bodied Hecate and Diana's three faces,
Virgin huntress, Moon, and pale Proserpina.
She sprinkled water as being from Avernus
And with a bronze knife harvested by moonlight
Herbs selected for their milky, black poison.   600
She calls for the love charm of a newborn foal
Torn from his forehead before his mother can eat it.
Dido herself, sacred cakes of barley in her pious hand,
Stands close to the altars, one foot unsandaled,
Her dress unbound. Then she calls to witness,   605
As one about to die, first Gods and then Stars
Who share Destiny's secrets. And then she prays
To whatever Power makes a final reckoning
For lovers who love on unequal terms.

It was night, and all over earth weary bodies   610
Lay peacefully asleep. Woods and wild seas
Had fallen still, and the stars were midway
In their gliding orbits. Ox and meadow were quiet,
And all the brilliant birds who haunt
The lapping lakes and tangled hedgerows   615
Were nestled in sleep under the dark, silent sky.

But not Dido, unhappy heart. She never drifted off
Into sleep, nor let night settle on her eyes or breast.
Her anxiety mounts, and her love surges back
And seethes, wave after wave on a furious sea.   620
At last she breaks into speech, debating in her heart:

"What am I doing? Should I entertain once more
My former suitors—and hear them laugh at me?
Go begging for a marriage among the Nomads,
After scorning their proposals time and again?   625

Shall I follow the Trojans' fleet and be subject
To their every command? After all, aren't they
So grateful for the help I gave them
That they could never forget my past kindnesses?
Even if I wanted to, who would let me on board,   630
Welcome someone so hated onto their ships?
Poor Dido, do you not yet appreciate
The treachery bred into Laomedon's race?
What then? Shall I crew with the Trojans
Cruising cheerfully away, all on my own?   635
Or should I, at the head of my own Tyrian fleet,
Give them pursuit, order my people to hoist sail
Into the wind again, a people I could scarcely persuade
To abandon their city back in Phoenicia?
No, Dido, die as you deserve, end your sorrow   640
With a sword.
                   You, my dear sister, caving in to my tears,
First loaded my frenzied soul with these sorrows
And put me in the enemy's path. It was not my lot
To live a blameless life as a widow, as free
As a wild thing, untouched by these cares.   645
I have not kept my vow to Sychaeus' ashes."

As these cries erupted from Dido's heart,
Aeneas, bent on leaving, with everything in order,
Was catching some sleep on his ship's high stern,
And in his sleep he had a vision of Mercury,   650
Returning to him in the same form as before,
The same voice and face, the same golden hair
And graceful body—and, as before, with a warning:

"Goddess-born, how can you sleep in a crisis like this?
Are you blind to the perils surrounding you,   655
Madman? Don't you hear a sailing breeze blowing?
Dido's heart revolves around evil. Determined
To die, she seethes with tides of raw passion.
Will you not flee now, while flight is still possible?
You will soon see this sea awash with timbers   660
And the shore in flames—if Dawn finds you

Lingering here. Push off, then, without delay.
A woman is a fickle and worrisome thing."

And with these words he melted into the dark.

Aeneas was deeply shaken by this apparition.   665
He tore himself from sleep and woke his crew:

"On the double, men, unfurl those sails
And get to the benches! A god has come down
From heaven again, urging us to cut the cables
And get out of here as fast as we can.   670
We will follow you, Holy One, whoever you are,
And gladly obey your commands again.
Be with us once more, grant us your grace,
And set propitious stars in the sky before us."

He spoke, drew his sword   675
Flashing from its sheath, and severed
The stern cable. Aeneas' fervor
Spread through the fleet. They ran to their posts
And shoved off from the shore, blanketing the sea
With their hulls. Leaning into the oars,   680
They swept the blue water and churned it to foam.

Dawn left Tithonus' saffron bed
And sprinkled the world with early light.
The Queen, in her tower, watched the day whiten
And saw the fleet moving on under level sails.   685
She knew the shores and harbors were empty,
The oarage gone. She beat her lovely breast
Three times, four times, and tore her golden hair.

"O God!" she said. "Will he get away,
Will this interloper make a mockery of us?   690
To arms, the whole city, after him!
Launch the fleet! Bring fire, man the oars!
What am I saying? Where am I?
What has come over me? Oh, Dido, only now

Do you feel your guilt? Better to have felt it   695
When you gave away your crown. Behold
The pledge, the loyalty, of the man they say
Bears his ancestral gods, bore on his shoulders
His age-worn father! Could I have not torn him
Limb from limb and fed him to the fishes?   700
Murdered his friends? Minced Ascanius himself
And served him up as a meal to his father?
The battle could have gone either way: What of it?
Doomed to die, whom did I have to fear?
I should have torched his camp with my own hands,   705
Annihilated father and son and the whole race,
And thrown myself on top of the conflagration.
      O Sun, fiery witness to all earthly deeds,
And Juno, complicit in my unhappy love,
Hecate, worshiped with howls at midnight crossroads,   710
Avenging Furies, and gods of dying Elissa—
Attend to this, turn the force of your wrath
Upon sins that deserve it—O hear my prayer!
If this criminal is destined to make harbor again,
If this is what the Fates and Jupiter demand,   715
May he still have to fight a warlike nation,
Be driven from his land and torn from Iülus.
May he plead for aid and see his people slaughtered.
And when he has accepted an unjust peace,
May he not enjoy his reign or the light of day   720
But die before his time and lie unburied
On a desolate shore. This is what I pray for.
These last words I pour out with my blood.
And you, my Tyrians, must persecute his line
Throughout the generations—this your tribute   725
To Dido's ashes. May treaties never unite
These nations, may no love ever be lost between them.
And from my bones may some avenger rise up
To harry the Trojans with fire and sword,
Now and whenever we have the power.   730
May coast oppose coast, waves batter waves,
Arms clash with arms, may they be ever at war,
They themselves and their children forever."

Dido said these things and then set her mind
On a quick escape from the hated light. She exchanged   *735*
A few words with Barce, Sychaeus' nurse; her own
Was black ashes back in the old country.

"Dear Nurse, bring my sister Anna here.
Have her sprinkle her body with river water
And bring along the victims for expiation. You   *740*
Come with her, and wreathe your brows with wool.
I intend to complete the rites to Stygian Jove
That I have begun, and so end my troubles,
And to send the Trojan's pyre up in flames."

She spoke. The old woman quickened her step.   *745*
Dido trembled, panicked at the enormity
Of what she had begun. Eyes bloodshot,
Blotched cheeks quivering, pale with looming death,
She burst into the innermost part of the house,
Climbed the pyre like a madwoman, and unsheathed   *750*
The Trojan sword—a gift not sought for such a use.
The sight of the familiar bed and the clothes he wore
Made her stop in tears. Struggling to collect herself,
She lay upon the couch and spoke her final words:

"Love's spoils, sweet while heaven permitted,   *755*
Receive this soul, and free me from these cares.
I have lived, and I have completed the course
Assigned by Fortune. Now my mighty ghost
Goes beneath the earth. I built an illustrious city.
I saw my walls. I avenged my husband   *760*
And made my evil brother pay. Happy,
All too happy, if Dardanian ships
Had never touched our shores!"

                              Dido spoke,
And pressing her face into the couch:

"We will die unavenged, but we will die.   *765*
This is how I want to pass into the dark below.
The cruel Trojan will watch the fire from the sea
And carry with him the omens of my death."

With these words on her lips her companions saw her
Collapse onto the sword, saw the blade   770
Foaming with blood and her hands spattered.
A cry rises to the roof, and Rumor
Dances wildly through the shaken town.
The houses ring with lamentation
And the wails of women. Great dirges   775
Hang in the air. It was as if Carthage itself
Or ancient Tyre had fallen to the enemy,
And flames rolled through the houses of men
And over the temples of the gods.

Anna, in great distress, heard the cries.   780
She rushed through the crowd, clawing her face
With her nails, and beating her breasts
With her fists, and then spoke to her dying sister:

"So this is what it was all about, Sister.
You cheated me, didn't you? This is what   785
Your pyre was for, your altars, your fire—
To deceive me. What should I lament first,
Deserted like this? Did you scorn my company
In death? You should have called on me
To share your fate, to die by the sword   790
With the same agony, at the same moment!
Did I build this pyre with my own hands
Calling upon the gods of our fathers,
So that when you were lying upon it like this
I would not be here? Cruel! You have destroyed   795
Yourself, me, the Sidonian elders, and your city.
     Ah, let me bathe her wounds, and if any last breath
Still lingers on her lips, let me catch it on mine."

She had reached the top of the pyre by now
And was holding her sister close to her bosom,   800
Sobbing as she used her dress to stanch
The blood's dark flow. Dido, trying to lift
Her heavy eyes, grew faint again. The wound hissed
Deep in her chest. Three times she struggled
To prop herself upon her elbow,   805

Three times she rolled back on the bed.
With wandering eyes she sought the light
In heaven's dome and moaned when she found it.

Then Almighty Juno, pitying Dido's long agony
And hard death, sent Iris down from Olympus   810
To free her struggling soul from its mortal coils.
Her death was neither fated nor deserved
But before her day and in the heat of passion.
Proserpina had not yet plucked from her head
A golden lock, nor allotted her a place   815
In the Stygian gloom. And so Iris flew down
Through the sky on sparkling, saffron wings,
Trailing in the sunlight a thousand changing hues,
And then stood above Dido's head.

                              "This offering
I consecrate to Dis and release you from your body."   820

As soon as she had cut the lock, all the body's warmth
Ebbed away, and Dido's life withdrew into the winds.

AENEID FIVE

By now Aeneas was out at sea with his fleet,
Holding course through waves darkening
Under a cold North Wind—and looking back
At the walls of Carthage lit with the flames
Of Dido's pyre. The cause of the fire   5
Was hidden, but the terrible pain
Of a great love defiled and knowledge
Of what a frenzied woman could do
Gave the Trojans grim presentiments.

When the ships were out on deep water,   10
With no land in sight, but only sea and sky,
A cobalt cloud loomed overhead
Bringing night and storm, and the waves
Shuddered with shadows. Palinurus,
The pilot, cried from the high stern: 15

"Look at these storm clouds ringing the sky!
What are you doing, Father Neptune?"

                                                    With this,
He gave the order to bring in the rigging
And man the oars. Then he trimmed the sails
Aslant to the wind and spoke again: 20

"Noble Aeneas, not even if Jupiter
Promised me himself could I hope
To reach Italy with such a sky. The winds
Have shifted and are blowing across us,

Roaring in from the black west. The air   25
Is thickening, and for all our efforts
We cannot make headway into this storm.
We must follow Fortune and let her
Call our course. The friendly shores
Of your brother Eryx and Sicilian ports   30
Are not too far, if I remember my stars."

And Aeneas, steadfast:

                    "For some time now
I have seen what the wind wants. You can't steer
Against it. Set the sails for a new course.
What place could be more welcome to me   35
And my weary ships than the island
Of Trojan Acestes, the land that holds
My father's bones in her bosom?"

                              This said,
They headed for port, with the West Wind
Filling their sails. The fleet raced on   40
And turned at last toward the familiar shore.

Standing on a distant hilltop, Acestes
Marveled at the arrival of friendly ships.
He hurried down toward them, bristling
With javelins and a Libyan bearskin—   45
Acestes, born of a Trojan mother
To the rivergod Crinisus. Mentioning
Their family ties, he congratulated them
On their return and made them welcome
With his rustic riches and comforts of home.   50

Early the next day, when a clear dawn
Had put the stars to flight, Aeneas assembled
His men on the shore and spoke to them
From a high dune:

                    "Great sons of Dardanus,
My people born of the gods' high race,   55

A year of circling moons has passed
Since we laid in the earth the last remains
Of my divine father and hallowed his altars.
And now, by my count, the day has come
That I shall always keep as a day of mourning—   60
As you willed, O Gods—and a day of honor.
Were I spending this day as an exile
In the Gaetulian Syrtes, or the sea of Argos,
Or in Mycenae itself, still I would fulfill
My yearly vow with solemn rites   65
And pile the altars high with offerings.
But now we stand near my father's bones,
Not without, I think, the will of heaven,
Carried here to a safe and friendly haven.
Then let us all celebrate this day with joy,   70
Pray for favorable winds, and ask Anchises
For his blessing. May I offer these rites
Year by year when I found my city,
In temples consecrated to his memory.
Acestes, himself of Trojan birth, has given   75
Two head of oxen for every ship.
Summon to the feast the gods of your hearth
And the gods of Acestes. Moreover,
When the ninth day dawns with light for men
And reveals the world, I will propose   80
Games and contests for the Trojans:
First a regatta for our sailing ships,
And then a footrace, a javelin throw,
And a boxing match with rawhide gloves.
Come one and all, and compete for glory!   85
Now wreathe your brows and observe silence all."

Aeneas spoke, and crowned his own brows
With his mother's myrtle. Helymus
Did the same, as did aged Acestes
And the boy Ascanius. The others followed.   90
Aeneas returned to the mound, thousands
Thronging around him. He poured a libation—
Two goblets of undiluted wine, two

Of fresh milk, and two of the victims' blood—
And scattered flowers. Then he cried: 95

"Hail once more, venerable Father,
Hail, ashes rescued in vain, soul and shade
Of my sire. I was not destined to seek
The fields of Italy with you at my side,
Nor find with you the Ausonian Tiber."   100

He had no sooner spoken when there slithered
From the shrine's base a serpent trailing
Seven huge coils. It circled the mound
And glided tranquilly among the altars,
Its back spotted midnight blue and its scales   105
Shimmering with the iridescent gold
Of a rainbow refracting the cloud-scutched sun.
Aeneas was filled with awe. The serpent
Slid its length amid the bowls and polished cups,
Tasted the food on the altars, and at last   110
Crept harmlessly beneath the mound.
Aeneas renewed the rites with greater fervor,
Unsure whether it was the genius of the place
Or his father's spirit. He sacrificed
Two sheep, two swine, and as many   115
Dark-backed bullocks, all the while
Pouring wine from shallow bowls and calling
Great Anchises' soul and shades of Acheron.
His men gladly brought gifts and heaped them
On the altars. Others slaughtered steers,   120
Set out cauldrons, and, spread out on the grass,
Roasted the meat over glowing coals.

Dawn of the ninth, long-awaited day
Was escorted in by the horses of the Sun.
The games, and Acestes' illustrious name,   125
Brought in the crowds. They filled the shores
In a holiday mood, some coming to see
Aeneas and his men, others to compete.
The prizes were set out for all to see:

Ritual tripods, green wreaths and palms   130
For the victors, arms, robes dyed rich purple,
A talent of silver and another of gold.
A trumpet pealed from a central mound,
Signaling the start of the competition.

Four ships entered the first contest,   135
Well-matched in oarage, the pride of the fleet.
The swift Leviathan was captained by Mnestheus,
Namesake of the Italian clan of Memmius.
Gyas commanded the huge Chimaera,
A trireme the size of a city, rowed   140
By Dardanian youths sweeping their oars
In three ordered tiers and propelling her on.
Sergestus, namesake of the house of Sergius,
Rode in the great Centaur, and Scylla,
A sea-blue vessel, carried Cloanthus,   145
Whence your family, Roman Cluentius.

Far offshore lies a rock, pounded
By the waves. During winter storms
It is submerged, but in fair weather
It rises in stony silence from the still sea,   150
And cormorants sun themselves on its surface.
Father Aeneas wedged a leafy oak branch there
To mark the turning point for the sailors.
They drew for positions. The captains
High on the sterns gleamed in purple and gold,   155
And the rowers were wreathed in poplar,
Their bare shoulders glistening with oil.
They sat on the benches, hands tense on the oars,
And eagerly awaited the start, blood
Shaking their hearts in their lust for glory.   160
The instant the trumpet sounded they broke
From their places. The shouts of the rowers
Split the air, and the water churned and foamed
With each pull of their arms. Side by side
The ships plowed furrows, and the sea's plain   165
Was ripped to its depths by the cleaving oars
And the triple prongs of the vessels' beaks.

Chariot teams that break from the start
And eat up the plain are not so headlong
Even when their drivers shake out the reins   *170*
And lean forward to apply the whip.

The crowds applaud and cheer on their favorites,
And all the woodlands return the sound,
And it echoes off the hills and cliffs
And reverberates across the sheltered shore.   *175*

Gyas took the lead first, slipping through the waves
Amid all the roaring. Cloanthus was next,
With better rowers but a heavier ship. Then,
Equally far behind, Leviathan and Centaur
Battled for third. Leviathan would pull ahead,   *180*
Then huge Centaur would pass her by,
And then they would sail neck and neck
And cleave the salt sea with their curving keels.
They were drawing close to the rocky turn
When Gyas, the leader on the course,   *185*
Called out to his ship's pilot, Menoetes:

"Why are you going so far to the right?
Steer this way! Hug the shore, let the oars
Scrape the rock on the left. The others
Can have the deep water."

                        But Menoetes,   *190*
Fearing blind rocks, swung the prow out to sea.

"Where are you veering? Hug the rocks,
Menoetes!"

            As Gyas was shouting,
He looked back and saw Cloanthus
Coming up fast, cutting a course
Between Gyas' ship and the roaring rock.   *195*
He surged past in an instant, turned the goal,
And was safely out on the open sea.
Gyas' dismay burned in his bones,

And tears streamed down his face. Forgetting
His own honor and his sailors' safety,   200
He pushed the sluggish Menoetes
Off the stern into the sea headfirst
And took the rudder himself. Urging on his crew,
The captain, now pilot, turned the prow toward shore.
Menoetes, heavy and old, bobbed up   205
From the depths and pulled himself out
Dripping wet onto the rock and sat there.
The Trojans laughed when he fell, laughed
As he swam, and were laughing now
As he vomited up buckets of seawater.   210

Sergestus and Mnestheus, bringing up the rear,
Now brightened with hope of catching Gyas.
Sergestus was ahead coming up to the turn
But not by much: Leviathan's prow
Overlapped his keel and was pushing hard.   215
Mnestheus strode up and down mid-ship
Exhorting his crew:

                    "Lean on those oars, men!
Comrades of Hector, men I handpicked
For Troy's last stand—show me the strength,
The spirit you had in the shoals off Carthage,   220
In the Ionian Sea and Cape Malea's currents!
We can't win this race, we're not shooting for first,
(If only!—but Neptune decides the winners)
But coming in last is a total disgrace. Your victory
Is to not let that happen!"

                    And they fell on the oars   225
With a supreme effort. The bronze-beaked ship
Shivered under their strokes, and the sea
Slipped away beneath them as they panted for breath,
Mouths dry, sweat pouring down their bodies in rivers.
It was an accident that gave them the glory.   230
As Sergestus rashly squeezed his prow inside
And into the danger zone, he ran out of luck
And caught the jutting rock. The oars

Splintered on its jagged edge, and the prow
Crashed hard and hung out over the water.   235
The sailors rose with a shout and steadied her
By rowing backward, then they pushed her off
With iron-tipped poles and fished out their oars.
Mnestheus, flushed with success, broke free
With oars flashing and winds at his call,   240
Running shoreward on the open sea.

                                   A dove
        Flushed from its nest in a cave's porous rock
        Flies out with a tremendous explosion of wings
        Into the open fields and then starts gliding
        In pure, still flight on the quiet air.

                                        Thus Mnestheus,   245
And thus the Leviathan, cutting through
The final stretch of water and flying along
On her own momentum. First she left behind
Sergestus, struggling on the craggy rock
And vainly calling for help on the shoals   250
While he learned how to row with broken oars.
Then she caught Gyas on the huge Chimaera,
Which, without her pilot, soon fell behind.

At the finish, only Cloanthus was left,
And Mnestheus went after him with all he had.   255
The noise from the crowd doubled, all rooting
For the ship behind. The sky rang with their cheers.
The leading crew cringed to lose the glory
Now in their grasp, and would trade their lives for it.
The other feeds off success. They can   260
Because they think they can, and perhaps
They would have won when they drew up level
If Cloanthus had not stretched out both hands
Over the sea and made this prayerful vow:

"Gods of the sea, upon whose plains I race,   265
I will place before your altars on this shore

A shining bull to discharge this my vow,
Cast entrails in the waves, and pour forth wine."

He spoke, and the gods deep in the water
Heard his prayer, all the Nereids, Phorcus,   270
And his daughter, Panopea. And as the ship
Moved on, Father Portunus himself
Reached out his great hand and drove her forward.
Swifter than wind or a speeding arrow, she flew
To the land and came to rest deep in the harbor.   275

Then Aeneas, true son of Anchises,
Summoned all the crews in ritual fashion
And, proclaiming Cloanthus the victor,
Wreathed his brows with fresh green laurel.
Then he had each ship select three bullocks   280
And gave to each wine and a great bar of silver.
The two leading captains he singled out
With special honors. To the victor he gave
A gold-embroidered cloak with a wavy border
Of Meliboean purple and the woven design   285
Of a royal youth on wooded Mount Ida,
A boy keen in the hunt, chasing down stags
With his javelin. As he ran, out of breath,
An eagle of Jove swooped down from Ida
To snatch him up in his hooking talons.   290
The boy's aged guardians lifted their palms
In vain to the stars, and his dogs barked at the wind.
To Mnestheus, who won second place,
Aeneas gave a corselet with burnished links
Interwoven with triple-meshed gold   295
That he himself had stripped from Demoleos
By the rushing Simois under Ilium's walls,
A prize of honor and a protection in war.
Sagaris and Phegeus could barely carry
The multilayered corselet on their shoulders   300
To give to Mnestheus, yet Demoleos
Ran in it when he routed the Trojans.
Third prize was a pair of bronze cauldrons
And finely finished cups chased in silver.

They all had their gifts and were gleaming with pride,   305
Their temples bound with crimson ribbons,
When Sergestus, having with consummate skill
Wrenched his boat from the pernicious rock,
Was bringing her in missing an entire tier of oars,
A crippled vessel without any honor.   310

> *Sometimes a snake caught crossing a road*
> *Is run over by a bronze wheel or struck by a rock*
> *Thrown by a passerby who has left it half-dead.*
> *It twists and writhes in an attempt to flee,*
> *And although its eyes burn with ferocity*   315
> *And its tongue hisses in its upreared head,*
> *The rest of its wounded body is coiled*
> *As it struggles along in trailing knots.*

So too this ship and her oars, moving slowly,
Yet she made sail and pulled into the harbor.   320
Aeneas gave Sergestus the promised gifts,
Glad to see the ship saved and her men returned,
And added a slave woman, a Cretan named Pholoë,
Skilled in crafts and with two infants nursing.

This contest done, pious Aeneas   325
Strode to a grassy field ringed by hills
That formed a natural stadium,
And thousands came with him. Here the hero
Took his place on a raised platform
And invited all comers who had enough spirit   330
To compete in a sprint for the prizes set forth.
A crowd of Teucrians and Sicanians
Stepped up to enter, first and foremost
Nisus and Euryalus. . . .
Euryalus stood out for his youthful beauty,   335
And Nisus for his pure love for this boy.
Diores, a son of Priam, was next in line,
And then Salius and Patron, one of them
From Acarnania, the other an Arcadian.
Then two Sicilians, Helymus and Panopes,   340
Woodsmen both and attendants of Acestes,

And many more, whose names oblivion hides.
Standing in their midst Aeneas addressed them:

"Hear my words, men, and be of good cheer.
No one will leave here without winning a prize: 345
Two Cretan arrows with burnished steel tips
And a two-headed axe embossed with silver,
The same award for all. The first three finishers
Will receive other prizes and will be wreathed
In golden olive. The winner will get a horse   350
With splendid trappings. The prize for second
Is an Amazonian quiver full of Thracian arrows
Slung on a belt with a broad gold band
And a gemstone buckle. Third place will be content
To leave the field with an Argive helmet."   355

When he finished speaking they took their places,
And when the signal was given they were off,
Streaming out from the line like pouring rain.
When the finish was in sight Nisus took off,
Leaving them all behind, faster than wind   360
Or the wings of lightning. Next, but far behind,
Was Salius, and trailing behind him
Euryalus ran third. Helymus was in fourth,
And hard on his heels was Diores, leaning
Over his shoulder; in a longer race   365
Diores would have passed him
Or they would have finished dead even.
They were in the final stretch, tiring
As they came up to the line, when Nisus
Had the bad luck to slip on a patch of grass   370
Wet with the blood of slaughtered oxen.
He was already celebrating his victory
When he lost his footing and fell face first
Into the filthy gore from the sacrifice.
But he did not forget Euryalus   375
Or his love for the boy. He slid through the slime
Into the path of Salius and knocked him
Head over heels onto the hard-packed sand.
Euryalus shot ahead and thanks to his friend

Flew on to victory to the sound of applause.   380
Helymus finished second and Diores third.
But Salius protested loud and long
Before the spectators, filling the ears
Of the elders in front with his complaints
That he had been cheated and robbed of his prize.   385
Euryalus was saved by his popularity
And becoming tears, and by the manly spirit
All the more pleasing in so handsome a frame.
And Diores gave him strong vocal support.
He had finished third but would have no prize   390
If Salius were awarded first place.
Then Father Aeneas:

                    "Your prizes are fixed,
And no one will change the finishing order.
But I do have a consolation prize
For our friend who did not deserve to fall."   395

And he presented the hide of a Gaetulian lion
To Salius, a huge shaggy skin with golden claws.
At this Nisus put in:

                    "If the losers are to get
These great prizes, and you feel so sorry for falls,
What about me, Nisus? I would have won   400
If I had not had the same bad luck as Salius."

As he spoke he displayed his face and arms
Filthy with muck. Aeneas, like a good father,
Smiled at Nisus and had a shield brought to him,
The work of Didymaon, a shield the Danaans   405
Had removed from the door of Neptune's temple,
Now a splendid prize for this noble youth.

The races were done, the awards completed.

"Now, if there is a man here with any heart,
Come out with gloves on and hands held high."   410

Aeneas spoke and put up a double prize
For the boxing match: for the victor,
A bullock with gilded horns and woolen fillets;
A sword and fine helmet to console the vanquished.

Without delay, Dares muscled himself up   *415*
To a chorus of cheers. He was the only man
Who used to hold his own against Paris,
And who at the funeral of Hector
Fought Butes, the great Bebrycian champion,
And laid him out dying on the yellow sand.   *420*
It was this Dares who now held his head high
For the first match, flexed his arms for his fans,
And began to shadowbox, punching the air.
Not a man stepped forward, out of all that crowd,
To put on gloves and go up against him.   *425*
Thinking everyone had conceded the prize,
He went up to Aeneas and without hesitation
Grasped the ox's horn with his left hand, saying:

"Goddess-born, if no one dares to fight me,
What are we standing here for? Give me the word   *430*
To lead away my prize."

                          The Dardanians
All yelled that he should be given his prize.
And then Acestes, sitting next to Entellus
On the green grass, said to him sternly:

"Entellus, you were once the bravest of heroes,   *435*
But it means nothing now if you are willing to let
Prizes like this be won uncontested.
What about the divine Eryx, your teacher?
Honored in memory only? What about your fame
Throughout Sicily, all your trophies at home?"   *440*

And Entellus:

                "It's not that my love of glory
Has given away to fear. But I'm old and slow

And don't have any juice. I'm all worn out.
If I had the youth that gives this rascal
His confidence, if I had my youth back,   445
I wouldn't need any prize, no prettied-up bull,
To make me fight. I don't care about prizes."

And he threw into the ring a pair of gloves
Of enormous weight, gloves that fierce Eryx
Would bind onto his hands for use in battle.   450
They all stared in wonder at the outsize leather,
Seven-ply rawhide stiff with lead and iron.
Dares stared the hardest and backed off fast
While Aeneas, Anchises' great-souled son,
Turned the huge, heavy gauntlets over and over.   455
Then old Entellus' voice boomed out:

"What if you had seen the gloves of Hercules
And the grim fight on this very shore?
Your half-brother, Eryx, wielded these weapons
(You can still see on them spattered blood and brains)   460
And stood against great Hercules with them.
I used them too, when my blood was hotter,
Before jealous old age sprinkled grey in my hair.
But if Trojan Dares objects to these gloves,
And if that sits well with pious Aeneas   465
And Acestes approves, we can even up the fight.
Relax; I'll give up Eryx's gloves
And you take off your Trojan mitts."

With that he flung his mantle from his shoulders,
Baring his heavy-boned, knotted arms,   470
And stood like a giant in the middle of the sand.
Father Aeneas, Anchises' true son,
Brought out two pairs of well-matched gloves
And bound the thongs to each boxer's hands.
They were up on their toes in an instant,   475
Both fearless, hands lifted skyward,
They held their heads high and well out of range
And began mixing it up, sparring for an opening,
Dares relying on fancy footwork and youth,

Entellus a heavyweight with a longer reach,   *480*
But his knees were going and his breath came hard.
They threw many knockout punches that missed
But landed many hard body blows, thudding
Into the rib cage and chest, and made frequent jabs
To head and ears; their jaws snapped with the impact.   *485*
Entellus stood his ground, tense and poised,
Swaying away from punches, eyes on his opponent.
Dares fought

       as if attacking a city
With high, massive walls, or laying siege
To a hilltop fortress, trying first one approach,   *490*
Then another, using all of the arts of war
And mounting various assaults in vain.

Entellus showed a high right hand and stepped in
For a hard downward blow. Dares saw it coming
And twisted out of the way. Entellus spent   *495*
All his force on the air and fell heavily
Onto the ground,

       like a vaulted pine
Uprooted and falling to the ground
On Erymanthus or great Mount Ida.

Trojans and Sicilians were on their feet,   *500*
Their shouts reaching the sky. Acestes
Ran out to lift his old friend from the ground,
But the great hero was unfazed by the fall
And returned to the fight with even more spirit,
Pumped up by anger, fortified by shame,   *505*
And fiercely proud. He drove Dares
All over the arena, hitting him with a right,
With a left, pelting him without letting up,
Like stinging hail. Both fists flying, the hero
Pounded Dares until he sent him spinning.   *510*

Father Aeneas did not allow Entellus
To pursue his bitter rage any further.

He stopped the fight, took Dares aside,
And spoke to him these soothing words:

"What happened out there? Didn't you sense   515
The powers had shifted? Yield to the gods."

Then he announced that the boxing was over.
Dares' supporters led him to the ships, dragging
His weak knees and lolling his head
As he spat out teeth clotted with blood.   520
They took the sword and helmet, leaving
First prize for Entellus. Towering over the bull
In pride of victory, the hero said:

"Goddess-born, and Trojans all, observe
The strength I had when I was young   525
And the kind of death you saved Dares from."

He spoke, then stood facing the ox
That was his prize, and, lifting his right hand,
Poised the hardened glove high between its horns,
Struck, and crushed its skull. The bull trembled   530
And then sank to the ground, a lifeless heap.
And Entellus spoke these heartfelt words:

"This life rather than Dares' I offer to you, Eryx.
I retire a champion and hang up my gloves."

Aeneas now announced the archery contest,   535
Invited all comers, and listed the prizes.
He set up a mast from Serestus' ship,
Holding it in one great hand, and tied
A dove to a cord suspended from its top.
This was the target. The contestants gathered   540
And threw their names into a bronze helmet.
The crowd cheered when Hippocoön,
Son of Hyrtacus, was sorted first. Mnestheus,
Who had just won the boat race, drew second,
Mnestheus, crowned with green olive leaves.   545
Eurytion drew third, your brother,

Most glorious Pandarus, who broke the truce
As bidden, first to shoot into the Achaean ranks.
The last position was drawn by Acestes,
Who had the courage to try his hand   550
In a young man's game.
                              Each man bent his bow
And took arrows from his quiver. The first shot
Was taken by Hippocoön. His bowstring twanged,
And his arrow whipped through the air,
Hitting the mast and sticking in the wood.   555
The mast quivered, and the frightened dove
Fluttered her wings. The crowd applauded.
Then Mnestheus eagerly took his stance,
Drawing his bow back for a high shot,
Intent on his aim. But he had no luck at all,   560
His iron-tipped arrow missed the bird, slicing instead
Through the knotted cord where it was attached
To the tip of the mast. The freed dove flew off
Into the warm wind and up toward the clouds.
Eurytion, who already had an arrow in his bow,   565
Spotted the carefree bird flapping her wings
In the empty sky and, with a quick prayer
To his brother Pandarus, shot her as she flew
Beneath a dark cloud. The dove fell lifeless,
Leaving her spirit in the stars, and in her fall   570
She returned to its owner the piercing arrow.

Only Acestes was left. He had no chance
For a prize but shot an arrow nonetheless
High into the air, the old patriarch
Displaying his skill and his sounding bow.   575
Then a sudden marvel appeared, destined to be
A mystic portent in days to come,
When seers chanted of late-fulfilled omens.
For as the arrow flew through the wispy clouds
It caught fire and marked its trail with flames   580
Until it was consumed in the thin upper air,

   Like a star that has come unfixed from heaven
   And flies across the sky with long, streaming hair.

Sicilians and Trojans stood rooted in wonder,
Murmuring prayers, and great Aeneas himself   585
Acknowledged the omen. He embraced Acestes
And lavished gifts upon him, saying:

"These are yours, sir. God on Olympus
Has shown with these auspices his high will
That you should receive exceptional honors.   590
As tribute from long-lived Anchises himself,
Accept this embossed bowl, which Cisseus,
The Thracian king, gave to my father
As a memorial and pledge of his love."

So saying, he wreathed Acestes' head   595
With verdant laurel and proclaimed him
Foremost champion. The good Eurytion
Did not begrudge him this preference
Even though he alone had shot down the dove.
Second prize went for severing the cord,   600
And third for piercing the mast with an arrow.

Before the archery contest was over
Aeneas had a private word with Epytus,
Young Iülus' trusted companion and guardian:

"Go find Iülus, and if the boys' column   605
Is ready for the equestrian parade,
Tell him to put on his best dress armor
And lead the procession in his grandfather's honor."

Aeneas himself had the crowd pull back
And form a large circle around the open field.   610
The boys entered on their bridled horses
And shone in their parents' eyes. Teucrians
And Trinacrians murmured in admiration.
The boys were all crowned in trim-cut wreaths,
And each bore two iron-tipped cornel spears.   615
Some carried polished quivers, others wore
Twisted gold collars around their throats—
All in ceremonial style. Three troops

Of riders each with a leader rode in formation,
Each troop in two files of six, each with a trainer,   620
All gleaming in the light. The first troop
Of triumphant boys was led by a little Priam,
Polites' noble son, named after his grandfather
And destined to increase the Italian race.
His mount was a dappled Thracian stallion,   625
White above the hooves and with a white forelock.
The second troop was led by Atys, founder
Of the Latin Atii. Young Atys
Was a dear friend of the boy Iülus,
And Iülus, the handsomest of them all,   630
Led the last troop, riding a Sidonian horse
Given to him by the lovely Dido
As a memorial and pledge of her love.
The other boys were given Sicilian mounts
By old Acestes.   635
They received the crowd's applause nervously,
And the Dardanians, watching them,
Recognized their ancestors' faces.
After they had happily paraded around
The entire assembly before their parents' eyes,   640
The son of Epytus gave the signal, first a shout,
Then the crack of a whip, and the riders split
Into separate sections, each of the three troops
Dividing in half. At a second command
The two new formations wheeled around   645
And advanced on each other, spears leveled.
Then they performed other maneuvers,
Attacks and counterattacks mirroring each other,
Weaving in and out of circular patterns,
Fighting mock battles in full battle gear,   650
Retreating, attacking, then calling a truce
And riding along side by side.

The Labyrinth
In lofty Crete is said to have been
A route woven within blind walls, a maze
With a thousand irretraceable paths   655
Designed to foil any map for escape.

So too the patterns the sons of the Trojans
Wove in their mock attacks and retreats

> *Like dolphins crisscrossing the Carpathian Sea*
> *Or the sea off Libya in their playful swimming.*   660

The tradition of this equestrian display
And these mock battles was first revived
By Ascanius, who taught the native Latins
How to perform them when he built the walls
Of Alba Longa. The Albans taught their sons   665
To do as Ascanius and the Trojans had done
When they were boys. In the course of time
Great Rome itself received and preserved
This ancestral tradition. It is now called "Troy,"
And the boys are called "the Trojan Troop."   670

> Thus the funeral games of Anchises,
>   Venerable father of Aeneas.

Fortune now shifted. While they celebrated
The funeral games, Juno sent Iris
Down from the sky to the Trojan fleet   675
And blew her along with a favoring wind.
The goddess was scheming, her old grievance
Still unsatisfied. Iris, herself unseen,
Soared through a thousand arcing colors,
Descending when she saw the great assembly.   680
She passed along the shore and saw the fleet
Unattended in the empty harbor.
Farther along, alone on the deserted beach,
The women of Troy wept for Anchises
And wept as they looked out at the boundless sea.   685
How weary they were, with so much water
Still to cross! All of them agreed,
It was a city they yearned for. The tedium
Of the sea had them sick at heart. Iris,
Who knew how to cause trouble, put aside   690
Her goddess's appearance and dress

And became Beroë, the aged wife
Of Doryclus of Tmarus, a woman
Nobly born, with a good name and fine sons.
In this guise Iris mingled   *695*
With the women of Troy and said:

"Trojan women, your tragedy
Is that Greek hands did not drag you off
To be killed before the walls of your city.
O my unhappy people, for what destruction   *700*
Is Fortune preserving you? Seven summers
Since the fall of Troy have we been driven
On the wind, measuring every sea and land,
Every inhospitable rock and hostile star,
Rolling in the waves as we search the ocean   *705*
For an ever-receding Italy. Now we are here
In the land of Eryx, our brother,
And Acestes is our host. Who is there
Who would prevent us from laying foundations,
Building walls, and giving our people a city?   *710*
O my country, O gods of my country,
Snatched from enemy hands to no purpose,
Will there never again be a city called Troy?
Will I never see the streams that Hector saw,
The Xanthus and the Simois? Come with me,   *715*
Women, and set fire to these accursed ships,
Burn them up! Cassandra, our prophetess,
Came to me in a dream and gave me torches,
Saying, 'Find Troy here, here is your home.'
It is time to act; we cannot delay   *720*
With portents like this. Look, Neptune's
Four altars! The god himself provides torches!"

So saying, she seized the deadly fire
And, from where she stood, whirled the torch high
And let it fly. The women of Ilium   *725*
Were astounded, their minds tense and alert.
The eldest among them, Pyrgo,
Nurse of so many of Priam's children,
Now spoke:

"This is not Beroë, women,
Not Doryclus' Trojan wife, I tell you.   730
Don't you see the marks of divinity,
Her burning eyes, the high spirit, that face,
The sound of her voice, her step when she walks?
I just left Beroë, sick and fretting
That she alone was missing our ceremony   735
And not paying her last respects to Anchises."

At first the women were uncertain and gazed
Upon the ships with angry eyes, wavering
Between wretched love for the present land
And kingdoms calling with the voice of Fate.   740
Then the goddess rose through the air on wings
And cut a huge rainbow beneath the clouds.
Now the women, frenzied by this portent,
Began to shriek and scream. They ransacked
The camp's hearth-fires, despoiled the altars,   745
And hurled torches made of twigs and branches.
Vulcan raged unbridled through the pine benches,
The banks of oars, and the painted sterns.

The herald Eumelus brought the news
To the assembly at Anchises' funeral mound   750
That the ships were burning. Looking back,
They saw black ash eddying up in a cloud;
And first of them all Ascanius,
Just as he was, gaily mounted for the games,
Rode furiously to the Trojan camp,   755
The breathless trainers unable to restrain him.

"What madness is this, what are you doing?"
He asked. "My pitiable countrywomen,
This is not an enemy Argive encampment
But your future that is going up in smoke.   760
Look, it is I, your Ascanius!"

And he threw at their feet the plumed helmet
He had worn in the war games.

Now Aeneas,
At the head of columns of Teucrians,
Was riding up fast. The women scattered   765
All over the shore, afraid, seeking the woods
And the shelter of rocks. They were ashamed
Of their deed, ashamed to be seen. Then,
Their mood altered, they recognized their menfolk,
And Juno was shaken from their breasts.   770

But the fire was not so easily tamed.
Beneath the wet wood the caulking
Was still alive, slowly belching out smoke,
And the smoldering heat ate at the keels
And spread through the frames, resisting   775
The men's heroic efforts and all the water
They sluiced onto the ships.
                              Then pious Aeneas
Rent his garments and stretching out his palms
Called on the gods:

        "Almighty Jupiter,
If you do not yet hate the Trojans to a man,   780
If you have any feeling for human suffering
As you did of old, save the fleet from fire,
Now, Father, and snatch Troy's slim fortunes
From utter perdition. Or finish what is left,
And if I deserve it, strike me dead with lightning   785
Here and now, and blot me out with your hand."

He had scarcely spoken when a black tempest
Began to rage. Rain poured down without limit,
Plains and steep hills trembled with thunder,
And the whole sky fell in a turbulent deluge   790
Swept with darkest winds. The ships' decks
Were inundated, the charred beams soaked,
The fire's last traces all extinguished, and
All the ships but four saved from destruction.

But Aeneas, stunned by this bitter blow,   795
Turned his immense troubles over and over

In his great heart. Should he settle in Sicily
And ignore Fate or seek Italy's shores?
Then old Nautes came to him. Pallas Athena
Had instructed this man above all in her lore,   800
Teaching him what might be portended
By the gods' wrath and what Fate demanded.
He comforted Aeneas and said to him:

"Goddess-born, we must follow Fate's lead.
All fortune is overcome by endurance.   805
You have Dardanian Acestes, of divine stock.
Take him into your counsel, a willing friend.
Entrust to him as many as the lost ships carried,
Those who are weary of your great enterprise,
The elderly, the mothers sick of the sea,   810
And whoever is weak or afraid of danger.
Choose them; let the weary have their own city here
And call it Acestes, if that name is permitted."

Old Nautes' friendly advice made Aeneas
Even more anxious. His mind was on fire.   815
Night's black horses had reached the zenith
When suddenly there glided down from heaven
An apparition of his father, Anchises,
Who poured these words from his heart:

"My son, once dearer to me than life   820
While life remained, my son, steeled in Ilium's fall,
I come here at Jove's command, Jove who drove the fire
Away from the ships, finally taking pity on you
From high heaven. You must follow the counsel,
Most fair, that old Nautes gives. Choose   825
The bravest hearts and take them to Italy.
There is a rough and sturdy race in Latium
You must defeat in battle. But before that,
Come to the realms of Dis, the deeps of Avernus,
To meet with me. For sinful Tartarus   830
Does not hold me, nor doleful shade.
I live in Elysium, in the pleasant company
Of the souls of the blessed. Virgin Sibyl

Will lead you here for the price of the blood
Of many black cattle. Then you will learn   835
All your race to come and the walls that await you.
And now, farewell. Dewy Night is turning
Past the middle of her course, and cruel Dawn
Breathes upon me with her panting horses."

He finished and was gone like a wisp of smoke.   840

"Where are you going? Why are you leaving
So quickly? Why can't we hold each other?"

As Aeneas spoke he was rekindling
The hearth-fire, and he paid reverence
To the Lar of Pergamum and to Vesta   845
With salted meal and clouds of incense.

Moments later he met with his comrades,
Acestes foremost, and explained to them
His beloved father's instructions
And how he himself now stood. The discussion   850
Was brief, and Acestes had no objections.
They registered the women and made citizens
Of those souls who had no need of glory.
The ships' crews rebuilt the benches,
Replaced the timbers charred in the fire,   855
And refit the oars and rudders. These men
Were few in number but ready for battle.
Meanwhile, Aeneas marked out with a plow
The city's boundaries and allotted homesteads,
Designating one neighborhood as Ilium,   860
Another as Troy. Trojan Acestes gladly
Called an assembly and handed down laws
To the new city fathers. High on Mount Eryx,
Near to the stars, a temple was dedicated
To Idalian Venus, and a sacred grove   865
Was annexed to the burial mound of Anchises.

For nine days all the people feasted
And sacrificed at altars. The water was calm

And a steady South Wind summoned the Trojans
Out to sea again. The sound of weeping   *870*
Curved along the shore. A day and a night
The people prolonged their farewell embraces.
Now the women themselves, and the same men
To whom the very mention of the sea
Had been abhorrent, wanted to go   *875*
And endure exile's toil. All of these
Good Aeneas consoled and, weeping himself,
Commended them to Acestes, their kin.
Then he ordered sacrifices—
Three calves to Eryx, and to the Storms a lamb—   *880*
And the ritual of untying the stern cable.
He himself stood on the prow, his head wreathed
In olive branches, holding a shallow bowl.
He poured out wine and cast the entrails
Into the salt sea. They got underway   *885*
And caught a rising tailwind. The crews
Outdid each other sweeping the sea with oars.

Venus, meanwhile, anxious and worried,
Was pouring out her heart to Neptune:

"Juno's iron anger and implacable heart   *890*
Force me, Neptune, to exhaust every prayer.
Neither time nor worship mollify her;
Neither at Jove's command nor broken by Fate
Does she acquiesce. It is not enough for her
To have eaten out the heart of the Phrygian nation,   *895*
Not enough to have dragged Troy's remnant through every
Conceivable chastisement: she must persecute
The city's very ashes and bones. The cause
Of such a monumental obsession
She knows best herself. You yourself saw   *900*
The wreckage she made of the sea off Libya,
Embroiling sea and sky, exploiting Aeolus—
All in vain—and daring this in your realm!
She drove the Trojan matrons to crime
And shamefully burned the ships, forcing Aeneas   *905*

To abandon his people in a strange land.
From now on, let them entrust their sails
And safety to you and reach Laurentine Tiber,
If what I request has been ordained by Fate."

And Saturn's son, Lord of Sea, replied: 910

"Cytherean, it is entirely proper
That you trust my realm, whence, after all,
You emerged at birth. And I have earned your trust.
I have often quelled the fury of sea and sky,
And no less on land (Simois and Xanthus   915
Can testify to this) has your Aeneas
Been under my care. When Achilles
Stampeded the Trojans into their city,
Robbing thousands of life, and all the streams
Were choked with corpses, and the river Xanthus   920
Could not roll its water into the sea—then,
Just as Aeneas was about to do battle
With Peleus' strong son, equal in neither
Gods nor strength, I whisked him away
In a hollow cloud, even though I yearned   925
To tear down the perjured city's walls,
Which my own hands had built.
                              Dispel your fears;
My mind has not changed. Your son will arrive
Safely at Avernus, just as you wish.
One man only will be lost at sea,   930
One life given for many."

                    So Neptune
Gladdened Venus' heart with soothing words.
Then the lord yoked his horses with gold,
Put bits into their foaming mouths,
And let out the reins, gliding lightly   935
Over the whitecaps in his chariot blue.
The sea flattened its swollen waves
Under the thundering axle, and the clouds
Fled from the threatening sky. Then came
The many shapes of his retinue, creatures   940

From the deep, old Glaucus and his train,
Ino's son Palaemon, swift Tritons,
And all the company of Phorcus. On the left,
Thetis and Melite and virgin Panopea,
Nisaea, Spio, Cymodoce, and Thalia.   945

Now a quiet joy came over Aeneas
And his tension ebbed away. He ordered
The masts to be raised and the sails hung.
The crews set the sheets and let out their sails,
First to the left, then to the right, swinging   950
The yardarms in unison as the fleet tacked
Into the wind. Palinurus kept the ships
In tight formation. The other captains
Had orders to set their course by him.

Dewy Night had almost reached its midpoint,   955
And the sailors were slumped over their oars
Up and down the hard benches, when Sleep
Drifted down from the stars of heaven,
Parting the shadows as he moved through the air
Seeking you, Palinurus, bringing grim dreams   960
To your innocent soul. The god settled
On the high stern, the image of Phorbas,
And said in a soft, insinuating voice:

"Palinurus, son of Iasius, the sea
Bears the fleet onward, steady blows the wind.   965
It is time for rest. Put your head down
And steal your weary eyes from their vigil.
I'll fill in for you for a little while."

And Palinurus, hardly lifting his eyes:

"Are you asking me to forget what I know   970
About a sea that looks calm? Asking me
To trust this monster? What, entrust Aeneas
To the vagaries of wind and weather?
I've been fooled too often by a calm, clear sky."

Saying these things, he held the rudder tight   975
And did not move his eyes from the stars above.
But the god shook a branch soaked in Lethe
Above both his temples, a branch drowsed
With the power of Styx, and he nodded off,
Closed his swimming eyes. His limbs   980
Had just begun to relax when the god,
Looming over him, threw him headfirst
Into the water along with part of the stern
And the rudder he still held. He called
His unhearing shipmates over and over   985
As the god soared upward into thin air.

The fleet sailed on safely without alarm,
As Neptune had promised, and now approached
The cliffs of the Sirens, formerly perilous
And white with men's bones but now just rocks   990
Roaring and echoing in the ceaseless surf—
When Aeneas sensed the ship was drifting
Without its master. He steered it himself
Through the midnight waves, sick at heart,
Lamenting the loss of his friend: 995

                    "O Palinurus,
You trusted the sea's calm too much, and now
Your corpse will lie naked on an unknown shore."

AENEID SIX

Aeneas wept as he spoke, and let the fleet
Glide along until it reached Cumae. Keels
Backed into the long arc of Euboean beach,
Prows seaward, as the anchors bit
Into the sea's shelving floor. Crews flashed ashore   5
Onto the banks of Italy. Some kindled fire
From veins of flint, some foraged timber
From the wilderness, others located streams.
But Aeneas, on a mission of his own,
Sought the high, holy places of Apollo   10
And the Sibyl's deeps, the immense caverns
Where the prophetic god from Delos breathes
Into her mind and soul and opens the future.
Aeneas and his men were soon within
The groves of Trivia and under golden eaves.   15

Daedalus once, fleeing Minoan Crete
On beating wings, trusted himself
To the open sky, an unused path,
North toward the Bears and a light landing
On this Chalcidian height,   20
And dedicated here his airy oarage
To you, Phoebus, and founded this temple.

On the doors, the murder of Androgeus
And the annual penalty for the Athenians,
Seven of their sons offered for sacrifice.   25
The urn stands ready, the lots are drawn. Opposite,

130

Rising from the sea, the island of Crete,
Raw passion for a bull, and Pasiphaë
In her furtive position, raising her knees.
And there too the mixed breed, the Minotaur,   30
Hybrid monument to unspeakable desire.
Here the Labyrinth winds its inextricable course,
And here is Daedalus himself, pitying
Princess Ariadne's great love, unraveling
The twisted skein of the maze, guiding Theseus'   35
Blind footsteps with a thread. And you also,
Icarus, would have played a great part
In this masterpiece, if grief had allowed:
Twice the artist attempted your fate in gold,
Twice the father's hands fell.

— comparing him to Icarus or Theseus

                    Aeneas' eyes   40
Would have scanned every last detail.
But Achates, sent ahead, was back,
And with him was Deïphobe, Glaucus' daughter,
Priestess of Phoebus and Trivia. A figure
Of divine awe, she had this to say to Aeneas: 45

"This is no time for looking at pictures.
You should be sacrificing seven bulls
From a sacred herd, and seven chosen sheep."

She spoke, and when Aeneas' men
Had seen to the sacrifice the priestess   50
Called the Trojans under the looming temple.

The flank of that Euboean cliff was carved
Into a hundred cavernous mouths, gaping orifices
That roar the Sibyl's oracular responses.
The virgin priestess greeted them at the threshold: 55

"It is time to demand your destiny. The god! Behold,
The god!"

        And as she spoke there before the gates
Her color changed, her hair spread out

Aeneas does as he was told

Into fiery points, she panted for air,
And her breast heaved with feral madness.   60
She was larger than life now, and her voice
Was no longer human, as the god's power
Took possession of her:

                "You hesitate
To pray, hesitate, Aeneas of Troy?
The great mouths of this thunderstruck hall   65
Will not open until you pray."

                   And she was silent.
Fear seeped like icy water through the Trojans' bones,
And their lord poured forth his heart in prayer:

"Phoebus, who has always pitied Troy
In its darkest times, who guided the arrow   70
From Paris' hand into the body of Achilles,
And who guided me through so many seas
Pounding so many distant shores,
The remote Massylian tribes, the lands
Fringed by the shoals of the Syrtes—   75
Now at last we have in our grasp
The ever-receding shore of Italy.
May Troy's fortune follow us no farther.
You also, gods and goddesses
Whom Ilium's great glory offended,   80
May now justly spare the Dardan race.
And you, most holy prophetess, who hold
The future in your mind, grant the realm
That has been pledged to me by Fate,
Grant that the Teucrians settle in Italy   85
With the wandering, harried gods of Troy.
Then to Phoebus and Trivia I will dedicate
A temple of solid marble and holy days
In Phoebus' name. And a great shrine
Awaits you in our realm, gracious priestess,   90
An inner sanctum where I will deposit
Your prophecies and the mystic sayings

Told to my people and ordain your priests.
Only do not entrust your verses to leaves,
Playthings swirling when the wind gusts,   95
But chant them out loud."

                    Aeneas finished.
But the priestess had not yet taken Apollo's
Bit in her mouth, and she convulsed like a maenad
Monstrous in the cave, desperate to shake
The great god from her breast. All the more,   100
Though, he tired her rabid mouth, tamed   — show his
Her wild heart, and molded her to his will.   frightening
And now the cave's hundred mouths   power
Opened of their own accord and transmitted
The oracle's response through the empty air: 105

"You have escaped the perils of the sea,
But perils more grave await you on land.
The Dardanians will enter Lavinium—
Be sure of that—but will wish they had never come.
War, I see horrible war, and the Tiber   110
Foaming with blood. You will have another
Simois and Xanthus, another Doric camp.
A second Achilles has been born in Latium
To a goddess mother, and Juno will
Continue to afflict the Teucrians,   115
While you, a suppliant, shall beg for help
Throughout Italy. And the cause
Of all this suffering for the Trojans   — golden apple
Shall be once more a foreign bride,   all over
An alien marriage.   again   120
Do not yield, but oppose your troubles
All the more boldly, as far as your fate
And fortune allow. Salvation will come first
From where you least expect it—
A Greek city will open wide its gates."   125

In words such as these the Sibyl of Cumae
Chanted eerie riddles from her shrine
In the echoing cave, shrouding truth

oracle tells Aeneas what
will happen

In darkness, as Apollo shook the reins
And twisted the goad in her raving heart.   130
As soon as her frenzy ceased, and her lips
Were hushed, the Trojan hero began:

"Virgin priestess, trouble of any kind,
However strange, no longer surprises me.
I expect it, and I have thought this through.   135
I ask for one thing. It is said that here
Are the dark lord's gate and the murky swamp
Of Acheron's backwater. Let me pass.
Open the sacred doors and show me the way,
So that I might see my father face to face.   140
I saved him, I carried him on my shoulders
Through fire and a thousand enemy spears.
He was at my side through the long journey,
Sharing the perils of sea and sky, crippled
As he was, beyond what his age allowed.   145
It was his pleas that convinced me to come
As suppliant to you. Pity father and son,
Gracious one, for you have the power.
Not in vain did Hecate appoint you
Mistress of the groves of Avernus.   150
If Orpheus could call forth his wife's ghost,
Enchanting the shades with his Thracian lyre,
If Pollux could ransom his brother, taking turns
With death, traveling the way so many times—
Not to mention Theseus and Hercules.   155
I too am descended from Jove most high."

So Aeneas prayed, clutching the altars.
And the Sibyl answered:

                                        "Goddess-born son
Of Trojan Anchises, the road down
To Avernus is easy. Day and night   160
The door to black Dis stands open.
But to retrace your steps and come out
To the upper air, this is the task,
The labor. A few, whom Jupiter

[handwritten annotations: "every greek/minor world myth"; "Aneas asks for access to the underworld"]

Has favored, or whom bright virtue   165
Has lifted to heaven, sons of the gods,
Have succeeded. All the central regions
Are swathed in forest, and Cocytus
Enfolds it with its winding, dark water.
But if you have such longing, such dread desire 170
To cross the Styx twice, twice to see
Black Tartarus, and if it pleases you
To indulge this madness as a sacred mission,
Listen to what you must do first.
Hidden in a darkling tree there lies   175
A golden bough, blossoming gold
In leaf and pliant branch, held sacred
To the goddess below. A grove conceals
This bough on every side, and umber shadows
Veil it from view in a valley dim.   180
No one may pass beneath the earth
Until he has plucked from the tree
This golden-leaved fruit. Fair Proserpina
Decrees it be brought to her as a gift.
When one bough is torn away another   185
Grows in its place and leafs out in gold.
Search it out with your deepest gaze
And, when you find it, pluck it with your hand.
It will come off easily, of itself,
If the Fates call you. Otherwise you will not   190
Wrench it off by force or cut it with steel.
Farther, there lies unburied (ah, you do not know)
The lifeless body of your friend,
Defiling the entire fleet with his death
While you seek counsel at my doorstep.   195
Bear him to his resting place and bury him
In the tomb. Then lead black cattle here
As first victims to expiate your sins.
Only then will you see the Stygian groves
And realms closed to the living."

                    She spoke,   200
Closed her lips, and said no more.

Aeneas
Left the cave and walked on with downcast eyes,
Pondering these mysteries. Loyal Achates
Walked with him, just as worried, and the two
Talked with each other, trying to sort out   205
Which comrade might be dead, whose unburied body
The seer spoke of. Then they came to the shore
And saw on the beach the body of Misenus,
Dead before his time—Misenus, son of Aeolus,
Second to none at rousing men to war   210
With his bugle's call. He had been the companion
Of great Hector and fought at his side,
As good with a spear as he was with his horn.
But when Achilles deprived Hector of life,
Misenus joined the ranks of Aeneas,   215
Unwilling to follow a lesser hero.
But today he had been sounding a conch shell,
Making it blare and sing like the sea, insanely
Challenging the gods to a contest. Triton
Was jealous and, if the tale is true, caught   220
The man and drowned him in the rocks and surf.
And so they gathered around and mourned,
And Aeneas led the echoing dirge,
Since this also was his duty. Then,
In tears, they hurried to carry out   225
The Sibyl's orders, piling up trees
For his tomb's altar and rearing it skyward.
Then into the primeval forest, the deep lairs
Of wild things—and down fell the pines,
The ilex rang with the axe, ash logs and oak   230
Were split with wedges, and enormous trunks
Rolled down the mountainside.

Aeneas
Led the way in this work also, wielding
The same tools and cheering on his men.
But his heart was heavy, and as he gazed   235
At the deep woods a prayer came to his lips:

"Let the golden bough show itself now

On a tree in this forest, since the prophetess
Was all too right about you, Misenus!"

He had scarcely spoken when twin doves   240
Came fluttering down from heaven
Before his very eyes and settled
On the green grass. Aeneas' mind soared
When he saw his mother's birds, and he prayed:

"Show me the way, float on the air to the heart   245
Of the forest, where the earth lies soft
In the shadow of the radiant bough
And you, Goddess and Mother, do not fail me
In these doubtful times."

                    And he stood quietly,
Watching, tracking their direction in the trees.
The doves, as they fed, flew only as far   250
As someone following could keep them in sight.
But when they came to the jaws of Avernus,
With its foul smell, they ascended swiftly,
And then, gliding down through the limpid air,   255
They sat side by side on their chosen perch,
A tree through whose branches there shone
A discordant halo, a haze of gold.

During winter's cold, deep in the woods,
Mistletoe blooms with strange leafage   260
On a tree not its own and entwines
The burled branches with its yellow fruit.

Such was the gold seen on the dark ilex,
And so rustled its foil in the gentle breeze.
Aeneas seized it at once, and though the bough   265
Hesitated, he broke it off eagerly and brought it
Safely back beneath the Sibyl's roof.

The Trojans were still lamenting Misenus
There on the shore, performing final rites
For thankless ash. First, they built a huge pyre   270

[Handwritten annotations: "isn't this changing fate by leading him to the golden?"; "I think Venus is intervening and he shouldn't have this. he never fully finished mourning."; "Aeneas with Venus's help finds the golden bough"]

Out of resinous pine and split oak,
Then trimmed its sides with gloomy foliage
And set up before it funereal cypresses.
They adorned the top with glittering arms.
Others heated water in bronze cauldrons   275
And bathed and anointed the cold body.
A cry went up. And then they placed the corpse,
Wet with their tears, onto the couch
And draped it with his familiar purple robes.
A small group lifted the heavy bier,   280
A poignant service, and with eyes averted
In ancestral manner, lit the fire. Flames crackled
Around the gifts heaped on the pyre—frankincense,
Platters of food, bowls filled with olive oil.
After the embers collapsed and the flames   285
Died away, they doused the remnant
Of glowing ash with wine. Corynaeus
Gathered the bones and placed them in an urn.
Then he circled the company three times,
Sprinkling them with water fresh as dew   290
From an olive branch, and so purified the men.
Then he spoke some last words. Aeneas,
In an act of piety, heaped above Misenus
A huge burial mound—with the hero's arms,
Horn, and oar—beneath a soaring hill   295
That is still called Misenus
And will bear that name throughout the ages.

The funeral was finished. Aeneas turned all his attention
To the Sibyl's commands.

                         There was a deep cave
With a jagged, yawning mouth, sheltered   300
By a dusky lake and a wood's dark shade.
Over this no winged thing could fly, so putrid
And so foul were the fumes that issued
From the cave's black jaws and rose to the sky
(And so the Greeks called the place Avernus).   305
Here the priestess set in line four black bulls,
Poured wine upon their brows, and plucked

[handwritten annotation: trying to show Romans are compassionate perhaps?]

[handwritten annotation: Aneas completes the funeral]

The topmost bristles from between their horns.
They set them on the sacred fire as first offerings,
Calling on Hecate, mistress of the moon   310
And of Erebus below. Others slit the bulls' throats
And caught their warm blood in bowls
While Aeneas himself sacrificed a lamb,
Black-fleeced, to Night, the Eumenides' mother,
And to Earth, her great sister. To you,   315
Proserpina, he offered a barren heifer.
Then began a sacrifice to the Lord of Styx,
As at night's darkest hour the hero lay
Carcasses of bulls on the altars, pouring rich oil
On their burning entrails. But, look, under   320
The threshold of the rising sun the ground rumbled.
The wooded ridges trembled, and dogs howled
As through the gloom the goddess drew near.

                                          "Begone,
Begone, you uninitiated!" shrieked the seer.
"Stand off from the grove! And you, Aeneas,   325
Onto the road and unsheathe your sword. Now
Is the time for courage and a heart of iron."

She spoke, then plunged wildly into the cave,
And Aeneas matched her stride for stride.

Gods of the world below, silent shades,   330
Chaos and Phlegethon, soundless tracts of Night—
Grant me the grace to tell what I have heard,
And lay bare the mysteries in earth's abyss.

On they went, shrouded in desolate night,
Through shadow, through the empty halls   335
Of Dis and his ghostly domain, as dim

   As a path in the woods under a faint moon
   When Jupiter has buried the sky in gloom
   And night has stolen color from the world.

Just before the entrance, in the very jaws   340
Of Orcus, Grief and avenging Cares

Have set their beds. Pale Diseases
Dwell there, sad Old Age, Fear, Hunger—
The tempter—and foul Poverty,
All fearful shapes, and Death and Toil,
And Death's brother Sleep, Guilty Joys,   345
And on the threshold opposite, lethal War,
The Furies in iron cells, and mad Strife,
Her snaky hair entwined with bloody bands.

In the middle a huge elm stands, spreading   350
Its aged branches, the abode of false Dreams
That cling to the bottom of every leaf.
At the doors are stabled the monstrous shapes
Of Centaurs, and biform Scyllas, and Briareus
With a hundred heads, the Lernaean Hydra,   355
Hissing horribly, the Chimaera armed with flame,
Gorgons, Harpies, and the hybrid shade of Geryon.
Suddenly panicked, Aeneas drew his sword
And turned its edge against their advance,
And if his guide had not observed   360
That they were hollow, bodiless forms,
Flitting images, he would have charged
And slashed vainly through empty shadows.

From here a road led to the Tartarean waters
Of Acheron, where a huge whirlpool,   365
Churning with mire, belched all its sand
Into Cocytus. The keeper of these waters
Was Charon, the grim ferryman, frightening
In his squalor. Unkempt hoary whiskers
Bristled on his chin, his eyes like flares   370
Were sunk in flame, and a filthy cloak hung
By a knot from his shoulder. He poled the boat
Himself, and trimmed the sails, hauling the dead
In his rusty barge. He was already old,
But a god's old age is green and raw.   375

And now a whole crowd rushed streaming
To the banks, mothers and husbands, bodies
Of high-souled heroes finished with life,

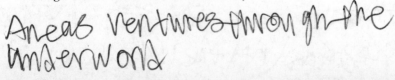

Boys and unwed girls, and young men
Placed upon the pyre before their parents' eyes.   380

> As many as leaves that fall in the woods
> At autumn's first frost, as many as birds
> That teem to shore when the cold year
> Drives them over the sea to sunny lands.

There they stood, begging to be the first   385
Ferried across, hands stretched out in love — *desperate*
For the farther shore. But the grim boatman
Culled through the crowd, accepting some,
But keeping the others back from the sand.

Aeneas, shocked by this mob of souls, said: 390

"What does this mean, priestess, the spirits
Crowding to the river? How is it decided
That some must leave the banks while others
Sweep the bruised water with oars?"

And the priestess, ancient of years: 395

"Son of Anchises and true son of the gods, — *that's a stretch*
You are looking at the lagoons of Cocytus
And the river Styx, by whose name
Even the gods fear to swear falsely. — *strength of it*
The crowd you see are the unburied dead;   400
The ferryman is Charon; his passengers
Are the dead entombed. He may not carry
Any across the raucous, dread water — *why they buried*
Until their bones are at rest. Else, *Misnews*
A hundred years they must roam the shoreline   405
And only then may return to cross these shoals."

The son of Anchises stopped in his tracks,
Pondering all this, and pitied in his heart
Their unjust lot. He saw among them,
Sad and bereft of death's due, Leucaspis,   410
And Orontes, captain of the Lycian fleet,

Aeneas sees the dead unable to cross Styx

Overwhelmed by the storm that engulfed their ships
As they sailed the windy seas out of Troy.

And now there came Palinurus, who
While reckoning their course from Libya   415
By the stars had fallen from the stern
Into the waves. Aeneas hardly knew him,
Forlorn in the deep gloom, but finally
Recognized him and called out:

                         "Palinurus,
What god tore you from us and plunged you   420
Into the open sea? Apollo, never before
Found false, deluded me when he foretold
You would escape the sea and reach Ausonia."

And Palinurus:

                    "Delphi did not mislead you,
My captain, nor did any god drown me.
The rudder I was holding to steer our course   425
Ripped apart, and as I fell headlong I
Dragged it down with me. I swear by the wild sea
I was not so afraid for myself as for your ship,
Afraid that stripped of its gear and its pilot overboard   430
It might founder and sink in the heavy weather.
Three stormy nights the South Wind drove me
Over boundless seas. As the fourth dawn broke
I rode the crest of a wave and sighted
Italy. I fought my way toward land and thought   435
I had safety in my grasp. I hooked my fingers
On a crag of shore, but weighed down
By my dripping clothes I was easy prey
For a band of marauders. Wind and surf
Now roll my body along the tide line.   440
By the sweet light and the air of heaven,
By your father, by the promise Iülus holds,
Save me from these woes, Aeneas unconquered!
Either cast earth upon me—it is in your power
If you sail back to Velia—or if your divine mother   445

[Handwritten annotations: "Apollo is their true god and can never be wrong"; "their reason for landing in Italy"; "Aeneas learns what happened to Palinurus"]

Shows you how (surely it is not your plan
To sail the great Styx without divine power),
Give me your hand and take me with you
Across these waves, so that I may at least
Find in death my final resting place."   450

Thus Palinurus, and the Sibyl answered him:

"Where did you get this outrageous desire?
Are you, unburied, to look upon the Styx,
The Furies' stream, and approach these shores
Unbidden? Stop hoping that the gods' decrees   455
Can be bent with prayer. But hear this
And bear it in your heart as consolation.
The neighboring peoples, in cities far and wide,
Will be driven by portents to appease your bones,
Will build a tomb, and to the tomb will tender   460
Solemn offerings, and forever the place
Will be called Palinurus."

                    By these words
His anguish was relieved, his grief dispelled.
And the land rejoices in the name Palinurus.

Continuing their journey, they drew near the river.   465
Out on the water the boatman saw them
Heading to the bank through the silent wood,
And before they could speak he rebuked them:

"Hold it right there, whoever you are
Coming to our river in arms! Why are you here?   470
This is the Land of Shadows, of Sleep
And drowsy Night. Living bodies
May not be transported in this Stygian keel.
I was not happy to take Hercules
Across the lake, or Theseus and Pirithoüs,   475
Invincible sons of the gods though they were.
One of them wanted to drag off in chains
The Tartarean watchdog from Pluto's throne—

[handwritten marginalia: Why is it outrage when everyone wantes this?]

[handwritten marginalia: seems like living bodies can cross]

[handwritten marginalia: Aeneas prepares to cross the river Styx]

And dragged him off trembling. The others tried
To carry off the queen from the bedroom of Dis."   480

Apollo's prophetess responded briefly:

"There is no such treachery here. Calm down.
Our weapons offer no threat of violence.
The giant watchdog may howl from his cave
Eternally and frighten the bloodless shades.   485
Proserpina may keep her chastity intact
Within her uncle's doors. Aeneas of Troy,
Famed as a warrior and man of devotion,
Goes down to his father in lowest Erebus.
If this picture of piety in no way moves you,   490
Yet this bough" (she showed it under her robe)
"You must acknowledge."

                    Charon's engorged rage
Subsided. No more was said. Marveling
At the venerable gift, the fateful bough
So long unseen, he turned the dark-blue prow   495
Toward shore. There he cleared the deck,
Pushed the shades from the benches, and laid out
The gangplank. He took aboard his hollow boat
Huge Aeneas. Groaning under his weight,
The ragtag craft took on water. At last,   500
The swamp crossed, the ferryman disembarked
Hero and seer unharmed in the muddy sedge.

Crouching in a cavern on the farther shore
Cerberus made these regions resound,
Barking like thunder from all three of his throats.
The seer, close enough now to see the snakes
Bristling on his necks, flung a honeyed cake
Laced with drugs into his ravenous jaws.
Cerberus snatched it from the air and then
Went slack, easing his huge, limp bulk   510
To the ground, stretching out over all his den,
Dead to the world. Aeneas entered the cave
And left behind the water of no return.

[handwritten annotations: "seems very dramatic", "really trying to make him seem like the best guy ever", "poor Cerberus", "somehow, I think he will return", "Aeneas bribes charon and crosses the river"]

Now came the sound of wailing, the weeping
Of the souls of infants, torn from the breast   *515*
On a black day and swept off to bitter death
On the very threshold of their sweet life.
Nearby are those falsely condemned to die.
These places are not assigned without judge
And jury. Minos presides and shakes the urn,   *520*
Calls the silent conclave, conducts the trial.

In the next region are those wretched souls
Who contrived their own deaths. Innocent
But loathing the light, they threw away their lives
And now would gladly bear any hardship   *525*
To be in the air above. But it may not be.
The unlovely water binds them to Hell,
Styx confines them in its nine circling folds.

Not far from here the Fields of Lamentation,
As they are called, stretch into the vastness.   *530*
Here those whom Love has cruelly consumed
Languish concealed in sequestered myrtle glades,
Sorrow clinging to them even as they wander
These lost paths in death. In this region of Hell
Aeneas makes out Phaedra, Procris,   *535*
And mournful Eriphyle, displaying the wounds
She received from her son. He sees Evadne
And Pasiphaë and, walking with them,   —YOOO
Laodamia, and Caeneus, a young man once,
Now a woman, returned to her original form.   *540*
And among them, her wound still fresh,
Phoenician Dido wandered that great wood.
The Trojan hero stood close to her there
And in the gloom recognized her dim form

As faint as the new moon a man sees,   *545*
Or thinks he sees, through the evening's haze.

He broke into tears and spoke to her
With tender love:

Aeneas sees those who died from love

              "Oh, Dido, so the message was true
That you were dead, that you took your own life
With steel. Was I really the cause of your death?   550
I swear by the stars, by the powers above,
And by whatever faith lies in the depths below,
It was not my choice to leave your land, my Queen.   — crwel
The gods commanded me to go, as they force me now   gods
With their high decrees to go through this shadowland,   555
This moldy stillness, the abyss of Night.
I could not believe that I would cause you
Such grief by leaving. Stop! Don't turn away!
Who are you running from? Fate will never
Let us speak with each other again."   560

With such words Aeneas tried to soothe
Her burning soul. Tears came to his eyes,
But Dido kept her own eyes fixed on the ground,
As unmoved by his words as if her averted face
Were made of flint or Marpesian marble.   565
Finally she left, a stranger to him now, and fled
Into a darkling grove, where her old husband,
Sychaeus, comforted her and returned her love.
But Aeneas, struck by the injustice
Of her fate, wept as he watched her   570
Disappear, and pitied her as she went.

Aeneas and the Sibyl now made their way
To the farthest fields, a place set apart
For the great war heroes. Here Tydeus
And renowned Parthenopaeus met Aeneas,   575
And the pale shade of Adrastus. And here,
Lamented on earth and fallen in war,
Were many Dardanians. Aeneas moaned
When he saw their long ranks:
Glaucus, Medon, and Thersilochus,   580
Antenor's three sons; Polyboetes,
Priest of Ceres, and Idaeus,
Still with his chariot, still bearing arms.
They crowded around him, right and left,
And it was not enough for these shades   585

Aeneas ventures throngs
the underworld

To have seen him: they want to linger,
To walk beside him and learn why he came.
But as soon as the foremost Danaans
And the battalions of Agamemnon
Saw Aeneas' arms flashing in the gloom,   590
They trembled with fear. Some turned to run,
As if fleeing again to their beachhead camp.
Others tried to shout, but their voices,
Thin and faint, mocked their gaping mouths.

And here Aeneas saw Deïphobus,   *once again* 595
Son of Priam, his whole body mangled   *wounds of war.,*
And his face cruelly mutilated, shredded,   *Greeks are*
And both hands gone. His ears had been torn   *monsters*
From the sides of his head, and his nostrils lopped
With a shameful wound. Aeneas scarcely   600
Recognized him as he trembled, struggling
To hide his brutal disfigurement. He paused
But then addressed him in familiar tones:

"Deïphobus, mighty warrior
Of Teucer's high blood, who took delight   605
In such torture? Who dared treat you like this?
Word reached me that on that last night, weary
With endless slaughter of Greeks, you fell
On a heap of tangled corpses. I set up for you
An empty tomb on the Rhoetian shore   610
And called three times upon your ghost.
Your name and your arms guard the place.
You, my friend, I could not see, nor bury you
In your native soil before I had to leave."

And Priam's son responded:

                    "My friend,   615
You have left nothing undone but have paid
All that is due to Deïphobus' shade.
My own fate, and that lethal Spartan woman,
Plunged me into this misery. She left
These memorials! You know how we spent   620

Aeneas speaks to Deïphobus

That last night in delusive joy. You know,
You remember all too well. When the Horse
Leapt to the city's high, holy place, its womb
Heavy with infantry, Helen feigned
A ritual dance and led the Trojan women   625
Crying in ecstasy around Pergamum's heights
While she herself held the huge, blazing torch
That signaled the Greeks from the citadel.
I was asleep in our ill-starred bedroom,
Worn out with care, wrapped in slumber   630
As peaceful as death, while Helen,
My incomparable wife, was busy removing
Every weapon from the house and even slipped
My trusty sword from under my head.
Then she called Menelaus inside,   635
Hoping this would please her lover
And wipe out the memory of her old sins.
Why draw it out? They burst into my room,
Ulysses with them, the evil counselor.
                         O Gods,
If my face is pious enough to pray for vengeance   640
Make the Greeks pay in kind!
                         But you,
Tell me now, what has brought you here,
Alive? Were you driven here while roaming the sea,
Or by Heaven's command? Why do you visit
The drear confusion of this sunless realm?"   645

While they were talking, Dawn had climbed
High up the sky in her roselight chariot,
And they might have spent all their allotted time
On these matters had not the Sibyl warned:

"Night is coming on, Aeneas, yet we   650
Weep away the hours. Here is the place
Where the road splits into two. To the right,
Winding under the walls of great Dis,
Is the way to Elysium. But the left road

Takes the wicked to their punishment   655
In Tartarus."

      Deïphobus responded:

"Do not be angry, great priestess. I will go
And return to my place in the shadows. But you,
Glory of our race, go. Go to a happier fate."

And on this word he turned away.   660

Aeneas suddenly looked back and saw,
Under a cliff to the left, a great fortification
Surrounded by a triple wall and encircled
By a river of fire—Phlegethon—
That rolled thunderous rocks in its current.   665
The Gate was flanked by adamantine columns
That could not be destroyed by any force,
Human or divine. High on a tower of iron,
Tisiphone sat, draped in a bloody pall,
Sleeplessly watching the portal night and day.   670
Groans, the crack of the lash, iron clanking,
And dragging chains grated on the ear.
Stunned by the noise, Aeneas froze in his tracks.

"What evil is here, priestess, what forms of torture,
What lamentation rising on the air?"   675

And the Sibyl began:

       "Teucrian hero,
No virtuous soul may ever set foot
On this accursed threshold, but when Hecate
Made me mistress of the groves of Avernus
She showed me all of the punishments   680
The gods inflict.
      Cretan Rhadamanthus
Rules this iron realm. He queries each soul,
Hears his lies, and forces him to confess

Aeneas comes to the place of torture

The sins whose atonement he has postponed,
In his deluded vanity, until too late. At once,   685
Tisiphone pounces upon the guilty soul
With her avenging scourge, brandishing
Glaring serpents in her left fist as she calls
Her sister Furies. Then, metal grinding
Upon metal, slowly open the Gates of Hell.   690
Do you see the face of the Fury who guards
The vestibule? The Hydra lurking within
Is much worse—fifty gaping black throats.
    Then there is the pit of Tartarus itself,
Plunging down into darkness twice as deep   695
As Olympus is high. Here Earth's ancient brood,
The Titans, struck down by the thunderbolt,
Writhe in the abyss. And here too I saw
The twin sons of Aloeus, the Giants who tried
To tear open the sky and pull Jupiter down.   700
And I saw Salmoneus suffering torment
For aping the Olympian's thunder and lightning.
Torches shaking, he drove his chariot
Through all the cities of Greece in triumph,
And he brought his show of smoke and mirrors   705
Home to Elis, demanding a divinity's honors
For mimicking with bronze and horses' hooves
The inimitable rumble of thunderheads.
But the Father Almighty hurled his bolt—
No smoky torch—through the thick clouds   710
And blasted the sinner into perdition.
And Tityos is there, another son of Earth,
His body stretched over nine full acres,
And a monstrous vulture with a hooked beak
Gnaws away at his immortal liver   715
And tortured entrails, pecking deep for its feasts.
The bird lives in his bowels while his flesh,
Like his pain, is renewed endlessly.
And then there are the Lapiths, Ixion
And Pirithoüs, above whom a black rock   720
Totters, ever about to fall. Before their eyes
A banquet fit for a king is spread,
And high festive couches gleam with gold.

Reclining there, the eldest Fury
Keeps their hands from touching the table,   725
Rearing up with a torch and roaring 'No!'
    Here are those who hated their brothers,
Struck a parent, or betrayed a client;
Those who hoarded the wealth they had won,
Saving none for their kin (the largest group this);   730
Those slain for adultery; those who did not fear
To desert their masters in treasonous war—
All these await their punishment within.
Do not ask its form, or what fortune undid them.
Some roll huge stones, or hang outstretched   735
On the spokes of a wheel. Theseus sits
And will sit forever. Phlegyas in his agony
Lifts his voice through the gloom, admonishing all:
'Learn justice, beware, do not slight the gods.'
This one sold his country for gold and installed   740
A tyrant; another made and unmade laws
For a price. This one went to his daughter's bed.
All dared a great crime, and did what they dared.
Not if I had a hundred mouths, a hundred tongues,
And a voice of iron, could I recount   745
All the crimes or tell all their punishments."

Thus the aged priestess of Apollo.

"But come, pick up your pace, and complete
What you came for," the Sibyl continued. "Hurry!
I see the walls forged by the Cyclopes   750
And the gates in the archway opposite, where
We have been told to place our offering."

They went side by side down dusky paths
And drew near the doors. Aeneas
Stood on the threshold, sprinkled his body   755
With fresh water, and fixed the bough in place.

The offering to the goddess complete,
Aeneas and the Sibyl now came
To regions of joy, the green and pleasant fields

essentially heaven

Of the Blissful Groves. Air and sky   760
Are more spacious here, and the light shines
With an amethyst glow. The land here knows
Its own sun and stars.

               Some are at exercise
On the grassy wrestling ground, some contend
On the yellow sand, others tread a dance   765
And chant a choral song. And Orpheus,
In the long robes of a Thracian priest,
Accompanies them on his seven-toned lyre,
Plucking notes with his fingers and ivory quill.
Here too is the ancient race of Teucer,   770
A people most fair, high-souled heroes
Born in better times—Ilus, Assaracus,
And Dardanus, founder of Troy. — *seem significant*

               Aeneas
Wonders at their weapons and chariots,
Mere phantoms, and yet their spears   775
Stand fixed in the ground, and their horses
Graze unyoked over all the plain.
The pleasure they took in arms and chariots
When they were alive, in keeping sleek horses,
Is still theirs now beneath the earth.   780
And he sees others, to the right and left,
Scattered on the grass, feasting, or singing
Songs of joy in a fragrant grove of laurel
Where the Eridanus rolls its mighty waters
Through forests to the world above.

              Here too are those   785
Wounded fighting in their country's defense,
Those who in life were priests and poets,
Bards whose words were worthy of Apollo;   *gods deemed them worthy*
Also, those who enriched life with inventions
Or earned remembrance for service rendered—   790
Their brows bound with bands as white as snow.
When they had gathered around, the Sibyl
Addressed them, Musaeus especially,
Who stood head and shoulders above the others:

Aeneas comes to Elysium

"Tell me, blessed souls, and you, best of poets,   *795*
Which part of this realm harbors Anchises?
For him we have crossed the rivers of Erebus."

The great soul Musaeus answered her briefly:

"We have no fixed homes but dwell in shadowed
Groves, recline on riverbanks, and live in meadows   *800*
Freshened by streams. But if you so wish,
Over this ridge I can show you an easy path."

He led them up and pointed out to them
Shining fields below. The pair went down.

Anchises, deep in a green valley, was reviewing   *805*
As a proud father the souls of his descendants
Yet to be born into the light, contemplating
Their destinies, their great deeds to come.
When he saw his son striding toward him
Through the grass, he stretched out   *810*
His trembling hands, tears wet his cheeks,
And these words fell from his lips:

"You have come at last! I knew your devotion   *loving family is important*
Would see you through the long, hard road.
I can look upon your face, and we can hear   *815*
Each other's familiar voices again.
I have been counting the hours carefully
Until this day, and my love has not deceived me.
All the lands and seas, all the dangers
You have been through, my son! How I feared   *820*
You would come to harm in Libya."

And Aeneas:

        "You, Father, your sad image,
Kept appearing to me, leading me here.
Our ships stand offshore in the Italian sea.
Let me hold your hands in mine, Father,   *825*
Do not pull away from my embrace!"

Aeneas finally sees his father

As Aeneas said this he began to weep.
Three times he tried to put his arms
Around his father's neck. Three times
His father's wraith slipped through his hands,   830
As light as wind, as fleeting as a dream.

[handwritten margin note: Still can't to see him]

While they talked in this sequestered valley
A secluded grove caught Aeneas' eye.
A stream drifted past its rustling thickets—
The river Lethe—and around it hovered   835
Nations of souls, innumerable

> *As bees on a cloudless summer day*
> *That settle upon wildflowers in a field*
> *And swarm so thickly around the white lilies*
> *That the whole meadow hums and murmurs.*   840

[handwritten margin note: building a calm and beautiful tone]

Aeneas was shaken at the sight
And asked, in his ignorance, the reason
For this congregation. What was the river,
And who were the men crowding its banks?
Father Anchises answered: 845

"These are souls owed another body by Fate.
In the ripples of Lethe they sip the waters
Of forgetfulness and timeless oblivion.
I have been longing to show them to you,
The census of my generations, so that you   850
May rejoice as I do at finding Italy."

"Father, can it be that souls go from here
To the world above and return again
To their gross bodies? What is this yearning
For these poor souls to taste the light?"   855

[handwritten margin note: reference to pythagoras beliefs?]

Aeneas asked this.

           "I will tell you, my son,
And not keep you in doubt."

[handwritten note at bottom: Aeneas witnesses the fields of Elysium]

Anchises answered,
And he revealed the mysteries one by one.

"First, heaven and earth, the sea's expanse,
The moon's bright globe, the sun and stars   860
Are all sustained by a spirit within.
Every part is infused with Mind,
Which moves the Whole, the source of life
For man and beast and all winged things
And the monsters of the marmoreal deep.   865
A divine fire pulses within those seeds of life,
A celestial energy, but it is slowed and dulled
By mortal frames, earthly bodies doomed to die.
And so men fear and desire, sorrow and exult,
And, shut in the shade of their prison-houses,   870
Cannot see the sky. Nor, when the last gleam
Of life flickers out, are all the ills
That flesh is heir to completely uprooted,
But many corporeal taints remain,
Ingrained in the soul in myriad ways.   875
And so we are disciplined and expiate
Our bygone sins. Some souls are hung
Spread to the winds; others are cleansed
Under swirling waters or purged by fire.
We each suffer our own ghosts. Then we are sent   880
Through spacious Elysium, and a few enjoy
The Blessed Fields, until the fullness of time
Removes the last trace of stain, leaving only
The pure flame of ethereal spirit.
                                   All these,
When they have rolled the wheel of time   885
Through a thousand years, will be called by God
In a great assembly to the river Lethe,
So that they return to the vaulted world
With no memory and may begin again
To desire rebirth in a human body."   890

Anchises paused, and he led his son,
Along with the Sibyl, into the heart

Of the murmuring crowd. He chose a mound
From which he could scan all their faces
As they passed by in long procession.   895

"Now I will set forth the glory that awaits
The Trojan race, the illustrious souls
Of the Italian heirs to our name.
I will teach you your destiny.

[handwritten: what awaits him in afterlife or life?]

That youth you see leaning on an untipped spear   900
Is first in line to be reborn, first in the upper air
From Italian blood mingled with ours,
Silvius, an Alban name, your last child,
Born in your twilight years and reared by your wife,
Lavinia, in a sylvan home,   905
To be a king and father of kings.
We shall rule through him in Alba Longa.

Next comes Procas, pride of our race,
Then Capys and Numitor, and then
Your avatar, Aeneas Sylvius,   910
Equal to you in piety and arms,
If ever he succeeds to Alba's throne.
Look at these young men, their strength,
Their brows shaded with civic oak!
They will build for you Nomentum, Gabii,   915
And the town of Fidena. They will crown
Collatia's hills with towers and will found
Pometii and Inuus, Bola and Cora,
Famous names someday, now places without names.
Then a son of Mars will support his grandsire—   920
Romulus, born to Ilia from the line of Assaracus.
Do you see the double plumes on his head,
And how the Father of Gods honors him
As one of his own? Under his auspices,
My son, Rome will extend her renowned empire   925
To earth's horizons, her glory to the stars.
She will enclose seven hills within the wall
Of one city, blessed with a brood of heroes

[handwritten: Rome was written in the stars, glorious destiny]

[handwritten: Anchises describes Aeneas + Romes]

As the Berecynthian Mother
Is blessed with a brood divine, riding   930
In her chariot through Phrygian towns,
Wearing her turreted diadem, and embracing
A hundred grandsons, <u>all of them gods,</u>   — *referencing*
<u>All of them with homes in high heaven.</u>   *Roman emperors*

Now turn your gaze here and let it rest upon   935
Your family of Romans. Here is Caesar,
And here are all of the descendants of Iülus
Destined to come under heaven's great dome.
And here is the man promised to you,   *wow, this is*
<u>Augustus Caesar, born of the gods,</u> — *not subtle*   940
Who will establish again a Golden Age
In the fields of Latium once ruled by Saturn
And will expand his dominion
Beyond the Indus and the Garamantes,
Beyond our familiar stars, beyond the yearly   945
Path of the sun, to the land where Atlas
Turns the star-studded sphere on his shoulders.

Even now the Caspian Sea trembles   *Jesus christ*
<u>At the oracles that foretell his coming,</u> — *this is a lot*
As does Persia, and the seven-mouthed Nile.   950
Not even Hercules ranged so far
Though he shot the bronze-hooved stag, brought calm
To Erymanthus' groves, and made Lerna quake
At his bow. Nor did Bacchus, though he drove
Tigers yoked with vine shoots from Nysa's heights.   955
And still we shrink from extending our virtue,
And fear to take our stand in Ausonia?

But who is this in the distance, resplendent
In his olive crown and sacred insignia?
I know that white hair and beard.   960
This is Numa, who will lay a foundation
Of law in our city, sent from a small town
In Sabine country to command a great nation.

Augustus Caesar uses
a not subtle way of saying
he's the best

Coming up after Numa is Tullus,
Who will shatter his country's leisure   965
And rouse to war men sunk in idleness
And an army unaccustomed to triumphs.

Hard upon Tullus' heels is Ancus,
Flaunting himself, blowing even now
In winds of popular favor.
                    Would you like to see   970
The Tarquin kings, the proud, avenging
Spirit of Brutus, and the rods of office
He will recover? He will be first to receive
The power of consul, and the stern axes.
When his sons stir up rebellious war   975
Their own father will exact punishment
In sweet liberty's name, an unhappy man
However the future might judge his deeds.
Love of country will prevail with him,
And a boundless desire for glory.   980

Look at the Decii and Drusi, still in the distance,
And Torquatus ferocious with his battle-axe,
And Camillus with the legion's standards regained.

But the two you see there, a match for each other
In resplendent armor, harmonious souls   985
While they are buried in night—what wars will they wage
Against each other, what civil slaughter
Should they ever reach the light, the bride's father
Marching down the Alps from Monaco,
His son-in-law drawing up his Oriental troops!   990
Do not inure yourselves to such war, my sons,
Nor rend your country's body with strife.
And you, child of Olympus, should show
Clemency first. Cast down your weapons,
My own flesh and blood. . . .   995

There is Corinth's conqueror, whose chariot
Will ascend the Capitoline Hill in triumph
After the slaughter of his Greek enemies.

Anchises continues his description

And here is the Roman who will uproot Argos
And Agamemnon's Mycenae, and even the blood   1000
Of Aeacus, mighty Achilles' grandsire,
Avenging Troy and Minerva's temple.
Who, great Cato, could leave you unsung,
Or you, Cottus? Or the Gracchi brothers;
Or the two Scipios, twin thunderbolts of war   1005
And bane of Carthage; or Fabricius,
Whose power will be thrift, or you, Serranus,
Who left your plow? And you Fabii,
Where do you draw my weary gaze? Ah,
You are Fabius Maximus, whose strategy   1010
Was delay, and who alone saved our state.

Others will, no doubt, hammer out bronze
That breathes more softly, and draw living faces
Out of stone. They will plead cases better
And chart the rising of every star in the sky.   1015
Your mission, Roman, is to rule the world.
These will be your arts: to establish peace,
To spare the humbled, and to conquer the proud."

Thus Anchises, and as they marvel he adds:

"Look at Marcellus, proud in choice spoils   1020
Torn from the vanquished enemy commander,
Towering triumphant over all the crowd!
When the Roman state is falling in ruin
He will set it upright; he will trample down
The Carthaginians, crush the rebel Gauls,   1025
And offer to Quirinus a third set of arms."

At this, Aeneas, seeing a youth pass by
Beautiful in his gleaming armor
But with downcast eyes and troubled brow,
Asked his father:

                    "Who is this,   1030
At the hero's side? His son, or another
In his great line of descendants? What

[Handwritten annotations: "though that state is now ruined", "shows that Rome is spreading its wonderful messages", "Anchises describes the wonder of Rome"]

An impression he makes with his crowd of followers!
But the shadow of death enshrouds his head."

And Anchises, tears welling up in his eyes: *1035*

"Son, do not seek your people's great grief.
Fate will permit him on earth a brief while,
But not for long. Gods above, you thought Rome
Would be too powerful had your gift endured.
What lamentation of the brave will hang   *1040*
Over the Field of Mars. O River Tiber,
What a funeral you will see as you glide past
His new tomb. No boy bred of Troy will ever raise
The hope of his Latin forefathers so high,
Nor the land of Romulus ever be so proud   *1045*
Of any of its sons. O, lament
His devotion, lament his pristine honor
And his sword arm invincible in war!
No enemy would have faced him unscathed,
Whether he fought on foot or dug his spurs   *1050*
Into the flanks of a foaming stallion.
If only you could shatter Fate, poor boy.
You will be Marcellus! Let me strew
Armfuls of lilies and scatter purple blossoms,
Hollow rites to honor my descendant's shade."   *1055*

And so they wandered every region of the wide,
Airy plain, surveying all it contained.
When Anchises had led his son
Through every detail and enflamed his soul
With longing for the glory that was to come,   *1060*
He told him of the wars he next must wage,
Of the Laurentine people and Latinus' town,
And how to face or flee each waiting peril.

There are two Gates of Sleep. One, they say,
Is horn, and offers easy exit for true shades.   *1065*
The other is finished with glimmering ivory,
But through it the Spirits send false dreams
To the world above. Anchises escorted his son

As he talked, then sent him with the Sibyl
Through the Gate of Ivory.   *1070*
Aeneas made his way to the ships,
Rejoined his men, and sailed along the coast
To Caieta's harbor. They cast anchor
From the prow; the sterns faced the shore.

AENEID SEVEN

You too Caieta, nurse of Aeneas,
Have by your death given eternal fame
To our shores. Still your resting place
Is honored, and if bones can lie in glory
So lie yours beneath your name   *5*
In great Hesperia.

        When the last rites
Were done, and her burial mound heaped up,
Godly Aeneas set sail from the haven
As soon as the high seas had subsided.
Breezes blew on into the night, and the moon   *10*
Shone white on the tremulous water below,
Lighting their voyage. Hugging the coastline,
They passed the land where Circe,
Daughter of the Sun, lived in opulence.
The woodland rang with her perpetual song,   *15*
And in her high house she burned fragrant cedar
To illumine the night while she worked the loom,
Combing her shrill shuttle through delicate threads.
And from those shores could also be heard
Lions roaring and snapping at their chains   *20*
Late into the night, the raging of bristled boars
And caged bears, and huge wolf-shapes howling.
All these were men whom Circe had cruelly drugged
And clad in the hides and faces of beasts.
But Neptune, to save the good Trojans   *25*
From these monstrous transformations,

Kept them from landing on those deadly shores,
Filling their sails with wind, and bearing them past
The seething shoals and out of danger.

Now the sea was reddening, and Dawn,   30
Saffron in her rosy chariot, shone in the sky,
When the winds fell and every breeze died down.
As the oars struggled in the smooth, marble water,
Aeneas, still far offshore, looked out and saw
A vast forest, and flowing through it   35
The beautiful Tiber, its current swirling
With golden sand as it broke into the sea.
Above and all about, birds of many kinds
That haunted the banks and bed of the river
Flew through the woods, enchanting the air   40
With their trilling.
                    Aeneas ordered his men
To change course and turn their prows landward,
And with joy he drew into the shady river.

And now, Erato, who were the kings
And what was the state of ancient Latium   45
When this foreign army landed in Italy?
Help me, Goddess, your sacred poet,
Recall the prelude to the hostilities,
For I will tell of war's horror, of pitched battle,
Heroes driven by courage to meet their doom,   50
Of Etruscan squadrons, and all Hesperia
Pressed into arms. A higher order of things
Opens before me; a greater work now begins.

King Latinus, old and grey, ruled over lands
And cities through a long twilight of peace.   55
He was born, we are told, from Faunus
And the Laurentine nymph Marica.
Faunus' father was Picus, and Picus
Looked to you, Saturn, as his father:
You were the founder of the royal line.   60
Latinus' son, his sole male heir, was gone,

Torn away by Fate in the springtime of youth.
He had only a daughter to keep his great house,
A daughter ripe for marriage, a bride to be,
Courted by many in broad Latium, by many   65
From all Ausonia, and the handsomest of all
Was Turnus. He was from old blood, powerful,
And Latinus' queen was strangely passionate
To join him to herself as her son in marriage.

But portents from the gods warned otherwise.   70

A sacred laurel stood in the inner courtyard
Of the palace, tended in awe for many years.
Latinus himself is said to have found this tree
When he first built the citadel. He dedicated
Its foliage to Phoebus Apollo   75
And from its name called his people
The Laurentines. A thick swarm of bees
Buzzing and humming through the crystal air
Settled in the top of this tree, and—
A sign and a wonder—hung with feet interlaced   80
From the highest branch—a sudden hive.
At once the seer cries:

              "I see an outlander—
Troops arriving from the same direction
As these bees, seeking and mastering the citadel."

And again, while Lavinia at her father's side   85
Kindled the altar with a hallowed torch,
Her long hair, to everyone's horror, caught fire.
Flames crackled in her headdress, her jeweled tiara
Flared with heat, and the princess herself,
Shrouded in glowing yellow smoke,   90
Scattered Vulcan's sparks throughout the palace.
This ghastly miracle was reported widely
And taken to mean that the princess's future was bright,
But that a great war would come upon her people.

The king was troubled by these portents   95
And consulted the oracle of Faunus,
His prophetic father, the vatic grove
Beneath high Albunea, a great forest
That echoes with the sound of a sacred spring
And breathes mephitic vapors from its shadows.   100
The people of Italy and all Oenotria
Come to consult this oracle in time of doubt.
It is here the priest brings his offerings,
And when he has lain down to sleep
Upon the fleeces of slaughtered sheep   105
In the still of the night, he sees many phantoms
Flitting about in strange ways, hears
Many voices, converses with the gods,
And speaks to Acheron in Avernus' depths.
Father Latinus came to consult this oracle.   110
He slaughtered a hundred yearling sheep
In ritual order and lay himself down
Cushioned by their woolly fleece. Suddenly,
A voice came from deep within the grove:

"Seek not, my son, to marry your daughter   115
Into a Latin family. Trust not a wedding
Already prepared. A stranger will come
To be your son-in-law. His blood will exalt
Our name to the stars, and his children's children
Will see the world turn under their feet,   120
And their rule will stretch over all that the Sun
Looks down upon, from sea to shining sea."

Thus the response of father Faunus,
His warning given in the dead of night.
And Latinus did not keep it a secret. Rumor   125
Took flight and had already spread the news
Through all the cities of Ausonia
When the men of Laomedon's Troy
Were mooring their ships to the Tiber's grassy banks.

Aeneas and his captains, and fair Iülus,   130
Reclined in the shade of a towering tree

And spread out a feast on the grass below,
Heaping fruits of the field—Jupiter himself
Gave them this notion—on wheat flatbread
To supplement the meal. When they had eaten   *135*
Everything else, their appetites drove them
To break the scored, fateful rounds into sections
And sink their teeth into the crusty bread.

"We're so hungry we're even eating our tables!"

Iülus said this in jest and said no more,   *140*
But Aeneas heard it as the first sign
That their trials were ending. Awestruck,
He seized upon his son's words and cried:

"Hail to the Promised Land and faithful gods
Of Troy! Here is our home, this is our country.   *145*
My father Anchises foretold this to me—
I remember it now—one of Fate's secrets:
'When you are borne, my son, to shores unknown,
And hunger compels you to eat your tables,
Then in your weariness hope for a home.   *150*
Build your first houses there, roof them well
With your own hands, and bank them with mounds.'
This was that hunger, the final stretch
Of all our misfortunes.
                    Come, then, be happy!
With the sun's first light we will explore these lands,   *155*
Find out who lives here, locate their city.
We will fan out from the harbor. For now, though,
Pour libations to Jove, pray to Anchises,
And set the wine again on the tables!"

                                        Aeneas spoke
And wreathed his temples with leaves.   *160*
Then he prayed to the place's indwelling spirit,
And to Earth, first of the gods, and to nymphs
And rivers yet unknown; then to Night
And Night's wheeling constellations,
To Jove of Ida and the Phrygian Mother,   *165*

And his two parents, one in heaven,
One in Erebus below. And at his prayer
The Father Almighty sent three peals of thunder
From a clear sky, set in the ether
A cloud glowing with shafts of gold,   170
And shook the cloud with his own great hand.
Word spread quickly through the Trojan ranks
That the day had come for them to found
Their promised city. They outdo each other
To renew the feast and, cheered by the great omen,   175
Fill the bowls with wine to the beaded brims.

Dawn touched the sky with her early light,
And Aeneas and his men fanned out
To reconnoiter the exact location
Of the city, its borders and coasts.   180
Some found the pool of Numicia's spring,
Others the Tiber, and still others the home
Of the brave Latin people. Aeneas ordered
A hundred ambassadors from every rank
To go to the king's majestic city,   185
All of them shaded with olive branches,
To offer gifts and beg peace for the Trojans.
They strode off quickly on their mission,
And Aeneas marked off walls for his city
With a shallow trench and started building,   190
Encircling this first settlement on the coast
With the ramped stockades of an army camp.

Now the envoys could make out the rooftops
Of Latinus' city. Outside the walls,
Young men and boys in life's early bloom   195
Were breaking in horses, riding them hard
On the dusty plain, or practicing archery,
Hurling javelins, squaring off to box,
Or running footraces—when, galloping up,
A messenger brought word to the aged king   200
That a great company had arrived, huge men
In strange dress. The king ordered them in
And took his seat upon his ancestral throne.

Stately, immense, column upon column,
Latinus' palace crowned the whole city.   205
Once the palace of Laurentine Picus,
It bristled with groves and religious awe.
Here it was auspicious for kings to receive
Their scepters and first lift the fasces. This shrine
Was their senate, here they held holy feasts,   210
And here, after the slaughter of rams,
The elders sat at long rows of tables.
Their ancestors' images, carved in cedar,
Lined the walls: aged Saturn, Italus,
And father Sabinus, who first planted the vine,   215
Pictured holding his long pruning hook,
And double-faced Janus—all of them standing
In the vestibule. And there were other kings
From the early days, and heroes who had suffered
Wounds while defending the fatherland.   220
And many arms were hung from the sacred doors,
Chariots taken in war, curved axes, helmet crests,
Massive bars of gates, javelins and shields,
And beaks wrenched from ships. And there too
Sat a figure holding the Quirinal staff,   225
In his robes of office, his left hand wielding
A sacred shield. This was Picus,
Breaker of horses. His lovesick bride, Circe,
Later struck him with her rod of gold,
And with poisonous drugs transformed him   230
Into a bird of colorful plumage.

It was into this temple of the gods
That Latinus, seated on his ancestral throne,
Summoned the Teucrians and as they entered
Welcomed them in calm and measured tones: 235

"Sons of Dardanus—for we do know your race
And your city and have heard of your sea voyage—
Tell us why have you come. What purpose, or need,
Has borne you over so many dark-blue seas
To the shores of Ausonia?   240
Whether you lost your bearings, or storm winds

Blew you off course, as often happens to those
Who sail the high seas, and so entered our river,
Do not refuse our hospitality.
Know that the Latins are Saturn's race,   245
A people just not by laws or constraints
But of their own free will, keeping the ways
Of their ancient god. And I seem to recall,
Though time has dimmed the old Auruncan tale,
How Dardanus was born in this land   250
And went from here to Phrygian Ida
And to Samothrace. It was from here he came,
From the Tyrrhenian town of Corythus.
And now he sits in the golden palace
Of the starry sky, while here on earth   255
There is one more altar to the gods above."

And Ilioneus, in response to Latinus:

"My lord, illustrious heir of Faunus,
No black storm has driven us here
To seek shelter in your land, nor has star   260
Or coastline deceived us. We have come
To your city on purpose, with willing hearts,
Exiled from a realm once the mightiest
The sun has seen from the circle of sky.
Our race is from Jove; the sons of Dardanus   265
Glory in Jove as their forebear; our king himself
Is of Jove's highest race—Trojan Aeneas,
Who sent us to you. How fierce was the storm
That swept from Mycenae over Ida's plains,
How the worlds of Europe and Asia clashed   270
In fateful conflict, has been heard the world over,
From the farthest shore lapped by Ocean
And the farthest region of the globe's five zones
Severed from us by the tropical sun.
From that deluge we have sailed the barren seas   275
And now we ask a safe strip of shore,
A little land for the gods of our country,
And water and air that are common to all.
We will hardly be a shame to your realm,

Nor shall you be lightly praised, nor shall gratitude 280
For such a deed grow dim, nor shall Ausonia
Ever regret taking Troy to her breast.
By the fortunes of Aeneas I swear,
And by his right hand steadfast in loyalty
And mighty when tested in war, 285
That many nations, many peoples have sought
Alliance with us. Do not hold us in scorn
Because we come with garlands in our hands
And words of entreaty. The fateful decrees
Of the gods in heaven have driven us 290
To seek your shores. Dardanus came from here;
Apollo calls us back and urges us on
To Tuscan Tiber and Numicia's sacred springs.
Further, Aeneas offers to you these tokens
Of our former fortune, rescued from Troy 295
As it burned. With this gold his father Anchises
Poured libation at the altars. These Priam bore
When he decreed laws to the nations—
Scepter, sacred tiara, and royal robes
That were the work of the women of Troy." 300

Ilioneus finished, and at his words Latinus
Held his face downward, reflecting deeply.
It was not Priam's embroidered purple robes
Or his scepter that moved the king. His thoughts
Were on his daughter and her marriage 305
As he brooded over Faunus' ancient oracle.

"This," he thought, "must be the foreigner
Whom the Fates have destined to be
My son in marriage and to share my power
Equally. His descendants will excel 310
In virtue, and rule the world with might."

At last, in joy, he spoke:

                    "May the gods favor
What we enter upon and their own prophecy.
You shall have what you ask for, Trojan,

And I do not spurn your gifts. While Latinus is king   315
You shall not lack rich fields or the wealth
You had at Ilium. However,
If Aeneas is eager for this alliance,
Let him come himself and not shrink
From friendly eyes. My condition for peace   320
Is that I have touched your master's hand!
Now take this message back to your lord.
Tell him I have a daughter whom oracles
From my ancestral shrine, and countless signs
From heaven, do not allow me to marry   325
To any of our race. It is Latium's destiny
That a son-in-law will come from foreign shores,
And that his blood will exalt us to the stars.
It is my belief that he is the chosen one,
And if I augur true, it is my desire."   330

And the old king picked out horses
From the three hundred in his stables
And ordered them to be led forth,
One for each of the Teucrians,
Horses swift of foot and caparisoned   335
With embroidered purple. Golden chains
Hung below their chests, their saddle cloths
Were gold, and gold the bits they champed.
For absent Aeneas he chose a chariot
And a matched pair of fire-breathing horses   340
Reared by Circe, daughter of the Sun,
Who had stolen one of her father's stallions
And mated it with a mortal mare.
And so Aeneas' men rode back to him
High on their mounts, bearing gifts   345
And words of peace from Latinus.

But now Jupiter's ferocious wife
Was returning from Argos, striding
The level air, when she saw from afar—
All the way from Sicilian Pachynus—   350
Aeneas, his spirits high, with all his people.
They were already building a city,

At home on the land, their ships empty.
She stopped in midair, pierced with grief,
And, shaking her head, poured forth these words: 355

"Ah, hated race, Phrygian fates
At odds with mine! Couldn't they have died
On the Sigean plain? Defeated,
Couldn't they have endured defeat?
Didn't burning Troy cremate these men?   360
No! They found a way through fire and foe.
My divinity must be wearing thin,
Or I have grown content, my wrath appeased.
Not exactly! When they were thrown out
Of their country, I persecuted the outcasts   365
All over the deep blue sea. All the powers
Of sea and sky have been used against them.
But what did the Syrtes get me, or Scylla,
Or gaping Charybdis? They have found shelter
In Tiber's long-sought channel, safe from the sea   370
And safe from me. Mars could destroy
The giant Lapith race; the Father of the Gods
Sacrificed Calydon to Diana's wrath,
But what did the Lapiths or Calydon do
To deserve such punishment? But I,   375
Jove's great consort, who have left nothing
Undared, have tried every trick and turn,
Am bested by Aeneas! But if my powers
Are not great enough, why should I hesitate
To seek help from any source whatever?   380
If I cannot sway Heaven, I will awaken Hell!
I concede Aeneas the rule of Latium,
And Lavinia is his bride by iron fate,
But to draw it out and delay the issue,
That I may do, and destroy both nations.   385
Their people's lives will be the price
For father and son-in-law to form a union.
Trojan and Rutulian blood will be your dowry,
Bride of Aeneas, and Bellona
Your matron of honor! It was not only Hecuba   390
Who conceived a firebrand and gave birth

To nuptial flames. Venus' own child
Is a second Paris, a funeral torch for New Troy."

With these words Juno descended to earth,
A terrifying presence, and called forth Allecto   *395*
From the home of the Dread Goddesses
And the shadows below, gruesome Allecto
Whose heart is set on war and wrath,
Intrigues and crime. She is hateful
Even to Pluto, who sired her, hateful   *400*
To her Tartarean sisters: so many shapes
She assumes, so cruel her faces, so vile
The black vipers that sprout from her scalp.
Juno enflamed her with words such as these:

"Daughter of Night, grant me a favor,   *405*
A special service that will preserve my honor.
Prevent Aeneas from winning over Latinus
Through marriage, or from invading Italy.
You are able to make like-minded brothers
Arm for battle, to overturn homes with hate,   *410*
To bring lash and funeral torch to the hearth.
You have a thousand names, a thousand ways
To cause harm. Ransack your teeming heart.
Shatter the peace, sow the seeds of war.
Make each man want to grip a weapon,   *415*
Demand one and seize one all in one breath."

And so Allecto, venomous as any Gorgon,
Makes for Latinus' palace in Latium
And occupies the still threshold
Of Amata. The queen was inside, seething   *420*
With a woman's fury at the Teucrians' coming
And sick at heart over Turnus' marriage.
The goddess plucks a snake from her dark hair
And throws it on Amata, thrusting it
Deep into her bosom to drive her mad   *425*
And so bring down the entire house. Gliding
Between her clothes and smooth breasts,
It insinuates itself unseen and unfelt

By the frenzied woman and hisses into her
Its viperous breath. The huge serpent becomes   430
The twisted gold around her neck, becomes
The long band about her brows, entwines itself
Into her hair, and slithers down her limbs.
As the first taint of the poison is absorbed—
Assailing her senses and enflaming her bones   435
But not yet engulfing her soul in fire—
Softly, as mothers do, she murmurs, weeping
Over her daughter's wedlock with Aeneas:

"Will you give Lavinia to Teucrian exiles,
You, her father? Have you no pity left   440
For your daughter or yourself? No pity
For her mother, whom this traitor will desert
With the first North Wind, sailing away
With our girl as plunder? Wasn't this how Paris
Entered Lacedaemon and bore off Helen   445
To Ilium? What of your solemn promise?
What of your old love for your own, what of
Your hand so often pledged to Turnus,
Your kinsman? If it has been decided
That we need a son-in-law of foreign stock,   450
If the words of your father Faunus
Are so important, then I maintain
That every land not under our rule
Is a foreign land, and the gods agree.
Turnus himself, if you trace his lineage,   455
Is descended from Inachus and Acrisius
With roots in Mycenae, the heart of Greece."

Amata's words had no effect on Latinus.
When she saw her husband standing against her,
And when the venom had infected her deeply,   460
Pulsing through her veins, the ill-starred queen
Was swept away by monstrous horrors
And raged in her frenzy all through the city.

   A top kept spinning by a twisted cord,
   As boys, intent on their game, drive it along   465

In great loops through an empty courtyard,
Will whip around curve after curve as the throng
Of entranced children hovers above it,
Mesmerized by the whirling boxwood toy.

Likewise Amata, driven through the cities   470
Of the fierce Latian peoples and through the forests,
Feigning the spirit of Bacchus, a greater sin,
And reaching new heights of madness.
She hid her daughter in the wooded mountains
To forestall her wedding to the Teucrian,   475
Shrieking:

            "Hail, Bacchus! You alone
Are worthy of her. She waves the thyrsus
For you, worships you in the dance,
Grows her sacred tresses for you, Bacchus!"

Rumor spreads, inflaming the Latian mothers   480
With fury, and they rise as one, abandoning
Their homes, hair streaming in the wind
As they fill the air with their quavering cries,
Dressed in fawnskins and carrying spears
Entwined with vines. The frenzied queen   485
Lifts up a blazing torch of pine and sings
A wedding song for her daughter and Turnus,
Rolling her bloodshot eyes and suddenly
Shouting:

            "Hear me, mothers of Latium,
Wherever you are! If your hearts are still loyal   490
To unhappy Amata, if you still care about her
And a mother's rights—unbind your hair
And celebrate the revels along with me!"

Such was the queen, driven by Allecto
With Bacchic goads through the haunts of wild beasts.   495

When the dark goddess thought she had put
A fine enough edge on the first shafts of frenzy

And had undone Latinus and all his house,
She flew on dusky wings to the walls
Of the bold Rutulian's city.   500
The story is told that Danaë,
Driven ashore by the strong South Wind,
Built this city with her Acrisian settlers.
Ardea it was called, and the great name remains,
But the place is desolate now.
　　　　　　　　　　　　　　Midnight,   505
And Turnus was asleep in his high palace.
Allecto sloughed off her fiend's body
And changed herself into an old woman.
She creased her brow, made her hair white,
And bound it with wool and an olive chaplet.   510
She was Calybe now, aged priestess
Of the temple of Juno, and with these words
She offered herself to the young hero's eyes:

"Turnus, will you allow all your work
To be washed away, and the scepter handed   515
To these Dardanian settlers? The king
Denies you the bride you won with your blood,
And a stranger is sought as heir to your throne.
Go ahead, face danger unrewarded, you fool,
Smash Tuscan ranks, shield the Latins with peace!   520
Saturn's almighty daughter in person
Told me to tell you this while you lay abed
In the still of the night. Up then, smile,
Arm your lads, march them through the gates
Into the fields, and burn the painted Phrygian ships   525
Lying at anchor in our beautiful river!
Heaven commands it. And unless King Latinus
Honors his word and gives you your bride,
Let him feel the full force of Turnus as foe."

And Turnus, mocking the seer:

　　　　　　　　　　　　　　"So a fleet   530
Has entered the Tiber's mouth, and you think
I don't know? Don't invent a crisis

For my benefit. Queen Juno does not forget me.
Old age has rotted your mind and deludes
Your prophetic soul with false alarms.   535
See to the gods' temples and statues.
War is the work of the men who wage it."

Allecto's hair spread out in fiery points,
And as Turnus spoke a sudden spasm
Seized his limbs. He stared in horror   540
At the Fury's hissing snakes and the face
That loomed before him. Her eyes rolled in flame
As she pushed him back. Turnus stumbled,
Tried to say more, but the Fury pulled
A pair of snakes from her hair, cracked her whip,   545
And spoke again from her rabid lips:

"Behold me, mind rotted with old age,
Prophetic soul deluded with false alarms.
Look on this! I come from the Dread Sisters,
And in my hand I bear War and Death."   550

And she threw a torch at the young hero,
Sticking it in his chest, where it smoked
With black light. Turnus woke in terror,
Sweat pouring down, drenching him
To the bone. He called madly for arms,   555
Groped wildly in the bed for weapons,
Lusting for steel and the rut of battle,
Rage crowning all.

                    A fire crackling
        Under a bronze cauldron heats the water
        Until it seethes and bubbles, unable to contain itself,   560
        And a cloud of dark steam rises into the air.

And so Turnus, peace be damned, ordered his captains
To march on Latinus. His battle cry rang out:

"For Italy! Drive the enemy out!
Turnus is here, a match for Teucrians   565
And Latins alike!"

And he called on the gods
To witness his vows. The Rutulians
Outdid each other in the call to arms,
Stirred by Turnus' good looks, his high lineage,
And his prowess in battle, second to none.   570

While Turnus steeled the Rutulians' hearts
Allecto was flying on shadowy wings
To the Trojan camp, surveying the region
With new wiles in mind. There on the shore
Iülus was hunting with horses, nets,   575
And a pack of dogs. The dark goddess
Threw the hounds into a sudden frenzy
And touched their nostrils with a familiar scent
That sent them off in pursuit of a stag.
This was the first cause of war in the countryside.   580

There was a stag of surpassing beauty,
With towering antlers, that had been torn
From its mother's breast and raised by Tyrrhus
And his children. Tyrrhus was the keeper
Of the king's herds and far-flung pastures.   585
His daughter, Sylvia, had trained the animal
And would lovingly twine its antlers with flowers,
Comb its coat, and bathe it in a spring.
Tame, and used to eating from its master's table,
It would wander the woods but always come back   590
To the door it knew, however late at night.

The stag had wandered far from home
And, having swum downstream, was cooling off
On the green riverbank when Iülus' dogs
Started it running. Ascanius himself,   595
Eager for glory, aimed an arrow
From his curving bow, and the goddess steadied
His trembling hand. The reedy shaft
Whistled through the air and pierced
The stag's belly and flank. The wounded animal   600
Fled to its familiar home and dragged itself
All bloody into its stall, and its moans

Filled the house like the cries of a suppliant.
Silvia, the sister, slapping her arms in fear,
Called for help from the hardy county folk,   605
Who came instantly, prompted by the fiend
Lurking in the silent woods. They were armed
With burnt-out torches, knotted clubs: whatever
Came to hand wrath turned into a weapon.
Tyrrhus, who was splitting oak with wedges,   610
Called to his men as he snatched up an axe,
His breath coming in huge gulps of rage.

But the cruel goddess, watching for the moment
She could do the most harm, scaled the rooftop
And sounded the shepherds' call, her hellish voice   615
Blaring through the twisted horn. All the groves
Quivered with fear, and the woods echoed
To their very depths. Trivia's lake
Heard the sound from afar, white Nar heard it
In his sulfurous water, and the springs of Velinus.   620
Fearful mothers clasped their sons to their breasts.
But their husbands, unruly farmers,
Quickened their pace at the trumpeted signal,
Snatching up weapons as they ran in from all sides.
And, from their camp's open gates,   625
The Trojans poured out to help Ascanius.
The battle-lines formed. This was no longer
A country quarrel fought with stakes and clubs,
But combat with sharp steel. The field bristled
With a dark crop of drawn swords, and flaring bronze   630
Reflected the sunlight up to the clouds.

The first wave begins to whiten in wind,
And then the swells rise higher and higher
Until they arch from the seafloor up to the stars.

An arrow whined through the foremost ranks   635
And hit the firstborn of Tyrrhus' sons,
Young Almo, full in the throat, blood choking
Speech and breath. He lay in the dust,
And around him lay many bodies of men,

Old Galaesus among them, cut down   640
As he threw himself between the two lines,
Pleading for peace. He was of all men
The most just, and once the wealthiest
In all Ausonia. Five flocks of sheep
Bleated in his fields, five herds of cattle   645
Returned from his pastures, and his soil
Was turned over by a hundred plows.

So the battle raged across the whole plain.
Allecto's promise was fulfilled. Blood
Had been spilled in battle, deaths inflicted.   650
She left Hesperia and turned through the sky
To address Juno in triumphant tones:

"I have crowned discord with grim war,
As you wished. Tell them to unite in friendship
Now that I have painted the Trojans   655
With Ausonian blood! And more,
If I am assured of your intention,
I will draw in the bordering towns with rumors
And inflame their minds with battle lust.
War will spread. I will sow the fields with arms."   660

And Juno answered her:

                    "Enough of treachery
And terror. The causes of war are in place.
They are fighting man to man, and the weapons
Chance first gave are now stained with fresh blood.
This is the wedding they must celebrate,   665
Venus' perfect son and great king Latinus!
The Lord of Olympus would not approve
Of your roaming too freely in the upper air.
Leave these regions. I will deal myself
With whatever troubles remain."

                    Thus Juno,   670
Daughter of Saturn. Serpents hissed
In Allecto's wings as she spread them wide, leaving

The world above for her home in Cocytus.
There is a place in the heart of Italy,
Beneath towering mountains, the famed   675
Vale of Amsanctus. Dark woods surround it,
And a stream roars through its center,
Spilling over rocks and swirling in eddies.
Here can be seen a dread cavern, and fissures
Through which the Dark Lord breathes,   680
And a vast gorge that belches out Acheron.
Here the Fury disappeared, relieving
Heaven and earth of her abhorrent presence.

Now Juno put the finishing touches
On her nascent war. A company of shepherds   685
Poured into the city from the battlefield,
Bearing the dead—the boy Almo
And Galaesus' mangled body. They called
On the gods and held Latinus to account.
Turnus was there, and amid the riot,   690
The passions, and the shouts of 'Murder!'
He multiplied their terror:

                    "Teucrians
Are called in to rule! We are becoming
Phrygian half-breeds, and I am shut out!"

The Bacchic women were still in their frenzy,   695
Mothers dancing through the trackless woods—
The name of Amata carried some weight.
And now their men were coming together
From all sides, wearying Mars with their pleas.
Defying the omens and the sacred oracles,   700
Their minds twisted, they all clamored
For an unholy war. Latinus' palace
Was soon besieged by an ugly crowd.
He stood as a cliff stands on an ocean shore,

    Motionless as a cliff in the crashing ocean.   705
    Its sheer bulk holds steady as the sea below

Howls and roars in the foaming crags,
And it flings back the seaweed that strikes its face.

But when he saw that he was powerless
To change their blind resolve, that all was going   710
As cruel Juno wished, old Latinus
Called the gods and the empty air to witness:

"We are being broken by Fate, swept away
By the storm. You will pay for this in sorrow
With your sacrilegious blood. You, Turnus,   715
You will suffer punishment severe. Too late
Will you supplicate the gods with vows.
As for me, my rest is won, but at the gate
Of the harbor, I am robbed of a happy death."

Saying no more, Latinus shut himself   720
In the palace and dropped the reins of power.

There was a custom in ancient Latium,
Held sacred later by the Alban cities
And now by Rome most high, whenever Mars
Is first roused—be it the Getae   725
Or Arabs or Hyrcanians against whom
They prepare to bring the tears of war,
Or to march on India, pursue the Dawn,
And reclaim their eagles from the Parthians.
There are twin Gates of War (so men call them)   730
Sanctified by faith and fear of Mars,
Held shut by a hundred bronze bolts
And the eternal strength of iron. Janus,
Their guardian, never leaves the threshold.
Here, when the Fathers declare war,   735
The Consul, wearing Quirinal robes
And a toga with a Gabine cincture,
Unbars the grating doors and calls forth War.
The rest of the army then takes up the cry,
And brass horns blare in hoarse accord.   740
Latinus was charged to declare war on Aeneas
In just this way and open the grim gates;

But the old man would not touch them, recoiling
From such service, and hid himself in shadows.
It was the Queen of the Gods, gliding down   745
From the sky, who with her own hand pushed
The hesitant doors on their turning hinges
And burst open the ironbound Gates of War.

Now all Ausonia was in burning motion.
Some were starting to cross the plain on foot,   750
Others rode out furiously on war-horses,
Raising clouds of dust. All lusted for weapons.
You could see men burnishing shields,
Polishing spears, and whetting axes on stones,
Glad to bear standards and hear the trumpets call.   755
Five great cities started to forge new weapons—
Mighty Atina, high Tibur and Ardea,
Crustumeri, and turreted Antemnae.
They molded helmets, framed shields in wicker,
Hammered bronze into breastplates,   760
And crafted smooth greaves of pliant silver.
They beat their plowshares into swords
And re-tempered the swords of their fathers.
The trumpet sounds, the password goes around,
Signaling war. A man anxiously snatches   765
A helmet from his home; another harnesses
His trembling horses, puts on his golden,
Triple-linked armor, and straps on his sword.

Now open the gates of Helicon, Goddesses,
And lift my song. Who were the kings   770
Incited to war, and the fighting men
Who filled the plain? With what heroes
Did sweet Mother Italy even then bloom,
With what armies did she burn? For you know,
Divine ones; you can remember and tell,   775
While we hear only the whisper of fame."

First into war came the fierce Etruscan,
Mezentius, scorner of the gods,

And he marshaled his troops. At his side
Stood his son, Lausus, in glory of youth   780
Second only to Turnus.
                            Lausus,
Breaker of horses, led into battle
A thousand men from Agylla's town
Who followed him in vain, a son worthy
Of a father better than Mezentius.   785

Next came Aventinus, handsome son
Of handsome Hercules, his chariot
And prizewinning horses on parade
In the fields of glory, and on his shield
His father's insignia—a hundred serpents   790
Surrounding the Hydra. The priestess Rhea
Gave birth to him in the Aventine's woods,
Bringing him secretly into the world of light,
A woman who lay with a god. Hercules,
Having slain Geryon, had just arrived   795
At the Laurentian fields and was watering
His Iberian cattle in the Tuscan stream.
Aventinus' men bore javelins
And great battle-pikes while he himself
Marched on foot, a huge lionskin   800
Swinging from his shoulders, its white teeth
Crowning his head. This was how Aventinus
Would enter the hall, an unnerving sight,
Bristling with the cloak of Hercules.

Next, the twins Catillus and Coras,   805
Brave Argives, came from Tibur,
Named after their brother, Tiburtus.
They worked their way to the front lines
Through a forest of weapons,

                            Like cloud-born
    Centaurs racing down a mountain,   810
    Leaving Homole or snowy Orthys behind,
    The woods parting before them
    As they crash through the thickets.

There too was Caeculus, Praeneste's founder,
The king, as every age has believed,   815
Born to Vulcan among rustic herds
And found on the hearth. With him marches
A vast militia drafted in the field,
Warriors from steep Praeneste,
From the farms of Juno who guards the Gabii,   820
From the cool Anio and Hernica's rocks,
And men whom you feed, rich Anagnia,
And you, Amasenus. Not all of these have
Weapons or shields or clanging chariots.
Most of them fight by slinging lead pellets.   825
Some carry two spears and wear wolfskin
Helmets. Their left foot is bare,
The right protected by a rawhide boot.
Messapus, breaker of horses, son of Neptune,
Whom none may lay low with fire or steel,   830
Calls to battle sedentary tribes, troops
Long idle, and once again grips a sword himself.
These are men of Fescennium
And of Aequi Falisci; from Soracte's heights
And the fields of Flacinia; near Ciminus' lake   835
And the groves of Capena. They all marched
To the beat and chanted praise to their king.

> Snowy swans high in the misty air,
> On their way back from feeding, issue
> Melodious cries from their outstretched throats,   840
> And the sound echoes from the Asian wetlands
> Far below.

No one would think that bronze troops
Were massing here, but that vast clouds
Of raucous birds were pressing toward shore.

Next comes Clausus, of old Sabine blood,   845
Leading a great army, and equal in stature
To a great army himself, ancestor
Of the Claudian clans that spread through Latium
After Rome was given in part to the Sabines.

With him marched Amiternum's troops   850
And the ancient Quirites, the whole band
Of Eretrum and of olive-bearing Mutusca;
Citizens of Nomentum and the inhabitants
Of the Rosean country around Velini,
And those who live on the cliffs of Tetrica   855
And Mount Severus, in Casperia
And Foruli, and by the river Himella;
Those who drink the Tiber and Fabaris,
Those sent from cold Nursia, Ortine troops,
The Latin peoples, and those whom Allia   860
(Name of ill omen) parts with its waters,

> *Multitudinous as the foaming waves*
> *That roll on the Libyan sea, when Orion sinks*
> *Into the wintry water; or as dense as wheat*
> *Scorched by the sun in Hermus' plain*   865
> *Or in the golden fields of Lycia.*

                                        Shields clang,
Earth trembles under tramping feet.

                                        Next, Halaesus,
Son of Agamemnon, Troy's nemesis,
Yokes horses to his chariot, leading
A thousand warlike tribes in Turnus' cause: 870
Men who hoe the wine-rich Massic country;
Men whom their Auruncan fathers sent
From the high hills and the Sidicine plains;
Men from Cales and the Volturnus' shallows
Marching alongside tough Saticulans   875
And Oscan bands. They were armed
With smooth javelins, their shafts entwined
With throwing-thongs. Shields protected
Their left sides; their sickled swords
Were for close combat.

                                Nor will you, Oebalus,   880
Pass by unsung. The nymph Sebethis
Bore you to Telon when he was king

Of Teleboan Capreae and already old.
But not content with his ancestral fields,
His son even then extended his rule   885
Over the Sarastrians, the Sarnus valley,
Rufrae, Batulum, and Celemna's fields,
Where men throw spears in Teuton style,
And all those under the walls of Abella,
Rich in apples. Their headgear   890
Is made from cork, but their shields
Flash bronze, and bronze flash their swords.

Mountainous Nersae sent you also to war,
Noble Ufens, a good man with a spear
And from a tough breed of men, raised   895
On Aequia's rocky soil and inured
To hard days of hunting in the woods.
They work the land in arms, and all their joy
Is to bear away spoils and live on plunder.

Archippus, lord of the Maruvians,   900
Sent a priest to war, helmet wreathed in olive,
Umbro most brave, who could charm to sleep
Vipers and hydras, with their venomous breath,
And cure their bites. But he could not heal
The bites inflicted by Dardanian spears,   905
Nor did his entrancements or herbs culled
On Marsian hills aid him with his wounds.
For you wept Angitia's grove,
For you the glassy wave of Fucinus,
For you the clear lakes . . .   910

Virbius too went to war, Hippolytus'
Beautiful son, sent forth by his mother,
Aricia. He had grown up in Egeria,
On the marshy shores where Diana's altar
Stands rich in sacrifice. Hippolytus   915
Had been undone by his stepmother's wiles
And paid the price to his father in blood,
Ripped apart by his own frightened horses.
But he was called back to heaven's air

Under the stars by the Healer's herbs   920
And Diana's love. Then the Almighty,
Vexed that a mortal should rise from the shades
To the light of life, blasted the Healer,
Son of Phoebus, to the waters of Styx.
But Diana in mercy hid Hippolytus   925
And sent him away to the nymph Egeria
And her sacred grove to live out his days there
In the woods of Italy, alone and unknown
Under the name of Virbius. This is why
Horses are banned from Diana's temples   930
And groves: panicked by a sea monster,
They strewed youth and chariot along the shore.
Still, his son was pushing his fiery stallions
Along the plain, driving his chariot to war.

In the foremost ranks moved Turnus himself,   935
Incomparable, sword in hand, head crowned
With a plumed helmet bearing a Chimaera
That breathed from her jaws Aetnean fire,
Flames all the more fierce the more blood is shed.
On his polished shield Io, horns uplifted,   940
An emblem blazoned in gold—Io,
Covered in bristles, already a heifer,
With Argus her warden and her father, Inachus,
Pouring his stream from a figured urn.
A cloud of foot soldiers followed him,   945
And shielded columns crowded the plain,
Argive troops and Auruncan platoons,
Rutulians and veteran Sicanians,
Lines of Sarcanians and Labicians
With painted shields; tillers of your glades,   950
O Tiber, and the sacred shore of Numicius,
Farmers from the Rutulian hills
And Circe's ridge, whose fields are ruled
By Jupiter Anxur and by Feronia,
Gay in her greenwood, where the black swamp   955
Of Satura lies and the cold Ufens
Winds through valleys and down to the sea.

Last of all rode Camilla the Volscian,
Leading her mounted troops and squadrons
Flowering in bronze. This princess warrior   960
Had not trained her hands to women's work,
Spinning and weaving, but trained to endure
The hardships of war and to outrun the wind.
She could sprint over a field of wheat
And not even bruise the tender ears,   965
Could cruise above the open sea's waves
And never wet the soles of her feet.
All the young men, and their mothers too,
Flocked from their houses and left their fields
To watch her ride by, mouths open in wonder   970
At how the royal purple draped
Her smooth shoulders, how her hair
Was bound in gold, and how she carried
A Lycian quiver and an iron-tipped spear.

AENEID EIGHT

When Turnus raised the flag of war
From Laurentium's high citadel;
When the horns blared, and he whipped
His horses to a fury and clashed his arms,
There was an instant, spirited reaction.   5
All of Latium rose to swear allegiance.
Young men raged to fight. Their leaders,
Messapus and Ufens, with Mezentius,
Who held the gods in contempt, mustered troops
From all over and ransacked the wide fields   10
Of their farmers. They even sent Venulus
To great Diomedes' city to seek aid
And to announce that Trojans were settling
In Latium, that Aeneas had arrived
With his fleet and his vanquished gods,   15
Proclaiming himself king by divine right,
And that many tribes were joining
The Dardan hero as his name spread wide.
All to what end, should Fortune favor him,
Would be clearer to Diomedes himself   20
Than to either Turnus or King Latinus.

Thus Latium. And Aeneas, hero in the line
Of Laomedon, saw it all, and was tossed
On a great sea of troubles. His mind darted
This way and that, turning and shifting.   25

   Sunlight, or the radiant moon, reflected from water
   Trembling in a bronze bowl, will glance and flit

190

All over a room—and then flash suddenly
Onto the coffered ceiling high above.

It was night, and all over earth deep slumber   30
Held weary creatures of the air and field.
Father Aeneas, heart troubled by war,
Lay down on the riverbank under a cold sky
And drifted off at last to sleep. He dreamed
That Tiberinus, the old rivergod himself,   35
Lifted his head amid the poplar leaves
Draped in a fine, grey-linen mantle,
His hair crowned with shady reeds,
And spoke to him, calming his fears:

"Child of the gods, you bring us our Troy   40
Back from the enemy, and you preserve
Pergamum forever. You have been awaited
On Laurentine soil, in Latin fields.
Here your home is sure—do not draw back!—
And sure are your gods. Do not be frightened   45
By threats of war. All the swollen wrath of the gods
Has ebbed away. . . .
To assure you this is no empty dream,
I offer a sign. Lying under oaks
You will find a sow, near a hidden stream,   50
With a litter of thirty, a white mother
Lying on the ground and white young nursing.
Here shall be your city, and surcease from sorrow.
The sign foretells that in thirty circling years
Ascanius will found a city, glorious Alba.   55
My prophecy is sure. As to the present ills,
I will explain in brief how you may emerge
Victorious. On these shores Arcadians,
Descended from Pallas and led by King Evander,
Have built a city in the hills and called it   60
Pallanteum after their forefather Pallas.
They are ever at war with the Latin race.
These Arcadians you must take as allies.
I myself will conduct you straight upstream
So that your oars will overpower the current.   65

Now rise, Goddess-born, and as the stars set
Pray to Juno and prevail upon her
To end her angry threats. And when you win out,
Pay tribute to me. I am he whom you see
Gliding through my banks in full flow   70
And cutting through the rich plowland—
The blue Tiber, river most beloved by Heaven.
Here is my great home, and my headwaters
Flow from high cities."

                              Thus the River,
And he plunged into a deep pool,   75
Seeking the depths. Night and sleep left Aeneas.
He rose and, looking at the rising sun,
Lifted water from the river with cupped palms
In ritual fashion and prayed aloud:

"Nymphs, Laurentine Nymphs at the source   80
Of all streams, and you, Father Tiber,
With your sacred water—receive Aeneas
And keep him from harm. Whatever spring,
Whatever pool holds you, from whatever soil
You flow forth in all your beauty, pitying   85
My trials, you will be honored forever
With my gifts, O horned Rivergod, lord
Of Hesperian waters. Only be with me now,
And confirm your divine presence."

                              Thus Aeneas,
And, choosing two galleys from his fleet,   90
He picked out crews and equipped the men.

And then a sudden marvel met his gaze.
Gleaming through the wood and as white
As her milk-white litter, a sow lay outstretched
On the green riverbank. Pious Aeneas   95
Offered her to you, Juno most mighty,
Setting her with her brood before your altar.

All the night long Tiber calmed his current,
Flowing backward until the water stood so still

It might have been a pool or quiet lake   *100*
Offering no resistance to the dipping oars.
The crews cheered as the ships sped along
And the well-caulked pine glided on the water.
The waves wondered, and the woods too, unused
To such a sight, the shields glittering on the water   *105*
And the painted hulls floating upriver.
The men rowed night and day, around the long bends
And under changing trees, their oars cutting
Through the green woods on the river's calm surface.
The burning sun had reached heaven's meridian   *110*
When they sighted walls off in the distance
And a few scattered huts, which Roman might
Has now raised to the sky but at that time
Were King Evander's humble domain.
They turned their prows and drew up to the town.   *115*

The Arcadian king was making sacrifice
To Hercules that day, and to all the gods,
In a grove outside the city. With him were
His son, Pallas, all the men of rank,
And the humble senate, offering incense   *120*
As the blood and warm meat smoked on the altar.
When they saw the tall ships gliding up
Between the shady banks, and the crew
Rowing noiselessly, they rose up in alarm
And left the feast. But Pallas kept his nerve,   *125*
And, ordering them not to break off the rites,
He seized his spear and ran out to meet
The strangers himself. Standing on a mound,
He cried out to them:

          "Men at arms,
What has forced you to travel routes unknown?   *130*
Where are you heading? What is your race,
Your home? Do you come in peace or war?"

Then Father Aeneas, holding out a branch
Of peaceful olive, spoke from his high stern:

"You see before you men of Troy, and arms   135
At war with the Latins, who in their arrogance
Have driven us to flight. We seek Evander.
Tell him that Dardanians, men of rank,
Have come to propose an alliance at arms."

Pallas was stunned when he heard the name   140
'Dardanian,' and he said:

                    "Come forward,
Whoever you are, and speak to my father
Face to face, as a guest at our hearth."

And he clasped Aeneas' hand. Together,
They left the river and entered the grove.   145

Then Aeneas addressed the king graciously:

"Noblest of the Greeks, it is my good fortune
To make my prayer to you and offer boughs
Hung with sacral wreaths. I have no cause to fear
Your lineage as a Danaan lord   150
And an Arcadian with ties to Atreus' sons.
My own nobility and heaven's oracles,
Our forefathers' kinship and your fame,
Which has spread throughout the world—all this
Has bound me to you and brought me here,   155
Consenting to Fate.
                    Dardanus, as the Greeks tell it,
Was Ilium's founding father, born of Electra,
Who herself was the daughter of Atlas,
Upon whose shoulders rests the celestial sphere.
Your ancestor is Mercury, whom shining Maia   160
Conceived and bore on Cyllene's cold peak.
Maia herself, if we can trust the tales,
Was the child of Atlas, the same Atlas
Who supports the star-studded sky. And so,
Our bloodlines branch from a common source.   165
Relying on this, I did not approach you
Through ambassadors or artful overtures.

I have come myself and offer you my life,
A suppliant at your door. The same Daunians
Pursue us both in bitter war, thinking that   170
If they drive us out nothing will stop them
From subjugating all Hesperia
And controlling the seas that wash her shores.
Take my pledge and give me yours. Our hearts
Are brave in war, our manhood tested."   175

As Aeneas was speaking Evander
Was watching him, scanning his face and eyes
And entire body. Then he replied briefly:

"Bravest of the Teucrians, how gladly
I receive you—and recognize you!   180
How I recall your father's words, the voice
And the face of great Anchises!
I remember it all—how Priam,
Laomedon's son, on his way to Salamis
Stopped to see his sister Hesione   185
And went on to visit cold Arcadia.
I was young then, my cheeks just bearded,
And I wondered at the Trojan princes,
Wondered at Priam himself, but Anchises
Towered above them all. My heart burned   190
With youthful love. I yearned to meet him,
To clasp his hand, and I did approach him
And led him eagerly to Pheneus' city.
When he left he gave me a beautiful quiver
With Lycian arrows, a cloak woven with gold,   195
And a pair of golden bits that my Pallas now has.
So the hand you seek is now joined with yours,
And when tomorrow's light has dawned
I will send you forth with men and means.
Until then, since you are here as friends,   200
Celebrate with us this annual rite,
Which may not be deferred, and join our feast."

So saying, he ordered the table reset
And arranged his guests on seats in the grass.

Aeneas, as guest of honor, he showed   *205*
To a lionskin cushion on a maple throne.
Then chosen youths and the priest of the altar
Outdid each other serving roast beef, piling
Baskets high with Ceres' bread, and pouring
The wine of Bacchus. Aeneas and his Trojans   *210*
Feasted on long chine and consecrated sweetbreads.

When they had satisfied their appetites,
King Evander spoke:

               "These solemn rites,
This traditional feast, this altar sacred
To a Power divine do not come to us   *215*
From some empty superstition, ignoring
The gods of old. No, my Trojan guest,
Rescued from savage dangers, we observe
This annual rite in memory of our deliverance.
Look first at this rocky overhang,   *220*
How the huge boulders are scattered,
How the mountain stands in desolation
And the crags have crumbled in avalanche.
There was once a cave here, its depths
Never fathomed by sunlight, the lair   *225*
Of a half-human monster, an ogre named Cacus.
The ground there always smoked with fresh blood,
And nailed to the door hung human heads
Moldering in decay. The monster's father
Was Vulcan; it was his black fires Cacus belched   *230*
As he moved his hulking form. Time at last
Answered our prayers in the person
Of a god, the mightiest avenger, Hercules,
Glorying in the slaughter of Geryon
And driving that triform ghoul's huge bulls   *235*
In triumph, filling the Tiber's valley with cattle.
Cacus, whose fiendish mind could leave
No crime undared or trick untried,
Rustled four superb bulls from their corral
And as many equally outstanding heifers.   *240*

He dragged these cattle by their tails to his cave
So no one could track them back to him,
Then he hid the animals in the rocky gloom.
No one searching could find any telltale marks
Leading to that cave. Amphitryon's son,   245
Meanwhile, was moving the well-fed herds
Out of their pens, rounding them up for the trail.
The cattle lowed as they headed out,
And the woods and hills were filled with their bellowing
Until the echoes began to die away.   250
And then one heifer lowed in response
From the depths of the cave, undoing Cacus.
The wrath of Hercules flared with black bile.
He seized his weapons, his heavy, knotted club,
And ran straight up the slope like the mountain wind.   255
It was then we first saw Cacus afraid,
Eyes shifting with terror. He flew to his cave
Faster than the East Wind; fear lent wings to his feet.
He shut himself in and broke the chains
That held the giant rock suspended in iron   260
By his father's craft. The rock dropped down,
Blocking the entrance, at just the moment
When Hercules arrived, raging mad.
He scanned every approach, looking around
And gnashing his teeth. Three times he traversed   265
The Aventine Mount, three times he tried
The rock-solid entrance, three times he sank down
In the valley, exhausted.
                          On the cave's ridge
Stood an immense dagger of flint, tall
Sheer rock, a perfect nesting place for vultures.   270
It leaned left with the ridge's slope toward the river.
The hero pushed from the right, shook it loose,
Wrenched it up from its roots, and abruptly
Heaved it forward. With that heave
Heaven thundered, the banks below split apart,   275
And the astonished river recoiled in terror.
Cacus' immense lair lay open, revealing
The shadowy depths of the cavern below,

As if Earth itself were split apart
By some unknown power, disclosing the Pit   280
And the moldy horror loathed by the gods.
The Abyss is laid open, and the pale ghosts
Tremble at the light streaming in from above.

Cacus was caught in the unexpected daylight.
Penned in by rock walls, he howled eerily   285
As Hercules rained down upon him
Everything he could throw—weapons,
Branches, colossal millstones. Cornered,
Cacus did the only thing he could, belching out
Clouds of smoke (an amazing display)   290
That enshrouded his subterranean home
In blinding smog shot through with dark flames.
Undeterred, Hercules hurled himself
Into the inferno where the huge cave was choked
With roiling smoke. He found Cacus there   295
Spewing forth his fiery vapors in vain.
Hercules gripped him in a knotted hold
And squeezed until Cacus' eyes bulged out
And his throat was drained of blood. Then,
With hardly a pause, he tore off the doors,   300
And the den was laid bare. The stolen oxen
(A theft Cacus had denied) were exposed
To the sky, and the gruesome carcass
Was dragged out by the feet. Men could not get enough
Of looking at those terrible eyes, that face,   305
The brute's bristled chest and his throat's quenched fires.
From that time on this has been a festival day
Kept by every generation, foremost by Potitius,
Who founded the rite, and the Pinarian house,
Priests of Hercules. The hero himself   310
Established this altar, which we will always call
Mightiest, and always mightiest shall be.
Come then, young men, wreathe your hair with leaves
In honor of these glorious deeds. Hold out your cups,
Call on the god to share our feast, and pour the wine."   315

Thus Evander, wreathing his head with poplar,
Whose green twilight shade is dear to Hercules.

The sacral goblet filled the king's hand, and all
Poured libation and prayed to the gods.

The great sky turned and evening came on.   320
The priests went forth, Potitius at their head,
Dressed in ritual skins and bearing torches.
They renewed the feast with welcome offerings
And heaped the altars with laden platters.
The Salii, leaping priests of Mars, chanted   325
In the glow of the altars, poplar weaving their brows,
One chorus of youths, another of elders,
And they sang the exploits of Hercules:
How in his crib he strangled the twin serpents
His stepmother sent; then how he tore down   330
Great cities in war, Troy and Oechalia;
How he performed a thousand hard labors
Under King Eurystheus by Juno's will.

"Unconquered hero, you slew with your hand
The cloud-born centaurs Hylaeus and Pholus,   335
The monsters of Crete, the huge lion
Beneath Nemea's high rock. The Stygian pools
Trembled before you; the watchdog of Orcus,
Stretched out in his cave on half-gnawed bones,
Trembled before you. No face of evil   340
Ever daunted you, not even Typhoeus
Towering in arms. Your wits did not fail you
When surrounded by the Hydra's swarm of heads.
Hail, true son of Jove, glory added to the gods!
Bless us with your presence, favor your rites."   345

Such were their songs, and they capped it all
With the tale of Cacus, the fire-breathing monster.
The woodland rang, and the hills echoed their song.

The rites were over, and they all returned
To the city. The king, worn with age,   350
Walked with Aeneas and his son, Pallas,
And lightened the journey with conversation.
Aeneas ran his eyes over the entire landscape,

Charmed by the various locales. He asked for,
And was delighted to hear, the stories   *355*
Behind each one, the races of the men of old.
King Evander, founder of Rome's citadel,
Was speaking:

                    "These woods were once haunted
By native Fauns and Nymphs, and a race of men
Sprung from tough oak trees. They had no rules or arts,   *360*
Did not know how to yoke an ox, or lay up stores
Or manage them. They lived off trees and hunting.
Then Saturn came down from highest heaven,
Fleeing Jove's weapons, exiled from his realm.
He brought together the unruly race, scattered   *365*
Across the mountain slopes, and gave them laws.
He called the area Latium, since he had hidden
Safely there, a latent presence within its borders.
The Golden Age, as men call it, existed
Under his rule, so peaceful was his reign.   *370*
Little by little a worse sort of people
Rose up, dimmer and duller, and with them came
Passion for war and love of possessions.
Then came the Ausonians, the Sicanians,
And the land of Saturn often changed its name.   *375*
Then kings arose, and Thybris, harsh and huge,
From whose name we Italians called
Our river the Tiber, and the old Albula
Lost its true name. As for myself,
Fortune almighty and ineluctable Fate   *380*
Drove me from my fatherland to follow
The sea to its end, and set me down here.
And the dread warnings of my mother,
The nymph Carmentis, and of Apollo,
August divinity, led me to this very spot."   *385*

As Evander finished he pointed out the altar
And what Romans call the Carmental Gate,
An ancient tribute to the nymph Carmentis.
This prophetic being first sang the greatness
Of Aeneas' sons, and Pallanteum's glory.   *390*

Next he showed a vast grove, which Romulus
Later would make a refuge; showed him too
The Lupercal, a cave beneath a cold cliffside
With the Arcadian name of Lycaean Pan.
He showed him the wood of holy Argiletum   395
And, calling the place to witness, recounted the death
Of Argus, his guest. From here Evander led him
To Tarpeia's home and the Capitol,
Golden now, but then bristling with thickets.
Even then the religious power of this place   400
Awed the country folk; even then they shuddered
At the woods and stones.

                              "This grove,"
Evander cried, "this tree-crowned hill,
Shelters a god, although which god it is
We do not know. But the Arcadians believe   405
They have seen Jupiter himself here, shaking
His darkening aegis and gathering the clouds.
Within the crumbling wall of these two towns
You can see the relics and memorials
Of men of old. This holy height was built   410
By father Janus, and that by Saturn.
Janiculum this was called, that Saturnia."

Talking in this way they came to Evander's
Humble dwelling and saw cattle
Milling about in the Roman Forum   415
And lowing in the fashionable Keels.
When they reached his house Evander said:

"The conquering hero, Hercules, passed through
This door; this palace had room enough for him.
Dare to despise riches, my guest; make yourself, too,   420
Worthy of godhood; do not scorn my poverty."

He spoke, led immense Aeneas
Under his low roof, and set him on a couch
Spread with leaves and a Libyan bearskin.
Night fell, enfolding the earth in dusky wings.   425

Venus, her mother's heart troubled
By the very real Laurentine threat,
Spoke to Vulcan in their golden bedroom,
Breathing into her words immortal love:

"While the Argive warlords ravaged Troy   430
And her walls doomed to fall in enemy fire,
I asked no aid for the victims, no weapons
Forged by your art. No, dearest husband,
I did not wish to trouble you in vain,
However much I owed to Priam's children,   435
And however much I wept for Aeneas
In his distress. Now, by Jupiter's commands,
He stands in Rutulian territory. Now, therefore,
I come, as suppliant to your sacred power,
Begging arms, a mother for her son. Thetis   440
Could sway you with tears, and Aurora.
See the nations mustering, the walled cities
Whetting steel to destroy my people!"

Vulcan hesitated, but when the goddess
Wrapped her snowy arms around him   445
And fondled him in her soft embrace,
He felt the familiar heat flash though his bones,

> *Like lightning splitting a thunderhead,*
> *A crackling flash in the rumbling sky.*

Venus felt it and smiled to herself.   450
And Vulcan, chained by eternal love:

"Why reach so far back for reasons?
What happened to your faith in me, Goddess?
If you had been as anxious then,
It would have been right for me to arm the Trojans.   455
Neither the Father almighty nor Fate forbade
That Troy stand or Priam live ten years more.
Now, if your mind is set on war,
All the care I can promise in my craft,
All that can be done with iron or electrum,   460

All that fire and air can avail—well, stop praying
And just trust your powers!"

                        Saying this,
He gave her the embrace they both wanted
And melted into sleep on his wife's bosom.

Vulcan woke in the middle of the night.   465

> *In the waning darkness, when sleep*
> *Gives way to rest, a housewife who subsists*
> *On spinning and weaving stirs the embers,*
> *Adding night to her workday, and has her women*
> *Toil long hours by lamplight, so she may keep*   470
> *Her husband's bed chaste and rear her sons.*

So too the Lord of Fire, no slower at that hour,
Rose from his soft bed and went to his smithy.

There is an island off the Sicilian coast
Hard by Aeolean Lipare. Smoking rocks   475
Rise to a peak, and subterranean vaults
Thunder in its bowels, hollowed out
By Cyclopean forges. Strong hammer strokes
Echo from anvils, smelted lumps of iron
Hiss through caverns, fire pants in the furnace.   480
To this island, called Vulcania from its master's name,
Down came the Fire Lord from heaven's height.

The Cyclopes were forging iron in the vast cave,
Brontes, Steropes, and bare-armed Pyracmon.
They had just shaped a thunderbolt, part polished—   485
Like the many Jupiter hurls down from heaven—
Part still unfinished. They had twisted in three rays
Of pelting hail, three of watery cloud, and added
Three of red fire and winged South Wind.
Now they were blending in terrifying flashes,   490
Noise and fear, wrath with pursuing flames.
Elsewhere they were busy with a flying chariot
For Mars to use when he inflames men and cities.

And they bent over the petrifying aegis of Pallas,
Burnishing it with golden scales of serpents,   *495*
And polishing the goddess's breastplate,
Which writhed with serpents around the severed head
And rolling eyes of the Gorgon Medusa.

"Stop all work!" he cried. "Cyclopes of Aetna,
Turn your minds now to arms for a hero. I want   *500*
Strength, fast hands, master craftsmanship—
And no delays!"

                    That was all they needed to hear.
They divided the work equally and bent down to it.
Bronze and gold flowed in streams of hot metal,
And Chalyb iron, the raw material   *505*
For so many wounds, was melted down in the furnace.
They formed a great shield, one shield against
All the weapons of the Latins, seven welded layers,
Circle upon circle. Some worked the bellows,
Others tempered the hissing bronze in the lake.   *510*
The cave groaned with the thud of anvils.
The Cyclopes' great hammers rose and fell
In cadence, and they turned the metal with tongs.

While the Lord of Lemnos was busy
On Vulcania, the gentle light of morning   *515*
And the songs of swallows beneath the eaves
Roused Evander from his humble home.
The old man put on a tunic and strapped
Tyrrhenian sandals on his feet, buckled on
His Tegean sword, and flung back a leopardskin   *520*
To hang from his left shoulder. Two hounds,
One trotting ahead and one at his heels,
Accompanied the hero as he left his threshold
And made his way to Aeneas' lodging,
Mindful of the aid he had promised the Trojan.   *525*
Aeneas was up just as early. With him
Walked Achates, as with Evander walked his son,
Pallas. They clasped hands when they met and sat

In the courtyard, conversing freely at last.
The king began:

> "Trojan commander—   530
> For while you live I will never admit
> That Troy's realm has been conquered—
> Our strength to aid you in war is weak
> Compared to our great name. We Arcadians
> Are hemmed in on one side by the river,   535
> And on the other by Rutulians
> Rattling their weapons around our walls.
> But I propose to form a coalition,
> To link with you an army of royal forces,
> A salvation no one could have guessed.   540
> The Fates must have called you here.

> Not far
> From where we sit is the city of Agylla,
> Built of ancient stone in the Tuscan hills.
> The Lydians, a warlike race, settled there
> Long ago, and long it prospered,   545
> Until an arrogant king, Mezentius,
> Came into power and ruled with iron hand.
> Why recount the tyrant's acts of butchery?
> May it fall on his own head and on his brood!
> He would even bind living men to corpses,   550
> Hand to hand and mouth to mouth, until
> By slow torture the living met their death
> In the putrefaction of that ghastly embrace.
> At last the weary citizens rose in revolt,
> Besieged the unspeakable monster   555
> In his palace, cut down his men, and fired the roof.
> In the mayhem Mezentius escaped
> And found refuge on Rutulian soil
> Under the protection of Turnus.
> All Etruria has risen in righteous rage.   560
> Their terms are extradition of the king
> Or immediate war. I will make you
> Commander of these thousands, Aeneas.
> Their troopships line the shore and clamor

For the standards to advance. However,   565
An old soothsayer holds them in check,
Intoning Fate:

> 'Chosen warriors,
Flower of Maeonia's ancient race,
Just resentment sends you forth to war,
Mezentius inflames your indignant rage.   570
The gods forbid that any Italian
Should be in command of so great a race.
Choose leaders from abroad.'

     The Etruscans
Are encamped on the plain, in awe of heaven.
Tarchon himself has sent me envoys   575
With the crown and scepter of the realm,
Inviting me to command the army
And succeed to the Etruscan throne.
But my old age, cold and slow, begrudges me
Military command. I am too weak for war.   580
I would urge my son to do it, but his mother
Is Sabine, and so his blood is mixed. But you,
Blessed by Fate in years and race, called by heaven,
Do your duty, lead the Italians and Trojans both.
Further, I will put Pallas at your side, Pallas,   585
Our hope and comfort. Let him learn from you
To endure the work of war. Let him observe
All you do and respect you from his early years.
To Pallas I will give two hundred cavalry,
Arcadia's finest, and he will give you   590
As many more himself."

     Evander finished.
Aeneas, son of Anchises, and loyal Achates
Would have sat a long time, eyes fixed,
Brooding on troubles of their own,
But Venus gave them a sign. Lightning   595
Flashed with thunder in the open sky,
And everything suddenly seemed to reel.
A Tuscan trumpet pealed through the sky.

They looked up as thunder split the heavens
Again and again. In a clear patch of sky   600
They saw arms gleaming like red fire
Through the pure air and clashing in thunder.
The others gaped with fear, but Aeneas
Knew the sound, and the promise of his mother,
And said:

       "Ask not what the portents forebode,   605
My dear host; in truth, do not ask. It is I
Who am summoned by heaven. The goddess
Who bore me foretold she would send this sign
If war was near, and that she would aid me,
Bringing through the air arms forged by Vulcan.   610
Ah, the slaughter in store for the poor Laurentines!
What a price you will pay me, Turnus! How many
Shields and helmets and bodies of the brave
Will you, Father Tiber, roll beneath your waves?
Let them call for battle and break their treaty!"   615

With this Aeneas rose and rekindled the fire
On Hercules' altar, approaching with joy
The Lar of yesterday and the small household altar.
Evander and the Trojans, side by side,
Sacrificed ewes ritually culled from the herd.   620
Then Aeneas went to his ships and handpicked
The best men on board to follow him to war,
Leaving the rest to ride the current downstream
And bring word to Ascanius of his father's fortunes.
The Teucrians bound for Etruscan fields   625
Were given horses. Aeneas' spirited mount
Was caparisoned in a lionskin
Tawny and glittering with claws of gold.

Rumor flew through the little town,
Spreading the news that horsemen were storming   630
To the shores of the Tyrrhenian king.
Mothers redoubled their vows, their fear
More immediate now, and the image
Of the War God loomed larger.

Then Evander,
Clasping the hand of his departing son,   635
Clung to him and, weeping beyond measure:

"If only Jupiter could turn back the years
And make me what I was under Praeneste's walls
When I cut down the enemy's foremost ranks
And burned their shields in triumph. This right hand   640
Sent King Erulus down to Tartarus.
His mother, Feronia, had given him at birth
Three lives, three changes of armor,
So that he had to be faced three horrifying times
And laid low in death each time. Yet this right hand   645
Stripped him of all his lives and of his armor.
If I could be as I was then I would never be torn
From your sweet embrace, nor would Mezentius ever
Have heaped such scorn upon his neighbor's head,
Or put so many to the sword, or widowed the town   650
Of so many of her sons.
                          You powers above,
And Jupiter, supreme ruler of the gods,
Pity the king of the Arcadians and hear
A father's prayer. If it is your will
To keep my Pallas safe, if it is his destiny,   655
If I will see him and come to him among the living,
Then I pray for life. I can endure any trial.
But if, Fortune, you threaten some dire mischance,
Cut off my cruel life now—now, while fears
Are still unsure and hope uncertain,   660
While you, dear child, my late and only joy,
Are in my arms. Then no ill-omened words
Could wound my ears."

                 As Pallas' father
Poured forth these words at their last parting
He fell unconscious, and his servants   665
Lifted him up and bore him into the house.

The horsemen rode out from the open gates,
Led by Aeneas and loyal Achates

And the other foremost Trojans.
Pallas himself rode in the column's center,   670
Conspicuous in his cloak and figured armor,

> *Like the Morning Star, loved by Venus*
> *As no other star, when it rises from Ocean,*
> *A sacred light in the sky melting the dark.*

On the walls mothers stood trembling,   675
Eyes following the cloud of dust
And the gleaming bronze squadrons
Heading off through the brush by the shortest path.
A shout went up, the column tightened,
And the horses thundered across the plain.   680

Near Caere's cold stream stands a vast grove
Steeped in religious awe. It lies in a hollow
Ringed by dark fir trees that march up the hills.
Rumor has it that the old Pelasgians
Who first held Latium in ages past   685
Dedicated the grove and a festal day
To Silvanus, god of fields and flocks.
Not far from this grove Tarchon encamped
With his Tyrrhenians, who pitched their tents
Throughout the fields. Their encampment   690
Could be seen from the hilltops, and Aeneas
Made his way there with his elite troops.
They watered their horses and took their rest.

Venus, a brightness in the air, drew near,
Bearing gifts through the clouds. She saw her son   695
In the hidden valley, standing alone by a cold stream,
And, making herself visible to him, she said:

"Here are the gifts I promised, forged to a wonder
By my husband's skill. Now you need not hesitate,
My son, to challenge the proud Laurentines   700
Or engage Turnus in combat."

The Cytherean spoke
And went to receive her son's embrace.
Then she set out before him under an oak tree
The refulgent armor. Aeneas gloried
In the gifts from heaven, in this high honor,   *705*
And he could not satisfy his eyes as they moved
From one part to another. He was lost in wonder
As he turned each piece over in his hands
And cradled it in his arms: the flaring helmet
With its threatening crest, the lethal sword,   *710*
The stiff, bronze corselet, as red as blood,
Glowing from within like a cobalt thunderhead
When it catches fire from the rays of the sun;
Then the smooth greaves in electrum and gold,
The spear—and the shield's ineffable design.   *715*

On it the Fire God had prophetically wrought
The future of Italy, and Roman triumphs
In the coming ages, every generation,
In order, still to be born from the stock
Of Ascanius, and all the wars they would fight.   *720*

On it he made the she-wolf, lying in Mars' green cave,
With the twin boys playing as they suckled fearlessly
At their mother's breast. Her sculpted head turned back
To nuzzle each in turn and lick them into shape.

Close by he put Rome, and the Sabine women   *725*
Carried off lawlessly from the seated crowds
At the great Circus games.
                                And then sudden war
Between the sons of Romulus and aged Tatius
With his stern Cures.
                                Next, peace between them,
The same kings standing armed before Jupiter's altar,   *730*
Holding shallow bowls as they made their treaty
Over a sacrificed sow. The roof
Of Romulus' palace bristled with fresh thatch.

Not far from there, four-horse chariots

Were driven in opposite directions, and a man   735
Chained between them had been torn apart,
Mettus (you should have kept your word, Alban!).
Tullus was dragging the traitor's entrails
    Through brambles spattered with drops of blood.

    And there was Porsenna, besieging the city   740
To restore by force the exiled Tarquin to Rome.
Aeneas' descendants rushed on the sword
For freedom's sake. You could see Porsenna
Portrayed as scowling, portrayed as threatening,
Because Cocles dared to tear down the bridge,   745
    And Cloelia broke free and swam the river.

    At the top, Manlius, captain of the Tarpeian fort,
Stood before the temple and held the high Capitol.
And here the silver goose was fluttering
Through gilded porticoes, cackling that the Gauls   750
Were at the gate. You could see the Gauls
Lurking in thickets, under cover of darkness
And the shadows of night. Their hair was gold
In the gloom, their cloaks shimmered
With golden stripes, and their milk-white necks   755
Were circled with gold. Each of them wielded
    Two Alpine pikes and a body-length shield.

    And here he had forged the leaping Salii,
The naked Luperci, their ritual caps bound with wool,
The shields fallen from heaven, and the solemn procession   760
    Of chaste Roman matrons in cushioned chariots.

    Far below he set the hells of Tartarus,
The high gates of Dis, and the wages of sin.
You, Catiline, were hung from the frowning
Face of a cliff and trembled at the Furies   765
    While Cato, set apart, gave laws to the good.

    These scenes were lapped by the swelling sea,
Pure gold, yet the water was blue and flecked

With whitecaps. Circling dolphins picked out in silver
   Cut through the waves, and their tails flicked the spume. 770

   In the center, bronze ships: the Battle of Actium.
You could see all Leucate seething with War,
   And the waves glistening with golden fire.

   On one side, leading Italy into battle,
With the Senate, the People, the city's Penates, 775
And all the great gods, stood Caesar Augustus
On his ship's high stern, a double flame
Licking his temples, and above his head
Shone his father's star.
               Elsewhere, Agrippa,
Backed by winds and gods, towered over 780
His fleet of ships, and on his brow gleamed
   The beaked Naval Crown, his proud insignia.

   On the other side, Antony, Conqueror of the East,
Fresh from the Red Sea, marshaled his armies,
A rich mélange of all the Orient's might 785
From Egypt to Bactria, and in his convoy—
   To his eternal shame—was his Egyptian wife.

The ships all rushed on at once, and the whole sea foamed,
Ripped by the oars and the triple-pronged beaks
As they made for deep water. You would think the Cyclades, 790
Uprooted from the seafloor, were floating there,
Or that high mountains crashed upon mountains,
So massive the assault launched by seamen
From one turreted ship upon another,
Flaming pitch raining down, steel flying, 795
   As Neptune's fields turned crimson with blood.

   Among them the Queen, rattling Egyptian timbrels,
Called up her warships, still unaware
Of the twin snakes at her back. Barking Anubis
And monstrous gods of every description 800
Fought against Neptune, Minerva, and Venus.
Chiseled in iron at the eye of the battle

Mars raged, the Furies swooped from the sky,
And exultant Discord, robe torn, strode forward
    Followed by Bellona with her bloody scourge.   805

    Apollo looked down on all this from Actium
And was bending his bow. In shock and awe,
Egypt and India, all the Sabaeans and Arabs,
Were in full retreat. The Queen herself
Was calling for wind, spreading her sails,   810
And hurrying to pay out the slackened ropes.
The Fire God had made her pale as death
Amid all the carnage, driven over the waves
By winds from Apulia toward the mourning Nile.
The great rivergod had opened all the folds   815
Of his copious robe and welcomed the vanquished
    Into the sheltering waters of his azure lap.

    But Caesar entered Rome in triple triumph
And consecrated his immortal votive offering
To the gods of Italy: three hundred great shrines   820
Throughout the city. The streets rang
With joyful festivities. At every temple
Was a chorus of matrons; there were altars
At every temple, and slaughtered steers
    Blanketed the ground before each altar.   825

    Caesar himself, seated at the polished
Marble threshold of Phoebus Apollo,
Reviewed the gifts from the world's nations
And hung them high on the temple's doorposts
While the conquered peoples marched on past   830
In long procession, each as different
In their clothes and gear as in the tongues they spoke.
Here the immortal blacksmith had fashioned
The Nomads, and the loose-robed African people,
The Leleges and Carians and the quivered Scythians.   835
The Euphrates now flowed with a softer current,
The Morini were here from the ends of the earth,
The two-horned Rhine, the indomitable Dahae,
    And the Araxes, vexed at his stream being bridged.

Such was the design of the shield Vulcan made,   *840*
Venus' gift to her son. Aeneas was moved
To wonder and joy by the images of things
He could not fathom, and he lifted to his shoulder
The destiny of his children's children.

AENEID NINE

While Aeneas was admiring his shield,
Juno sent Iris down from heaven
To bold Turnus, who was sitting
In the sacred grove of his sire, Pilumnus.
And Thaumas' daughter, with pale-rose lips: 5

"Turnus, what no god dared promise you
Time in its turning has brought unasked!
Aeneas has left his town and his fleet
To visit Evander's Palatine realm.
Not only that, he has gone deep   10
Into Etruria to recruit the country folk,
All the way to Lydian Cortona.
What are you waiting for? Now is the hour
To call for your chariot. Quit stalling,
And take their camp by surprise."

                Iris spoke,   15
Rose into the air on wings, and in her wake
Left a huge arc beneath the clouds.

                Turnus
Knew it was the goddess and, spreading
Both his upturned palms to the stars, implored:

"Iris, sky's glory, which god sent you to me   20
Down along the clouds? What is this sudden
Brightness in the air? The mists have parted,

And I see the stars that roam the sky's field.
Whoever you are that calls me to arms,
I follow the omen!"

          And with these words   25
He went to the river, scooped up water,
And prayed to the gods over and over,
Burdening heaven's air with his vows.

And now the whole army was advancing
Over the open plain, rich in horses, rich   30
In embroidered robes and gold. Messapus
Rode point, Tyrrhus' sons brought up the rear,
And Turnus rode in the company's middle,

    Like the Ganges River rising high in silence
    Fed by its seven solemn streams, or the Nile   35
    Sinking into its channel after it has flooded
    All the bottomland with its rich water.

The Teucrians saw a sudden cloud of dust
Gathering on the plain and darkness rising.
Caicus shouted from the foremost rampart: 40

"Something big is rolling this way, black as night.
Every man to arms and on the walls!
The enemy is here!"

          And with a roar
Every last Teucrian came inside the gates
And took his position on the wall,   45
Just as Aeneas had ordered when he left.
If anything should happen before the return
Of their general, the Trojans were not
To take the field but only hold the fort,
Protected by the walls and mound. Even if   50
Shame and anger prompted them to retaliate,
They were under orders to bar the gates
And await the enemy in the towers.

Turnus now was flying ahead
Of his lagging column, twenty picked horsemen   55
Riding with him, and arrived at the city
Unexpectedly. He was mounted
On a white-flecked Thracian stallion,
And his golden helmet was plumed in crimson.

"Which of you men will be first with me   60
To attack the enemy? Watch this!"

                              As he spoke
He rifled a javelin into the wind
To start the battle and, towering on horseback,
Scoured the plain. His company
Cheered the throw and followed after him   65
With bone-chilling screams. They were amazed
That the Teucrians still lay up in camp,
Unwilling to join battle on a fair field.
Turnus rode wildly back and forth
And around the walls, searching   70
For a way in, but there was none to be found.

> *A wolf lies in wait by a crowded sheep pen,*
> *Growling through midnight wind and rain.*
> *Huddled beneath their mothers, the lambs*
> *Keep bleating, and the wolf rages and snaps*   75
> *At the prey it cannot reach, tormented*
> *By long hunger, its jaws thirsting for blood.*

So too the Rutulian as he scanned the walls,
His iron bones burning with grief and rage.
How can he get in? By what strategy   80
Can he flush the Trojans out onto the plain?
The fleet lay close to one side of the camp,
Hemmed in by mounds and the running river.
Turnus attacked it, calling to his men
To bring fire. He wrapped one huge hand   85
Around a blazing pine, and his whooping comrades,
Inspired by his sheer presence, stripped
The campfires and armed themselves

With smoking torches. The lurid glare
Spread toward the ships, and the god Vulcan   *90*
Lifted the swirling ashes to the sky.

What god, O Muses, turned these flames
Away from the Trojans? Who drove
This conflagration from their ships?
Tell the old tale as it has ever been told.   *95*

Long ago, when Aeneas was building his fleet
On Phrygian Ida, preparing to sail the seas,
The Berecynthian Mother of Gods herself
Interceded with Jupiter:

                    "My son,
Now Lord of Olympus, grant the prayer   *100*
Of your own dear mother. Once I had a grove,
Beloved through the centuries, a pine forest
On the mountain's crest, a sacred wood,
Dim with dark fir and black trunks of maple.
I gave it all gladly to the Trojan hero   *105*
When he needed ships. But now I am anxious.
Relieve my fear, let a mother's prayer prevail:
Battered and blasted, let these ships not fail.
Let their birth in our hills win them this grace."

And in reply, her son, who spins the stars: *110*

"Mother, where are you summoning Fate?
What do you want for these ships of yours?
Should keels crafted by mortal hands
Have immortal rights? Should Aeneas
Pass through perils unimperiled?   *115*
What god has such power? No,
But one day, their duty discharged,
As they lie moored in an Ausonian harbor,
All the ships that have escaped the deep
And brought their Dardanian captain   *120*
To the fields of Laurentum I shall transmute,

Tearing away their mortal forms
And bidding them be goddesses
Of the great sea, like the Nereid Doto
Or Galatea, breasts shearing the brine."   125

Jupiter spoke, and, ratifying his oath
By the black, swirling waters
Of his Stygian brother, he nodded assent
And with his nod made Olympus tremble.

And so the Fates parsed out their time,   130
And on the promised day Turnus' outrage
Signaled the Mother to repel the fire
From her sacred ships. First, an eerie flash of light
Blinded the eye, and then, coming out of the east,
An immense cloud, circled by Ida's mystic dancers,   135
Rushed across the sky, and the voice that fell
From the ocean of air sent shock waves through the ranks
Of Trojans and Rutulians alike:

"Do not trouble, Teucrians, to take up arms
In defense of my ships. Turnus will sooner   140
Burn up the sea than scorch my sacred pines.
Go free now, go, goddesses of the deep.
The Mother commands it."

                    The ships at once
Ripped their cables free of the banks
And, dipping their beaks, dove like dolphins   145
Into the depths. And then each, a great wonder,
Rose as a mermaid and swam in the waves.

Awe shriveled the Rutulians' souls. Even
Messapus panicked, and his horses shied,
Wide-eyed with fear. The river itself fell silent   150
As Father Tiber stepped back from the sea.
But Turnus did not lose his nerve. He responded
By seizing this chance to steel his men's spirits:

"It is the Trojans these portents are meant for!
Jupiter himself has taken away   155
Their usual crutch. They're as good as dead,
Even without Rutulian sword and fire.
With no escape by sea, no hope of flight,
They have lost half the world, and we hold
The other half, the land, with so many thousands   160
Of Italy's people taking up arms!
The oracles these Phrygians boast of
Don't scare me one bit. Venus and Fate
Were paid in full when the Trojans first touched
The fields of Ausonia. And I have my own fate: 165
To cut the heart out of a race guilty
Of stealing my bride! It is not only
The sons of Atreus who feel that pain,
Not only Mycenae that gets to go to war.
'Oh, but Troy has already suffered enough.'   170
One offense would have been enough—
If only they didn't deeply despise
Every woman on earth. These are men
Who put their hope in half-built walls,
Puny ramparts that merely delay their death.   175
Didn't they see Troy's walls, built by Neptune,
Go down in flames?
                        But which of you,
My chosen troops, is ready to chop down
This fence with me and terrorize their camp?
I don't need arms made to order by Vulcan,   180
Or a thousand ships, to face the Trojans.
They can have all the Etruscan allies they want,
And they don't have to fear stealth by night,
Or theft of their Palladium—and we won't skulk
In the hollow belly of a wooden horse.   185
No, I mean to ring their walls with fire
In broad daylight, and I will make sure they know
They are not dealing now with the youth of Greece,
Whom Hector held off for ten long years.
        The better part of this day is done, men.   190
Use what's left for some well-earned rest,
And rest assured we are preparing for war."

Messapus was in charge of blockading the gates.
He posted sentries along a ring of watch fires
Encircling the walls. Fourteen Rutulians   195
Captained these stations, and each was attended
By a hundred men, purple-crested, gleaming in gold.
They trotted to their posts, and when not on guard
Lay in the grass draining bronze bowls of wine.
The fires shone bright, and the sentries spent   200
The sleepless night in games. . . .

The Trojans looked down on this from the wall.
Although they held the high, fortified ground,
They were anxious, restless, testing the gates,
Building gangways out to the towers,   205
Hauling up weapons. In command here
Were Mnestheus and the intense Serestus.
Aeneas had put them in charge of the troops,
And the state as well, should adversity knock.
The entire army camped out along the wall,   210
Sharing duties, peril, and the watch by night.

Stationed at one of the gates was Nisus,
Fierce in his bronze. His father
Was Hyrtacus, and the huntress Ida
Had sent him to be Aeneas' companion,   215
Quick as lightning with a javelin or bow.
Next to him was Euryalus. No one
More beautiful followed Aeneas
Or wore Trojan armor. Still a boy,
His face showed the first hint of a beard.   220
One love united them. Side by side
They would charge into battle, and now
They were on watch together at the gate.
Nisus was speaking:

                    "Do the gods
Put this fire in our hearts, Euryalus,   225
Or do our passions become our gods?
I've been eager to do battle, or to do

Some great thing. My mind just won't rest.
You see how the Rutulians are getting careless?
Just a few fires winking, the troops flat on their backs,   230
Drunk and half asleep. Dead quiet for miles.
This is what I'm thinking. Everyone,
The elders and the people, is demanding
That scouts be sent to summon Aeneas
And brief him. Well, if they promise   235
What I want for you (the glory will do for me),
I think I can find beneath that mound
A path that leads to the walls of Pallanteum."

And Euryalus, struck by a great love
Of praise, said to his ardent friend: 240

"Are you refusing to let me join you
In this supreme adventure, Nisus?
Am I supposed to send you out alone
Into danger like this? My father, Opheltes,
The old warrior, didn't raise me that way   245
During all our struggles with the Greeks,
All the terror at Troy. Nor have I been that way
With you, following great Aeneas
To his utmost destiny. Before you one
Who scorns the light, who believes that honor,   250
Which you too strive for, is bought cheaply with life."

And Nisus:

            "I have no doubts about you,
Nor should I. No. And I pray that Jupiter,
Or whichever god might look on this with favor,
Will bring me back to you in triumph. But if,   255
As does happen in business like this,
Some god, or just bad luck, takes me down,
I want you to survive me. Someone your age
Is worthier of life, and I'll need someone
To commit me to the earth after my corpse   260
Is dragged out of battle, or perhaps ransomed—
Or if circumstance prohibits the usual rites

To perform them in my honor by an empty tomb.
And I would not want to be the cause of grief
For your mother, who alone of many mothers   265
Followed her boy and left Acestes' haven."

But Euryalus said:

                    "Stop offering excuses.
I'm not going to change my mind. Let's get going."

With that he roused the guards for the next watch.
They took their positions, and Euryalus   270
Went with Nisus to find the prince Ascanius.

All creatures throughout the land were asleep,
Their cares forgotten.
                    Not so the Teucrian captains.
They were deep in council, debating what to do
And whom to send to bring word to Aeneas.   275
They were standing in the middle of the camp,
Leaning on their long spears, shields shouldered.
Nisus and Euryalus burst in on them,
Begging to be heard on urgent business.
It was Iülus who came forward and welcomed   280
The nervous pair. He asked Nisus to speak,
And the son of Hyrtacus began:

                         "Please listen to us
With open minds, men of Aeneas, and don't judge
What we have to say by our age. The Rutulians
Have succumbed to sleep and wine. We see   285
A place to ambush them in the fork by the gate
Nearest the sea. The fires have gone out there
And black smoke rises to the sky.
If you let us take this chance you will soon
See us here again with spoils from a great slaughter.   290
Then we can follow the path to Pallanteum
And to Aeneas. On our hunting trips
Down those dark valleys we have sighted
The city's walls, and we know the whole river."

Then Aletes, the grave old counselor, said: *295*

"Gods of our fathers and of Troy,
You do not intend after all to blot out our race,
Not if you have brought us youths with such spirit
And steady hearts."

             Saying this, he held them both
By their shoulders and clasped their hands. Tears   *300*
Flowed down his cheeks as he said:

            "What rewards can match
Such glorious deeds? The gods will give you
The most precious rewards, the gods
And your own good character. The rest Aeneas
Will bestow upon you, as will young Ascanius,   *305*
Forever mindful of service so great."

And taking up his words, "No, I will go further,"
Ascanius said: "My sole safety lies
In my father's return, and so, Nisus,
By the great gods of the house of Troy,   *310*
By the Lar of Assaracus,
And by the inner sanctum of hoary Vesta,
I implore you both and place in your hands
My hope and my fortune. Call my father
Back into our sight. Our gloom will be gone   *315*
At his return. As for gifts, I will give you
A pair of silver goblets, richly embossed,
That my father got at the sack of Arisba,
Two matching tripods, two great bars of gold,
And an ancient bowl that he received   *320*
From Sidonian Dido. And if it is our lot
To take Italy and divide the spoils of war—
You have seen the horse that Turnus rides,
And his armor, all gold—that horse, that shield,
And those crimson plumes I hereby set aside   *325*
As your reward, Nisus. And besides this
My father will give you twelve chosen matrons,
Beautiful all, and men too, captives of war,

Each with his armor. And on top of this,
Whatever land King Latinus holds.   *330*
And you, Euryalus, revered in your youth,
Which is close to my own, I welcome you
With all my heart, with open arms,
As my friend and companion in every deed.
No glory will be mine that is not yours,   *335*
In war and peace, in word and in action
My greatest trust will be placed in you."

And Euryalus answered him with this:

"Never shall a day prove me unfit
For such valor; only let fortune fall   *340*
In my favor. But more than all you offer
There is one thing I ask. My mother,
Of Priam's ancient line, unhappy woman,
Left Ilium's land and Acestes' city
Rather than leave me. I now leave her   *345*
Ignorant of whatever peril this may be
And without telling her good-bye, because—
I swear by Night and your own right hand—
I could not bear a mother's tears. So I beg you,
Comfort her in her need and desolation.   *350*
Let me hope this of you, and I will go
More boldly into danger."

                         The Dardanians
Were moved to tears, Iülus most of all.
This picture of a son's devotion
Touched his heart, and he said:

                              "Rest assured   *355*
That all will be worthy of your great endeavor.
Your mother will be mine, lacking only the name
Creüsa. No small gratitude awaits
The woman who bore such a son. Whatever
The outcome of your action, I swear   *360*
By this head, by which my father once swore,

That what I promise to you on your return
Will be there for your mother and family as well."

And with tears in his eyes he unbuckles his sword,
The gold-crusted wonder forged by Lycaon   365
And fitted by him with an ivory sheath.
Mnestheus gives Nisus a shaggy lionskin,
And loyal Aletes swaps helmets with him.
They head out at once, and the whole company,
Young and old, escort them to the gate with prayers.   370
Iülus, young and beautiful, but mature
Beyond his years, carefully gives them
Messages for his father, but the winds
Would scatter them all to the clouds above.

They leave, cross the trenches, and make their way   375
Through night's shadows to the enemy camp,
Where soon they will be the death of many.
Everywhere they look they see drunken men
Asleep in the grass, chariots tilted upright,
Soldiers sprawled among wheels and reins,   380
Weapons and wine jars lying about.
The son of Hyrtacus was first to speak:

"This is it, Euryalus. Cover our rear
And keep your eyes open. I'll lead,
And I'll make a road of blood you can't miss."   385

Then he closed his mouth and addressed Rhamnes
With his sword. This proud man, propped
On a pile of blankets and snoring loudly,
Was a king himself and served King Turnus well
As his augur, but could not augur his way   390
Out of death. Nisus killed his three attendants first,
And Remus' armor-bearer, and the charioteer,
Finding him at the horses' feet, and then severed
The horses' drooping necks. Then he decapitated
Rhamnes himself and left the trunk spurting blood.   395
The couch and the ground were soaked
With warm black gore. Nisus killed also

Lamyrus, Lamus, and young Serranus,
A handsome boy who had played late that night
But was mastered by Sleep, happy—   400
If only he had played his game until dawn.

A lion that has not fed rages through a sheep pen,
Mad with hunger. As it mangles the flock,
The weak animals stand dumb with fear,
And the lion roars from its bloodstained mouth.   405

So too Euryalus, burning with rage,
Fell upon the faceless multitude.
Fadus, Herbesus, and Abaris
Never knew what hit them. Rhoetus, though,
Was awake and saw it all, cowering   410
Behind a large mixing bowl. As he rose
Euryalus buried his sword in his chest
Up to the hilt and then drew the blade out
Drenched in death. Rhoetus belched forth
His purpled life, bringing up wine   415
Mixed with blood as Euryalus pressed on,
Seething in the dark. He was approaching
Messapus' troops and by the fire's dying light
Was watching the tethered horses graze
When Nisus, who felt his friend   420
Was being carried away by blood lust, said:

"Let's get out of here. It's almost light.
We've had our revenge, and we've cut a way
Through the enemy lines."

                   They left behind
Whole sets of solid silver armor, bowls too,   425
And beautiful carpets. Euryalus did take
Rhamnes' gear, with his gold-studded sword-belt,
Gifts that long ago wealthy Caedicus sent
To Remulus of Tibur as a pledge of friendship.
As Remulus lay dying he passed them on   430
To his grandson, and then the Rutulians
Took them as spoils of war. This gear Euryalus

Tore away and put on—all for nothing—
And he put on his head Messapus' plumed helmet.
Then the pair left the camp and ran for cover.   435

Meanwhile, a company of horsemen,
Sent ahead from the Latin city
While the rest of the troops halted on the plain,
Rode up with a reply for Turnus—
Three hundred strong, all under shield,   440
With Volcens in command. The walls of the camp
Were just ahead when off in the distance
They saw the pair turning off on a path to the left.
And in the dim shadows the helmet
Euryalus thoughtlessly wore betrayed him.   445
Volcens caught its gleaming reflection
And shouted from the head of the column:

"Halt! Who are you? Why are you armed,
And what mission are you on?"

                      They made no response
But hurried into the woods and trusted to night.   450
The horsemen rode to block the crossways
And seal the perimeter of the woods with guards.
It was a wide and dense forest, with thickets
Of dark ilex and brambles everywhere,
And trails that glimmered through open patches.   455
The dark branches and his ponderous spoils
Hampered Euryalus, and the network of trails
Confused and panicked him. Nisus got through
In a blind rush and would have escaped the enemy
And those regions later called Alban   460
(At that time part of Latinus' pasture)
When he stopped and looked back,
To no avail, for his missing friend.

"Poor Euryalus, where did I leave you?
How can I find you?"

                  And Nisus retraced   465
His tangled path through the treacherous forest,

Wandering through the silent thickets
Until he heard the horses and the telltale sounds
Of men in pursuit. A few moments later
A cry reached his ears, and he saw Euryalus.   470
Misled by the terrain, betrayed by the night,
And overpowered in the sudden tumult,
Euryalus struggled desperately
As the band dragged him away.
                                        Nisus
Was at a loss. How could he possibly   475
Rescue his friend? With what weapons, what force?
Or should he charge right into their swords
To a swift and beautiful death? Pumping
His spear arm, he looked up to the moon and prayed:

"Be with me now, Goddess, and help me   480
In my need, O daughter of Latona,
Glory of the stars and guardian of groves.
If ever my father brought you offerings
On my behalf, if ever I myself hunted
In your honor, hung sacrifices in your dome,   485
Or fastened them to your temple's roof—
Guide my weapons through the air
And let me break up that party over there."

Nisus spoke, and put all of his weight
Into the throw. The spear split the dark air,   490
Hit a warrior named Sulmo in the back,
And snapped. The splintered shaft
Punched through to his chest, and Sulmo
Spun around, hemorrhaging warm blood
In heaving gasps until he collapsed   495
Into cold death. The Rutulians looked around
In every direction. Breathing more sharply,
Nisus balanced another spear over his shoulder,
And while they hesitated it went hissing
Through both of Tagus' temples   500
And warmed itself deep in his cloven brain.
Volcens seethed with rage but could not see
Who threw the spear or where to unleash his fury.

"All right, then you will pay me with hot blood
For both their deaths."

        As he spoke   505
He went for Euryalus with drawn sword.
This was too much for Nisus. Out of his mind
With terror and no longer able to remain
Hidden in darkness or endure such pain,
He shouted:

        "Me—I did it—turn your swords on me,   510
Rutulians! It was all my idea.
He couldn't have done it, wouldn't have dared,
I swear by the sky and the stars that see all.
He only loved his unlucky friend too much."

Thus Nisus, but the sword, driven home with force,   515
Sliced through the ribs and gashed the white breast.
Euryalus rolled over, dead. Dark blood
Ran over his beautiful limbs, and his head
Sank down onto one shoulder,

    As a purple flower cut by a plow   520
    Droops in death, or as a poppy bows
    Its weary head, heavy with spring rain.

Nisus rushed among them, going only
For Volcens. Volcens alone was his care.
The troops surrounded him, tried to push him back,   525
But he kept on coming, his sword
Flashing like lightning, until he buried the blade
Full in the face of the shrieking Rutulian
And, dying himself, deprived his enemy of life.
Then, pierced and slashed, he threw himself   530
Upon his lifeless friend and there finally
Rested quietly in easeful death.

            Happy pair,
If my poetry has any power
Never shall you be blotted from memory,

As long as the house of Aeneas still stands   535
On the Capitol's unmoving rock,
And the Roman Father rules supreme.

The Rutulians went back to their camp
Victorious and weeping, carrying their spoils
And the lifeless body of Volcens.   540
Their lamentation was still louder in the camp
When they found Rhamnes' pale corpse
And so many of their best men—Serranus,
Numa—massacred. A great throng rushed
To the dead and dying men. The ground   545
Steamed with slaughter, and the foaming blood
Ran in rivulets. Talking among themselves
They recognized the spoils, Messapus' shining helmet,
Other bits of gear won back with so much sweat.

Dawn left Tithonus in his saffron bed   550
And showered new light over all the lands.
When the sun streamed in and unveiled the world,
Turnus, in full dress armor himself,
Called his men to arms. The commanders
Marshaled the bronze lines into battle formation   555
And honed their anger with the latest reports.
They fixed the heads of Nisus and Euryalus
On upright spears—a soul-wrenching sight—
And fell in behind them with a roar.

                                        The Trojans
Formed up on the left flank of their walls—   560
The river protected the right side—
Manning the wide trenches. The troops
Posted in the towers stood in stark grief
At the sight of the transfixed heads they knew
So well, heads now dripping with dark gore.   565

Meanwhile, Rumor winged her way
With the news through the fearful town,
Swift to the ears of Euryalus' mother.

Her bones turned to ice, the shuttle fell
From her hands, and the thread unreeled.   570
She flew out of the house, tearing out her hair,
Her voice quavering in high lamentation,
And in her madness made for the ramparts
And front lines of battle, ignoring the men,
The danger, the weapons flying, and then   575
She filled the sky with her plaintive cries:

"Is this you I see, Euryalus, you,
My last and only comfort in old age?
How could you leave me alone like this?
And when you were sent into danger,   580
Not even to tell your poor mother good-bye!
Now you will lie in a strange land,
Prey to the dogs and birds of Latium,
And I, your mother, did not bury you,
Or close your eyes, or bathe your wounds.   585
I did not shroud you with the robe I made for you,
Working at the loom night and day
To console an old woman's sorrow.
Where am I to go? What land now holds
Your dismembered body? Is this all, my son,   590
You bring back to me of yourself? Is this
What I have pursued by land and sea?
Rutulians! If you have any decency,
Run me through, throw all your spears at me.
Or you, our Father in heaven, be merciful   595
And blast this hateful life into Tartarus,
Since I cannot myself break life's cruel bonds."

Her speech stunned their souls. Too shaken to fight,
The entire army gave way to grief
Until Ilioneus and the weeping Iülus   600
Had Idaeus and Actor gather up the poor woman
And carry her indoors.

                    Trumpets sounded
Their terrible bronze call, and the shouting
That followed echoed in the sky. The Volscians

Locked shields and charged, determined   605
To fill the trenches and pull down the palisade.
One contingent attacked the Trojan lines
Where they were thinnest and threw up ladders
To scale the wall. The Trojans, experienced
At defending walls, threw down on them   610
Everything they could, thrusting with long poles
And rolling down stones of deadly weight
In an attempt to break their shield formation.
The Volscians were doing well under its protection,
But when the Teucrians rolled up a huge boulder   615
And rolled it down where the enemy was thickest,
The Volscians broke ranks and scattered,
No longer willing to fight blind. Standing back,
They now attacked the wall with javelins and arrows.
Elsewhere, Mezentius, a grim sight, was hurling   620
His Tuscan pine torches, and Messapus,
Son of Neptune, breaker of horses,
Was ripping down the rampart and calling for ladders.

Breathe into me, Muses, I pray, O Calliope,
As I sing the slaughter and death Turnus dealt   625
And whom each hero sent down to Orcus.
Unroll with me the great scroll of war.

Looming above the plain there was a tower
Connected to the wall by high gangways.
The Italians concentrated their attack here   630
And were doing their mightiest to topple it.
Inside, the Trojans' defense was to hurl
Stones and projectiles through open slits.
Leading the way, Turnus threw a blazing torch
That stuck in the tower's side. The fire,   635
Fanned by the wind, burned posts and planks,
Eating them away. The men trapped inside
Panicked and edged back en masse
To the tower's far side. Under the sudden
Shift in weight the entire structure collapsed,   640
And the whole sky thundered with the crash.

The men fell to the ground, dead and dying,
Crushed by the mass, impaled by their own weapons
And the splintered wood. Only two made it out,
By the skin of their teeth, Helenor and Lycus.   645
     Helenor, in the prime of youth, was the son
Of a Licymnian slave who had borne him
Secretly to the Maeonian king. His mother
Sent him to Troy, arming him as best she could
With a naked sword and a blank shield   650
As yet ungloried. When he found himself
Surrounded by Turnus' thousands
And hemmed in by the Latin lines, he charged.

     A wild beast hedged in by a circle of hunters
     Rages against them and, knowing it will die,   655
     Bounds into the air and onto their spears.

So too Helenor ran to meet his death
Where he saw the enemy was thickest.
Lycus, though, a far swifter runner,
Sprinted through a rain of weapons   660
And reached the wall. He was trying
To pull himself over the top, reaching
For his friends' hands, when Turnus,
Who had been following him with his spear,
Laughed at him, saying:

                    "You thought   665
You could get away, didn't you?"

                    And as he spoke
He pulled Lycus down with a large chunk of the wall.

     Think of a hare, or a snow-white swan,
     In the talons of an eagle; or a wolf
     Snatching from the fold a bleating lamb.   670

A shout went up, and the Rutulians
Pressed on, filling the trenches with earth
And throwing burning torches on the roofs.
Ilioneus hit Lucetius with a huge craggy rock

As he was coming up to the gate with fire   675
And laid him low. Liger killed Emathion,
Good with a spear; Asilas killed Corynaeus,
A skilled archer. Caeneus cut down Ortygius
And himself fell to Turnus, who went on to kill
Itys, Clonius, Dioxippus, Promolus,   680
Sagaris, and Idas, the latter as he stood
On the topmost tower. Capys then killed
Privernus, who had just been nicked
By Themilla's spear. Privernus panicked,
Threw down his shield, and moved his hand   685
To the wound, and Capys' arrow flew home,
Punching deep into his left side, a fatal wound
That tore through his lungs. Arcens' son stood
In splendid armor, his embroidered mantle
Dyed Iberian violet. Noble and handsome,   690
He had been reared in a grove of Mars
Near the Symaethus river and Palicus' altar.
Seeing him, Mezentius dropped both his spears,
Whirled his sling above his head three times,
And split the man's head open with slugs of lead,   695
Laying him out full length in the sand.

Then Ascanius, for the first time in war,
Took aim with an arrow. Until this moment
He had only shot at animals in the hunt,
But now he shot and killed Numanus Remulus,   700
Who had recently married Turnus' sister.
Numanus was striding out from the ranks,
Saying things both proper and improper.
His newfound royalty had gone to his head,
And he boasted loudly of his heroic stature: 705

"Shame on you, Phrygians! Twice now
Your city has been taken. Aren't you getting tired
Of being besieged and warding off death with walls?
Look at the great heroes fighting us for our wives!
What god, what insanity, has driven you   710
To Italy? There are no sons of Atreus here,
No lying Ulysses. No, just us, a tough breed.

We bring our newborn sons to the river
To toughen them up in the ice-cold water.
When they are boys they hunt day and night.   715
They break horses for fun, and shoot arrows.
But they know how to work and to do without,
Whether it's busting sod or shaking cities in war.
Our whole life is worn away with iron. We goad
Our oxen with spear butts, and old age   720
Doesn't slow us down either, or make us weak.
We press helmets onto white hair, and we love
To bring home new spoils and live on plunder.
But you! You wear embroidered saffron
And purple satin. You like to loaf and dance.   725
Your tunics have sleeves and your heads bonnets.
You are really Phrygian women! Go over
To Dindymus, where they play those double pipes
You are used to hearing. The tambourines
Are calling you, and the Berecynthian   730
Boxwood flutes of the Mother on Ida.
Get out of here and leave war to men."

Ascanius did not take these boasts and taunts.
Facing Numanus, he fit the arrow's notch
To the horsehair string, drew it back,   735
And paused to invoke Jupiter with vows:

"Almighty Jupiter, assent to my bold start
And I will bring gifts yearly to your temple,
Set before your altar an ox with gilded brow,
White as the moon, head as high as its mother's,   740
Already butting horns and scuffing the sand."

The Father heard and thundered on the left
In the clear sky, and in the same moment
The lethal bow twanged and the arrow whined
As it bored through the air and Remulus' skull,   745
Iron cleaving both of his temples.

                              "So you want
To mock our valor with haughty words? This

Is the answer the twice-captured Phrygians
Give the Rutulians."

               Ascanius said no more.
The Teucrians cheered, and their spirits soared.   *750*

And in the high regions of the sky, Apollo,
His rich hair streaming, was looking down
From his seat on a cloud at the Ausonian lines
And the Trojan town. He addressed
The triumphant Iülus in words such as these: *755*

"This is the way to the stars, noble young hero,
Born of the gods and with gods to come in your line.
All destined wars will justly subside
Under the descendants of Assaracus.
Your fate is greater than Troy's."

               Apollo spoke   *760*
And shot down from high heaven, parting
The gusty air. He found Ascanius
And then transformed himself into aged Butes,
Who had been Anchises' armor-bearer
And trusted companion. Aeneas later   *765*
Assigned him to Ascanius. Apollo
Strode on exactly like the old man—
The same complexion, voice, white hair,
Even the harsh clank his armor made—
And he spoke these words to fiery Iülus: *770*

"Let it be enough, child of Aeneas,
That Numanus has fallen to your arrow
Unavenged. Apollo grants you this honor,
Your first, and is not jealous of your archery,
Which rivals his own. But now, my son,   *775*
Stay out of the war."

              While he was speaking
Apollo left the sight of men and vanished
Into thin air. The Dardanian princes

Knew it was the god, and as he flew off
They heard the quiver rattle on his back.   780
And so, in accordance with the will of Phoebus,
They reined in Ascanius, eager as he was for war,
And went themselves back to the fighting
And put their lives on the line. A shout
Ran all along the wall's perimeter,   785
From tower to tower. They bent their bows
And rifled javelins with leather thongs.
Spears littered the ground, shields and helmets
Clashed and rang. The battle surged,

> *Like lashing rain that comes out of the west*   790
> *When the watery Goat Stars rise in the sky;*
> *Or hail that showers into the sea*
> *When Jupiter, bristling with southerly gales,*
> *Stirs up a storm and explodes the clouds.*

Pandarus and Bitias, tall as pine trees   795
On their native Ida, were sons of Alcanor
And the wood nymph Iaera, who bore them
In a grove of Jupiter. Now they opened the gate
Their captain had put them in charge of
And, confident in their strength of arms,   800
Waved the enemy in. They themselves stood
On either side of the gate, sheathed in iron,
Plumes rippling on their towering heads,

> *As twin oaks on the banks of the river Po,*
> *Or the pleasant Athesis, lift their unshorn heads*   805
> *Into heaven's air and nod their leafy crowns.*

When they saw the entrance was clear,
The Rutulians rushed in. They did not last long.
Quercens and Aquicolus, a handsome warrior,
And the daredevil Tmarus, and Haemon,   810
Whose father was Mars, were all routed
Along with their troops. They turned tail
And ran, or lost their lives in the very gateway.
The Trojans, their spirits rising,

Massed at the gate; engaging the enemy   815
Hand to hand, they ventured farther out.
Turnus was creating havoc of his own
In another sector. When word reached him
That the enemy had tasted blood
And were leaving the gates wide open, he quit   820
What he was doing and, his rage flaring,
Ran to the Trojan gate and the twin giants.
First out to meet him was Antiphates,
Sarpedon's bastard son by a Mysian woman.
Turnus killed him with a spear-cast, the hard   825
Italian cornel gliding through the soft air
To enter Antiphates' gullet and tunnel deep
Into his chest. The dark, gaping wound surged
With foaming blood, and the steel grew warm
In the transfixed lung. Meropes next,   830
Then Erymus and Aphidnus fell to Turnus,
And then Bitias, eyes burning, rage in his heart.
It was not Turnus' spear that undid Bitias—
He would never have lost his life to a spear—
But a whirling battle-pike of lead and iron   835
That split the air like a bolt of lightning.
Two layers of oxhide and a corselet
Of double-plated gold could not withstand it.
Bitias' gigantic frame collapsed. Earth groaned
When he fell, and his shield crashed like thunder.   840

> *A huge mass of rock falls on Baiae's shore*
> *As men construct seawalls, and as it falls*
> *It trails ruin behind it, crashing down*
> *Into the water to rest in its depths. The sea*
> *Churns with black sand, and the sound rumbles*   845
> *Through high Prochyta and Inarime's lava bed,*
> *Laid on Jove's orders above Typhoeus.*

And now Mars, the War God, multiplied
The Latins' courage and twisted his sharp goads
Deep in their hearts. But among the Trojans   850
He unleashed black Terror and Panic.
The Latins, with the War God in their souls,

Saw their chance and converged. . . .
When Pandarus saw his brother crumple
And how the day's fortunes were going,   855
He put his shoulder to the gate and swung it closed,
Leaving many of his comrades shut outside
In the bitter fighting, but enclosing many
With himself, and welcoming them
As they rushed in. But in his madness   860
He did not notice the Rutulian prince
Bursting in among the streaming ranks
And unwittingly shut him up in the town,
Like a great tiger let into a sheep pen.
A new light gleamed in Turnus' eyes,   865
And his armor rang terribly. The bloody crests
On his helmet quivered, and his shield
Flashed with lightning. In one awful moment
The Trojans recognized that hateful face,
That massive form, and were thrown into a panic.   870
Then gigantic Pandarus sprang forward
Seething with rage for his brother's death
And spoke out:

                    "This is not Amata's
Bridal palace, or downtown Ardea.
You are looking at the enemy's camp,   875
And there is no way for you to escape."

And Turnus, smiling calmly at the man:

"Bring it on, if you have the guts. You can
Tell Priam there is another Achilles here."

Thus Turnus. Pandarus threw his spear,   880
Knotty and rough, with all his might,
But the wind took it—Saturnian Juno
Deflected the shot—and it stuck in the gate.
And Turnus:

                    "Right! But don't think I'll miss.
Nobody dodges my weapons."

                                    With that he leapt high   885
And put his weight into his sword, cleaving
Pandarus' brow in two between the temples
And splitting open his boyish face. He fell
With a crash, and the earth trembled
Under the impact of his enormous body.   890
Stretched on the ground in brain-spattered armor
Pandarus lay dying, his neatly parted head
Dangling equally to each of his shoulders.

The Trojans, terrified, beat a hasty retreat,
And if it had occurred to the victorious hero   895
To burst the gate's bars and let in his troops,
That day would have been the last for the war
And the Trojan people. But passion for slaughter
Made him rage on.
First he took out Phaleris, and then Gyges,   900
Hamstringing the latter. Seizing their spears
He threw them at the backs of the escaping enemy.
Juno multiplied his strength, and he dispatched
Halys and Phegeus, piercing his shield;
And then Alcander, Halius, Noemon,   905
And Prytanis, who were up on the wall
Urging men on. They never knew what hit them.
When Lynceus, rallying his troops, made a move,
Turnus came at him from the wall on the right
And with one swipe of his flashing sword   910
Severed the man's head, which came to rest
Some distance away, still in its helmet.
Amycus was next, a formidable hunter
Who excelled in the art of poisoning arrows;
And then Clytius, son of Aeolus,   915
And Cretheus, dear to the Muses—
The Muses' companion, Cretheus,
Who was forever tuning his lyre,
Setting verses to music, and singing
Of horses, the arms of men, and war.   920

When word of the carnage reached them,
The Teucrian captains Mnestheus and Serestus

Came forward to see their men scattered
And their enemy within the gates.
And Mnestheus, sharply:

                          "Where are you going?   925
Do you have some other walls to protect you?
Countrymen, shall one man, trapped inside,
Slaughter a whole town unpunished? Send so many
Of our best young men to Orcus? Cowards!
Have you no shame, no pity for your country,   930
For your ancient gods, for great Aeneas?"

This speech steeled their spirits. They halted
In dense formation, and Turnus gave ground
Step by step, making for the part of the town
Bounded by the river. The Teucrians pressed him   935
All the harder, shouting loudly and closing in.

> *Hunters crowd around a savage lion,*
> *Their spears ready. The lion is wary*
> *But glares angrily as it gives ground,*
> *And although its valor will not allow it*   940
> *To turn its back it cannot, for all its desire,*
> *Break through the hunters and their spears.*

So too Turnus, hesitantly retracing
His steps, his heart seething with rage.
Even then he attacked twice, routing them   945
Along the wall each time. But when
The entire army gathered together,
Juno did not dare give Turnus the strength
To oppose them all, for Jupiter sent Iris
Down from heaven with stern warnings for his sister   950
That Turnus must leave the Teucrian camp.
And so the hero could not hold his own
With sword or shield, not with all the missiles
Raining down on him. His helmet rang
Incessantly, stones cracking the solid bronze open.   955
The horsehair plumes were torn from his crest,
And his shield could no longer withstand the blows.

The Trojans, and Mnestheus himself,
Struck like lightning, hurling spear after spear.
Sweat poured down Turnus' entire body   *960*
In black streams; his breath came in gasps;
And his arms and legs shook convulsively.
At last, in full armor, he dove headfirst
Into the river. Tiber welcomed him,
And buoying him up in his yellow water   *965*
He washed away the blood and floated Turnus
Back to his comrades on a gentle current.

AENEID TEN

Meanwhile, highest Olympus opened,
And the Father of Gods and Men called a council
In the starry halls from which he surveyed
All lands, the Dardan camp, and the Latin peoples.
The gods took their seats, and their lord began: 5

"Why have you gone back on your word,
Divine ones, and fight among yourselves?
I forbade Italy to go to war with Troy.
This quarrel thwarts my will. What fear
Has caused these humans to rush to arms?   10
There shall come a time (do not hasten it)
When wild Carthage will open the Alps
And pour down upon Rome. Then may they fight
And ravage each other. For now, cease your strife
And assent with good will to my covenant."   15

Thus Jupiter, briefly. But golden Venus
Made no brief reply:

"Father Eternal, Power of the Universe—
For what else may we appeal to now?—
Do you see how insolent the Rutulians are,   20
How Turnus, swollen with pride,
Rides his chariot through the crowds,
Rushing into war with Mars at his back?
The Teucrians are no longer protected
By their walls. The fighting has moved   25

244

Inside the gates, and the trenches flow with blood.
Aeneas, far away, does not know of these dangers.
Will you never allow this siege to be lifted?
A second army threatens the walls
Of an infant Troy, and again there rises   30
From Aetolian Arpi a son of Tydeus.
I feel I myself will be wounded again,
I, your child, will stop another mortal spear.
If the Trojans have sought Italy
Without your leave, abandon them   35
And let them pay for their sin. But if
They have followed all the oracles
Given by gods above and shades below,
How can anyone now subvert your will
And establish destiny anew?   40
Why should I even mention the fleet
Burned on the shores of Eryx, or the storms
Stirred up by Aeolus, or Iris
Sent from the clouds? And now Juno
Is mobilizing Hell—a sector   45
Of the universe as yet untried—
And Allecto is turned loose on the upper world
And raves through the cities of Italy.
I no longer care about empire, my hope
While Fortune still smiled. Let those win   50
Whom you want to win. If there is no country
Your hardened wife will allow the Trojans,
Then by the smoking ruins of Troy, I pray,
Let me at least withdraw Ascanius, Father,
Unscathed from war; let my grandson   55
Survive! Aeneas, yes, may be tossed
On unknown seas and follow Fortune's lead,
But let me protect this child and rescue him
From this terrible conflict. Amathus
Is mine, high Paphus and Cythera,   60
A shrine in Idalia. He can live out his life
There, without weapons or glory. Let it be
Your grand decision that Carthage crush Italy.
Nothing then would hinder the Tyrian cities.
But what good has it done him to survive the war,   65

Escape Greek fire, endure endless perils
On land and sea, while his Teucrians sought
To found a new Troy in Latium?
Better to have settled on the dying ashes
Where Troy once stood. You might as well   70
Give them back their Simois and Xanthus
And let them suffer forever Ilium's sorrows!"

Then regal Juno, furious:

                                "Why do you force me
To break my silence and tell the whole world
My heart's deep sorrow? Did any man or god   75
Compel Aeneas to make war on the Latins?
'He sought Italy at the call of the Fates.'
Yes—driven on by Cassandra's raving.
Did I advise him to leave his camp or entrust
His life to the winds? To put a boy in charge   80
Of their defenses at the height of war?
To tamper with Etruscan loyalties
Or stir up peaceful nations to war? What god,
What cruel power of mine, undid Aeneas?
Where is Juno in all of this, or Iris   85
Sent from the clouds? It is indeed monstrous
That Italians are burning your infant Troy,
And that Turnus has taken a stand
In his native land, Turnus, a mere grandson
Of old Pilumnus and whose mother is only   90
The goddess Venilia! But what about
The Trojans torching the Latin people
And pillaging their fields? Dragging a bride
Away from her betrothed? Offering peace
In one hand and arming ships with the other?   95
You have the power to whisk Aeneas
Away from the Greeks and substitute
Empty mist for the man. You are as well
Perfectly capable of turning their ships
Into so many nymphs. But for us to help   100
The Rutulians is disgraceful? You say,
'Aeneas is far away and doesn't know.'

Let him be utterly ignorant and really far away!
Paphus is yours, Idalium, high Cythera.
Why bother with a city teeming with war   105
Or with savage hearts? Is it because I
Am toppling the tottering Phrygian state?
Is it I? Or is it he who dumped the Trojans
Right in front of the Greeks? What cause was there
That Europe and Asia should rise up in arms   110
And ravage their peace treaties in treachery?
Was it I who led Paris, the Dardan adulterer,
To rape Sparta? Did I arm the man
And goad him on with lust? All this was you!
It was then that you should have been afraid   115
For your people. And now you come on late
With your unjust complaints and petty bickering."

Thus Juno's plea, and all the celestials
Murmured various assent,

                    a sound like wind
        Rising in the forest with whispers and moans   120
        That tell the sailors a great storm is coming.

Then the Father Almighty, the greatest power
In the universe, begins, and as he speaks
The high house of the gods grows silent,
Earth's foundations tremble, still goes the air,   125
The winds are hushed, and the high seas calmed:

"Take my words to heart and keep them there.
Since Ausonians and Teucrians cannot form
An alliance, and your dissension has no end,
I shall make no distinction between the hopes   130
And fortunes of either, Trojan or Rutulian,
Whether it be Italy's fortune that holds the camp
Or Troy's tragic error and false prophecies.
Nor do I absolve the Rutulians. The efforts
Of each will bring suffering or success.   135
Jupiter rules over all alike. The Fates
Will find their way."

                    And he nodded assent
By his brother's Stygian waters, by the banks
That seethe with black and swirling waters.
Then Jupiter rose from his golden throne   140
And the gods escorted him to the threshold.

Meanwhile, the Rutulians pressed on
At every gate, intent on slaughtering men
And ringing walls with fire. The Trojans
Were penned inside with no hope of escape.   145
They made a desperate stand on the high towers,
Barely able to man the wall's perimeter.
Asius, Thymoetes, the two Assaraci,
Castor, and old Thymbris were in the lead.
At their side were Sarpedon's two brothers   150
Out of high Lycia, Clarus and Thaemon.
Acmon of Lyrnesus, his whole body straining,
Came up with a huge chunk of mountain,
Himself as huge as his father, Clytius,
Or Mnestheus his brother. They defended   155
With spears and stones, notched arrows and fire.
In their midst the Dardanian boy himself,
Venus' most rightful care, his glorious head
Unhelmeted glittered like a jewel
Set in yellow gold to adorn neck or brow,   160
Or as ivory gleams inlaid in boxwood
Or Ocrian ebony: hair streaming over
His milk-white neck encircled in gold.
You also, Ismarus, your highborn kinsmen
Saw inflicting wounds with poisoned arrows,   165
You, Ismarus of Lydia, where men work rich fields,
And the Pactolus irrigates them with gold.
And Mnestheus was there, yesterday's hero,
Exalted for driving Turnus from the wall;
Capys too, who gave his name to Campania.   170

Thus the struggles of war. Aeneas, though,
Was cutting through shallow seas at midnight.
When he had left Evander and entered

The Tuscan camp, he met the king and announced
His name and race, what he sought, what he offered.   175
And he informed the king of the forces
Mezentius was recruiting, and of Turnus'
Violent heart. He spoke to him about the trust
That could be placed in things human, and as he talked
He entreated. Without delay Tarchon   180
Joined forces and struck an agreement.
Freed from the prophecy, the Lydians
Boarded ship under divine ordinance
And entrusted themselves to a foreign leader.
Aeneas sailed in the flagship, Phrygian lions   185
Crouched under her beak; above rose Ida,
A sight most welcome to Trojan exiles.
There sat great Aeneas, pondering
The fortunes of war. And Pallas,
Staying close to his left, questioned him,   190
Now about the stars that guided them through the night,
And now of his trials on land and at sea.

Now open Helicon, Muses, and chant
The roll call of the men from Tuscan shores
Who armed the ships and sailed with Aeneas.   195

At their head Massicus cut through the water
In the bronze-plated Tiger. A thousand men
Served under him, from Clusium and Cossae,
Armed with quivers of arrows and deadly bows.

With him was Abas, whose entire contingent   200
Bore dazzling arms, and his ship gleamed
With a gilded Apollo. To this grim general
Populonia had given six hundred warriors,
And Ilvia three hundred, an island rich
In the Chalybes' inexhaustible ore.   205

Third came Asilus, the great interpreter
Between gods and men, a man to whom
Sacrificial entrails revealed their meaning,

As did stars, birdsong, and prophetic lightning.
He hurried a thousand men to war   210
In close formation, bristling with spears,
Men placed under his command by Pisa,
A city born by the river Alpheus
But transplanted in Tuscany.

                         Astur
Came next, second to none in looks, Astur   215
Who trusted his mount and flickering weapons.
Three hundred men, all of one mind,
Followed him, whose homes were in Caere,
In the plains of Minio, and in ancient Pyrgi,
And who breathed the heavy air of Graviscae.   220

Nor would I pass you by, Cunerus,
Bravest of the Ligurian warriors,
Or you, Cupavo, with your few followers,
Swan plumes on your crest, the insignia
Of his father's form but a reproach to you,   225
O God of Love. For they say that Cycnus,
Grieving for his beloved Phaethon,
Was singing in the shade of his sisters' poplars,
And while he consoled his sorrow with music,
Whitened not with age but downy plumage,   230
And then left the earth, seeking the stars with his cry.
Now his son with a band of men his own age
Rowed the mighty Centaur, a looming figure
That threatened the water with a massive stone
While the ship's long keel furrowed the sea.   235

Great Ocnus, too, marshaled an army
From his native shores. He was the son
Of the seer Manto and the Tuscan river,
And he gave you, Mantua, your city walls
And his mother's name—Mantua,   240
Rich in ancestry from many stocks,
Three races of men, each with four peoples,
And she herself the mistress of all,
With her strong Tuscan blood.

　　　　　　　　　　　　From here too
Were the five hundred men Mezentius armed—　　　　　245
Against himself. The rivergod Mincius,
Benacus' son, crowned with grey sedge, captained them
Across the sea on their ships of war.

And on came Aulestes, ponderously,
Surging through the water on a hundred oars　　　　　250
That churned the marble surface of the sea.
His ship was the Triton, whose conch alarmed
The indigo waves. The figurehead was a man
With a shaggy chest fronting the whitecaps
But turning into scales and fins below the waist.　　　255
The water murmured under the half-human form.

And so these captains with their thirty ships
Sailed to Troy's aid, cutting the brine with bronze.

Day had left the sky, and the gracious Moon
Was treading mid-heaven with steeds of the night.　　　260
Aeneas, too anxious to sleep, sat at his post,
Manning the rudder and trimming the sails.
Halfway across, a band of his own company
Met him in the waves: the nymphs whom Cybele
Had transformed from ships to deities,　　　　　　265
Powers of the sea. They came swimming abreast,
Equal in number to the brazen keels
Once moored to Latin shores. They recognized their king
From far off and encircled him in a dance.
The most eloquent of them, Cymodocea,　　　　　270
Swam behind the ship, grasped the stern
With her right hand, and rose breast high
While her left hand paddled the silent water.
She spoke to Aeneas, who was caught by surprise:

"Are you awake, Aeneas, son of the gods?　　　　　275
Wake, and haul in tight the sheets to the sails.
We—pines from the sacred crest of Ida,
Now nymphs of the sea—were once your fleet.

When the treacherous Rutulian attacked us
With fire and sword we reluctantly broke   280
Our mooring chains and have been seeking you
Over the sea. The Great Mother, out of pity,
Gave us this form and granted to us
Divinity beneath the waves.
                              But your son,
Ascanius, is hemmed in by wall and trench,   285
Surrounded by Latins bristling for war.
Arcadian horsemen, joined by brave Etruscans,
Are in position. Turnus has resolved
To keep these troops from reaching the camp.
Rise, then, and with the coming Dawn   290
Order your men to arms. Then take the shield
That the Fire God gave you, invincible
And rimmed with gold. Tomorrow's light,
If you do not think my words are useless,
Will look upon heaps of Rutulian dead."   295

Cymodocea spoke, and as she departed
Gave the stern a push with a knowing hand.
The tall ship sped over the water
Faster than a javelin or a wind-swift arrow,
And the other ships picked up their speed.   300
The Trojan son of Anchises was astonished,
But the omen lifted his spirits. Looking up
At the vaulted sky, he said this brief prayer:

"Lady of Ida, Mother of the Gods,
To whom Dindyma is dear,   305
Turreted cities, and harnessed lions,
Lead me now in battle. Fulfill this omen
And be propitious, Goddess, to your Phrygians."

As Aeneas prayed the returning day
Ripened with light and the darkness fled.   310
He commanded his men to prepare to attack
On his signal and to steel their hearts for battle.
He stood on the high stern, and when he had
The Trojan camp in sight he lifted his shield

High in the morning light. The Dardanians   315
Shouted from the walls, new hope kindling fury,
Javelins now flying thick from their hands,

> Like Strymonian cranes calling back and forth
> Under dark clouds. Their clamor pierces the air
> As they cry in triumph and ride the South Winds.   320

Turnus and the Ausonian captains
Did not know what to make of this
Until they saw sterns facing the shore
And the whole sea crawling with ships.
The apex of Aeneas' helmet shot flames   325
Into the sky, and his shield's golden boss
Was a radiant bolt of fire, glowing

> As a comet glows, bloodred and baneful,
> In the dark, liquid night; or like Sirius rising,
> The star that brings drought and fever to men   330
> When it saddens the sky with its baleful light.

But Turnus did not back off. Determined
To seize the shore and drive the invaders into the sea,
He raised his troops' courage with these scalding words:

"This is what you have been praying for, men—   335
The chance to break the enemy's ranks. The war
Is in your hands! Remember your wives,
Remember your homes and your ancestors' glory.
We will engage the enemy in the surf
While they're still unsure of their footing.   340
Fortune favors the brave!"

                    As Turnus spoke
He decided who would lead the attack
And whom he could trust to maintain the siege.

Meanwhile, Aeneas was landing his men.
Crews were coming down gangways, leaping   345
Into the shallows, vaulting down with oars.

Tarchon spotted a beach with low surf,
Where the waves glided easily onto the sand.
He made a quick decision, turned his prow,
And implored his crews:

                    "You're elite troops!   350
Lean on those oars and ram these ships
Straight onto the shore! Cut the sand with the beaks
And force the keels to plow up the beach.
Shipwrecks won't matter once we're on land!"

Tarchon's men took him at his word. Pulling hard,   355
Backs arched, they drove their ships through the foam
And onto the Latin fields. Most of them made it,
Their hulls coming to rest high on dry land.
But not your ship, Tarchon. Driving hard
Into shallow water, it hung up on a sandbar,   360
Teetered there in the battering waves,
And finally broke up, plunging its crew
Into the breakers, where they floundered
Among broken oars and floating benches
While a riptide sucked their feet from under them.   365

Turnus wasted no time getting his army
Onto the shore and making a stand
Against the oncoming Trojans. Trumpets blared.

Aeneas attacked first, charging the Latin ranks,
Field-hands mostly and raw recruits.   370
He ran them over—an omen of what was to come—
Killing Theron, who more than other men
Itched to face the hero. Aeneas' sword
Found the seams in Theron's bronze armor,
Crunched through the shirt's stiff, gold embroidery,   375
And drank from his slashed side.
                              Lichas was next.
Cut from his dead mother's womb, as a child
He was consecrated to you, Phoebus. Why
Did you let him escape steel as a baby, but not now?
    Aeneas moved on to Cisseus and giant Gyas,   380

Who were clubbing down troops. The weapons
Of Hercules could not help them now, nor
Their strong hands, nor their father, Melampus,
Hercules' companion during all his labors.

    Leaving them dead, Aeneas launched a javelin   385
At Pharus, who was strutting and boasting,
And planted it in the man's bawling mouth.

    And you, poor Cydon, trailing after
Your new joy, Clytius, with his downy, golden cheeks,
You would have fallen under the Trojan's hand   390
And lain on the ground most pitiably,
Forgetful of your love for boys. But your brothers,
All seven of them, children of Phorcus,
Closed ranks around you and threw seven spears.
Some glanced off Aeneas' helmet and shield,   395
Some Venus diverted so that they only grazed
The hero's body, who then called to Achates:

"Keep feeding me spears. I'm not going to miss
A single Rutulian with these spears that quivered
In Greek bodies on Ilium's plain."

                     And he let fly a heavy shaft   400
That crashed through the bronze of Maeon's shield
And punched a hole through his corselet and chest.
Maeon's brother Alcanor came to his aid,
Supporting the fallen man with his right arm,
Which Aeneas' next spear immediately pierced.   405
The spear kept going and completed
Its bloody course, leaving Alcanor to examine
His own dead hand, dangling by sinews.
Numitor, another brother, pulled the spear out
And threw it at Aeneas, but his aim was off   410
And it grazed the thigh of great Achates.

Now Clausus of Cures came to the front,
Confident in his strength, his youth.
He hit Dryops under the chin with a hard throw
At some range. The spear pierced his throat   415
As he was speaking and robbed him of voice

And life together. His forehead hit the ground,
And clotted blood spewed from his mouth.
Clausus went on to kill three Thracians
Of Boreas' high race, and three more   420
Far from their native Ismarus, and their father, Idas,
Dispatching each of them in different ways.
Halaesus joined him, and Auruncan bands,
As Messapus, descendant of Neptune,
Came driving up with his glorious horses.   425
All of them fought to drive back the enemy
In this battle on the very threshold of Italy.

> *As clashing winds in the sky's great reaches*
> *Rise to battle, matched in spirit and strength,*
> *And will not yield, nor will clouds or sea,*   430
> *But all nature is deadlocked in struggle,*

So too the Trojan and Latin ranks
Clashed together in hand-to-hand combat.

On another front, a river in torrent had strewn
Boulders and bushes torn from its banks   435
Across the debris. Pallas saw his Arcadians
Turn and run before the pursuing Latins.
Pallas' men were not used to fighting on foot,
And the terrain, roughened by the flood,
Had forced them, this once, to dismiss their horses.   440
Pallas had only one hope left—to use
Whatever words he could to restore their courage:

"Where are you running, my friends? I beg you,
By your own brave deeds, by the name of Evander,
By the wars you have won, and by my own hope,   445
Which rises to match my father's renown—
Do not put your trust in your feet!
We have to hack our way through with swords.
There, where the enemy is thickest,
Is where your country calls you, with Pallas   450
At your head! We are not fighting gods.

We are mortals under attack by mortals.
We have as many lives and hands as they do.
And now we have the ocean at our backs,
The barrier of the sea, and no more land.   455
Should we run across the sea all the way to Troy?"

Pallas spoke, and charged into the enemy lines.
The first man unlucky enough to cross his path
Was Lagus, who was trying to uproot a stone
Of considerable weight. Pallas' spear   460
Went into his spine just below the rib cage.
He pulled the spear out from the bones
Where it stuck and was ready for Hisbo,
Who failed to take him by surprise, although
This was his hope. As he rushed in from above,   465
Hell-bent with rage at his companion's death,
Pallas buried a sword in his wheezing lungs.
He got Sthenius next, and Anchemolus,
Of Rhoetus' ancient line, a man who had dared
To sleep with his stepmother.
                              And you, too,   470
Larides and Thymber, twin sons of Daucus,
Fell on the Rutulian plain. As boys
You were indistinguishable from each other—
A sweet perplexity to your parents—
But Pallas made you easy to tell apart,   475
Lopping off your head, Thymber, with Evander's sword,
While your severed hand longed for you, Larides,
Its dying fingers shifting their grip on your sword.

The spectacle of these glorious deeds shamed
The Arcadians into battle. But Pallas was not done.   480
His spear caught Rhoetus as he was flying past
In his chariot, a chance shot, but a reprieve for Ilus,
Whom Pallas had lined up with his long, hard throw.
Rhoetus intercepted the spear in its flight
From you, noble Teuthras, and your brother, Tyres,   485
And rolled from his chariot,
Heels kicking the Rutulian fields in death.

Summer winds the shepherd has hoped for
Begin to rise, and he sets fires here and there
In the woods. Suddenly, the spaces between   490
Are ablaze, and when Vulcan's battle-lines
Have spread across the fields, the shepherd smiles
As he sits and watches the reveling flames.

So too your soldiers' valor converged,
To your joy, Pallas.
               Halaesus countered them.   495
Collecting himself behind his shield, this bold warrior
Brought down Ladon, Pheres, and Demodocus;
Sliced off Strymonius' hand with bright steel
And smashed in Thoas' face with a stone,
Scrambling the bones with blood and brains.   500
Halaesus' father, prophesying his fate,
Had hidden the boy in the woods. Later,
When his hollow, ancient eyes closed in death,
The Fates laid their hands on Halaesus
And marked him out for Arcadian spears.   505
Pallas went after him, praying first:

"Father Tiber, grant to this iron,
Which I am about to throw, safe passage
Through Halaesus' ribs. Your oak
Will hold this weapon and the hero's spoils."   510

The god heard this prayer. While Halaesus
Shielded Imaon he left his own chest exposed
To the Arcadian spear.
               Lausus,
A major part of the Rutulian offensive,
Did not allow his troops to be panicked   515
By Pallas' killing streak. His first move
Was to cut down Abas, a node of the battle,
And then more youth of Arcadia
Began to fall, Etruscans fell,
And you Trojans too, you whose bodies   520
The Greeks had not destroyed. The armies
Closed on each other, closely matched,

Rearguard crowding front lines, so close
The soldiers could not lift their weapons.
On one side Pallas presses forward, strains,   *525*
Confronted by Lausus, the young heroes
Nearly equal in age, handsome beyond all,
Neither destined to return to his homeland.
But the Lord of Olympus did not permit them
To meet face to face. Each was fated   *530*
To fall soon to a greater adversary.

Turnus had a sister, the nymph Juturna,
Who warned him now to bring aid to Lausus.
The hero split the ranks with his swift chariot
And called to his men:

                        "Stand down from battle.   *535*
Pallas is mine, and mine alone.
I only wish his father could watch."

When Turnus said this, his men withdrew,
And Pallas stood there, marveling
At this arrogant command, amazed at Turnus.   *540*
His eyes took in that giant frame. He scanned
The whole scene with a fierce glare
And made this response to the great Rutulian:

"The praise is mine soon, either for prime spoils
Or a glorious death. My father can live   *545*
With either fate. Away with your threats."

And he strode out to the middle of the field.
The Arcadians felt their blood turn to ice,
And Turnus vaulted down from his chariot
Ready to fight on foot in hand-to-hand combat.   *550*

   A lion, poised on a high vantage point,
   Has caught sight of a bull meditating battle
   And charges.

This was how Turnus charged.
When Pallas thought he was within spear range
He began his own charge, hoping to balance　　　　　*555*
This mismatch in strength with daring and luck,
And he prayed to bright heaven:

　　　　　　　　　"I beseech you,
Hercules, by the welcome you received
In my father's house, come to me now
And help me in my need. Let Turnus see me　　　　*560*
Strip the bloody armor from his dying limbs,
Victorious over him as his eyes close in death."

Hercules heard the boy's prayer and stifled
A heavy groan, shedding useless tears. Jupiter
Addressed his son with fatherly words:　　　　　*565*

"Each has his own day. Brief is the time
And irretrievable the life of every man. Yet,
To lengthen fame by deeds is the task of valor.
Under Troy's high walls fell many sons of gods,
My Sarpedon among them. Fate calls Turnus too,　　*570*
And he has reached the end of his allotted years."

Thus Jove,
Who then turned his eyes from the Rutulian fields.

Pallas threw his spear with all his strength,
And his sword flashed from its sheath. The spear　　*575*
Flew on and struck the top edge of Turnus' shield,
Forced its way through and nicked his shoulder.
Turnus shrugged and balanced his spear
For what seemed an eternity. When he threw
The iron-tipped oak at Pallas, he said:　　　　*580*

"See if my spear goes in farther."

　　　　　　　　　No sooner spoken
Than the spearpoint slashed through the center
Of Pallas' shield, with all its layers of iron,

Of bronze, all the folds of oxhide, and then pierced
His corselet and burrowed into his chest.   585
Pallas pulled the warm shaft out, but with it came
His blood and his life. He fell onto the wound,
Armor clattering, and his bloody mouth
Struck the hostile earth. He was dying
When Turnus, standing above him, said: 590

"Remember, Arcadians, to bring my words
To Evander. I send him the Pallas he deserves.
The honor of a tomb, the solace of burial
I freely grant, but he will pay dearly
For welcoming Aeneas."

                    Turnus spoke   595
And, bracing his left foot on Pallas' corpse,
He tore away the massive belt engraved
With crime—the sons of Aegyptus murdered
By Danaus' daughters on their nuptial night,
The rooms reeking with blood—the work   600
Of Clonus, son of Eurytus, who chased it in gold.
Turnus now exulted in this belt and gloried
In its possession.
                    The mind of man
Knows neither fate nor future doom
Nor moderation when elated by fortune.   605
The hour will come when Turnus will wish
He had paid handsomely for an unharmed Pallas
And will curse the day he won those spoils.
But now Pallas was surrounded by his friends,
Moaning and weeping as they bore him back   610
Lying on his shield. O Pallas, you will go home
To your father a great grief and great glory.
This day brought you to war and took you from it,
Yet you left behind mounds of Rutulians dead.

It was no vague rumor of disaster   615
That reached Aeneas but sure intelligence
That his men were inches from death
And that it was time to rescue the Teucrians.

He mowed down everything before him
With his sword, burning a broad path   620
Through the enemy, seeking you, Turnus,
Flush with slaughter. Pallas, Evander,
Everything swam in Aeneas' eyes—the table
He came to as a stranger, the right hands pledged.
Four youths, sons of Sulmo, and four of Ufens,   625
He took alive, to sacrifice them to the shades
And pour their blood on the funeral flames.
Then he took aim at Magus, who ducked
As the spear trembled through the air above him,
Then he fell in supplication at Aeneas' knees: 630

"By your father's ghost, and by your hopes
For growing Iülus, spare my life for my own son
And father. Buried deep inside my high house
Lie talents of chased silver, masses of gold
Wrought and unwrought. Troy's victory   635
Does not turn on me, one life won't matter!"

He spoke, and Aeneas answered him:

"You can save all that silver and gold
For your sons. Turnus did away with
Such traffic in war when he took Pallas' life.   640
This is the judgment of my father's spirit,
Of great Anchises, and of Iülus my son."

With these words, he grasped Magus' helmet
With his left hand and, bending back
The suppliant's neck, buried the sword   645
Up to its hilt.
            Close by was Haemonides,
Priest of Phoebus and Trivia, head bound
With a sacred band, shining in white robes
And gleaming armor. Aeneas drove him
Over the plain, and when the priest fell   650
Bestrided the body and slaughtered it
In his own great shadow. Serestus

Gathered up the armor and carried it off,
A trophy for Mars, who walks the lanes of war.

Caeculus, born of Vulcan's race, and Umbro,   655
From the Marsian hills, filled in the ranks.
The Trojan attacked furiously. His sword
Had already severed Anxur's left arm,
Which fell to the ground along with his shield—
Anxur had been talking big and hoped his strength   660
Would match his words, or perhaps he was just
Raising his spirits and had promised himself
A ripe old age—when Tarquitus, strutting
In gleaming arms, crossed paths with Aeneas.
The nymph Dryope had borne this man   665
To Faunus, who haunts the woods. The Trojan
Pinned his heavy shield and corselet together
With a hard spear-cast, and as the boy tried
To get some words of supplication out,
He sent his head whirling to the ground.   670
Then, as he rolled the warm torso over,
He said in a voice without a trace of pity:

"Lie there, you hulk. Your sweet mother will never
Heap earth above you back home in your country.
No, you will be left here for the vultures,   675
Or thrown into the sea, rolled by waves,
And hungry fish will nibble at your wounds."

He caught Lucas and Antaeus next, two
Of Turnus' front-line men, and brave Numa,
And blond Camers, son of noble Volcens,   680
The richest man in all Ausonia
And ruler of silent Amyclae.

Aegaeon, men say, had a hundred arms,
A hundred hands, and shot flames from fifty mouths
And chests, when against Jove's thunder he clanged   685
Fifty shields and drew as many swords.

So Aeneas in triumph savaged the field
Once his blade grew warm. Even the horses

That pulled Niphaeus' chariot, when they saw
The hero advancing in his rage, turned in terror,   690
Spilling their master as they raced for the shore.

Meanwhile, Lucagus and his brother, Liger,
Entered the combat zone in a chariot drawn
By two white horses, Liger handling the reins,
Lucagus swinging a sword. Aeneas   695
Took exception to their ardor for battle
And bore down on the duo, towering above them
As he pumped his spear. Liger spoke:

"These aren't Diomedes' horses you see,
Or Achilles' chariot, or the plains of Troy.   700
Your war and your life now end in this land."

Insane words from Liger, but Aeneas responded
With no words at all. He let his javelin fly,
And as Lucagus leaned forward with his sword,
Stepping into the stroke with his left foot,   705
The point came through the lower rim of his shield
And punctured his left groin. He rolled to the ground,
Dying, while loyal Aeneas offered him bitter words.

"Your horses didn't shy, Lucagus, or run
From a shadow. No, you made a flying leap   710
And deserted your team."

                          And he seized the horses
As Lucagus' brother bailed out and stood,
A picture of misery, with outstretched hands:

"By the Trojan hero that you are,
And by the parents who bore such a son,   715
Spare this life and have pity on a suppliant."

He had more to say, but Aeneas:

                          "That's not
What you said before. Now die with your brother."

And Aeneas' sword laid bare Liger's soul.

Such were the deaths the Dardanian leader   720
Left in his wake, raging like a torrent
Or a black whirlwind over the plain. At long last,
Ascanius and the besieged Trojans
Burst from the camp and left it behind.

Jupiter now turned to Juno and said: 725

"Dearest sister and wife, you were clearly right
When you said Venus alone sustains the Trojans
And not their own right hands alive to war
Or their brave hearts enduring of peril."

And Juno, submissively:

                              "My noble lord,   730
Why do you provoke me when I am sick at heart,
Terrified already of your stern commands?
If my love possessed the force it once had—
And still should have—you would not forbid me,
Almighty One, to take Turnus from the war   735
And keep him safe for his father, Daunus.
As it is, let him perish and pay the Trojans
With his innocent blood! And yet his name
Is of our lineage, for Pilumnus sired him
Four generations back. And he has been generous   740
In heaping your temple's threshold with gifts."

The Lord of Olympus briefly replied:

"If you are requesting a reprieve from death
For this doomed youth, in complete awareness
It is a respite only, with no further illusions,   745
Take Turnus away from Fate and Doom.
There is this much room for indulgence. However,
If your prayers conceal an ulterior motive
And you think the course of the war can be changed,
You are badly mistaken."

                    And Juno, weeping: 750

"What if you were to grant with your heart
What you cannot bear to say, and Turnus' life
Were assured? Now doom is upon
This guiltless man, if I am in my right mind. Oh,
I would rather be deluded by a baseless fear!   755
And you, who can, change your mind for the better."

Juno said these things and launched herself
Down from high heaven robed in clouds,
Driving storms before her. She sought and found
Ilium's army and the camp at Laurentum.   760
Then the goddess fashioned a phantom
Out of mist and shadow, a strengthless image
Of Aeneas, and she counterfeited
Trojan weapons—a shield and a plumed helmet—
For this wondrous apparition. Then she gave it   765
Empty words, a voice without thought,
And an imitation of Aeneas' gait.

   It was like the flitting shapes of the dead,
   Or dreams that mock the slumbering mind.

The phantom stalked the front ranks, exultant,   770
And defied the enemy to come forth and fight.
Turnus attacked it, hurling a spear
That hissed through the air, and the phantom turned,
Showing its back. Turnus thought he had Aeneas
On the run and, drunk on empty hope, he shouted: 775

"Where are you going Aeneas? Don't run out
 On your marriage. Come here. This right hand
Will give you the land you sought through the seas."

With cries like this he gave chase, brandishing
His drawn blade, and did not see   780
That the winds were blowing his joy away.

Moored to a rock ledge stood the ship
That Osinius had sailed from Clusium,

Ladders down and gangway in place.
The phantom of a terrified, fleeing Aeneas   785
Hurried onto this ship to hide, and Turnus,
Not a step slower, followed aboard,
Taking the gangway in a single stride.
He had barely touched the prow when Juno
Snapped the cable, sweeping the unmoored ship   790
Out with the tide. The phantom hid no longer
But soared high to blend with a dark thunderhead.
While Aeneas was challenging his absent foe
And dealing death to all who crossed his path,
The gale carried Turnus far out to sea.   795
Ignorant of how things stood, and ungrateful
For his reprieve, he looked back toward shore
And, lifting his hands to heaven, prayed:

"Almighty Father, am I so unworthy,
And is it your will I be punished like this?   800
Where am I bound? What path is taking me—
If this is me—so far from home?
Where have I come from?
Will I see the walls of Laurentium again?
What about the men who followed me to war?   805
I have abandoned them all—a disgrace beyond words!—
To an ignominious death. I see them scattered now,
Hear their groans as they fall. What can I do?
How could the earth gape deep enough for me?
Winds, take pity on me and drive this ship   810
Aground on a reef—I implore you—push it
Onto a shoal, where neither the Rutulians
Nor Rumor herself will ever know my shame."

As Turnus said these things his mind rocked
Back and forth. Should he, because of his disgrace,   815
Impale himself on his pitiless sword,
Or dive into the waves and swim to shore
To fight the Trojans again? He tried each way
Three times, and three times great Juno
Held him back, restraining him in heartfelt pity.   820

He glided on, cutting through the waves,
And the tide bore him back to his ancestral city.

Jupiter now prompted fiery Mezentius
To take the battle to the jubilant Trojans.
But it was the Tyrrhenians who responded,   *825*
Focusing all their hatred and all their weapons
On this one man. He took it all,

> *Like a high cliff that juts out*
> *Into the ocean, exposed to the winds' fury*
> *And the pounding surf, enduring all the menace*   *830*
> *Of sea and sky, but motionless itself.*

So too Mezentius, as he laid out on the ground
Hebrus, son of Dolichaon, and with him
Latagus and Palmus, a man fast on his feet.
Latagus he caught full in the face and mouth   *835*
With a huge slab of granite; Palmus, though,
He hamstrung and left him writhing slowly
While he gave his armor to Lausus, his son,
Along with the plumes to fix on his helmet.
Evanthes was next, the Phrygian, and Mimas,   *840*
The same age as Paris and his constant shadow
When they were boys. Theano bore him to Amycus
On the very night that Hecuba, pregnant
With a firebrand, gave birth to Paris.
Paris now sleeps in his ancestral city,   *845*
And Mimas rests in an unmarked grave
On Laurentium's shore.

> *When a boar,*
> *Driven from a mountain by dogs,*
> *(It has lived for years on piney Vesulus,*
> *Or has fed on reeds in the Laurentine marsh)*   *850*
> *Reaches the hunters' nets, it halts and snorts*
> *And raises its hackles. No one has the courage*
> *To come near enough to vent his rage,*
> *So they throw their javelins and shout at it*

From a safe distance. The boar is undaunted 855
And turns in all directions, gnashing its teeth
As it shakes off the javelins stuck in its back.

Just so, none of those who harbored
Righteous rage had courage enough to draw a sword
And face Mezentius, preferring instead 860
To launch spears and insults from a safe distance.

Acron, a Greek, had come from ancient Corythus,
Leaving his home and an unfinished wedding.
Mezentius saw him wrecking battalions,
Helmet's crest shining with his bride's purple. 865

A lion that has not fed will range
The deep woods mad with hunger, until
He spots a timid roe or an antlered stag.
Mouth agape in exultation, mane bristling,
He crouches intently over the warm viscera, 870
And foul gore bathes his cruel jaws.

So too Mezentius,
Charging into the massed enemy ranks.
Acron had no chance. He went down hard,
Hammering the black earth with his heels,
His splintered spear dyed red with his blood. 875
This put Orodes on the run. Mezentius,
Disdaining a cheap shot from the rear,
Caught up with Orodes and faced him man to man,
Besting him not with stealth but superior strength.
Then he planted his foot on the body, and, straining 880
To pull out his spear, he cried to his troops:

"Great Orodes is down, men, no small part of the war!"

Shouting in unison his men raised the victory cry,
But Orodes, breathing his last, said:

"I shall not die
Unavenged, and you, whoever you are, 885

Will not celebrate long. The same fate awaits you.
You too will soon lie dead in these fields."

And Mezentius, with a sneering smile:

"Now die. As for me, the Lord of Gods and Men
Will see to my fate."

              And he pulled the spear out.   890
Iron slumber pressed hard on Orodes' eyes,
And their light faded into everlasting night.

Now Caedicus cut down Alcathoüs;
Sarcatur killed Hydaspes; Rapo—Parthenius
And tough Orses; Messapus both Clonius   895
And Lycaon's son Ericetes, the former
As he sprawled on the ground unhorsed, the latter
As he advanced on foot. Agis, a Lycian,
Also advanced on foot but was struck down
By Valerus, who had his ancestors' valor.   900
Salius killed Thronius and was killed by Nealces,
A good man with both a spear and a bow.

Stern Mars balanced the suffering and death.
Men on both sides killed and were killed,
Victor and vanquished, and neither side yielded.   905
Looking down from the high halls of Jove—
Venus sitting across from Saturnian Juno—
The gods pitied the senseless passion of men
While pale Tisiphone raged among thousands.

Still Mezentius, pumping his huge spear,   910
Stormed across the plain.

              Think of great Orion
Stalking on foot the deeps of Nereus, plowing
Through the water, shoulders above the waves;
Or hefting a mountain ash, his feet treading the earth,
His head shrouded in clouds.

So too Mezentius,   915
Gigantic in armor. Aeneas, spotting him
In the distance, closed ground quickly.
Mezentius waited for his noble opponent,
Standing unperturbed in his immovable bulk.
His eyes measured the space between them,   920
And, when Aeneas was in range, he said:

"May this right hand, which is my god,
And this spear, which I am about to throw,
Come through for me now. Lausus, you yourself,
Clad in the spoils torn from that robber's corpse,   925
Will be my trophy over Aeneas."

He spoke
And let fly. The spear hissed though the air
And, glancing off Aeneas' shield, pierced
Antores under his ribs—noble Antores,
An Argive companion of Hercules   930
Who had joined Evander and settled
In an Italian town. Now he lay dying
With a wound meant for another, gazing
At the sky and remembering sweet Argos.
Then Aeneas threw. The hero's spear   935
Punched through the curved shield's triple bronze,
Through the inwoven linen and oxhide layers,
And, losing speed, stuck low in the groin.
Aeneas was glad to see the Tuscan's blood
And, drawing his sword, moved in eagerly   940
On an anxious Mezentius. Lausus, watching,
Groaned deeply for love of his father,
And tears rolled down his face.
(Neither your death,
Nor your heroic deeds—if antiquity
Can confer belief in prowess so great—   945
Nor you yourself, noble young man,
So worthy of memory, will I leave in silence.)
Mezentius gave ground, disabled and hobbled,
Aeneas' spear still stuck in his shield.

His son ran into the space between them,   *950*
Hurling himself into battle, and just as Aeneas
Brought his sword sweeping down,
Lausus parried the blade from below
And held the hero in check. His comrades
Came up from behind with loud cries   *955*
And held off the enemy with a hail of missiles
Until the father, under the protection
Of the son's shield, could make good his retreat.
Aeneas raged, but took cover.

> *When the storm breaks*
> *And pours down clouds of hail, every plowman*   *960*
> *And farmer runs from the fields, and the traveler*
> *Huddles under a riverbank or rocky ledge*
> *While the rain falls on the lands. When the sun comes out,*
> *They go on with the day's work.*

So too Aeneas,
Overwhelmed by javelins, endured the war cloud   *965*
Until all its thunder was gone, but all the while
He taunted Lausus and threatened him:

"You're headed for death, Lausus! Why rush it
By daring what's beyond your strength?
Your filial devotion is blinding you."   *970*

But Lausus was much too wound up to think,
And now the Dardanian leader's rage
Was mounting higher, and the Fates
Gathered up the last threads of Lausus' life.
Aeneas drove his sword straight through   *975*
The young body he faced and up to the hilt,
The point piercing the shield (far too fragile
To counter this threat) and the tunic
His mother had woven of soft gold threads.
Blood filled his chest; his soul left his body   *980*
And sighed through the air to the shades below.

When Anchises' son looked on his dying face,
So strangely pale, he groaned in pity
And stretched out his hand. There shone in that face
The image of his own devotion to Anchises.   985

"For all his sense of duty, what now, poor boy,
Can Aeneas give you for such glorious deeds?
What is worthy of so great a heart?
Keep the arms in which you delighted,
And, if it matters to you now, I commit you   990
To the spirits and ashes of your ancestors.
And may this comfort you in death's sadness:
You fell by the hand of the great Aeneas."

Then he scolded Lausus' men for hanging back
And lifted their prince from the ground   995
Where blood was fouling his finely bound hair.

Meanwhile, his father was washing his wound
On the Tiber's bank, leaning back on a tree trunk.
His bronze helmet hung from a branch nearby,
And his heavy arms were at rest on the grass.   1000
His men stood around him as he gasped for breath
And tried to ease his sore neck. His combed beard
Flowed down on his chest. He asked for Lausus
Over and over and sent messengers
To call him back and deliver the commands   1005
Of his despondent father. But Lausus' men
Were bearing him back on his armor, dead,
A great warrior undone by a mighty wound.
They wept as they came, and Mezentius'
Foreboding heart knew their wail from afar.   1010
He defiled his white hair with dust, lifted
His hands to heaven, and, clinging to the corpse:

"Was life so sweet to me, Son, that I let you
Face the enemy in my place—you,
Whom I begot? Am I, your father, saved   1015
By your wounds, alive through your death?
Ah, now at last the bitterness of exile

Comes home to me, the wound is driven deep.
I have stained your good name, my son,
With my guilt—I, driven by resentment   1020
From the throne and scepter of my fathers.
The penalty I owe my native land
And bitter countrymen is overdue.
I should have given up my guilty life
Through any kind of death. Now I still live   1025
And have not yet left the light of day,
But leave I will."

        As he spoke he raised himself
On his injured leg, and though slowed by his wound
He held his head high and called for his horse,
His pride and solace, on which he rode   1030
Victorious from every battle. Now he spoke
To the grieving creature words such as these:

"Rhoebus, we have lived long, if anything
Lasts long for mortals. Today either you will
Bear off Aeneas' head and bloody spoils   1035
And avenge with me the suffering of Lausus
Or, if we cannot find our way through force,
You will die with me. For I do not think,
My brave one, that you would endure
A stranger's orders or a Trojan lord."   1040

He spoke, mounted, and settled into position,
Loading both hands with whetted javelins.
His head glittered with bronze and bristled
With horsehair crests as he galloped off
Into the thick of battle, his heart a seething mass   1045
Of shame, and of grief verging on madness.

Three times his voice boomed out, "Aeneas!"
Aeneas knew that voice and, filled with joy
He prayed:

        "May the Father of the Gods
And Apollo on high make this happen!   1050

It's your move, Mezentius."

                    Having said this,
Aeneas moved forward with leveled spear.

But Mezentius:

        "My son's gone,
And you try to frighten me? You murderer.
This was the only way you could destroy me.   1055
We do not fear death, nor do we hold back
For the gods. Break it off. I come to die,
But first I have these gifts for you."

                        He spoke,
And let fly with a javelin, then wheeling
In a circle, hit home with another, and another,   1060
But the shield's heavy gold withstood them all.
Three times he rode around a standing Aeneas,
Launching javelins as he circled to the left.
Three times the Trojan pivoted around
With a forest of spears on his shield's bronze skin.   1065
Then, weary of prolonging the fight—
And of plucking out javelins—and feeling the heat
Of this unequal combat, he considered his options
And struck suddenly, hurling his spear
Squarely between the war-horse's temples.   1070
The great stallion reared, pawing the air.
He threw his rider and then, falling himself,
Hit the ground headfirst, disjointing his shoulder
And entangling Mezentius. The Trojans and Latins
Lit up the sky with their cries. Aeneas ran up,   1075
Drew his sword, and standing over him cried:

"You're not so tough now, are you, Mezentius?"

The Tuscan lifted his eyes, drank in the bright air,
And, when he had recovered his senses, answered:

"Bitter enemy, why do you taunt me   1080
And threaten me with death? Killing me

Is no sin. I did not come into battle
For a truce. My Lausus did not seal such a pact
Between me and you. I ask only one thing,
If the vanquished have any claim to clemency: 1085
Let my body be covered by earth. I know
My people's hatred surrounds me. Guard me
From their rage; let me join my son in the tomb."

Mezentius said these things and did not flinch
When the sword entered his throat   1090
And his life sluiced out in streams of blood.

AENEID ELEVEN

Dawn left Ocean and ascended the sky.
Aeneas yearned to devote these hours
To the burial of his dead, but as victor
He must fulfill his vows in the day's first light.
He erected the trunk of a mighty oak   5
High on a mound and clothed the wood
In the gleaming arms stripped from Mezentius,
A trophy to you, O great Lord of War.
He nailed up the crests dewy with blood,
And the breastplate pierced a dozen times.   10
On its left side he bound the shield of bronze
And hung from its neck the ivory sword.
Then, surrounded by the army's generals,
He exhorted his triumphant comrades:

"Well done, men. We have nothing to fear now.   15
These are the spoils of a high and mighty king;
This is Mezentius, done by my own hands.
We march now to Latium and Latium's king.
Prepare your arms with a will and look forward
To battle, so that when the gods give us the nod   20
To raise our standards and lead our men
Out of camp we will not be delayed
By poor logistics or lack of resolve.
But now we must commit to earth
The unburied bodies of our comrades—   25
Their only honor in Acheron below.
Go, and dignify with final rites

Those noble souls who with their blood
Have claimed this land for us. But first
Send Pallas to Evander's mourning city,   30
Pallas, whom, brave though he was,
A black day has plunged into bitter death."

Aeneas wept as he spoke, and walked back
To the threshold where Pallas' lifeless body
Was laid, watched by old Acoetes. This man   35
Had once been Evander's armor-bearer.
Now, a sadder duty, he accompanied
His beloved ward in death. All around
Stood the funeral party, the Trojan throng
And the women of Ilium, their hair unbound.   40
When Aeneas entered the great doorway
They beat their breasts, and their lamentation
Filled the room and rose to the stars.
Aeneas looked at Pallas. His head
Was propped on a pillow, and his face   45
Was white as snow. His smooth breast
Gaped with the wound from an Ausonian spear.
Aeneas' tears welled up as he spoke:

"Was it you, poor boy, that Fortune begrudged
To look upon my realm and ride in triumph   50
To your father's home? This was not the pledge
I gave Evander when he embraced me
At my departure, sending me forth with you
To win great empire, and warning me in fear
That our enemy was a tough breed of men.   55
And now he might very well, in vain hope,
Be making vows and heaping the altars high
While we in sorrow bestow empty honors
Upon his dead son, who owes no more
To any of the gods above. Pitiable man,   60
You will see the bitter funeral of your son!
Is this our return, our awaited triumph,
My solemn pledge? But you will not,
Evander, look upon a son routed
By shameful wounds, nor as a father   65

Pray for death because your son chose life
Before honor. Ah, Ausonia, what a hero
You have lost, and, Iülus, what an ally!"

Aeneas ended his lament and ordered them
To lift the piteous corpse. He chose   70
A thousand men to attend the funeral
And share the father's tears, small solace
For sorrow so great but a grieving father's due.
A wicker bier was quickly fashioned
Out of arbute shoots and sprigs of oak   75
And covered with a canopy of leaves.
They lifted him high onto this rustic bed,

> *Like a flower plucked by a young girl,*
> *A tender violet or drooping hyacinth,*
> *Still glowing and beautiful, but no more*   80
> *Does Mother Earth sustain its life.*

Then Aeneas brought out two purple robes
That Sidonian Dido had made for him
With her own hands, a labor of love,
Embroidering them with stiff threads of gold.   85
He draped one of them around the youth
As a final honor, veiling the locks of hair
That the fire would burn. He heaped up
Many prizes from the Laurentine battle
And ordered that these spoils be carried   90
In a long procession. He added horses
And armor stripped from the enemy,
And he bound the hands of the captives he meant
To offer to the shades, sprinkling the flames
Of the funeral pyre with sacrificial blood.   95
He charged the captains to bear tree trunks
Covered with enemy weapons and infixed
With the enemies' names. Old Acoetes
Was led along, disfiguring his breast
With his fists, his face with his nails,   100
And prostrating himself full-length on the ground.
They led Pallas' chariot too, spattered

With Rutulian blood. Behind it
The war-horse Aethon, insignia laid aside,
Walked weeping, his face wet with big tears.   105
Two men carried Pallas' spear and helmet;
The rest of the armor Turnus, as victor, held.
There followed behind an army in mourning,
Teucrians, all the Tuscans and Arcadians,
With arms reversed. When the entire retinue   110
Had advanced far ahead, Aeneas halted
And with a deep groan spoke once more:

"War's grim duty calls me to other tears.
Hail for evermore, most noble Pallas,
And forever farewell."

               Saying no more,   115
He turned his steps toward the walls of the camp.

And now the envoys from Latium arrived,
Shaded with olive and asking for a truce.
They requested Aeneas to return the bodies
That lay on the field and allow them burial.   120
They pleaded that there could be no quarrel
With men who had lost the light of heaven,
Nor with men once called their hosts and kin.
Aeneas could hardly refuse this request
And generously granted it, adding: 125

"What undeserved ill fortune, Latins,
Has entangled you in a war so terrible
That you turn away from us, your friends?
You request peace for the war dead. Gladly
I would grant it for the living as well.   130
I would never have come had not Fate
Assigned me a home here, nor am I at war
With your people but with your king,
Who broke our alliance and trusted instead
To Turnus' arms. It would have been more just   135
For Turnus himself to face this death.
If he wanted to end the war by force

And drive out the Trojans he should have
Fought me with these weapons. Only one of us
Would have lived, whether by heaven's grace   140
Or his own strong hand. Go now,
And place your countrymen on the pyre."

Then aged Drances, who hated Turnus
And always denounced the younger man,
Answered in turn:

                    "Trojan hero, great in glory,   145
Greater in arms, how may I sing your praises?
Should I marvel first at your justice
Or your prowess in war? We will indeed
Gratefully bear these words to our city
And, if Fortune allows, unite you with our king,   150
Latinus. Let Turnus make his own alliance!
We will be pleased to raise your destined walls
And carry on our shoulders the stones of Troy."

Drances spoke, and all murmured their assent.
They set the truce at twice six days,   155
And in that settled peace Trojans and Latins
Roamed the wooded ridges side by side.
Tall ash trees rang under two-edged axes;
They felled pines whose crests swept the stars,
Cleaved oak and fragrant cedar ceaselessly,   160
And hauled the wood away in groaning carts.

Rumor took wing and heralded this sorrow
To Evander, filling his city with the news,
Rumor, who had just announced the triumph
Of Pallas to all of Latium. The Arcadians   165
Hurried to the gate, holding ritual torches.
The road gleamed with the long line of flames
Stretching through the fields. The Trojans
Advanced to meet them, and the mourners
Joined companies. When the women saw them   170
Approach their houses, their shrieks inflamed

The grieving city. Nothing could hold Evander back.
As soon as the bier was set down he flung himself
On Pallas and clung to him weeping and groaning,
Until at last he could speak through his anguish: 175

"This is not what you promised your father, Pallas.
No, you said you would be extra cautious
In committing yourself to the God of War.
I knew very well what the first taste of glory
Could do, how sweet the first battle could be.   180
But how bitter were the first fruits of your youth,
How hard the first lessons of war! My prayers
Were heard by none of the gods! O, my sainted wife,
How happy in the death that saved you from this grief!
But I have by living destroyed my destiny.   185
A father should not survive his son. If only
I had marched to war as an ally of Troy
And fallen beneath Rutulian fire!
If only I had given up my life, and this procession
Were bringing me, not Pallas, home!   190
I would not blame you, Trojans, nor our pact,
Nor our hands joined in friendship. This fate
Was owed to my white hair. But if an early death
Awaited my son, it will comfort me that he fell
After slaying thousands of Volscians   195
And while leading the Trojans into Latium.
Yes, my Pallas, I could think you worthy
Of no other funeral than loyal Aeneas does,
And the mighty Phrygians, the Tuscan captains,
And the entire Tyrrhenian army.   200
They bear great trophies of the men you killed.
And you also, Turnus,
Would now be just a great standing trunk
Decked with arms, if your strength of years
Had been like his. But why do I, poor wretch,   205
Keep the Trojans from war? If I drag out
A life hateful to me with Pallas gone,
The reason is your right hand, Aeneas,
Which you know owes Turnus to my son
And to me, his father. That is the only field   210

Of honor left to you, the only fortune.
I do not ask for joy in life—I do not ask
For the impossible—but only to bring word
Down to my son among the shades below."

Dawn lifted her gentle light for weary mortals,   215
Bringing back all their labors. Father Aeneas
And Tarchon had set up funeral pyres
On the curving shore. Here they each brought
The bodies of their men, each in the manner
Of their forebears, and, when the smoky fires   220
Were lit beneath, high heaven was buried
In the darkening gloom. Three times they circled
The burning pyres in their gleaming bronze;
Three times on horseback they rounded
The mournful death-fires and wailed aloud.   225
Earth was showered with tears, their armor
Glistened with tears. The cries of men
And the trumpets' blare mounted to heaven.
Some cast upon the fire spoils stripped
From slain Latins—helmets, ornate swords,   230
Bridles, and chariot wheels. Others burned
Offerings familiar to the dead—their own shields
And luckless weapons. All around, many cattle
Were sacrificed to Death. Bristling hogs
And stock taken in raids had their throats cut   235
Over the flames. Then, all along the shore,
Men watched their comrades burning
And kept vigil over the charred pyres, unable
To tear themselves away until dewy night,
Studded with blazing stars, rolled up the sky.   240

Elsewhere, the Latins built their own pyres
For their own innumerable dead. Some
They interred in the earth; others they lifted
And carried to neighboring farms or sent home
To the city. The rest, a huge mass   245
Of confused slaughter, they burned
Without distinction. Everywhere the wide fields

Outshone each other with clusters of fires.
When the third dawn dispelled the sky's cold shadow,
Mournfully they raked the ash-clotted bones   250
From the pyres and heaped warm earth above them.
The lamentation inside Latinus' rich city
Now reached a crescendo. Here mothers
And their sons' widows, here the loving hearts
Of sorrowful sisters and boys bereft of fathers   255
Cursed the terrible war and Turnus' marriage.
They wanted him to decide the issue in combat,
The very man who laid claim to Italy's realm
And its highest honors. Drances weighed in
And fiercely affirmed that Turnus alone   260
Was summoned to battle. At the same time,
Many voiced a different opinion,
In favor of Turnus. The queen's great name
Protected him, and many a tale
Of Turnus' prowess supported the hero.   265

The crowning touch for all this turmoil
Was the arrival of gloomy envoys
Reporting the response of great Diomedes.
Nothing had been gained. Their gifts of gold
And all their prayers had netted nothing.   270
Latium must look elsewhere for military aid
Or sue for peace with the Trojan king.

Latinus sank under his burden of grief.
Aeneas was a man of destiny. The gods
Were angry. He stared at the fresh graves.   275
Then he issued a royal command
For his councilmen to convene in his palace.
They streamed through the city's streets
And assembled under the king's roof.
In their midst, eldest in years and first in state   280
Sat Latinus, his brow furrowed. He summoned
The envoys who had just returned
From the Aetolian city, and he demanded
A full report from each in turn. Silence reigned.
And then Venulus, as ordered, began to speak: 285

"Citizens, we have seen Diomedes
And his Argive camp. We completed
Our journey, overcame all perils,
And grasped the hand by which Ilium fell.
He was still building his city, Argyripa—　　　　290
Named after his father's race—as victor
In the fields of Iapygian Garganus.
We entered, were given permission to speak,
Presented our gifts, told him our names,
The name of our country and its invaders,　　　　295
And the purpose of our visit to Arpi.
He listened, and replied with calm demeanor:

'Sons of Saturn and ancient Ausonia,
A people blessed, what has disturbed your peace
And leads you to provoke a dangerous war?　　　　300
All of us who profaned Ilium's fields with steel
Have suffered for it. I do not mention
What we endured in the war itself
Beneath Troy's high walls, or the heroes drowned
In the Simois river. No, I mean　　　　305
All the unspeakable punishments
Inflicted upon us throughout the world
For our transgressions. Even Priam
Would take pity on us. Witness Minerva's
Baleful star, the cliffs of Euboea,　　　　310
Avenging Caphareus. After the war
We were driven to distant shores,
Menelaus as far as the pillars of Proteus.
Ulysses has seen the Cyclopes on Aetna.
Then there is Neoptolemus' kingdom,　　　　315
Idomeneus' devastated home,
And Locrians living on Libya's shore.
Even the Mycenaean, Agamemnon himself,
Had scarcely crossed his threshold when he fell
By his evil wife's hand—the Conqueror of Asia　　　　320
Undone by a lurking adulterer.
To think that the gods begrudged me the sight
Of my longed-for wife and lovely Calydon,
Never to return to my country's altars!

I am still pursued by dreadful portents.   *325*
My lost comrades have taken wing to the sky
Or haunt the rivers as birds—O my people!—
And fill the cliffs with their tearful cries.
What else should I have expected,
Insanely assaulting celestial bodies   *330*
And profaning the hand of Venus with steel?
No, do not urge me into such battles.
I am not at war with the Trojans, not since
Pergamum's towers fell, and I find no joy
In remembering these ancient troubles.   *335*
The gifts that you bring me from your country,
Take them to Aeneas instead. I have faced
His steely weapons, fought him hand to hand.
Trust me to know how big he looms up
Above his shield, how he throws his spear   *340*
With whirlwind force. If Ida's land had borne
Two more like him, the Dardanians
Would have invaded Argos, and all Greece
Would be in mourning, the tables turned.
In all the time we spent besieging Troy,   *345*
It was only Hector and Aeneas
Who held us off, until the tenth year.
Both were preeminent in courage and arms.
Aeneas was first in loyalty. Join him
In peace; beware of meeting him in war.'   *350*

You have heard, my lord, Diomedes' reply,
And his counsel on this momentous war."

The envoys had just finished when troubled murmurs
Rippled through the Ausonian assembly,

>   *Like the sound that comes from a pent-up stream*   *355*
>   *That has been blocked by boulders; the current churns,*
>   *And the close banks echo the rushing water.*

When they had calmed down, Latinus spoke
From his high throne. After calling on the gods,
He said:

          "I wish we had already decided   *360*
This crucial issue, Latins. It is not good
To be holding council when the enemy
Sits outside our walls. This war, my countrymen,
Is ill-omened. We are fighting a race of gods,
Invincible men, unwearied in battle, unable   *365*
Even when beaten to release the sword.
If you had any hope for Aetolian aid,
Dismiss it. Each is his own hope, but you see
How slender is ours. Your complete ruin
Is before your eyes. You can reach out and touch it.   *370*
I do not blame anyone. What valor could do
Has been done. We have given all we have.
Now listen, and I will briefly lay out
My opinion as to what we should do.
There is an ancient tract of land I own   *375*
Beside the Tuscan river, stretching westward
Even beyond Sicania. Auruncans
And Rutulians work the fields, plowing
The hillsides and grazing the rough slopes.
Let this entire region, with a belt of mountain pine,   *380*
Be ceded to the Trojans in good will, on just terms,
With an invitation to share our realm.
Let them settle there, if that is their heart's desire,
And build a city. But if they have a mind
To seize other lands and can leave our soil,   *385*
Let us build twenty ships of Italian oak,
Or, if they can fill more, the timber lies
Hard by the sea. They themselves can prescribe
The number of vessels and their design.
We will provide bronze, labor, and shipyards.   *390*
Further, to bring word of this and seal the pact,
It pleases me to send a hundred envoys,
Latin nobles, holding boughs before them
And bearing gifts—talents of gold and ivory,
A throne and robe, insignia of our realm.   *395*
Take counsel now and save our weary state."

Then Drances, hostile as ever, bitter
With secret envy of Turnus' glory,

A wealthy man and a silver orator
But cold in battle; respected in council   400
But prone to faction; of noble lineage
On his mother's side but with a lowly father—
This Drances rose, and with these words
He magnified their anger and built their rage:

"This is no mystery you consult us on,   405
My good king, and needs no voice from us.
Everyone knows what is called for here,
But we all mumble in our beards. Let one man
Dismiss his pride and give us freedom to speak,
The man through whose perversity   410
And ominous generalship (I will speak out,
Even if he threatens me with death)
So many of our shining leaders have fallen
And the whole city is sunk in grief while he
Shakes his fist at heaven and attacks the Trojans,   415
Knowing he can bolt whenever he pleases.
Add one more gift for the Dardanians,
One more, my excellent lord, and let no man
Prevent you by force from giving your daughter,
As a father may, to a peerless husband   420
In a worthy marriage, an eternal covenant
And a bond of peace. But if the fear in our hearts
Is so great, we should entreat the prince himself,
Implore him, to renounce his own rights
And defer out of grace to country and king.   425
You, the source and cause of Latium's ills,
Why do you so often hurl its citizens
Into harm's way? There is no safety in war.
We ask for peace, Turnus, and we ask you
For the one inviolable pledge of peace.   430
I first, whom you imagine to be your enemy
(Which I do not deny), I am here before you
On bended knee. Pity your people,
Put down your pride, admit defeat, and withdraw.
We have seen enough death and desolation.   435
But if glory is everything to you, if you feel
Such strength in your heart, or if a royal dowry

Is so dear to your heart, be bold and shout
A fearless heart to the enemy. O yes, please,
So that Turnus can have his royal bride,   440
Let our worthless lives, the unburied
And unwept masses, be strewn on the field!
But you, my friend, if you have any might,
Any of your fathers' fighting spirit,
At least look your opponent in the eye!"   445

Turnus' rage now burst into flames.
He groaned, and then erupted into speech:

"You always have a full supply of words
Whenever battle calls for action, Drances,
Always first in line when council is called.   450
But there is no need to fill the council house now
With those big words that fly out of you
While you are safe behind our fortress walls
And the trenches have not yet filled with blood.
Go ahead, thunder in eloquence, your usual style,   455
And accuse me of cowardice, Drances—
When and if you have created mounds
Of slaughtered Teucrians and left fields everywhere
Marked with your trophies. Give it a try,
See what live valor can do. One thing is sure: 460
We have no shortage of enemies. Our walls
Are surrounded by them. What are you waiting for?
Are we going to attack, or will your God of War
Always be your windy words and flying feet?
I should admit defeat? You watch your tongue,   465
You dirty liar. Who's going to say I'm beaten
When he sees the Tiber swollen with Trojan blood,
Evander's house and all his line laid low,
And his Arcadian troops stripped of their armor?
Bitias and giant Pandarus didn't think   470
That I was beaten, or the thousand men
I sent to hell in one fighting day, even though
I was cooped inside the enemy's walls.
No safety in war? You fool. Sing that song
For the Trojan's head—and your own property.   475

Go on, keep throwing everyone into a panic,
Touting the prowess of a twice-conquered people
And running down Latinus' army.
Now the Myrmidons tremble before Phrygian arms—
There go Tydeus' son and Achilles of Larissa—   480
And Aufidus flows back from the Adriatic Sea.
What about when he pretends, the cunning bastard,
To fear my threats just to make me look bad?
You will never lose your pathetic life—don't worry—
By my right hand. Keep it, you gutless wonder.   485
        Now, Father, to return to your great question.
If you put no further hope in our arms,
If we are so utterly lost and ruined
After one setback, and Fortune cannot return,
We should sue for peace with outstretched hands.   490
But, O, to have any of our familiar valor!
The luckiest man on earth, and the finest,
Is the man who, to avoid such a sight,
Has fallen in death and bitten the dust.
But if we still have resources, and sound troops,   495
And the cities of Italy are still behind us,
If the Trojans too have paid for glory in blood
(They too have suffered casualties, the storm
Was the same for everyone), why do we falter
So ingloriously at the first steps? Why do we   500
Tremble before the trumpet sounds? Time
And the shifting tide of events have improved
Many situations. Fortune revisits many a man,
First mocking him and then setting him
Upon firmer ground. The Aetolian in Arpi   505
Will not help us, but Messapus will,
As will the prosperous Tolumnius,
And the leading men of many a nation.
Latium and Laurentium will send their best,
And we have Camilla too, leader   510
Of the glorious Volscians, with her cavalry
And squadrons flowering in bronze.
But if I am called out to single combat
By the Trojan, and this is your pleasure,
And I am so great an obstacle   515

To the common good, know that Victory
Has not deserted these hands of mine
With such loathing that I would refuse to dare
All that I have for a hope so high.
I will face him with spirit even though   520
He comes on like great Achilles himself
And wears armor made by Vulcan's hands.
To all of you and to Latinus,
Father of my bride, I, Turnus, second
In valor to none of my ancestors,   525
Dedicate my life. Aeneas calls me out?
I pray that he does, and that it is not Drances
But I who appease the gods with death,
If they are angry, or win glory for valor."

While the Latins fought among themselves   530
And debated an uncertain future, Aeneas
Was moving his troops from the camp.
A messenger rushed through the general uproar
In Latinus' halls and filled the city
With great alarm: Teucrians and Tuscans   535
Were sweeping down from the Tiber River
In battle formation and covering the plain.
The townspeople were stunned and then,
Bitten by the danger, gave way to panic.
Shaking with fear they called for weapons,   540
The young raged for weapons while their fathers
Wept and moaned, and a great din arose,
A discordant roar that rose to the sky,

> As when flocks of birds settle in a grove,
> Or when by the fish-filled stream of Padusa   545
> Raucous swans call out among clamorous pools.

Turnus seized the moment and cried:

"Right, convene a council, citizens,
And sit there praising peace. The enemy
Is attacking our kingdom!"

                        And he rushed out   *550*
From the high halls issuing commands:

"Volusus, get the Volscian squadrons armed
And lead out the Rutulians. Coras, you
And your brother, and you, Messapus, deploy
The cavalry on the plain. Post some guards   *555*
At the city gates and man the towers. The rest
Are going into battle under my command."

The whole city rushed to the walls. Latinus,
Overwhelmed by this grim turn of events,
Quit the council and abandoned his plans.   *560*
He blamed himself for not warmly welcoming
Dardanian Aeneas and adopting him as a son
For the good of the city. Details set to work
Digging trenches in front of the gates
And hauling stones and stakes. A horn sounded   *565*
Its bloody signal for battle. Mothers and boys
Ringed the walls: the final struggle
Summoned them all. The queen herself rode
With a throng of women to the temple of Pallas
On the high citadel, bearing gifts,   *570*
And at her side, eyes lowered modestly,
Was the maiden Lavinia, the cause
Of all this misery. The women went up
And filled the temple with clouds of incense.
Their sad voices drifted down from the threshold: *575*

"Mistress of War, Tritonian Maiden,
Break the spear of the Phrygian marauder
And lay him out on the ground before our gates."

Meanwhile, Turnus armed himself for battle,
And every move he made was an act of passion,   *580*
Strapping on the flashing bronze breastplate,
Sheathing his calves with gold, and, head still bare,
Buckling the sword to his side. He shone
Golden as he ran down from the high citadel,
His exultant mind already engaging the enemy.   *585*

A horse has broken his halter and bolted
Out of his stall, free at last, and now gallops
Over the plain, making for the mares in pasture
Or his accustomed swim in the river.
He holds his head high and whinnies with joy,   590
Mane streaming like wind on his shoulders.

Camilla, with her army of Volscians,
Rode to meet him, and when she reached the gates
The warrior queen leapt down from her horse.
Following her lead, her troops dismounted   595
And slid to the ground. Then Camilla spoke:

"Turnus, if the brave can trust themselves,
I commit myself to face Aeneas' cavalry
And ride alone against the Tuscan horsemen.
Let me try my hand at the first encounter   600
While you stay on foot to guard the city walls."

And Turnus, eyes fixed on this formidable woman:

"Glory of Italy, how can I ever give you
Sufficient thanks? But since your spirit
Outmatches all I could say or do to repay you—   605
Yes, share the work with me. That dog Aeneas,
As rumor has it and scouts confirm,
Has sent his cavalry ahead to scour the plain.
He himself has crossed the ridge and is now
Marching on the city through the mountain pass.   610
I am concealing units under the canopy
On the forest road to block both ends of the gorge.
Muster the troops and wait for the attack
By the Tuscan cavalry. With you will be
Messapus, a good man, the Latin troops,   615
And Tiburtus' squad. You're in command."

He spoke and with similar words encouraged
Messapus and the other allied captains,
And then he moved out against the enemy.

There is a jagged valley, a perfect place   620
For stratagems of war, both sides walled
With dark forest. It can be reached only
By a narrow path through a deep gorge,
A difficult approach. High above,
Among the mountain peaks, lies a plain   625
Invisible from below, a safe staging area
From which to launch sorties right or left,
Or to take a stand and roll down boulders.
Turnus hurried there by familiar roads
And lay in wait in the treacherous woods.   630

Diana, meanwhile, in the halls above,
Addressed Opis, one of her sacred sisterhood,
With these sorrowful words:

                    "Camilla
Is entering this bloody war, Opis,
And girding herself with our weapons in vain,   635
Camilla, whom I love as no other.
This is no new love for me, no sudden
Sweet infatuation on Diana's part.
        Metabus was driven from his throne
By his subjects' hatred of his tyranny,   640
And as he was fleeing ancient Privernum
In the heat of battle he took with him
His infant daughter to share his exile.
Casmilla, her mother's name,
Was changed by Metabus into Camilla.   645
Holding her to his chest he headed out
To a lonely stretch of mountain forest
With armed Volscians closing in on him
From every side. Blocking his flight
Was the Amasenus, which had flooded its banks   650
After a heavy storm. As the fugitive
Prepared to swim he was held back
By love and fear for his precious burden.
Quickly weighing his options, he settled on this:
He was holding in his hand a huge spear   655

With a hard, burly shaft of seasoned oak,
And to this shaft he fastened his daughter,
Swaddled in the bark of a forest cork tree,
Binding her tightly to the balance point.
Then, cradling the spear in his huge right hand,   660
He cried out to heaven:

                              'Lady of the Woods,
Gracious daughter of Latona, this child
I, her father, vow to your service. Yours
Is the first weapon she grasps as suppliant,
Flying through the air to escape her foe.   665
Accept her as yours, Goddess, I implore you,
As I commit her now to the perilous air.'

He spoke, drew back his arm, and hurled the spear,
Sending poor Camilla flying over the loud
Rushing water on the whistling shaft. Metabus,   670
Hard pressed, entrusted himself to the river
And emerged triumphant to pluck from the turf
The spear and the girl, his gift to Diana.
No cities welcomed him into their walls—
Not that he in his wild state would have accepted.   675
He lived among shepherds in the lonely hills,
And there, amid the woods and rugged lairs of beasts,
He nursed his child on a wild mare's milk,
Pressing the teats into her tender lips.
As soon as the baby could take her first steps,   680
He put into her hands a little sharp spear
And slung on her back a quiver and bow.
Instead of gold for her hair and a trailing robe,
A tigerskin hung from her head and shoulders.
Even then she hurled her childish spears   685
With tender hands and twirled her leather sling
Around her head to bring down snowy swans
And Strymonian cranes. Many a mother
In Tyrrhenian towns prayed for her
To marry her son, but she was always content   690
With Diana alone, inviolate in her love
For her weapons and her chastity. O,

That she had not been swept up in this war
Or tried to challenge the Teucrians!
She would still be my dear companion.   695
But now, since bitter Fate presses her hard,
Glide down from heaven, Nymph, to Latium,
Where battle is joined under an evil star.
Take these, and draw from the quiver
An avenging arrow. With this in his throat   700
May anyone, Italian or Trojan,
Who violates her sacred body with a wound
Pay me an equal penalty in blood.
Then in a hollow cloud I will bear the poor girl,
Body and armor all unspoiled, away to the tomb   705
And lay her to rest in her fatherland."

Diana spoke, and Opis swooped down
Through the light air of heaven,
Shrouding herself in dark, whirling wind.

The Trojans now were approaching the walls   710
With the Etruscan leaders and their squadrons
Of mounted troops. The war-horses neighed
And pranced, swerving all over the plain,
Fighting their reins, and the field was spiked
With lifted iron spearpoints flashing light.   715
Advancing toward them, the swift Latins,
Led by Messapus, by Coras and his brother,
And by Camilla, the warrior princess,
Came into view, pumping their spears.
The sound of horses and men intensified,   720
And then both armies halted, standing
Within a spear-cast of each other. Then,
With a sudden shout, both sides charged,
Spurring on their furious horses. Weapons
Showered down as thick as snowflakes   725
And their shadows darkened the sky.

Tyrrhenus and Aconteus, spears leveled,
Were first to charge each other and first to fall.
Their horses collided chest to chest

With a deafening crash, crippling both.   730
Aconteus was flung off like a thunderbolt
Or a stone shot by a catapult
And scattered his life into the air.

This sent a tremor through the battle-lines,
And the Latins, shields on their backs now,   735
Turned their horses toward the city walls.
The Trojans gave chase, Asilas in the lead.
When the Latins were almost to the gates
They shouted and wheeled their horses around,
Reins pulling their supple necks, and then   740
The Trojans turned and let their horses run.

>   *Picture the sea surging in and ebbing.*
>   *A huge swell rushes to shore, breaking*
>   *Over the rocks in a foaming arch of water*
>   *And drenching the farthest reach of sand,*   745
>   *Then seething back over the rolling stones*
>   *As the shallows recede and leave the shore dry.*

Twice the Tuscans drove the Rutulians
Back to the city, their shields slung behind.
But when they met for the third time, the lines   750
Interlocked, and they fought man to man.
The battle became a welter of bodies, weapons,
The groans of the dying, horses floundering
On their slaughtered riders and dying themselves,
Knee-deep in blood.
                        Orsilochus shot his spear   755
At Remulus' horse, too afraid to confront
The rider himself, and left the steel
Just beneath its ear. The horse reared in agony,
Pawing the air and unseating Remulus,
Who rolled to the ground. Catillus took down   760
Iollas and Herminius, a man of huge stature
And with courage to match. His blond head bare,
Chest and shoulders unarmored, unafraid of wounds,
He was an enormous target. Catillus' spear
Came quivering through his broad torso   765

And doubled him over, transfixed with pain.
Everywhere you looked, blood ran dark
As struggling men killed each other with iron,
Seeking through wounds a glorious death.

And in the center of all this slaughter   770
Camilla raged, an exultant Amazon,
One breast bared for battle, a quiver on her back.
Whipping javelins from her hand, or wielding
A heavy battle-axe for hours on end,
Diana's golden bow clanging on her shoulder.   775
And when she was forced by pressure behind
To withdraw, she turned in her saddle,
Bow in hand, and took aim as she fled.
Around her were her handpicked companions,
Virgin Larina and Tulla, and Tarpeia   780
Slicing the air with her bronze battle-axe,
Daughters of Italy whom godlike Camilla
Chose as her glory in both peace and war.

Think of Amazons in Thrace tramping across
The Thermodon's streams following Hippolyte   785
As they go to war with emblazoned weapons;
Or gathered around Penthesilea, daughter
Of Mars, when she returns in her chariot,
An army of women howling in triumph
As they leap exultantly with crescent shields.   790

Whom did you strike down first, fierce girl,
Whom last? How many dying bodies
Did you leave on the earth?
                          Euneus was first,
Clytius' son, whose exposed chest
Camilla ripped through with her long pine spear.   795
He fell, coughing up blood and chewing
The crimson dust as he writhed on his wound.
Then she brought down Liris, and Pagasus
On top of him. Liris was falling from his horse,
Which had just been hit, clutching at the reins,   800

When Pagasus rode up to lend a helping hand;
The pair crashed down headfirst together.
She quickly added Amastrus, son of Hippotas,
And, leaning into long-range spear-casts,
Tereus, Harpalycus, Demophoön, and Chromis,   805
Killing a Phrygian with every weapon
That left her hand.
                    The hunter Ornytus,
Wearing strange armor, rode at a distance
On a Iapygian horse. Oxhide protected
The warrior's shoulders; his head was covered   810
By the white-fanged jaws of a wolf's gaping mouth,
And he carried a rustic pike in his hands.
He was a full head above the other riders
Clustering around him. Camilla caught him—
Which was no great trouble—pierced him through,   815
And cried in a voice without a trace of pity:

"Did you think you were hunting animals,
Tuscan? This is the day all your big talk
Is squelched by a woman's weapons.
But you can boast of this to your ancestral shades,   820
That you went down by Camilla's spear."

Next were Butes and Orsilochus, two
Of the biggest bodies in the Trojan army.
Butes she got with a spear from behind
As he sat on his horse, the point going in   825
Where the neck shows between the helmet
And corselet, just above the shield's rim.
She let Orsilochus chase her in a wide circle
And then wheeled into a tighter ring
And pursued the pursuer. Rising in the saddle   830
She hacked away with her battle-axe
Through armor and bone while he begged
Over and over for mercy. His warm brain
Spattered his face.
                    Aunus' warrior son
Then fell in her way, terrified to see her.   835
He was from the Appenines, and not the least

Of the Ligurians while Fate allowed him
His deceitful life. When this man saw
He could not escape combat by outriding
Or outmaneuvering the princess warrior,   840
He resorted to a clever ruse, saying:

"What's so great about a woman who relies
On a strong horse? Why don't you meet me
On a level field and fight me on foot,
Hand to hand? You'll soon find out   845
Who is deceived by windy vanity."

Camilla, furious, burned with indignation.
She handed her horse's reins to a comrade
And, wholly unafraid, confronted the man
On foot, with equal arms, a naked sword   850
And plain light shield. Thinking he had won
By guile, Aunus' son pulled his horse around
And spurred him into a willing gallop.

"You Ligurian fool, your slippery tricks
Aren't going to work this time; cunning   855
Won't get you home safe to lying Aunus."

She spoke, and with feet like lightning
She intercepted the horse, seized the reins,
And took her vengeance in his hated blood.

> *A falcon, sacred to Mars, swoops down*   860
> *From a high rock and overtakes a dove*
> *Flying in a cloud. Clutching her*
> *In his hooked talons he rips her to pieces,*
> *And gore and torn feathers drift from the sky.*

The Father of Gods and Men saw these things   865
With all-seeing eyes as he sat on Olympus.
He roused Tyrrhenian Tarchon to battle,
Inflaming him with spite and rage. And so
Tarchon rode through the murderous lanes of war

Shouting encouragement to his faltering troops,   870
Calling each man by name, and rallied them:

"What are you afraid of, Tyrrhenians?
Where's your sense of shame? Are you just lazy,
Or is this rank cowardice? Letting a woman
Scatter you like this and drive you back!   875
Why do you think we carry these swords?
You're not lazy when it comes to the nightly
Wars of love, when the flute signals
Bacchic dances. You're waiting for the cups
To be set on the table for the feast, aren't you?   880
This is what you like. You can hardly wait
Until the priest announces the sacrifice
And the fattened ox calls you to the deep groves!"

And he spurred his horse into the melee,
Ready to die. He came at Venulus   885
Like a cyclone, tore him from his horse,
And holding him to his chest with one hand
Urged on his horse and carried the man off.
The Latins cheered when they saw this,
And Tarchon bolted over the plain carrying   890
Arms and the man. He snapped off the iron point
Of Venulus' spear and groped around
For an unarmored patch of his captive's skin
Where he could inflict a mortal wound.
Venulus struggled, keeping Tarchon's hand   895
Away from his throat, meeting force with force.

A golden eagle soars on an updraft
Carrying a snake she has caught, her talons
Entwined around it. The wounded serpent,
Writhing sinuously, scales bristling, lifts   900
Its hissing mouth high, but the eagle
Keeps attacking her struggling victim
With her hooked beak, and her wings beat the air.

So Tarchon carried off his prey triumphantly
From the Tiburtine army. His Maeonians   905

Followed their chief's shining example
And ran forward. Arruns, marked by Fate,
Circled Camilla warily, looking for a chance
To use his javelin. Whenever she attacked
In her fury, Arruns crept up from behind,   910
Stalking her silently; whenever, victorious,
She stepped out of battle, Arruns
Stealthily turned his horse in her direction,
Circling, probing, looking for an opening,
And always pumping his unerring spear.   915

It happened that Chloreus, a Trojan
And formerly a priest of Cybele,
Resplendent in his Phrygian armor,
Was charging ahead on his foaming stallion.
This horse was caparisoned in a skin plated   920
With bronze scales and buckled with gold.
Chloreus himself shone in exotic purple
And shot Cretan arrows from a Lycian bow,
Golden the bow, and golden his helmet,
And the rustling folds of his saffron cloak   925
Were clasped with gold. The tunic he wore
And his Asian leggings were finely embroidered.
Camilla wanted either to hang these weapons
As spoils in a temple or to wear the gold herself.
In any case she singled out Chloreus   930
And chased him down like a huntress,
Oblivious to all else and raging recklessly
Through the ranks of men with a woman's passion
For booty and spoils. Arruns saw his chance
And finally sprang into action, spear in hand,   935
As he prayed to heaven in words such as these:

"Lord God Apollo, guardian
Of holy Soracte, where we your votaries
Pass through the fire in our faith
And walk with bare feet over the embers,   940
Grant that this disgrace be effaced by our arms.
O Father Almighty!
I seek no plunder, no spoils,

No trophy for this woman's defeat.
Other feats will bring me fame.   945
If only this dread plague falls beneath my blow,
I will return inglorious to my fatherland."

Apollo heard his prayer, and in his heart
Granted half of it and scattered half to the winds.
Arruns would defeat Camilla, yes, and lay her   950
Low in death, but his high fatherland
Would never see his return. That prayer
The winds bore away to the southern storms.
And so, as the spear flew from his hand
And hissed through the air, all the Volscians   955
Turned their eyes and hearts to their queen,
But she herself noticed neither air nor sound
Nor weapon coming out of the sky
Until the spear transfixed her bared breast,
And drank her virgin blood from deep within.   960
Her comrades hurried around her in alarm
And caught their mistress as she fell. Arruns,
More frightened than any of them, ran away
In mingled joy and fear, unwilling to trust
His own spear or face Camilla's weapons.   965

> *Having killed a shepherd, or a great steer,*
> *A wolf will run before men can come after him*
> *With their hostile spears. Aware*
> *That he has done something reckless,*
> *He loses himself in the trackless mountains,*   970
> *Tucking his quivering tail beneath his belly.*

So too Arruns in his panic wanted only
To be out of sight, and to this end
He plunged into the thick of battle.

Camilla's dying hand pulled at the spear,   975
But the iron point was stuck deep in her ribs.
Drained of blood, she sank back; the chill light
Sank in her eyes; and her face, formerly
So radiant, turned pale in death.

As she drew her last breaths she called Acca,   *980*
Who was her own age, loyal to Camilla
Beyond all others and the only one
To share her cares, and said to her:

"I've been strong so far, sister Acca,
But now this bitter wound is finishing me,   *985*
And everything is growing dark
With shadows. Hurry and bring to Turnus
My last command: to take my place in battle
And keep the Trojans from the city.
And now, good-bye."

                    Camilla spoke,   *990*
Dropped the reins, and slipped to the ground
Unwillingly. As her body grew cold
She slowly freed herself from all its bonds,
Relaxing her neck and letting her head fall
Into the grip of Death. Finally,   *995*
She released her weapons, and with a moan
Her soul fled resentfully down to the shades.

The roar that followed broke through the sky
And struck the golden stars. With Camilla down,
The fight intensified, and all forces converged: *1000*
The Teucrian army, the Etruscan captains,
And Evander's Arcadian squadrons.

Opis, Diana's sentinel,
Had been calmly watching the war
A long time from her mountain seat.   *1005*
When she saw, far off in the din of combat,
Camilla pay the penalty of death,
She spoke these words from her heart's deep core:

"Ah, Camilla, you have paid too cruel
A penalty, too cruel, for challenging   *1010*
The Trojans in battle. It has not helped you
That you worshiped Diana alone in the woods,

Or wore our quiver on your shoulder.
But your queen has not left you dishonored
In the hour of death, and your doom   1015
Will be renowned among the nations.
Nor will you be disgraced as one unavenged.
Whoever violated your body with a wound
Will pay with his life."

             At the foot of the mountain
Stood the great burial mound of Dercennus,   1020
A Laurentine king of old, shaded by ilex.
The beautiful goddess touched down here
And from the high barrow spotted Arruns.
When she saw him swelling with pride
In his gleaming armor, she cried: 1025

"Why are you going off? Turn your steps
This way, come over here to die,
And receive for Camilla your just reward—
Not that you are worthy of Diana's arrows."

Thus the Thracian nymph, and she pulled   1030
From the gilded quiver a feathered arrow
And stretched the bow deliberately
Until its curving tips were almost touching,
Her left hand up against the arrow's metal point,
Right hand and bowstring back against her breast.   1035
Arruns heard the arrow whir through the air
At the same moment that it pierced his chest.
He gasped his life away in the nameless dust,
Forgotten by his comrades, and Opis
Winged her way to high Olympus.   1040

Their commander lost, Camilla's light cavalry
Was the first unit to retreat. The Rutulians
Then withdrew, as did the fighter Atinas.
Scattered captains and abandoned troops,
Seeking safety, wheeled their horses around   1045
And galloped back toward the city walls.
None of them could stop the Trojan onslaught

Or even stand against it. They slung
Their unstrung bows on their sagging shoulders,
And their horses' hooves pounded the crumbling plain.   1050
A dark cloud of dust rolled to the walls,
And in the watchtowers mothers beat their breasts
And raised their cries to the stars.
The first group to race inside the open gates
Was followed so closely by the enemy   1055
That their ranks mingled, and far from escaping
A piteous death they were sliced open
On the very threshold of their native city
And gasped out their lives under the shelter
Of their own homes. Some closed the gates   1060
And did not dare open them for their friends
No matter how much they pleaded.
The slaughter was heartbreaking, citizens
Rushing on the defenders' swords. Shut out
Before the eyes of their weeping parents,   1065
Some were stampeded into the trenches
While others charged blindly at the stout gates
And battered the strongly barred doors.
Even the mothers defended the walls,
Rivaling Camilla out of love of their country,   1070
Hurling missiles from their trembling hands—
Oak poles and seared stakes in place of hard steel.
Each burned to die first defending the walls.

Meanwhile, Acca brought her grim message
To Turnus, still in the forest, and filled his mind   1075
With a picture of immense devastation:
The Volscian ranks destroyed, Camilla fallen,
The enemy advancing relentlessly,
Sweeping everything before them in triumph,
And the panic that had spread to the town.   1080
Raging—and this was the stern will of Jove—
Turnus abandoned the ambush in the hills
And left the forest. He had just reached the plain
And was out of sight when Father Aeneas
Entered the open pass, scaled the ridge,   1085
And came out from the shadows of the wood.

So both men marched rapidly toward the city
With all their troops, no great distance apart.
Aeneas saw on the plain ahead clouds of dust
Tramped up by the Laurentine army,   1090
And at the same moment Turnus became aware
Of Aeneas' advance, heard the marching feet
And the snorting horses. They would have
Joined battle at once, but the rose-red Sun
Was already bathing his weary team   1095
In the western waters. And so as day ebbed
And night was coming on, one army encamped
Before the city, and the other strengthened its walls.

AENEID TWELVE

When Turnus saw that the Latin forces
Were beaten down, saw that his promises
Had now come due and that all eyes
Were on him, his pride hardened to iron
And his spirit burned.

> *A lion prowling*   5
> *The fields around Carthage is wounded in the chest*
> *By hunters and only then wakens to war.*
> *Tossing his shaggy mane with joy, he snaps*
> *The spear and roars with bloodstained mouth.*

So too the fury mounting in Turnus.   10
He stormed to King Latinus and said:

"I'm not waiting. There is no need
For Aeneas and his cowards to recant.
I'll meet him in single combat. Draw up
The pact, Father, and begin the rites.   15
Either this arm pitches the Asian tramp
Into Tartarus, with the Latins watching,
And my sword restores our nation's honor—
Or he rules with Lavinia as his bride."

And Latinus, steady and calm, replied: 20

"The more spirited you, our champion, are,
The more heroic, the more carefully must I

Ponder, and weigh every chance. You have
Your father Daunus' kingdom and all the towns
You have taken in war. Nor do I, Latinus,   25
Lack gold or influence. There are in Latium
Other brides of noble birth for you,
Now listen to me hard, and take this to heart.
All the oracles and augurs forbade me
To wed my child to any of the suitors   30
She had in the past. But I was overcome
By love for you and our ties of kinship,
Overcome by the tears of my sorrowful queen,
And I broke all bonds. I betrayed my child's betrothed
And took up impious arms. From that day on,   35
You see, Turnus, how I have been beset by war
And the burdens you, above all, must bear.
Defeated twice in battle, we can scarcely guard,
Even within our walls, the hopes of Italy.
The Tiber still flows warm with our blood,   40
The great plains are white with our bones.
Why do I waver? What madness possesses me?
If with Turnus dead I am ready to accept
The Trojans as allies, why not end the struggle
While he is still unharmed? What will they say,   45
Your Rutulian kinsmen, the rest of Italy,
If—Fortune avert my words—I deliver you
To death while you ask to marry my daughter?
Give some thought to war's hazards, pity
Your aged father, sorrowing in Ardea!"   50

Latinus' words did nothing to dispel
Turnus' fury. The very attempt
Inflamed his rage and made it mount higher.
When he could speak again, he had this to say:

"For my sake, sire, do nothing for my sake,   55
And permit me to purchase fame with death.
I too can throw spears, Father, and when I strike
Blood flows from the wound. His goddess mother
Won't be there for him, lurking in mist,
To hide his womanly flight in a cloud."   60

But the queen, reeling with horror
At the new rules of engagement, wept
And raved for death as she clung to the man
Betrothed to her daughter:

           "By these tears
I beg you, Turnus, by any reverence you have   65
For your beloved Amata—you are my only hope,
The only comfort of my sad old age,
And on you depend the honor of Latinus
And the declining fortunes of our house—
This one thing I beg of you: 70
Do not commit yourself to this combat.
Whatever fate awaits you in battle
Awaits me also, and together with you
I will leave this hateful light before I see
Aeneas as my captor and my son."   75

Lavinia heard her mother's words, tears
Stinging her cheeks, and the blood
Ran to her face,

      Like crimson dye
   Staining Indian ivory, or the blush
   Of white lilies mingled with roses.   80

Turnus stared at the girl, distraught
By his love for her. Then, more avid
Than ever for war, he turned to Amata
And said briefly:

        "Don't pester me with tears
Or be a bird of ill omen as I go off to battle,   .85
Mother. Turnus cannot delay his death.
    Idmon, take this message to the Phrygian,
A message he will not be glad to hear:
As soon as tomorrow's Dawn, riding
In her crimson chariot, reddens the sky,   90
Let him not lead his Teucrian troops
Against the Rutulians. Let Teucrian arms

And Rutulians rest. We will decide the war
With our own blood. On that field
Let Lavinia be wooed and won as bride!"   95

Turnus spoke and ran back into the palace.
He called for his horses and smiled to see them
Neighing and prancing, horses Orithyia herself
Had given to Pilumnus, glorious animals
Whiter than snow, faster than the wind.   100
The grooms were drumming on their chests
With cupped palms and combing their manes.
Turnus strapped on his shoulders a corselet
Plated with gold and pale bronze. He hefted
A shield, put on a crimson-crested helmet,   105
And slung on the sword that the Lord of Fire
Had made for Daunus, dipping the white-hot steel
In the waters of Styx. His spear was leaning
Against a column in the middle of the hall,
A spear taken as spoil from Auruncan Actor.   110
Turnus gripped the stout spear, shook it
Quivering, and cried out:

                    "Spear that has never
Failed my call, the hour has come! Actor
Once bore you mightily; now you are in the hand
Of Turnus. Grant that I lay the Phrygian eunuch   115
Out on the ground, rip away his corselet,
And grind into the dirt his pretty hair, crisped
With curling irons and dripping with myrrh!"

By these furies Turnus was driven. His face
Burned and spat sparks, and his eyes shot flames.   120

   When a bull prepares to fight, he bellows
   Horrifically and, concentrating his anger
   In his horns, charges a tree trunk and spars
   With the wind or scatters sand with his hooves.

Aeneas too was like this, a fierce presence   125
In the armor his mother had given him.

He whetted his soul for war, and he fanned
His anger, glad that the war would be settled
On the terms offered. Then he comforted
His comrades and Iülus, who was sad and afraid,   *130*
Reminding them of his destiny. And he ordered
That a firm and clear response be conveyed
To King Latinus, declaring the terms of peace.

Dawn scattered radiance on the mountaintops
As the horses of the Sun rose from the sea   *135*
Breathing light from flared nostrils.
                                    Rutulians
And Trojans had measured the field for combat
Before the city walls and in its center
Were preparing sod altars to their common gods.
Priests in vestments, verbena on their brows,   *140*
Were bringing springwater and fire.
The Ausonian army marched out from the gates
In close formation. Opposite them,
All the Trojan and Tyrrhenian troops
Streamed forward, variously equipped,   *145*
But each armed with steel as if for battle.
Amid these thousands the captains rushed,
Resplendent in gold and purple: Mnestheus,
Of the house of Assaracus, brave Asilas,
And Messapus, breaker of horses,   *150*
In the line of Neptune. They all withdrew
To their own side, stuck their spears in the earth,
And rested their shields against them. Then,
Eagerly pouring forth, the mothers,
The unarmed masses, and feeble old men   *155*
Sat on rooftops and towers and stood on the gates.

Juno was watching all this from the hill
Now called Alban (unnamed at that time
And without fame or glory). She gazed out
Over the plain at the double lines   *160*
Of Laurentum and Troy, and at Latinus' city.
Then she abruptly addressed, goddess to goddess,

Turnus' sister, mistress of still water
And sounding rivers, an honor Jupiter,
Lord of the Sky, had bestowed upon her   *165*
In return for taking her virginity:

"Nymph, glory of rivers, my heart's delight,
You know how I have given you preference
Over all the Latin girls who have climbed
Into Jove's thankless bed. You alone   *170*
I have gladly given a place in heaven.
Learn now, Juturna, your sorrow,
And do not blame me. While Fortune
Seemed to allow it, and Fates permitted
Latium to prosper, I protected Turnus   *175*
And your city. Now I see him facing
A destiny he does not deserve; his doom
Is upon him, and the fatal stroke is near.
I cannot look upon this ordained combat.
If you dare to help your brother now,   *180*
Go on; it becomes you. It may still be
That better fortune will befall the damned."

At this, Juturna wept profusely
And three times, four times, her hand
Beat her lovely breast. But Juno cried: *185*

"This is no time for tears. Hurry,
And if there is any way at all
Save your brother from death,
Or renew the war and strike the treaty
From their hands. I, Juno, order you to dare."   *190*

With this exhortation Juno left her,
Her mind stunned and her heart in pain.

And now the kings came forth. Latinus rode
In a four-horse chariot of impressive size.
Around his brows shone twelve golden rays,   *195*
Insignia of his ancestor the Sun.
Turnus drove a white pair and brandished

A brace of spears with broad iron heads.
From the camp opposite came Aeneas,
Father of the Roman race, his starry shield   200
And celestial arms a blaze of glory,
And with him was Ascanius, Rome's second hope.
A priest in immaculate vestments brought
A young boar and an unshorn sheep
And set them beside the blazing altars.   205
The heroes faced the rising sun,
Sprinkled the victims with salted meal,
Cut the forelocks, and poured libations
From shallow bowls upon the altars.
Then pious Aeneas, sword in hand, prayed: 210

"I call to witness the Sun, and this land
For which I have endured many trials,
And the Father Almighty, and you, his consort,
Saturnia—kinder at last now, Goddess, I pray—
And Mars in his glory, father of all war.   215
And I call upon the springs and rivers,
And the Powers of the air and the blue sea:
If victory falls to Turnus the Ausonian,
The vanquished will withdraw to Evander's city.
Iülus shall leave this land, and Aeneas' sons   220
Will never return to renew this war
Or challenge this realm with the sword.
But if Victory grants that we win the field
(As I think shall be, and may the gods so confirm)
I will not demand that Italians be subject   225
To Teucrians, nor seek dominion for myself.
Let both nations, unconquered, commit
To everlasting peace under equal laws.
I will ordain rites and gods. Latinus,
My father-in-law, will retain command.   230
Authority will remain with my father-in-law.
For me the Teucrians will raise my city walls,
And Lavinia will give the town her name."

Latinus spoke next. Looking up to heaven
He stretched his right hand to the stars, saying: 235

"By these same Powers I too swear, Aeneas,
By Earth, Sea, and Stars, by Latona's twins
And two-faced Janus, by the lords
Of the world below and the shrines of Dis.
May the Father of all, who sanctions treaties   240
With his thunderbolt, hear my words.
I touch the altars and swear by the fires
And gods between us: the day will not dawn
That will break this peace and truce for Italy,
However things may fall; nor shall any power   245
Change my will, though it may drown Earth
In flood and dissolve Sky into the Abyss.
Sooner will this scepter I hold sprout leaves
And branch again, though it has been cut
At the root, bereft of its mother, and the axe   250
Has pared off leaf and twig. Once it was a tree,
But now the craftsman's hand has sheathed it
In bronze for the elders of Latium to bear."

With such words they ratified the treaty
In the presence of the leaders. Then   255
They cut the throats of the consecrated beasts
Over the flames, tore out the living entrails,
And piled the altar high with platters of meat.

But it had long seemed to the Rutulians
That the fight was not fair. Their hearts   260
Were filled with doubt, and all the more when they saw
The ill-matched combatants up close.
Turnus added to their dismay
By walking quietly, like a suppliant
Approaching an altar with downcast eyes,   265
His cheeks hollow, youthful body pale.
When his sister Juturna saw the talk
Begin to spread and the whole crowd waver,
She entered their midst disguised as Camers—
A man of noble birth whose family had a name   270
For valor, and who was himself a warrior—
Entered their midst and, knowing well
The ways of men, let drop a few choice words:

"Aren't you ashamed, Rutulians, to risk
One man's life when we have an army like this?   275
Aren't we their match in numbers and strength?
Look, this is all of them: Trojans, Arcadians,
And the superstitious Etrurians, who hate Turnus.
Even if only every other man of us fought,
There would barely be enough of them.   280
Turnus' fame will lift him to the gods,
Upon whose altars he has sworn his life,
And shall be kept alive on the lips of men.
But we, our country lost, will become slaves,
We who today lounge around in the fields."   285

This brought their feelings to the boiling point,
And a murmur rippled through the ranks.
Not only the Rutulians but the Latins too
Were transformed, and the Laurentines.
Those who had been hoping for rest and safety   290
Now wanted their weapons, prayed for the truce
To be broken, and pitied Turnus' unjust fate.
Juturna showed them something more,
A sign in high heaven, none more potent
To confuse the minds of the sons of Italy   295
And cheat them with its portent. Flying across
The red sky, Jupiter's bird, a golden eagle,
Was chasing a clamorous flock of shorebirds,
When it swooped down suddenly to the water
And snatched in its talons a noble swan.   300
The Italians snapped to attention and saw,
To their amazement, all of the birds
Turn in flight with a rush of wings
That darkened the sky, pursuing their enemy
Until the eagle, overcome by the attack   305
And the swan's sheer weight, dropped its prey
Into the stream and took refuge in the clouds.

The Rutulians greeted this omen with a shout.
They were ready for battle. Tolumnius,
The augur, took the lead and cried: 310

"This is what I have been praying for!
I accept, I acknowledge the gods. With me,
With me as leader, take up your weapons!
You've suffered enough, like these frail birds,
Harassed by a shameless foreign invader   315
Who has been ravaging your shores.
He too will take flight and spread his sails
Far out to sea. Now close ranks with one heart.
Your king has been seized. Fight to defend him!"

With that Tolumnius ran forward   320
And rifled his spear at the enemy lines.
Men could hear the hiss of the cornel shaft
As it split the air. A thundering shout
Went up from the crowd and their hearts raced
As the spear flew on. Fate had it   325
That nine brothers stood in its path,
Beautiful boys born to Arcadian Gyllipus
By his faithful Tuscan wife. One of them,
Especially handsome in his gleaming armor,
Was hit by the spear, which pierced his ribs   330
Just above the buckle of the stitched belt
That cinched his waist and laid him out
On the yellow sand. His brothers,
A spirited band, were stung with grief
And rushed blindly ahead, some with swords drawn   335
And others with spears. A Laurentine column
Charged out to meet them, and these were countered
By a flood of Trojan and Agylline troops,
And Etruscans in their emblazoned armor—
All with one passion, to let cold steel rule.   340
The altars were stripped bare. The sky seethed
With javelins, and the iron rain fell hard.
Sacred vessels and fire were carried off,
And Latinus himself fled, bearing away
His defeated gods, the truce null and void.   345
Men were reining their chariots or leaping
Onto horseback, ready with drawn swords.

Messapus, in his zeal to overturn the truce,
Drove his horse straight at Aulestes,

An Etruscan. This man, a king   350
And wearing a king's insignia, backed away,
Tripped, and fell head and shoulders
Onto an altar behind him. Messapus
Was over him in a flash, spear in hand,
And although Aulestes, poor wretch,   355
Pleaded long, came down hard on him
With his beam of a spear and said:

"He's had it, one of our better victims
For the great gods."

                    The Italians
Crowded around and stripped the body   360
While it was still warm. Corynaeus
Was in their path, and as Ebysus came up
To hit him he snatched up a charred brand
From an altar and shoved it in Ebysus' face,
Igniting his huge beard, which gave off a stench   365
As it burned. Corynaeus followed this up
By clutching the hair of his bewildered foe
In his left hand and coming up hard with his knee
To bring him down, where he finished him off
With a sword stroke to his side.
                                  Podalirius   370
Had chased down the shepherd Alsus
As he was rushing through a hail of weapons
And now towered over him with naked sword.
But it was Alsus who, with a swing of his axe,
Cleaved through his enemy's brow and chin,   375
Spattering his armor with gore. Iron slumber
Pressed hard on Podalirius' eyes,
And their light was shrouded in eternal night.

But steadfast Aeneas, head bare, stood
Stretching out his unarmed hand and calling   380
In a loud voice to his men:

                    "Where are you going?
What is this sudden surge of strife? Hold in your rage!

The truce has already been struck, its terms set.
I alone have the right to fight. Let me do it,
Forget your fears; this hand will make the treaty true.   *385*
These rites have already given Turnus to me!"

As Aeneas was saying these things an arrow
Whistled through the air toward him
In a long falling arc, shot by whose hand
No one knows, nor whether it was pure chance   *390*
Or some god who brought the Rutulians
This glory. Credit for the deed is hidden,
And no one boasted of wounding Aeneas.

When Turnus saw Aeneas withdraw
And his captains in disarray, he burned   *395*
With new hope. He called for his horses
And arms, bounded into his chariot,
And proudly took the reins in his hands.
That chariot ride brought death to many,
Many he rolled over half-alive, crushing   *400*
Entire platoons under hooves and wheels,
And picking off those who tried to escape
With spear after spear.

> *Bloodstained Mars*
> *Thunders with his shield to rouse men to war*
> *As he gives his frenzied horses free rein*   *405*
> *Along the icy Hebrus river. They run so fast*
> *Over the open plain that not even the Winds*
> *Can keep up, and the land of Thrace moans*
> *With the beat of their hooves. Along with the god*
> *Drive his satellites, the dark shapes of Terror,*   *410*
> *And of Rage and Treachery.*

> So too Turnus,
Whipping his foaming, sweat-glazed horses
Through the lanes of battle, trampling his foes.
Pity those killed under the flying hooves
As they splashed through the blood and kicked up sand   *415*
Mingled with gore.

                    Sthenelus fell to Turnus
At long range; Thamyrus and Pholus
In close encounters. He also killed from a distance
Glaucus, and Lades, whom their father, Imbrasus,
Had raised in Lycia and equipped   420
With matched sets of arms, one for close combat,
The other for fighting from wind-swift horses.

Elsewhere, Eumedes rode into battle,
Dolon's famous son, named after his grandfather
But with the heart and hands of his father,   425
Who at Troy dared to ask as his reward
For going as a spy to the Danaan camp
The horses of Achilles. Diomedes
Gave him a quite different reward, and Dolon
No longer aspired to Achilles' horses.   430
When Turnus saw his son far off on the plain
He sent a spear after him through empty space
And then, catching up with the man, halted
His team and jumped from his chariot.
Standing over the fallen, dying Eumedes,   435
Turnus planted a foot on his neck, wrested
The sword from his hand, and reddened
The shining blade deep in his throat, saying:

"Take a good look, Trojan, at these fields,
The Hesperia you came to conquer in war.   440
Lie there and measure out every acre. This
Is the reward for those who try me with a sword,
And this is how they build their city walls."

Then, with a cast of his spear, Turnus sent
Asbytes to keep Eumedes company   445
And added Chloreus, Sybaris, Dares
And Thersilochus, and then Thymoetes,
Who fell from the neck of his bucking horse.

  The North Wind roars on the deep Aegean
  And drives the waves shoreward, and where the wind   450
  Swoops down clouds scud through the sky.

Wherever Turnus cut his path, the ranks fell back
And men turned and ran. His own momentum
Carried him on, and as his chariot
Split the air his plume streamed in the wind.   455
Phegeus could not bear to face his onslaught.
Half out of his mind, he threw himself
In front of the chariot and, grabbing the reins,
Wrenched aside the frothing jaws of the horses.
While he was dragged along hanging from the yoke,   460
Turnus' broad lance found his unguarded side
And ripped through the double-plated corselet,
Just grazing the skin. But as Phegeus
Twisted around and tried to engage his sword,
The turning wheel whirled him over   465
And onto the ground. As Turnus passed by
He swung his blade between the lower rim
Of Phegeus' helmet and the upper edge
Of his breastplate, slicing off his head,
And left his maimed body to lie in the sand.   470

While Turnus was dealing death all over the plain,
Mnestheus and loyal Achates, with Ascanius
At their side, led Aeneas into the camp,
Bleeding and limping as he leaned on his spear.
He grit his teeth as he struggled to extract   475
The head of the broken shaft. He called for
The most direct approach, telling them
To cut into the wound down to the dark recess
Where the point was lodged and send him back
Into battle.
                  And now Iapyx was there,   480
Iasus' son, dearest of all to Phoebus Apollo.
The god, deeply in love with the boy,
Had offered to give him all of his arts:
Prophecy, the lyre, his own swift arrows.
But Iapyx, whose father was dying,   485
Wanted to put off his fate and to that end
Preferred to know the virtues of herbs
And the skills of a healer, and to practice,
Without glory, the silent arts.

                              Aeneas leaned
On his great spear, chafing at the delay,   *490*
Surrounded by a crowd of warriors,
His sad Iülus among them. The hero stood
Unmoved by their tears. The aged physician
Tucked up his robes in Paeonian fashion
And treated Aeneas with his healing hands   *495*
And Phoebus' potent herbs, but all in vain.
In vain he pulled at the arrow with forceps,
With no good fortune, no help from Apollo.
Panic and rout were spreading more widely
Over the plains; war's horror was upon them.   *500*
The sky was a solid wall of dust; the horsemen
Were closing in fast; spears and arrows
Rained down on the camp; and the iron noise
Rose to heaven with the cries of men fighting
And of men falling under the fist of Mars.   *505*

Then Venus, shaken by her son's
Undeserved pain, plucked from Cretan Ida
A stalk of dittany with downy leaves
And purple flowers, an herb wild goats eat
When shot with an arrow. This herb   *510*
Venus brought down, her face shrouded in mist.
She steeped the plant in a gleaming cauldron
Full of river water to bring out its hidden
Medicinal virtues and sprinkled in juices
Of healing ambrosia and fragrant panacea.   *515*
Not knowing what he had, old Iapyx
Was bathing Aeneas' wound with this water.
Suddenly, all the pain went out of his body,
The wound stopped bleeding, the arrow
Slipped out easily in the healer's hand,   *520*
And all of Aeneas' old strength returned.

"Hurry and bring the man his weapons!
Why are you standing there?"

                              Iapyx said this,
And he was the first to fire them up for battle:

"This did not happen by any human power,   525
Nor was it my art that saved you, Aeneas.
A greater power, a god, is at work here
And is sending you back to do greater deeds."

Aeneas was hungry for the fight. Impatient
Of any delay, he clapped golden greaves   530
Onto his shins and started handling a spear.
As soon as his breastplate was strapped on
And his shield was fitted to his side,
He put his arms around Ascanius, kissed him
Lightly through his helmet, and said: 535

"Learn how to be a man from me, my son;
Learn good fortune from others. Today my hand
Will defend you in war and lead you
To great rewards. When you come of age,
See to it that you remember the example   540
Of your kinsmen, and that your father, Aeneas,
And your uncle Hector enliven your soul."

Aeneas spoke and then moved through the gates,
Huge himself and brandishing a massive spear.
Close by his side were Antheus and Mnestheus,   545
And behind them the entire army poured out,
Emptying the camp. The plain boiled
With blinding dust, and the shocked earth trembled
Under the tramping feet.
                          From the wall opposite
Turnus saw them coming; the Ausonians saw them,   550
And a cold shudder ran through their bones.
Before any of the Latins, Juturna
Heard the sound, knew it, and turned and fled.
Aeneas was flying, and his dark line of troops
Was drawn in his wake over the open plains.   555

   When a storm breaks at sea, and the rain cloud
   Moves toward land, pity the farmers,
   Whose prescient hearts know what is coming
   And shudder. Trees will be brought down,

> *Crops ruined, everything scattered. The winds*   560
> *Run before it and their howls carry shoreward.*

Just so the Trojan commander brought his troops
Up to the front, and they massed around him.
Thymbraeus landed his sword on Osiris,
Mnestheus killed Arcetius, Achates Epolo,   565
Gyas Ufens. Even Tolumnius fell,
The augur who was first to hurl a spear
In the enemy's face. A shout split the air,
And the routed Rutulians turned around
In a cloud of dust and ran through the fields.   570
Aeneas didn't bother with these fugitives,
Or even with those who opposed him,
On foot or mounted. Turnus alone
He tracked through the thickening gloom,
Turnus alone he called out to combat.   575

Juturna, in her deep distress,
Knocked Turnus' driver, Metiscus,
Out of the chariot and left him behind.
The warrior goddess assumed his form,
His voice and armor, and took the rippling reins.   580

> *A black swallow flits through the mansion*
> *Of a wealthy lord, winging her way*
> *Through the high halls to scavenge*
> *Scraps and crumbs for her chirping nestlings,*
> *Then twittering in and out of the porticoes*   585
> *And about the courtyard pools.*

                    So too Juturna
Guided the horses through the enemy ranks
And flew in the chariot all over the field,
Giving them glimpses of her exultant brother,
Now here, now there, never allowing him   590
To lock up in combat but always flitting away.
Still, Aeneas kept tracking Turnus down
Through the winding maze of war, calling him,
Calling, and when he spotted him, sprinting

To match the horses' speed, only to have   595
Juturna wrench the chariot aside.
What could he do? He was all at sea,
His mind pulled in contrary directions.
Meanwhile, Messapus, treading lightly
And carrying two javelins tipped with steel,   600
Rifled one of them at him with deadly aim.
Aeneas went down to one knee and crouched
Behind his shield as the spearhead sheared
The crest from his helmet. He felt a sudden
Surge of anger at this treacherous attack.   605
He saw Turnus' chariot pulling away.
Calling to witness Jupiter himself
And the altars of the broken treaty,
Aeneas plunged into the general combat
And, with Mars at his back, began to kill   610
Indiscriminately, giving his rage free rein.

What god could now unfold for me
So many bitter deaths, which poet could tell
Of all the captains who met their many dooms
Driven over the plain now by Turnus,   615
Now by the Trojan hero? Did it please you,
Jupiter, that nations destined to live
In everlasting peace should clash so harshly?

Aeneas, in the first combat that halted
The Trojans' onrush, paused only briefly   620
To take out Sucro, driving his steel
Through the rib cage, where death comes most quickly.
Turnus unhorsed Amycus and his brother, Diores,
And then advancing on foot struck down one
With his long spear, the other with his sword;   625
Then hanging their severed heads from his chariot,
He bore them off dripping dewdrops of blood.
Aeneas sent to their deaths Talos, Tanais,
And brave Cethegus, three in one assault,
And then dispatched the shocked Onites,   630
A Theban whose mother was Peridia.

Turnus' next victims were the brothers sent
From Apollo's Lycian fields, and Menoetes,
An Arcadian who hated warfare, in vain.
This man had been a humble fisherman   635
Near the pools of Lerna. He had no patrons,
And his father tilled a rented plot of land.

    Like fires set on different sides of a wood,
    A dry thicket of crackling laurels;
    Or like rivers roaring down a mountainside,   640
    Each destroying everything in its path,

So Aeneas and Turnus swept through the battle,
Each of them seething with rage within,
Hearts bursting, neither yielding an inch,
And all their desire was to wound men with steel.   645

Murranus was boasting of his ancient lineage
Stretching back to Latin kings, when Aeneas
Hit him with a huge stone that pitched him
Headfirst over his car, where he was trampled
By horses who did not remember their master.   650
Hyllus was charging forward with insane fury
When Turnus rifled a spear at his golden brow.
The point pierced his helmet and stuck in his brain.
And you, Cretheus, bravest of the Greeks,
Your right hand did not save you from Turnus;   655
Nor did Cupencus' gods protect him
When Aeneas came. He put his chest in the way
Of Aeneas' spear, and the slight reprieve
His bronze shield offered did not help him much.
You also, Aeolus, fell at Laurentum   660
And spread your body out in its fields,
You, whom the Argive army could not lay low,
Nor Achilles, destroyer of Priam's realm.
Here was your end. Your home was in Lyrnesus
Under Mount Ida; in Laurentum is your grave.   665

Now, all up and down the lines, both armies
Engaged—all the Latins and all the Trojans:

Mnestheus and intense Serestus;
Messapus, breaker of horses, and brave Asilas;
Tuscan troops and Evander's Arcadians,   670
Each doing his utmost, each at his limit,
No rest, no respite in the vast, open conflict.

Aeneas' mother now put it in his mind
To advance on the walls, attack the town
With abrupt force, and throw the Latins   675
Into confusion at the sudden slaughter.
Tracking Turnus through the lanes of battle,
He swept his eyes in every direction
And saw the city untouched by the war,
Quiet and at peace. At once a vision   680
Of a greater conflict burned in his mind.
Summoning Mnestheus, Sergestus,
And brave Serestus, he climbed up a mound
To which the rest of the Trojans came at a run,
Still holding their spears and shields. Aeneas,   685
Standing on this height, addressed them:

"I want no delay in carrying out my orders—
Jupiter is on our side—and I don't want anyone
Holding back because the decision is sudden.
That city, the cause of this war, the heart   690
Of Latinus' realm, unless they surrender
And submit to our rule—that city
I will today overthrow and lay its smoking roofs
Level with the ground. Am I supposed to wait
Until Turnus feels like doing battle with me,   695
Until he comes back for more, beaten though he is?
This is the crux of this accursed war, men.
Bring torches and reclaim the treaty with fire!"

They outdid each other in their eagerness,
Formed a wedge, and advanced to the walls en masse.   700
Ladders and torches appeared from nowhere.
One group stormed the gates and cut down the guards,
Others darkened the sky with their javelins.

Aeneas himself stood at the foot of the wall,
Stretched out his hands, and in a great voice   705
Accused Latinus, calling the gods to witness
That he was being forced into battle again,
That the Italians had twice become his foes,
Twice broken a treaty. Inside the walls
Strife arose among the anxious citizens.   710
Some wanted the city gates thrown open
To the Dardanians and called for the king
To be dragged to the walls. Others brought arms
And marched out to defend their city.

   A shepherd has followed bees to their hive   715
   In tunneled pumice and filled it with smoke.
   Anxious for their realm, the bees scurry
   This way and that through their wax fortress
   And with loud buzzing hone their rage.
   The black stench billows through their halls,   720
   The hollow rock resounds with a blind hum,
   And the smoke comes out into the empty air.

There was more grief for the weary Latins,
And it shook the city to its very foundations.
When the queen saw the enemy coming   725
Into the town, the walls breached, roofs aflame,
And no Rutulians, no troops of Turnus
Opposing them, the poor woman believed
That he had perished in battle. In her distress
She cried out that she was the cause and origin   730
Of all these evils, and said many other things
In her frenzied grief. Determined to die,
She tore her royal robes and from a high beam
Hung a noose for her hideous death.
When the Latin women found her dead,   735
First her daughter Lavinia tore out
Her golden hair and scored her cheeks,
Then all of the people around her raved,
And the house resounded with their laments.
The sad news spread through all the city.   740
Minds and hearts sank. Latinus went about

With rent garments, dazed by his wife's death
And his city's ruin, his white hair grimed with dust.

During all this time, Turnus was pursuing
A handful of stragglers at the edge of the plain,   745
Moving more slowly now, less and less happy
With his horses' brilliance. The wind carried to him
Unseen terrors in the clamor from the town.
Then, as he listened intently, a puzzle of sound
Struck his ears, the murmur of suffering.   750

"What are all these cries coming from the city?
It must be bad if I can hear it from here."

Distracted, he drew in the reins and stopped.
His sister, who still looked like Metiscus
And as such was steering the chariot,   755
Faced him and said:

                    "Let's keep after the Trojans
Out here, where we are already winning.
There are other troops to defend the town.
Aeneas is taking it to the Italians now,
And we should be dealing death to the Teucrians.   760
You'll kill just as many here, with no less honor."

To which Turnus replied:

                          "I knew it was you
Long ago, Sister, when you entered this war
And tricked us into breaking the truce,
And you don't fool me now, Goddess. But why   765
Come down from Olympus and endure all this?
So you can see your brother's miserable death?
What can I do? There are no guarantees.
I saw Murranus before my own eyes,
Calling me as he went down. No one   770
Meant more to me—Murranus,
A mighty man undone by a mighty wound.
Poor Ufens died so he wouldn't have to see
My disgrace. The Trojans have his body and arms.

And now I should allow our homes destroyed   775
(The final touch) and not refute Drances?
Turn tail and let this land see Turnus in flight?
Is it so bad to die? Shades below,
Be good to me, since the will of heaven
Has turned against me. I will go down to you   780
Holy in spirit, innocent of any guilt,
And never unworthy of my great forebears."

He had scarcely finished when Saces,
His face wounded by an arrow, came riding up
On a panting horse through the enemy lines,   785
Calling Turnus by name and imploring him:

"Turnus, you are our last hope. Pity your people.
Aeneas is storming in battle and threatening
To throw down the Italians' topmost towers
And destroy them utterly. Torches are already   790
Flying to the roofs. The Latins are turning
All eyes to you, Turnus. King Latinus himself
Mutters about whom to call his son
And to which alliance he should turn. Moreover,
The queen, who put all her trust in you, is dead   795
By her own hand, gone from the world of light.
Only Messapus and Atinas are holding the gates,
Surrounded by squadrons bristling with steel,
While you wheel your chariot in an empty field."

Turnus was stunned by this changed picture   800
Of his fortunes. He stood rooted in silence,
His great heart roiling with shame, with grief
Verging on madness, with frenzied love
And undeniable courage. When the shadows
Parted, and light returned to his mind,   805
He swept his blazing eyes toward the walls,
Furious, and looked back from his chariot
At the great city.

             Flames were spiraling skyward
From story to story, about to catch a tower—

A defensive bulwark he himself had built,   810
Set on wheels and hung with high gangways.

"Now, Sister, the Fates triumph at last.
Stop holding me back. We will follow
Where God and cruel Fortune call us.
My mind is made up. I will meet Aeneas   815
And bear death's bitterness. No longer,
Sister, will you see me shamed. But first,
Allow me to rage with furious rage."

Turnus spoke, leapt down from his chariot,
And careened madly through the enemy lines,   820
Leaving his sorrowing sister behind.

> *Think of a stone crashing down a mountain,*
> *Either a storm has washed it free, or time*
> *In its passing has loosened it, and now*
> *The shameless mass of rock sweeps down*   825
> *The steep slopes and bounds over the earth,*
> *Rolling along with it trees, herds, and men.*

So too Turnus scattering the ranks
In his rush to the walls, where the ground
Was most soaked with blood and the air   830
Whined with spears. Turnus lifted his hand,
Had their immediate attention, and spoke:

"Fall back, Rutulians; and you, Latins,
Hold your fire. Whatever fortune is here
Is mine. It is better for your sake   835
That I alone make good the treaty
And settle the issue with steel."

And the troops made room for him in the middle.

When Father Aeneas heard Turnus' name,
He left the walls and left the high fortress,   840
Jettisoned everything he had been doing,
And in great exultation clashed his weapons.
The sound was like thunder, and the hero

As vast as Mount Athos, vast as Eryx,
Vast as Father Apennine himself   845
With his shimmering oaks, when he roars in joy
And lifts his snowy head toward heaven.

Now every last man turned and stared—
Every Rutulian, Trojan, and Italian soldier,
Both those high on the walls and those below   850
Who were battering the walls—and they all
Took off their armor. Latinus himself
Was lost in wonder that these two great men,
Born in different parts of the world, had met
And now would settle the issue with steel.   855
As soon as the field was cleared out on the plain
They sprinted forward, threw their spears from afar,
Then waded into battle with a clash of bronze.
Earth groaned. Sword struck sword with stroke
After stroke, luck and valor blending into one.   860

In great Sila, or high on Taburnus,
Two bulls have locked horns in mortal combat.
The keepers fall back in fear, and all the cattle
Stand in silent dread, the heifers musing
On who will be lord of the entire herd.   865
The bulls butt heads with tremendous force
And gore each other, bathing their backs
And shoulders with blood, and the whole grove
Resounds with their bellowing groans.

So too the Trojan and Daunian heroes   870
Clashed shield against shield and filled the sky
With crashing thunder. Jupiter himself
Held up his balanced scales and placed on them
The destinies of each man to determine whom
The battle doomed, whose weight sank down to death.   875

Turnus, thinking he could get away with it,
Sprang forward with sword lifted high
And put all of his weight into a sweeping stroke.
A shout went up from both armies, Trojans

And Latins both straining to see, expectant,   880
But the treacherous sword only splintered
In mid-stroke. When Turnus saw
That his right hand held an unfamiliar hilt
He fled, faster than the East Wind.
The story is told that when Turnus   885
First mounted his chariot he neglected,
In his haste, to bring his father's sword,
And snatched up instead the blade of Metiscus,
His charioteer. This served him well enough
When he was chasing down Teucrian stragglers,   890
But when it came up against the divine armor
Forged by Vulcan, the mortal blade
Shattered like brittle ice into fragments
That glittered on the yellow sand.
                                Turnus
Ran like a madman this way and that   895
Across the plain, weaving in circles.
The Teucrians closed in, confining him
Between the walls and the desolate marsh.
Aeneas, though his knees were slowed
By the arrow wound and he was not at full speed,   900
Nevertheless stayed hot on his heels.

    A hunting hound has caught a stag
    Hemmed in by a stream, or by crimson feathers
    That hunters use to hedge in game. The dog
    Runs and barks and worries the stag,   905
    Who in terror of the snares and the high bank
    Runs back and forth in a thousand directions.
    But the keen Umbrian hound stays close,
    Mouth gaping wide. The hound almost seizes it,
    And snaps its jaws shut as if it had seized it,   910
    But bites only the empty air.

                        Another shout arose,
Echoed by the banks and pools, and the sky thundered
With the tumult below. While Turnus ran,
While he was in full flight, he reproached the Rutulians,
Calling them by name, and clamored for his sword.   915

Aeneas, though, promised instant death
For anyone who came near and made them tremble
By threatening to level their town. Wounded,
He pressed on as they ran in loops, circling five times
And doubling back he unwove all their circuits,   920
For they were not running for some trivial prize
At games but for the lifeblood of Turnus.

There was a bitter-leaved wild olive tree,
Sacred to Faunus, out on the plain,
Revered of old by mariners. Onto this tree   925
They would attach their offerings
To the Laurentine god and in its branches
Hang their votive garments. But the Teucrians,
With no regard for the tree's sanctity,
Had cut it down so that they could fight   930
On an open field. The spear Aeneas had thrown
Was stuck in the tough roots of this tree,
And the Trojan now stooped to pull it out
So he could take down with this weapon
The man he could not catch on foot.   935
Turnus, out of his mind with fear, cried out:

"Have pity on me, Faunus and Mother Earth.
Hold fast the spear, if ever I have honored you,
Whom the men of Aeneas now profane in war."

He spoke, and the gods heard his prayer.   940
Aeneas struggled long with the pliant root
But could not with all his strength force open
Its stubborn grip. And while he struggled,
Juturna, transformed again into Metiscus,
Ran up and handed her brother his sword.   945
Venus, outraged at the nymph's audacity,
Came and plucked the spear out from the root.
The two heroes, weapons and spirits restored,
One trusting his sword, the other towering
With his spear, both panting for breath,   950
Stood face to face in the arena of War.

Meanwhile, the Lord of Olympus
Addressed Juno as she watched the fighting
From a golden cloud:

            "Juno, my wife,
How will it end? What remains at the last?   *955*
You yourself know, and you admit that you know,
That Aeneas, the hero of his country,
Is destined to be exalted to the stars.
What are you preparing? With what hope
Do you cling to the chill clouds? Was it right   *960*
That a god be profaned by a mortal's wound?
That the sword be returned—Juturna could never
Have done it without you—which Turnus had lost,
Or that strength increase in the vanquished?
Desist, and yield at last to my prayers,   *965*
Lest your great grief consume you in silence,
Lest your bitter woes return to me often
From your sweet lips. We have come to the end.
You have had the power to pursue the Trojans
Over land and sea, to kindle a terrible war,   *970*
To disfigure a home and blend bridals with grief.
I forbid you to attempt more."

            Thus Jupiter;
And thus Saturn's daughter, with downcast eyes:

"It was because I knew that this was your will,
My mighty lord, that with great reluctance   *975*
I left the earth and left Turnus. Otherwise,
You would not see me sitting here alone
On my airy throne enduring all, right or wrong.
No, I would be standing cinctured in flame
In the front lines of battle, dragging the Trojans   *980*
Into mortal combat. As for Juturna,
Yes, I persuaded her to help her brother,
And for his life's sake I sanctioned daring deeds
But not to shoot the arrow, not to bend the bow.
I swear to this by the implacable water of Styx,   *985*
The one inviolable oath for the gods above.

And now I yield, and quit this loathsome war.
I have one solemn request of you, something
Not prohibited by Fate, for Latium's sake
And for your people's majesty. When soon   990
(Let it be) they make peace with happy weddings,
And form alliances with laws and treaties,
Do not command the native Latins
To change their ancient name, nor become
Trojans and be called Teucrians, nor to change   995
In language or in dress. Let Latium be,
Let Alban kings rule through the ages,
And let the Roman stock be strong
In Italian manhood. Troy has fallen.
Let the name of Troy be fallen too."   1000

Smiling at her, the world's Creator said:

"You are Jove's true sister, and Saturn's child.
The waves of wrath that roll deep in your breast!
Come, dismiss the fury that was aroused in vain.
I grant your request, and I willingly relent.   1005
The Ausonians will keep their native tongue
And ancestral ways; as their name is now,
So shall it be. The Teucrians shall be absorbed
In the body at large. I will establish
Their sacred rites and laws and make them all   1010
Latins, with a single tongue. From them shall rise
A race blended with Ausonian blood
That you shall see surpass both gods and men
In faith and loyalty. And no nation
Shall be more zealous in Juno's worship."   1015

The goddess nodded, happy to assent,
Then left the cloud and departed from the sky.

This done, the Father pondered how
To withdraw Juturna from her brother's side.

There are twin fiends, whom men call Dirae,   1020
Born to the Night Goddess in the same litter

As hellish Megaera. Their mother wreathed
The heads of all three with coiling snakes
And gave them wings to ride the winds.
These two Dirae attend the throne of Jupiter   1025
And whet the fears of feeble mortals
When the grim monarch visits them
With disease and death, or terrorizes
Guilty cities with war. Jove sent one of them
Down from high heaven with instructions   1030
To appear as an omen before Juturna.
The fiend flew down to earth in whirling wind,

   Like an arrow speeding from a bowstring
   Into a cloud bank, a poisoned arrow
   Shot by a Parthian archer, a Parthian   1035
   Or a Cydonian, an incurable shaft
   Whining unseen through the flitting shadows.

Thus the child of Night, speeding to earth.
When she came in sight of the Trojan ranks
And the troops of Turnus, she suddenly shrank   1040
Into the shape of an owl, the small bird
That often perches at night on tombs
And deserted rooftops, singing its late,
Unwelcome song through the shadows.
So transformed, the fiend flits and screams   1045
Before the face of Turnus, her dark wings
Beating his shield. A strange, numbing dread
Washed through Turnus' body; his hair
Bristled with fear; his voice stuck in his throat.

His sister, Juturna, recognized from afar   1050
The harsh whisper of the Dread One's wings.
She tore out her unbound hair, her nails
Clawed her face, and she pounded her breast
With her fists. Then she cried out to her brother:

"How can your sister help you now, Turnus,   1055
And what is left for my own hard life? Nothing
I can do will prolong the light for you.

Can I oppose this terrible portent?
Now at last I quit the field. Don't try to scare me,
You ill-omened vultures! I am already afraid.   *1060*
I know the beating of your wings,
The sound of death, and I do not mistake
The haughty commands of Jupiter.
Is this how he compensated me
For my lost virginity? Why did he give me   *1065*
Life everlasting? If I could only die
I could end this sorrow, go through the shadows
At my poor brother's side. I, immortal!
Nothing can be sweet without you, Brother.
What ground can gape deep enough   *1070*
To send a goddess to the deepest shades?"

So saying, Juturna covered her head
With a sea-grey veil, and moaning profusely
The goddess plunged into the river's depths.

Aeneas kept the pressure on, rocking   *1075*
His tree of a spear, and cried savagely:

"What's the delay now, Turnus? Why are you still
Holding back? This isn't a footrace, you know;
It's hand-to-hand combat with cold steel.
Go ahead, change yourself into all sorts of shapes,   *1080*
Collect all your courage and skill, fly away
High on wings if you want, up to the stars,
Or sink into the hollow earth—I'll get you still."

And Turnus, shaking his head:

                              "You don't scare me,
Big-mouth. The gods scare me, and having Jupiter   *1085*
As my enemy."

                  Turnus said no more.
Looking around he saw a huge stone
Lying on the plain, a stone ancient and huge
Set in place to settle boundary disputes.

Twelve chosen men could scarcely lift it   1090
Onto their shoulders, as men are now,
But the hero scooped it up quickly, rose
To his full height, and with a burst of speed
Hurled it at his adversary. But as he ran
He did not know himself, did not know who he was   1095
As he moved toward the immense stone, lifted it,
And sent it flying. His knees buckled,
His blood was like ice. The stone itself,
Rolling through empty air, fell short
And did not deliver its blow.

                In dreams,   1100
   When night's weariness weighs on our eyes,
   We are desperate to run farther and farther
   But collapse weakly in the middle of our efforts.
   Our tongue doesn't work, our usual strength
   Fails our body, and words will not come.   1105

So too Turnus. However bravely he tried
The Dread One would not let him win through.
Shifting images spun through his mind.
He looked at the Rutulians, and the town,
Frozen with fear. He saw death closing in   1110
And trembled, nowhere to escape, no way
To attack his enemy. He could not see
His chariot, or his sister, the charioteer.

While Turnus faltered Aeneas' fatal spear
Quivered in the light. Seeing his chance   1115
He put all his weight behind a long-range throw,
And his weapon flew with deadly force,
Faster than a stone hurled by a catapult
And with a sound louder than thunder.
Roaring through the air like a black tornado   1120
It tore through Turnus' seven-ply shield,
Ripped open his corselet, and with a hiss
Sliced through his thigh. Huge Turnus
Sank down on one knee. The Rutulians
Leapt up with a shout, and the woods and hills   1125

Echoed their groans. Humbled, Turnus
Lifted his eyes to Aeneas
And stretched forth his hand in supplication:

"Go ahead, use your chance. I deserve it.
I will not ask anything for myself,   1130
But if a parent's grief can still touch you,
Remember your own father, Anchises,
And take pity on Daunus' old age,
I beg you. Give me, or if you prefer,
Give my dead body back to my people.   1135
You've beaten me, and the Ausonians
Have seen me, beaten, stretch out my hand to you.
Lavinia is yours. Let your hatred stop here."

Aeneas stood there, lethal in his bronze.
His eyes searched the distance, and his hand   1140
Paused on the hilt of his sword. Turnus' words
Were winning him over, but then his gaze shifted
To the fateful baldric on his enemy's shoulder,
And the belt glittered with its familiar metalwork—
The belt of young Pallas, whom Turnus had killed   1145
And whose insignia he now wore as a trophy.
Aeneas' eyes drank in this memorial
Of his own savage grief, and then, burning
With fury and terrible in his wrath, he said:

"Do you think you can get away from me   1150
While wearing the spoils of one of my men?
                                            Pallas
Sacrifices you with this stroke—Pallas—
And makes you pay with your guilty blood."

Saying this, and seething with rage, Aeneas
Buried his sword in Turnus' chest. The man's limbs   1155
Went limp and cold, and with a moan
His soul fled resentfully down to the shades.

Glossary of Names

Acestes (A-kes´-teez): A Trojan who became a king in Sicily.

Achaeans (A-kee´-unz): General name for the Greeks.

Achates (A-ka´-teez): Companion of Aeneas.

Acheron (A´-ker-on): River in the Underworld.

Achilles (A-kil´-eez): A central character in Homer's *Iliad*. Son of Peleus and Thetis; killer of Hector.

Actium (Ak´-tee-um): A promontory in northwestern Greece near which Octavian defeated Antony and Cleopatra in 31 B.C.E.

Aeneas (Ee-nee´-as): Principal character in the *Aeneid;* Trojan warrior in Homer's *Iliad*. Son of Venus and Anchises; leader of the Trojans after the fall of Troy.

Aeneas Silvius (Ee-nee´-as Sil´-vee-us): Descendant of Aeneas; a future king of Alba Longa.

Aeolus (Ee´-oh-lus): God of the winds.

Agamemnon (A-ga-mem´-non): King of Mycenae; leader of the Greek army during the Trojan War. He was killed by his wife, Clytemnestra, when he returned home.

Agenor (A-gen´-or): Ancient king of Tyre; ancestor of Dido.

Agrippa (Ag-rip´-a): Marcus Vipsanius Agrippa; son-in-law of Augustus and commander under Augustus.

Ajax (Ay´-jax): Son of Oïleus; a Greek warrior in Homer's *Iliad*. He attacked Cassandra during the fall of Troy and was later punished for sacrilege toward the temple of Pallas.

Alba Longa (Al´-ba Lon´-ga): City founded by Ascanius in the Alban hills of Italy.

Allecto (A-lek´-toh): One of the Furies; bringer of war and wrath.

Amata (A-ma´-ta): Queen in Italy; the wife of Latinus and mother of Lavinia.

Amazons (Aʹ-ma-zonz): Women warriors. They were allies of the Trojans.

Anchises (An-keyeʹ-seez): Son of Capys; father of Aeneas by Venus. He escaped Troy on the shoulders of Aeneas.

Andromache (An-draʹ-ma-kee): Wife of Hector.

Anna (Anʹ-a): Sister of Dido.

Antenor (An-teeʹ-nor): Trojan prince who founded Patavium.

Antony (Anʹ-toh-nee): Marc Antony; rival of Octavian. He was defeated at the battle of Actium in 31 B.C.E.

Apollo (A-polʹ-oh): Son of Jupiter and Latona; brother of Diana. Patron god of music and prophecy; associated with the lyre and archery.

Arcadia (Ar-kayʹ-dee-a): Region in the Peloponnesus of Greece known for pastoral practices.

Arethusa (Ar-a-thooʹ-za): Nymph who was transformed into a fountain at Syracuse in Sicily.

Argos (Arʹ-gos): City or district in the northeastern Peloponnesus of Greece. The name "Argives" is derived from this city and refers to the Greeks.

Argus (Arʹ-gus): Hundred-eyed monster charged by Juno with the task of watching over the cow Io. Killed by Mercury.

Ascanius (As-kayʹ-nee-us): Son of Aeneas and Creüsa; also called Iülus. He eventually founds Alba Longa.

Assaracus (As-arʹ-ak-us): A king of Troy; son of Tros; great-grandfather of Aeneas.

Astyanax (As-teyeʹ-a-nax): Son of Hector and Andromache. Killed during the fall of Troy.

Atlas (Atʹ-las): Titan who holds up the sky; son of Iapetos.

Augustus (A-gusʹ-tus): Gaius Julius Caesar Octavianus Augustus; adopted by Julius Caesar. First Roman emperor; ruled from 27 B.C.E. to 14 C.E. He assumed the name Augustus in 27 B.C.E.

Ausonia (Ow-sohʹ-nee-a): Italy.

Avernus (A-ver´-nus): Lake near Cumae in Italy near which was said to be an entrance to the Underworld.

Bacchus (Bak´-us): God of wine; son of Jupiter and Semele. Also Liber in Latin. Greek Dionysus.

Baiae (Beye´-eye): Seaside town near Naples.

Belus (Bel´-us): A king of Tyre; father of Dido.

Briareus (Bree´-ar-ee-us): Hundred-handed giant; also known as Aegaeon.

Brutus (Broo´-tus): Lucius Junius Brutus; expelled the last Tarquin king from Rome in 510 B.C.E.

Cacus (Ka´-kus): Son of Vulcan. A giant who was killed by Hercules.

Caesar (Seez´-ar): Gaius Julius Caesar; a Roman statesman and general who adopted Octavian. Killed in 44 B.C.E.

Camilla (Ka-mil´-a): Warrior woman allied with Turnus. She was the leader of the Volscians.

Capitol (Kap´-it-ol): Top of the Capitoline Hill in Rome on which stood the temple to Jupiter Optimus Maximus.

Carthage (Kar´-thaj): City on the northwest coast of Africa; historically a rival of Rome. According to legend it was founded by Queen Dido after she fled her brother's violence.

Cassandra (Ka-san´-dra): Daughter of Priam and Hecuba. A prophetess whom no one believed.

Catiline (Kat´-a-lin): Lucius Sergius Catilina; a Roman conspirator who was exposed by Cicero in 63 B.C.E.

Cato (Kay´-toh): Marcus Porcius Cato; a conservative Roman statesman who strongly urged the destruction of Carthage.

Celaeno (Sel-eye´-noh): Chief of the Harpies.

Centaur (Sen´-tar): Half-man, half-horse mythological creature belonging to a race fathered by Ixion.

Cerberus (Ker´-ber-us): Three-headed dog that guards the gates of the Underworld.

Ceres (Seer´-eez): Goddess of crops and the harvest. Greek Demeter.

Charon (Kay´-ron): Ferryman who transports the dead across the river Styx in the Underworld.

Charybdis (Ka-rib´-dis): Whirlpool near Scylla in the straits of Messina.

Circe (Sir´-see): Sorceress whom Ulysses encountered in Homer's *Odyssey*. She changes Ulysses' men into swine.

Cocytus (Ko-kee´-tus): River in the Underworld.

Corinth (Kor´-inth): City in the northwest Peloponnesus of Greece; captured by the Romans in 146 B.C.E.

Crete (Kreet): Island in the Aegean Sea south of Greece. Aeneas landed here when searching for his destined land.

Creüsa (Kree-oos´-a): Daughter of Priam; first wife of Aeneas; mother of Ascanius. She was separated from Aeneas and lost during the fall of Troy.

Cupid (Kyoo´-pid): God of love; son of Venus.

Cybele (Kee´-bel- ee): (1) Phrygian mother-goddess of Asia Minor. (2) The mountain with which she is associated.

Cyclops (Seye´-klops): (1) Race of giants living in Sicily who have only one eye each. (2) The workers of Vulcan.

Cyprus (Seye´-prus): Eastern Mediterranean island; associated with Venus.

Cythera (Si-thee´-ra): Island southeast of Greece near which Venus was born, hence Venus' name Cytherean.

Daedalus (Deye´-dal-us): Craftsman who built the labyrinth for the purpose of containing the Minotaur on the island of Crete. He escaped Crete by fashioning wings of feathers and wax and using them to fly to Cumae in Italy.

Danaans (Da-nay´-unz): A general name referring to the Greeks.

Danaë (Dan´-ay-ee): Daughter of Acrisius, a king of Argos. She was set adrift in a chest by her father; she reached Italy and founded Ardea, the city of Turnus.

Dardanus (Dar´-dan-us): Ancestor of the Trojans and mythological founder of Troy. From his name the Trojans are called Dardanians.

Delos (Dee´-los): Island in the Aegean Sea; birthplace of Apollo and Diana.

Diana (Deye-an´-a): Daughter of Jupiter and Latona; sister of Apollo; goddess of the hunt and the moon. Greek Artemis.

Dido (Deye´-doh): Queen of Carthage in North Africa. She founded Carthage when she fled from her brother's violence. She killed herself after Aeneas left Carthage. Also called Elissa.

Diomedes (Deye-oh-mee´-deez): Son of Tydeus and Deïpyle. A commander and a foremost warrior in Homer's *Iliad*. He founded the city of Arpi in Italy after the Trojan War.

Drances (Dran´-seez): A Rutulian hostile to Turnus.

Elissa (A-lis´-a): A name of Dido.

Elysium (Ee-lees´-ee-um): Pleasant region of the Underworld reserved for those who led a good life.

Entellus (En-tel´-us): A boxer who defeated Dares.

Erebus (Er´-ab-us): Name of the Underworld.

Eryx (Er´-ix): (1) Son of Venus, and so a half-brother of Aeneas; a king at Sicily known for boxing. (2) The name of a mountain.

Etruria (Ee-tru´-ree-a): Region in Italy north of Rome.

Etruscans (Ee-trus´-cans): People who inhabit Etruria.

Eumenides (Yoo-men´-id-eez): Kind name for the Furies; avengers of crimes committed within a family.

Eurus (Yoo´-rus): Southeast Wind.

Euryalus (Yoo-ree´-a-lus): Trojan, son of Opheltes, beloved of Nisus.

Evander (Ee-van´-der): Son of Mercury; king of Pallanteum. His son, Pallas, fought as an ally of Aeneas.

Fates: Three goddesses who spin the fate of human lives. Also called the Parcae.

Faunus (Faw´-nus): Italian god of woodlands and a deified king.

Furies (Fyur´-eez): Avengers of crimes committed within a family; also called the Eumenides.

Ganymede (Gan´-ee-meed): Son of the Trojan Tros. Snatched up by the eagle of Jupiter, he became Jupiter's cupbearer.

Geryon (Ger´-ee-on): Giant with three bodies; killed by Hercules.

Gorgon (Gore´-gon): One of three sisters with snakes in their hair and the ability to turn anyone who looked at them into stone. Medusa, one of the Gorgons, was decapitated, and her head was attached to Minerva's aegis.

Gracchi (Grak´-eye): Prominent Roman family whence came two brothers, Tiberius and Gaius, who attempted to reform the Roman state.

Harpies (Har´-peez): Monsters with a bird's body and a woman's head.

Hecate (Hek´-at-ee): Goddess of the Underworld and witchcraft; associated with the moon and Diana.

Hector (Hek´-tor): Eldest son of Priam and Hecuba; husband of Andromache. Leader of the Trojan army at Troy in Homer's *Iliad*; killed by Achilles.

Hecuba (He´-kew-ba): Queen of Troy and wife of Priam; mother of Hector, Paris, Cassandra, and other children of Priam.

Helen (He´-len): Daughter of Leda and Jupiter; wife of Menelaus. The most beautiful woman in the world. Her abduction by Paris was believed to cause the Trojan War.

Helicon (He´-li-kon): Mountain in Greece that the Muses frequent.

Hercules (Her´-kyoo-leez): Son of Jupiter and Alcmene; a hero famed for his twelve labors.

Hesperia (Hes-per´-ee-a): A land in the west; a name for Italy.

Hesperides (Hes-per´-id-eez): Daughters of Hesperus. Keepers of a garden in the far west that contained a tree bearing golden apples.

Hippolytus (Hip-all´-ee-tos): Son of Theseus and Hippolyte. His stepmother, Phaedra, fell in love with him, and when her love was not returned she engineered his death.

Hydra (Heye´-dra): Monster with many heads; killed by Hercules.

Icarus (I´-ka-rus): Son of Daedalus. He escaped Crete with his father by means of wings assembled with feathers and wax; he flew too close to the sun, the wax melted, and he fell into the sea.

Ida (Eye´-da): (1) Mountain near Troy. (2) Mountain in Crete. (3) Mother of Nisus.

Ilia (Il´-ee-a): Mother of Romulus and Remus by Mars.

Ilium (Il´-ee-um): A name for Troy.

Ilus (Ee´-lus): (1) A name for Ascanius, the son of Aeneas. (2) A founder of Troy. (3) A Rutulian allied with Turnus.

Io (I´-oh): Daughter of Inachus. Jupiter fell in love with her; she was changed into a cow and was tormented by Juno.

Iris (Eye´-ris): Goddess of the rainbow; messenger for Juno.

Iülus (Ee-oo´-los): A name for Ascanius, the son of Aeneas.

Jove (Johv): Name of Jupiter.

Juno (Joon´-oh): Daughter of Saturn; wife and sister of Jupiter. She is hostile toward the Trojans. Greek Hera.

Jupiter (Joo´-pit-er): Son of Saturn; husband of Juno; ruler of the gods. Greek Zeus.

Juturna (Joo-turn´-a): A nymph; sister of Turnus.

Laertes (Lay-er´-teez): Son of Arcesius; husband of Anticleia; father of Ulysses.

Laocoön (Lay-ak´-oh-on): A Trojan priest of Neptune. He was devoured by serpents for warning the Trojans about the Trojan Horse.

Laomedon (Lay-om´-ee-don): A king of Troy; father of Priam. He refused to repay Neptune and Apollo for building the walls of Troy.

Lar (Lar): A tutelary deity of the Roman household, associated especially with the hearth.

Latinus (La-tine´-us): Son of Faunus; father of Lavinia; King of Laurentium in Latium.

Latium (Lay´-she-um): Region in west-central Italy; ruled by King Latinus.

Latona (La-tone´-a): Mother of Apollo and Diana.

Lausus (Lau´-sus): Son of Mezentius; ally of Turnus.

Lavinia (La-vin´-ee-a): Daughter of Latinus and Amata. She was courted by Turnus but was destined to be the wife of Aeneas.

Leda (Lee´-da): Mother of Helen. Jupiter impregnated her while he assumed the form of a swan.

Lethe (Lee´-thee): River of forgetfulness in the Underworld. Whoever drank of this river lost memories.

Libya (Lib´-ee-a): Region of North Africa.

Lycurgus (Lie-kur´-jus): A Thracian king.

Manlius (Man´-lee-us): Marcus Manlius Torquatus Capitolinus; Roman general who successfully defended the citadel at Rome from the Gauls in 390 B.C.E.

Marcellus (Mar-sel´-us): (1) Marcus Claudius Marcellus; Roman general during the Second Punic War. (2) Nephew and son-in-law of Augustus: he died at a young age.

Mars: Son of Jupiter and Juno; the god of war. Greek Ares.

Memnon (Mem´-non): Son of Aurora and Tithonus; a king in Ethiopia; ally of the Trojans.

Menelaus (Me-ne-lay´-us): Son of Atreus and Aerope; brother of Agamemnon; husband of Helen; ruler of Sparta.

Mercury (Mer´-kyoor-ee): Son of Jupiter and Maia; the messenger god and guide of souls of the dead. Greek Hermes.

Messapus (Mes-ap´-us): Son of Neptune; ally of Turnus.

Mezentius (Mez-en´-tee-us): Father of Lausus. An exiled king who was an ally of Turnus.

Minerva (Min-er´-va): Daughter of Jupiter; said to have been born from his head; goddess of wisdom, crafts, and battle. Greek Athena.

Minos (Meye´-nos): King of Crete; husband of Pasiphaë. After his death he was a judge of souls in the Underworld.

Mnestheus (Men-es´-thee-us): A comrade of Aeneas.

Mycenae (Meye-see´-nee): City in the Peloponnesus of Greece ruled by Agamemnon.

Myrmidons (Meer´-mi-donz): People from Thessaly; the troops who follow Achilles.

Neoptolemus (Nee-op-tal´-a-mus): A name of Pyrrhus, son of Achilles, that means "young warrior."

Neptune (Nep´-tune): Son of Saturn and Rhea; brother of Jupiter; god of the sea. Greek Poseidon.

Nisus (Neye´-sus): Trojan son of Hyrtacus, lover of Euryalus.

Ocean: Son of Uranus and Earth; thought to be the river that encircled the earth.

Olympus (O-lim´-pus): Mountain in Thessaly thought to be the home of the gods.

Opis (O´-pis): A nymph; follower of Diana.

Orcus (Oar´-kus): Name of Pluto, the god of the Underworld. Or used to refer to the Underworld.

Orestes (O-res´-teez): Son of Agamemnon and Clytemnestra. He killed his mother and her lover in order to avenge the murder of his father.

Orion (O-reye´-on): Mythical hunter who, after his death, was transformed into a constellation. The setting of the constellation signaled stormy weather.

Orpheus (Oar´-fee-us): Mythical poet and singer who attempted to bring his wife, Eurydice, back from the Underworld after she died from a snakebite.

Ortygia (Oar-tij´-ee-a): (1) A name for the island of Delos. (2) A region of Syracuse in Sicily.

Palinurus (Pal-ee-noor´-us): The pilot of Aeneas' fleet.

Pallas (Pal´-as): (1) Name of Minerva. (2) An ancestor of Evander. (3) The son of Evander.

Pan: God of forests and shepherds; half-man, half-goat.

Pandarus (Pan´-dar-us): (1) A Trojan warrior with Aeneas. (2) A Trojan warrior at the battle of Troy who broke the truce between the two armies.

Parcae (Par´-keye): Three goddesses who spin the fate of human lives. Also called the Fates.

Paris (Pa´-ris): Son of Priam and Hecuba; brother of Hector. He took Helen from Menelaus at Sparta.

Pasiphaë (Pas-if´-a-ee): Wife of Minos; queen of Crete. She mated with a bull and produced the Minotaur.

Pentheus (Pen´-thee-us): A king of Thebes. He denied the worship of Bacchus and was killed by maenads, among whom was his mother.

Phaedra (Fay´-dra): Wife of Theseus. She fell in love with Hippolytus, her stepson; when he refused to return her love, she engineered his death and then committed suicide.

Phlegethon (Fleg´-a-thon): Fiery river in the Underworld.

Phoebus (Fee´-bus): Name of Apollo meaning "bright."

Pluto (Ploo´-toh): God of the Underworld. Greek Hades.

Portunus (Por-toon´-us): God of harbors.

Praeneste (Preye-nes´-tee): City in Latium.

Priam (Preye´-am): King of Troy; husband of Hecuba. He was killed during the fall of Troy.

Proserpina (Pros-er´-peen-a): Daughter of Ceres; wife of Pluto. Greek Persephone.

Pygmalion (Pig-mail´-ee-on): Brother of Dido. He killed Dido's husband.

Pyrrhus (Peer´-us): Son of Achilles; a Greek warrior in the Trojan War.

Quirinus (Kweer-in´-us): Italian god. This became the name of Romulus when he was deified.

Remus (Ree´-mus): (1) Son of Ilia; brother of Romulus. He was killed by Romulus. (2) A Rutulian.

Rhadamanthus (Rad-a-man´-thus): Brother of Minos. He became a judge in the Underworld after his death.

Romulus (Rom´-you-lus): Son of Ilia; brother of Remus. Legendary founder of Rome and descendant of Aeneas.

Rutulians (Roo-tul´-ee-anz): People in Italy ruled by Turnus.

Sarpedon (Sar-pee´-don): Son of Jupiter; leader of the Lycians in the Trojan War. Killed by Patroclus.

Saturn (Sat´-urn): Father of Jupiter and Juno. He was driven from Olympus by Jupiter. Greek Cronus.

Scylla (Sil´-a): Sea monster that devoured the passengers of passing ships.

Serestus (Ser-es´-tus): Comrade of Aeneas.

Sergestus (Ser-ges´-tus): Comrade of Aeneas.

Sibyl (Sib´-il): Prophetess at Cumae in Italy. Aeneas consulted her about entering the Underworld.

Sparta (Spar´-ta): City in the Peloponnesus of Greece; ruled by Menelaus.

Styx (Stix): River in the Underworld. The gods swore oaths to this river and could not break the oaths.

Sychaeus (See-keye´-us): Dido's husband who was murdered by her brother, Pygmalion.

Syrtes (Sir´-teez): Sandbanks off the northern shore of Africa that were dangerous for ships.

Tarchon (Tar´-kon): An Etruscan leader; ally to Aeneas.

Tarquin (Tar´-kwin): The name of two kings of Rome. The second of the two, Tarquin the Proud, was driven out of Rome by Lucius Junius Brutus.

Tartarus (Tar´-tar-us): Region of the Underworld in which sinners were punished.

Tatius (Tay´-tee-us): Titus Tatius; a king of the Sabines who fought against the Romans but later made peace with them and joined Romulus as an ally.

Teucer (Too´-ser): (1) A king of Troy from Crete. From his name the Trojans are called Teucrians. (2) A Greek who fought in the Trojan War and later founded Salamis in Cyprus.

Theseus (Thee´-see-us): Son of Aegeas; a king of Athens. Killed the Minotaur. Attempted to help his comrade Pirithöus carry Proserpina from the Underworld.

Tiber (Teye´-ber): River in Italy near which Rome was founded.

Tibur (Teye´-bur): City in Latium.

Tithonus (Tith-oh´-nus): Son of Laomedon; husband of Aurora. He was granted eternal life but did not ask for eternal youth.

Triton (Treye´-ton): Son of Neptune; a sea-god.

Trivia (Triv´-ee-a): Name referring to Hecate and Diana as goddesses of crossroads.

Troy: City in northwestern Asia Minor ruled by Priam. It was the area of focus in Homer's *Iliad* and the city from which Aeneas fled when it was destroyed.

Turnus (Turn´-us): Son of Daunus and Venilia; king of the Rutulians. He was Aeneas' rival for Lavinia and led the armies opposing Aeneas in Italy.

Ulysses (Yoo-lis´-eez): A Greek leader in Homer's *Iliad* and the central character in Homer's *Odyssey*. Greek Odysseus.

Venus (Vee´-nus): Daughter of Jupiter and Dione; goddess of love and beauty. Mother of Aeneas by Anchises. Greek Aphrodite.

Vesta (Ves´-ta): Goddess of the hearth.

Vulcan (Vul´-can): Son of Juno; god of the forge and fire. He made armor for Aeneas. Greek Hephaestus.

Xanthus (Zan´-thus): River near Troy.

Zephyrus (Zef´-eer-us): The West Wind.

Suggestions for Further Reading

Fairclough, H. R. *Virgil*. 2 vols. Loeb Classical Library. Harvard University Press. Cambridge, Mass., 1978.

Mynors, R. A. B. *P. Vergili Maronis Opera*. Claredon Press. Oxford, 1972.

Page, T. E. *Aeneid*. 2 vols. Macmillan. London, 1900.

Williams, R. D. *The Aeneid of Virgil*. 2 vols. Macmillan. London, 1973.

Maffeo Vegio: Short Epics. Edited and translated by Michael Putnam. Harvard University Press (The I Tatti Renaissance Library). Cambridge, Mass., 2004.

Boyle, A. J., ed. *Roman Epic*. Routledge. London, 1993.

Broch, Hermann. *The Death of Virgil*. Translated by Jean Starr Untermeyer. Vintage Books. New York, 1995.

Cairns, Francis. *Virgil's Augustan Epic*. Cambridge University Press. New York, 1989.

Clausen, Wendell. *Virgil's Aeneid and the Tradition of Hellenistic Poetry*. University of California Press. Berkeley, 1987.

Commager, Steele, ed. *Virgil: A Collection of Critical Essays*. Prentice-Hall. Englewood Cliffs, N.J., 1966.

Dyson, Julia T. *King of the Wood: The Sacrificial Victor in Virgil's Aeneid*. University of Oklahoma Press. Norman, 2001.

Farrell, Joseph. "Which *Aeneid* in Whose Nineties." *Vergilius* 36 (1990): 74–80.

Feeney, D. C. *The Gods in Epic: Poets and Critics of the Classical Tradition*. Oxford University Press. New York, 1991.

Gransden, K. W. *Virgil's Iliad: An Essay on Epic Narrative*. Cambridge University Press. New York, 1984.

Gurval, Robert Alan. *Actium and Augustus: The Politics and Emotions of Civil War*. University of Michigan Press. Ann Arbor, 1995.

Hardie, Philip R. *Virgil's Aeneid: Cosmos and Imperium*. Clarendon Press. Oxford, 1986.

——, ed. *Virgil. Critical Assessments of Classical Authors*. Routledge. London, 1999.

Harrison, S. J. *Oxford Readings in Vergil's Aeneid*. Oxford University Press. New York, 1990.

Heinze, Richard. *Virgil's Epic Technique.* Translated by Hazel Harvey, David Harvey, and Fred Robertson. University of California Press. Berkeley, 1993.

Hinds, Stephen. *Allusion and Intertext: Dynamics of Appropriation in Roman Poetry.* Cambridge University Press. New York, 1998.

Horsfall, N. M. *A Companion to the Study of Vergil.* E. J. Brill. Leiden, 1995.

Jenkyns, R. *Virgil's Experience: Nature and History, Times, Names, and Places.* Oxford University Press. New York, 1998.

Johnson, W. R. *Darkness Visible: A Study of Vergil's Aeneid.* University of California Press. Berkeley, 1976.

Keith, A. M. *Engendering Rome: Women in Latin Epic.* Cambridge University Press. Cambridge, 2000.

Lyne, R. O. A. M. *Words and the Poet: Characteristic Techniques of Style in Vergil's "Aeneid."* Oxford University Press. New York, 1989.

Mackie, C. J. *The Characterisation of Aeneas.* Scottish Academic. Edinburgh, 1988.

Martindale, Charles, ed. *The Cambridge Companion to Virgil.* Cambridge University Press. New York, 1997.

McKay, Alexander G. *Vergil's Italy.* Adams and Dart. Bath, 1971.

Monti, Richard C. *The Dido Episode and the Aeneid: Roman Social and Political Values in the Epic.* E. J. Brill. Leiden, 1981.

Most, Glenn W., and Sarah Spence, eds. *Re-presenting Virgil: Materiali e discussioni No. 52: Special Issue in Honor of Michael C. J. Putnam.* Istituti editoriali e poligrafici internazionali. Pisa, 2004.

Nelis, D. *Vergil's Aeneid and the Argonautica of Apollonius Rhodius.* Francis Cairns. Leeds, 2001.

O'Hara, James J. *Death and the Optimistic Prophecy in Vergil's "Aeneid."* Princeton University Press. Princeton, N.J., 1990.

———. *True Names: Vergil and the Alexandrian Tradition of Etymological Wordplay.* University of Michigan Press. Ann Arbor, 1996.

Otis, Brooks. *Virgil: A Study in Civilized Poetry.* Clarendon Press. Oxford, 1963.

Perkell, Christine, ed. *Reading Vergil's Aeneid: An Interpretive Guide.* University of Oklahoma Press. Norman, 1999.

Pöschl, Viktor. *The Art of Vergil: Image and Symbol in the Aeneid.* Translated by Gerda Seligson. University of Michigan Press. Ann Arbor, 1962.

Putnam, Michael C. J. *The Poetry of the Aeneid: Four Studies in Imaginative Unity and Design*. Harvard University Press. Cambridge, Mass., 1965.

———. *Virgil's Aeneid: Interpretation and Influence*. University of North Carolina Press. Chapel Hill, 1995.

———. *Virgil's Epic Designs: Ekphrasis in the Aeneid*. Yale University Press. New Haven, 1998.

Quinn, Stephanie, ed. *Why Vergil? A Collection of Interpretations*. Bolchazy-Carducci. Wauconda, Ill., 2000.

Schmidt, Ernst A. "The Meaning of Vergil's *Aeneid*: American and German Approaches." *Classical World* 94.2, 145–71. Classical Association of the Atlantic States. New York, 2001.

Segal, C. P. "*Aeternum per saecula nomen,* The Golden Bough and the Tragedy of History," Part I, *Arion* 4 (1965): 615–57; Part II, *Arion* 5 (1966): 34–72.

Spence, Sarah, ed. *Poets and Critics Read Vergil*. Yale University Press. New Haven, 2001.

Stahl, Hans-Peter, ed. *Virgil's Aeneid: Augustan Epic and Political Context*. Duckworth. London, 1998.

Thomas, Richard F. *Reading Virgil and His Texts*: Studies in Intertextuality. University of Michigan Press. Ann Arbor, 1999.

———. *Virgil and the Augustan Reception*. Cambridge University Press. Cambridge, 2001.

Wigodsky, Michael. *Vergil and Early Latin Poetry*. F. Steiner. Wiesbaden, 1972.

Wilhelm, Robert M., and Howard Jones, eds. *The Two Worlds of the Poet: New Perspectives on Vergil*. Wayne State University Press. Detroit, 1992.

Williams, Gordon. *Technique and Ideas in the Aeneid*. Yale University Press. New Haven, 1983.

Wiltshire, Susan Ford. *Public and Private in Vergil's Aeneid*. University of Massachusetts Press. Amherst, 1989.

Ziolkowski, Theodore. *Virgil and the Moderns*. Princeton University Press. Princeton, N.J., 1993.